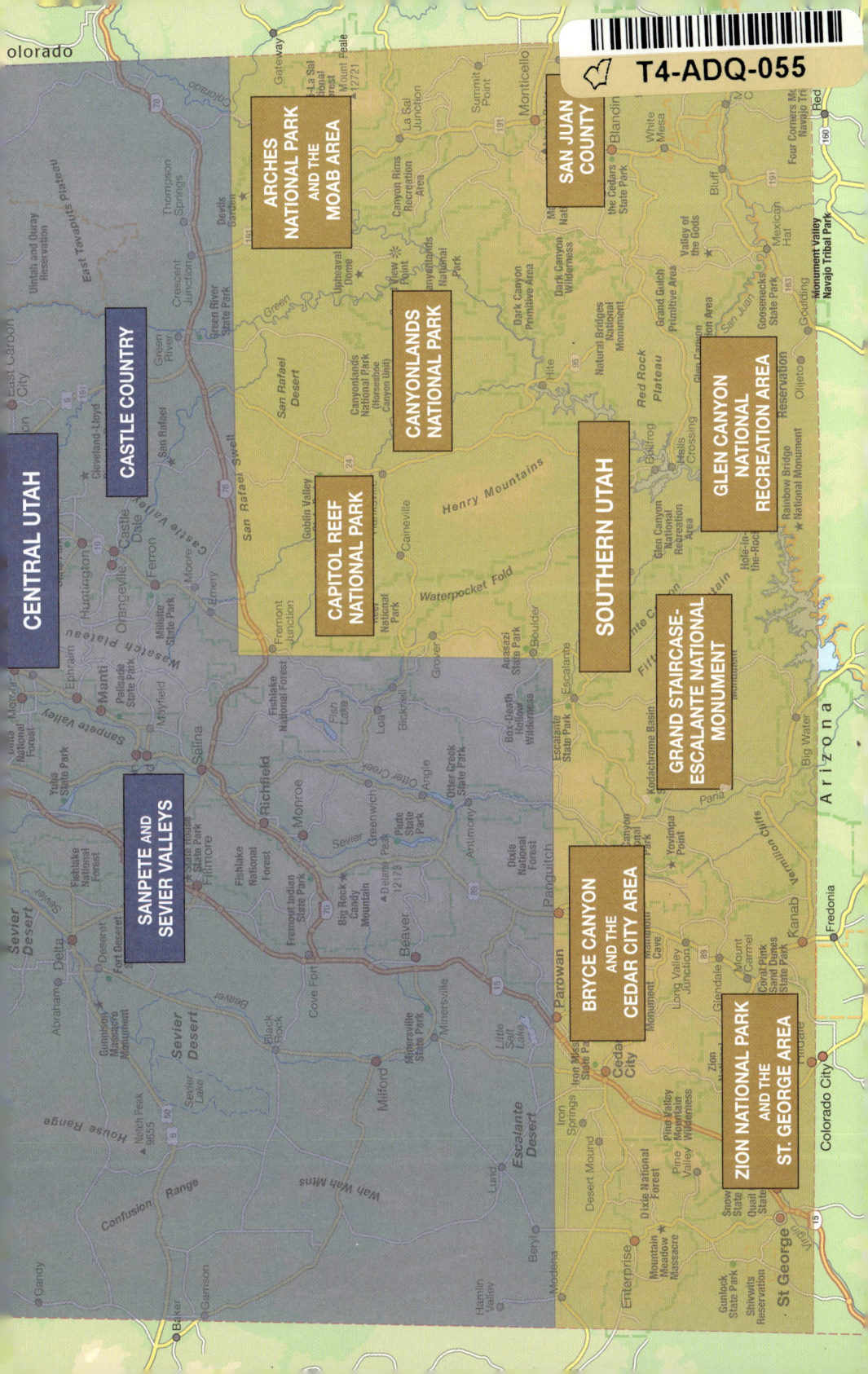

PLAN & BOOK
YOUR TAILOR-MADE TRIP

TAILOR-MADE TRIPS & UNIQUE EXPERIENCES CREATED BY LOCAL TRAVEL EXPERTS AT INSIGHTGUIDES.COM/HOLIDAYS

Insight Guides has been inspiring travellers with high-quality travel content for over 45 years. As well as our popular guidebooks, we now offer the opportunity to book tailor-made private trips completely personalised to your needs and interests. By connecting with one of our local experts, you will directly benefit from their expertise and local know-how, helping you create memories that will last a lifetime.

HOW INSIGHTGUIDES.COM/HOLIDAYS WORKS

STEP 1

Pick your dream destination and submit an enquiry, or modify an existing itinerary if you prefer.

STEP 2

Fill in a short form, sharing details of your travel plans and preferences with a local expert.

STEP 3

Your local expert will create your personalised itinerary, which you can amend until you are completely satisfied.

STEP 4

Book securely online. Pack your bags and enjoy your holiday! Your local expert will be available to answer questions during your trip.

BENEFITS OF PLANNING & BOOKING AT INSIGHTGUIDES.COM/HOLIDAYS

PLANNED BY LOCAL EXPERTS
The Insight Guides local experts are hand-picked, based on their experience in the travel industry and their impeccable standards of customer service.

SAVE TIME & MONEY
When a local expert plans your trip, you save time and money when you book, even during high season. You won't be charged for using a credit card either.

TAILOR-MADE TRIPS
Book with Insight Guides, and you will be in complete control of the planning process, from the initial selections to amending your final itinerary.

BOOK & TRAVEL STRESS-FREE
Enjoy stress-free travel when you use the Insight Guides secure online booking platform. All bookings come with a money-back guarantee.

WHAT OTHER TRAVELLERS THINK ABOUT TRIPS BOOKED AT INSIGHTGUIDES.COM/HOLIDAYS

Every step of the planning process and the trip itself was effortless and exceptional. Our special interests, preferences and requests were accommodated resulting in a trip that exceeded our expectations.

Corinne, USA

The organization was superb, the drivers professional, and accommodation quite comfortable. I was well taken care of! My thanks to your colleagues who helped make my trip to Vietnam such a great experience. My only regret is that I couldn't spend more time in the country.

Heather

DON'T MISS OUT BOOK NOW AT INSIGHTGUIDES.COM/HOLIDAYS

CONTENTS

Introduction

The best of Utah:
   Top Attractions 6
The best of Utah:
   Editor's Choice 8
The Beehive State 19

History & features

Decisive dates 22
Native Heritage 25
Trailblazers 33
   Butch Cassidy and the Sundance Kid 40
Promised Land 43
   The Origins of Mormonism 52
Utah in the Modern Age 55
The Cultural Landscape 63
   Utah Festivals 70
Empire of Saints 73
The Naked Earth 79
   There be Monsters 84
Life in a Dry Land 87
   Sea Monkey Business 92
   Puma Country 94
Outdoor Adventure 97
Snow Sports 105

Places

■ NORTHERN UTAH 119
Ogden and Environs 121
Salt Lake City 131
   Urban Wilderness 139
Provo, Park City and the Wasatch Range ... 141
   Hollywood in Utah 149
Dinosaur, Flaming Gorge
   and the High Uintas 151
■ CENTRAL UTAH 159
Castle Country 161
Sanpete and Sevier Valleys 169
   Rodeos 174
The Great Basin 177
■ SOUTHERN UTAH 183
Zion National Park and the
   St. George Area 185
Bryce Canyon and the Cedar City Area 197

Grand Staircase-Escalante National
   Monument **205**
Glen Canyon National Recreation Area **215**
   🔍 Hidden Life **220**
Capitol Reef National Park **223**
Canyonlands National Park **231**
Arches National Park and the Moab Area .. **239**
San Juan County **249**
   🔍 Navajo Art **259**

Travel tips

TRANSPORT
Getting There **262**
   By Air **262**
   By Road **262**
   By Rail **262**
Getting Around **263**
   By Rail **263**
   By Road **263**

A – Z
Accessible travel **265**
Accommodations **265**
Admission charges **267**
Age restrictions **267**
Budgeting for your trip **267**
Children **267**
Climate **267**
Crime and safety **268**
Customs regulations **269**
Eating out **269**
Electricity **270**
Embassies and consulates **270**
Emergencies **270**
Etiquette **270**
Festivals **270**
Health and medical care **271**
Internet **272**
LGBTQ+ travelers **272**
Maps **272**
Media **272**
Money **272**
Opening hours **273**
Postal services **273**
Public holidays **273**

Religious services **273**
Shopping **273**
Smoking **273**
Tax **273**
Telephones **274**
Time zones **274**
Tourist information **274**
Tour operators and travel agents **275**
Visas and passports **275**
Websites and apps **275**
Weights and measures **275**

FURTHER READING
History and society **276**
Fiction and Poetry **277**

Maps
Utah **116**
Ogden and Environs **122**
Salt Lake City **132**
Provo **142**
Dinosaur; Flaming Gorge, and the
   High Uintas **152**
Castle Country **162**
Sanpete and Sevier Valleys **168**
Great Basin **178**
Zion National Park **186**
Around St George and Cedar Key **192**
Bryce Canyon National Park **198**
Grand Staircase–Escalante National
   Monument and Glen Canyon National
   Recreation Area **206**
Capitol Reef National Park **224**
Canyonlands National Park **232**
Arches National Park **240**
Around Moab **250**

Inside front cover Utah
Inside back cover Utah's National Parks and
   Monuments

LEGEND
🔍 Insight on
📷 Photo story

THE BEST OF UTAH: TOP ATTRACTIONS

△ **Skiing in the Wasatch Range.** Utah boasts some of the best skiing anywhere in the world, with glitzy resorts set in atmospheric former mining towns such as Alta, Powder Mountain, Park City, and Snowbird. See page 141.

▽ **Salt Lake City.** The capital of Utah is rich in Mormon history and architecture, but is also home to the state's best museums, and culinary and nightlife scenes. See page 131.

△ **Zion National Park.** Zion's soaring cliffs, riverine forests and cascading waterfalls make this the most beautiful of Utah's national parks, culminating in the lush oasis of Zion Canyon, a spectacular narrow gorge. See page 185.

△ **Monument Valley.** Though the eerie sandstone monoliths of Monument Valley on the Utah/Arizona border are familiar the world over – thanks to countless Western movies – they still take every visitor's breath away. See page 257.

TOP ATTRACTIONS | 7

△ **Arches National Park.** This awe-inspiring slice of desert is studded with fins of red and golden sandstone and more than 1800 natural arches of various shapes and sizes, cut into the rock by eons of erosion. See page 239.

△ **Grand Staircase–Escalante National Monument.** The remote gorges of the Escalante River encompass some wonderful backpacking trails to plunging waterfalls and storm-gouged slot canyons, including smooth Peek-a-Boo Canyon and the aptly named Spooky Canyon. See page 205.

△ **Bryce Canyon National Park.** The surface of the earth can hold few weirder-looking spots than Bryce Canyon, a startling landscape of contorted stone pinnacles, "hoodoos" that poke out of technicolor ravines. See page 197.

△ **Alpine Loop Scenic Drive.** Utah is laced with scenic byways but this is one of the most rewarding, a 20-mile (32km) jaunt along Provo Canyon and the spectacular gorges of the Wasatch Range. See page 144.

▽ **Hovenweep National Monument.** Straddling the Utah-Colorado border, the six remote clusters of Ancestral Puebloan ruins within Hovenweep National Monument, all sprouting from the rims of shallow desert canyons, offer a haunting sense of timeless isolation. See page 258.

▽ **Canyonlands National Park.** Utah's largest and most magnificent national park lies at the confluence of the Green and Colorado rivers, a mind-bending tangle of canyons, fissures, buttes, monoliths, arches, and caverns. See page 231.

THE BEST OF UTAH: EDITOR'S CHOICE

Holeman Spring Canyon.

BEST SCENERY

Alpine Loop in fall. Closed by snow in winter, this dramatic drive through the Wasatch Mountains is best in fall when changing foliage in the aspen forests splashes color across Uinta National Forest. See page 144.

Calf Creek, Escalante Canyons. Utah's most popular wilderness destination has paved and four-wheel-drive backroads, slot canyon hiking, and gorgeous waterfalls. See page 209.

Island in the Sky (Canyonlands National Park). Hundred-mile views of canyons and a host of outdoor pursuits, from river running to hiking, biking, and jeep driving. See page 231.

Bryce Amphitheatre (Bryce Canyon National Park). Soak up the sensational canyon views from Sunrise Point or Sunset Point, with the pinnacle known as Thor's Hammer visible from the latter. See page 199.

Zion Canyon. A free shuttle bus system from Springdale makes viewing stunning Zion Canyon and accessing summer hiking trails a snap. See page 189.

BEST FAMILY ATTRACTIONS

American West Heritage Center. Visit this Wellsville living-history center where costumed interpreters bring 19th-century dancing, gunfighting, and woodworking to life. See page 128.

Clark Planetarium. Budding astronomers will love Salt Lake City's excellent planetarium and space museum, with moon rock samples and more on display. See page 135.

Monument Valley by jeep or horseback. Kids will be thrilled by an open-air Jeep tour or horseback ride through the West's most famous scenery. See page 258.

Natural History Museum of Utah. One of the state's most absorbing museums, with exhibits on Utah's native peoples and a massive dinosaur collection. See page 137.

The San Juan River. Easy paddling, great scenery, ancient Native American rock art, wildlife, swimming beaches, and access to the adjoining Navajo Reservation. See page 256.

Wall of Bones at Dinosaur National Monument. A Disney-like tram ride, ranger talks, and partially excavated dinosaur skeletons, some 1,500 bones in all, going back 149 million years. See page 152.

Bryce Canyon.

Natural History Museum of Utah.

EDITOR'S CHOICE | 9

BEST WILDLIFE VIEWING

American Bison, Antelope Island State Park.

Flaming Gorge National Recreational Area. Every August and September, thousands of bright-red kokanee salmon spawn in Sheep Creek and may be viewed along with bighorn sheep, bears, and other wildlife. See page 155.

Hardware Wildlife Management Area. You can view the hundreds of elk that come here to feed in the winter. See page 128.

Antelope Island State Park. Home to herds of free-roaming bison, pronghorn and bighorn sheep, and thousands of shorebirds attracted to the lakeshore by brine flies in summer and fall. See page 121.

Virgin River, Zion National Park. Mule deer and wild turkeys wander roadsides while peregrine falcons, red-tailed hawks, and California condors nest on cliffs above the river. See page 187.

BEST HISTORY AND CULTURE

Donner-Reed Museum, Grantsville. View the possessions of the ill-fated Donner Party abandoned during their disastrous crossing of the Great Salt Lake Desert. See page 179.

Highway 89 Scenic Byway, Sanpete and Sevier Valleys. Soak up the Scandinavian architecture, artist studios, and mining ghost towns in Central Utah's traditional Mormon strongholds. See page 169.

Museum of Peoples and Cultures, Provo. Artifacts from Utah and other parts of the world that relate to Mormon history are on display at Brigham Young University campus. See page 142.

Nine Mile Canyon, Castle Country. Narrow gorge containing the world's biggest outdoor museum of Fremont Culture rock art and other artifacts. See page 163.

Temple Square, Salt Lake City. Home to the most important Mormon churches, museums, libraries, and monuments, including Brigham Young's preserved residence. See page 131.

Salt Lake Temple.

OFF THE BEATEN TRACK

Brown's Park. Follow in the footsteps of Butch Cassidy and the Wild Bunch in Brown's Park, a remote outlaw's refuge on the Wyoming border. See page 154.

Cleveland-Lloyd Dinosaur Quarry. Getting there is half the fun for dinosaur lovers drawn to one of the world's biggest dinosaur die-off sites in the San Rafael Desert, east of Price. See page 163.

Pipe Spring National Monument. Set in the lonesome Arizona Strip, little-known Pipe Spring preserves an 1870s fortified Mormon ranch built atop a former Ancestral Pueblo village. See page 192.

Spiral Jetty. Robert Smithson created this unique spiraling earthwork on a remote section of Great Salt Lake coastline in 1970. See page 129.

Trail of the Ancients. Scenic byway that takes in the state's best Ancestral Pueblo ruins, working trading posts, the San Juan River, Lake Powell, and Monument Valley. See page 254.

Rozel Point.

10 | INTRODUCTION

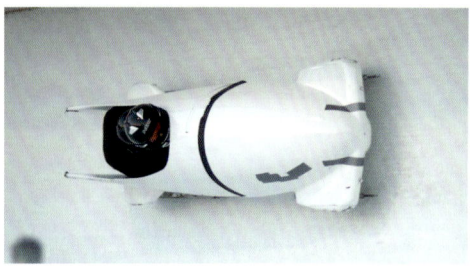

Bobsledding at Olympic Park.

Western meadowlark.

BEST OUTDOOR ADVENTURES

Best Snow on Earth. Skiers and snowboarders have their choice of world-class ski resorts, most within an hour or two of Salt Lake City. See page 105.

Cataract Canyon, Canyonlands National Park. River runners vie for a chance to "Waltz the Cat" on the last section of Colorado River whitewater before it enters Lake Powell. See page 233.

Escalante Canyons. Follow the Escalante River through its deep canyons on foot or horseback to view Fremont granaries and rock art as well as lush side canyons. See page 209.

Ride a Bobsled at Olympic Park. Pay big bucks to hop aboard a four-man bobsled steered by a certified driver and reach 80mph (130km/h) at Utah Olympic Park. See page 107.

Slickrock Trail, Moab. A favorite with fat-tire enthusiasts who come to Moab to challenge themselves on this hot and dusty but highly scenic desert bike trail. See page 245.

West Rim Trail, Zion National Park. This overnight trail across Zion's Kolob Plateau offers a chance to hike a part of the Zion backcountry few visitors experience. See page 191.

BEST FOR BIRDWATCHING

Bear River Migratory Bird Refuge. This Utah Valley preserve, on the edge of the Great Salt Lake, attracts hundreds of species of migratory and resident waterfowl. See page 127.

Dinosaur National Monument. Harpers Corner Scenic Drive, in the Canyons section, is an excellent place to see eagles, hawks, and other soaring raptors as well as sage grouse in spring. See page 151.

Fish Springs National Wildlife Refuge. Mineral-laden, saline warm springs are home to over 5,000 wintering birds in this remote area off the Pony Express Trail. See page 90.

Matheson Wetlands Preserve. Next to downtown Moab on the Colorado River, these wetlands are home to a huge variety of bird species as well as other riparian wildlife. See page 247.

Ouray National Wildlife Refuge. This Uinta Basin sanctuary is one of the best places in eastern Utah to view hundreds of birds attracted to wetlands. See page 157.

West Rim Trail.

EDITOR'S CHOICE | 11

Salt Lake City Public Library.

Vivint Arena.

BEST FOR CONTEMPORARY CULTURE

Gallivan Center. Salt Lake's cultural center hosts popular concerts, folkloric dance festivals, and a giant chess board. See page 134.
Golf Mecca. St George, in southern Utah, has 10 golf courses and perfect playing weather year-round. See page 194.
Salt Lake City Public Library. The award-winning Salt Lake City Public Library is one of Utah's top cultural attractions. See page 135.

Sundance Film Festival. The granddaddy of American Indie movie events, this weeklong celluloid celebration has become the biggest event of the year in Park City. See page 145.
Vivint Arena. Home of the NBA's Utah Jazz, this 18,000-seat arena is also the place to see rodeos, circuses, pop concerts, and other big events. See page 134.

BEST WINTER SPORTS DESTINATIONS

Brian Head Ski Resort. Southern Utah's premier ski and snowboard destination, and one of the highest anywhere, with a base elevation of 9,600 ft (2926 meters). See page 202.
Park City. This vast ski area has something for everyone, with its two major resorts of Park City Mountain and Deer Valley. See page 147.
Snowbasin. The three ski resorts east of Ogden are relatively uncrowded, with Snowbasin best known for its high-tech snowmaking systems. See page 125.
Soldier Hollow. Nordic skiing facility and 2002 Winter Games venue with miles of cross-country skiing and snowshoeing trails to explore. See page 146.
Utah Olympic Park. The primary 2002 Winter Games hub is now the best place to try bobsledding, Nordic jumping, slopestyle skiing, luge racing, and skeleton racing. See page 148.

Deer Valley Ski Resort.

The Watchman and the Virgin River, Zion National Park.

Canyon Overlook, Zion National Park.

Buckskin Gulch slot canyon.

Arches National Park.

INTRODUCTION | 19

THE BEEHIVE STATE

Utah is a land of beguiling landscapes, mesmerizing national parks, world-class skiing, and a rich history that includes Native American Indigenous people and Mormon pioneers.

Utah state border.

Utah holds something for everyone: From multicolored canyons and desert plains to densely forested and snow-covered mountains. Almost all this unmatched range of terrain is public land, making Utah the place to come for outdoor pursuits.

Led by Brigham Young, Utah's earliest white settlers – the Mormons or Latter-day Saints (LDS) – arrived in the Salt Lake area, which then lay outside the US, in 1847 and embarked on massive irrigation projects. At first, they provoked great suspicion and hostility back East. Relations eased when the Mormon Church dropped polygamy in 1890 and statehood followed in 1896; to this day, over 60 percent of Utah's 3-million-strong population are Mormons, and Salt Lake City has matured into an urbane, dynamic, and fast-growing metropolitan center with cultural and commercial assets rivaling those of any American city of similar size. Mormon history provides much of the interest here, but above all, there is the lure of the outdoors.

Indeed, driving into Utah, one can't help but be struck by the otherworldly nature of the landscape. Here the ruddy sandstone of the Colorado Plateau has been sculpted by water, wind, and ice into a fantasia of arches, spires and balancing rocks. In the north, the Wasatch Range runs like a spine down the center of the state, separating the forested peaks of north-eastern Utah from the sun-scorched flats of the Great Basin. The Wasatch Mountains are justly renowned for some of the finest and most abundant snow in the West – within an hour from downtown Salt Lake City you can be flying through mounds of fluffy powder at a world-class ski resort, or hiking a cool mountain trail shaded by pine and aspen. Because of all of Utah's blessings – and they are many – surely the richest is a landscape unlike any other in the world.

Utah's State Capitol.

⊘ A NOTE TO READERS

At Insight Guides, we always strive to bring you the most up-to-date information. This book was produced during a period of continuing uncertainty caused by the Covid-19 pandemic, so please note that content is more subject to change than usual. We recommend checking the latest restrictions and official guidance.

Mormon family portrait, Great Salt Lake Valley.

DECISIVE DATES

PREHISTORIC CULTURES

c.10,000 BC
A nomadic lifestyle is the cultural norm for the people who inhabit the region that includes present-day Utah.

c. AD 500
Ancestral Puebloans settle in villages in southern Utah, growing crops and flourishing as one of the main cultures of the Colorado Plateau.

c.1300
Ancestral Pueblo and Fremont cultures decline during a protracted drought. When Europeans arrive, Utah is home to the Northern Shoshone, Goshute, Ute, Paiute, and Navajo.

EUROPEAN ARRIVALS

1776
The first comprehensive exploration of Utah by Europeans is carried out under two Franciscan priests, Silvestre Vélez de Escalante and Francisco Atanasio Dominguez, searching for a route between the Spanish missions of New Mexico and California.

1821
Mexico wins independence from Spain, and inherits Utah.

1824
Mountain man Jim Bridger encounters the Great Salt Lake. Meanwhile, an annual rendezvous system for trappers and traders gets under way in Utah.

1826
Utah is traversed as part of the first overland journey to California by an American, the fur trapper Jedediah S. Smith.

THE WESTERN FRONTIER

1846
Trader Miles Goodyear establishes Utah's first Anglo-American settlement, Fort Buenaventura, which gives rise to the town of Ogden.

1847
Mormon pioneers led by Brigham Young arrive in the Salt Lake Valley after a

Mountain Meadows Massacre of September 1857.

1,200-mile (1,900km) journey from Nauvoo, Illinois.

1848
Land that includes modern-day Utah is ceded by Mexico to the United States, after its defeat in the Mexican–American War.

1850
Congress rejects a Mormon proposal for a State of Deseret and instead establishes the Territory of Utah, population 11,390.

1851
Brigham Young is appointed by President Millard Fillmore as governor of Utah Territory.

1857
Utah War – disapproval of Mormon separateness, aggravated by the practice of polygamy, causes President James Buchanan to send an army expedition to oust Brigham Young. Meanwhile, a massacre of non-Mormon emigrants at Mountain Meadows causes a national outcry.

Petroglyphs carved by the Fremont Indigenous people on McConkie Ranch.

CHRONOLOGY | 23

1865
Encroachment on native lands sparks the Black Hawk War in central Utah.

1869
America's first transcontinental railway is completed at Promontory Point north of the Great Salt Lake. Meanwhile, Major John Wesley Powell begins his breakthrough explorations of the Green and Colorado rivers.

1870
Women are granted voting rights by the Utah legislature.

1877
LDS president Brigham Young dies at age 76; succeeded by John Taylor.

1890
Mormon leaders forsake the doctrine of plural marriage, clearing the way for presidential pardons and statehood.

1896
Utah becomes 45th state on condition that a ban on Mormon polygamy be written into the state constitution.

THE 20TH CENTURY

1909
Creation of "Mukuntuweap National Monument," the basis for Zion National Park.

1939
Establishment of the Alta Ski Area, Utah's first ski resort.

1964
Completion of Flaming Gorge Dam on the Green River, creating Flaming Gorge Reservoir, and becoming a major source of hydroelectricity.

Mitt Romney speaks at Henderson Pavilion.

1966
Glen Canyon Dam opens on the Colorado River in Arizona, creating Utah's Lake Powell.

1978
A long-held Mormon policy whereby Black people are denied priesthood status in the Church is ended as the result of a revelation announced by its leader, Spencer W. Kimball.

1979
The NBA's New Orleans Jazz relocates to become Utah Jazz.

1996
A proclamation by President Bill Clinton sets aside 1.7 million acres (690,000 hectares) as Grand Staircase–Escalante National Monument.

THE 21ST CENTURY

2000
Southwestern megadrought begins.

2002
Salt Lake City hosts the XIX Olympic Winter Games; Mitt Romney leads the organizing committee.

2014
Utah legalizes same-sex marriage.

2016
A proclamation by President Barack Obama creates Bears Ears National Monument.

2018
Former presidential candidate – and devout Mormon – Mitt Romney is elected US senator for Utah.

2020
The Covid-19 pandemic hits the United States.

2022
Lake Powell reaches its lowest ever water level. With increased Covid vaccination rates restrictions are eased and tourism returns to Utah.

Mormon pioneers led by Brigham Young arrive in the Salt Lake Valley.

Native American feather head dress.

HISTORY & FEATURES | 25

NATIVE HERITAGE

From Ice Age hunters and ancient Pueblo civilizations to modern Native American Indigenous people, Utah's Indigenous people have left a singular mark on the land, and are still doing so.

In 1990, the Utah Democratic Party nominated an all Native American slate for elected offices in San Juan County – a first in American history. The campaign was led by San Juan County Commissioner Mark Maryboy, a young Diné (din-EH; Navajo) who, just four years earlier, had succeeded in becoming the first Native American to hold an elected position in Utah. With the exception of Maryboy, all the candidates were defeated. However, the campaign drew widespread media attention, resulting in a surge in voter registration on reservations in San Juan County.

Since then, the battle for voting rights and against discrimination toward Native American voters has continued in the courts and at the polls. Today, the chair and vice chair of San Juan's Board of County Commissioners are both Diné and Democrats in a primarily white, Republican state – Kenneth Maryboy (brother of Mark) and Willie Grayeyes were elected in 2018 to the first majority-Indigenous commission in county history. And in 2022, Davina Smith became the first Diné woman to run for the Utah State Legislature.

Statewide, the 33,000 members of Utah's Navajo, Southern Paiute, Northwestern Shoshone, Northern Ute, White Mesa Ute, and Goshute Indigenous people, concentrated in southeastern Utah, the Uintah Basin, and the Salt Lake City area, are showing their political strength after centuries of marginalization.

ANCIENT ROOTS

All the Indigenous people now living in Utah arrived there less than a thousand years ago, comparatively late in the human occupation of the Southwest. They moved onto lands that, for

An ancient petroglyph found in Land Hill.

millennia, had been used by Ancestral Pueblo and Fremont farmers, who built hundreds of villages, or pueblos, in southeastern Utah and the adjoining Four Corners that have been beautifully preserved on mesas and in canyons.

For the first humans on the North American continent at the end of the last Ice Age, 15,000 years ago, Utah's newly emerging grasslands and lakes and the wealth of big game must have seemed like the Promised Land. Paleo-Indian hunters crossed the Bering Land Bridge from Mongolia to modern-day Alaska, then traveled south in family groups. The hunters moved with herds of oversized animals such as woolly mastodons, camels, giant bison, and ground sloths that required strength and agility to bring

HISTORY & FEATURES

> As the lakes and grasslands disappeared and desert conditions took their place, the big game herds died out, doomed perhaps by the changing environment and overhunting.

down with spears. They slept in cave shelters, where they created stone tools and butchered big game, and left behind bones, stone flakes, and beautiful chert spear points. These people

A Navajo woman weaving.

are known as the Clovis and Folsom cultures, named after the towns in northeastern New Mexico where their spear points were first uncovered. The Pleistocene climate continued to warm and dry, and thousands of new plant species appeared.

People in Utah adopted a new lifestyle: that of hunter-gatherers. They hunted smaller game, such as modern bison and bighorn sheep, but also harvested wild plants. These people, dubbed the Archaic culture, fitted themselves gracefully into their surroundings and thrived for at least 6,000 years.

Knife blades, projectile points, milling stones, and firepits have been found in rock shelters at Danger, Smith Creek, and Deer Creek caves near the margins of lakes and water sources and offer the first clear archaeological evidence of human activity in Utah during the early Archaic period (9000–7500 BC). By the Middle Archaic (7500–4000 BC), people were using a greater variety of ecological zones, from mountains to desert, and inventing new technologies. Women processed wild foods using grinding stones and made twined baskets for harvesting plants, which they carried on the forehead using a tumpline, the same way they carried their babies. The men made nets to catch small game, such as rabbits, and used an *atlatl*, or "spear-thrower," which allowed them greater precision in bringing down game. Excavations at Hogup Cave indicate that they enjoyed a diverse diet. Archaeologists have uncovered the remains of four species of large mammals (deer, pronghorn, mountain sheep, and elk), 32 species of small mammals, 34 species of birds, and 36 plant species.

By 2000 BC, Archaic families were found throughout Utah, and the expanding population forced people to spread out in the Great Basin uplands, where plants and animals were more restricted. The more efficient bow and arrow replaced the *atlatl*, but something seems to have gone wrong. Hunters began leaving split-twig figurines of bighorn sheep in high cliff crevices where the sheep traveled, perhaps as hunting fetishes designed to attract the real thing. Game and plants may have been severely affected by drought, leading shamans to undertake long pilgrimages to sacred sites to pray for help.

Camped beneath sheer sandstone cliffs in southern Utah, they painted images in red hematite on the walls: herds of bighorn sheep, flowing water, and oversized triangular figures with long thin bodies and huge empty eyes. These limbless beings hover wraithlike above sandy washes in the labyrinthine canyons of the Maze District of Canyonlands National Park. They seem like the overwrought visions of a hungry, worried people calling to the gods for help.

EARLY FARMING

By AD 500, Archaic people were trying something new: cultivation of a domesticated wild grass from Mexico called maize. Agriculture

NATIVE HERITAGE

made its way to the Four Corners region from Mexico via traders from the south, beginning in the early Christian era. From the Hohokam culture, who practiced irrigation farming in southern Arizona, the Basketmaker culture learned how to use check dams, ditches, and dry farming techniques, and acquired hammers, axes, and exotic goods from Mexico. From the Mogollon culture of the southern New Mexico mountains, they learned how to make pots using the coiled clay method and to fire them at high temperatures to make strong, airtight

> By 1300, Ancestral Puebloans had left their homes in the Four Corners and headed southeast to live along the Rio Grande and other rivers in New Mexico and Arizona, where their descendants, the Pueblo people, remain today.

keep house, grind flour, cook, weave baskets, make pottery, raise children, and gather seeds, nuts, and fruits.

Ancient ruins, Chaco Culture National Park.

Northern Ute Veterans Memorial.

containers for storing and transporting grains and valuables. The refined decorated pueblo pottery from the Four Corners quickly became a sought-after trade item, reflecting the potter's aesthetic.

Farming required a sedentary life and was much more labor intensive than hunting. Nomadic families joined together to sow, water, and watch over crops in irrigated gardens. They built semi-subterranean shelters, or pit houses, with roofs made of branches covered in earth and held up by central supports, that were snug in winter and cool in summer. Corn and squash, and later beans, were harvested in fall, then stored in sealed granaries for winter. While men went off hunting, the women stayed behind to

During the early Pueblo I period (AD 700–900), families throughout the Four Corners began building hamlets of above-ground houses made of sandstone and adobe. Pit houses were used now as kivas, or "underground ceremonial rooms." Here clansmen gathered to weave cotton and discuss the most advantageous times to plant and harvest. Ritual specialists tracked the daily movements of the sun, moon, and planets across the sky. As the solstices approached, planting and harvesting ceremonies were announced. These priests quickly became the most important members of the village.

CHACO AND MESA VERDE

In a phenomenon never seen before or since, the powerful Chaco civilization, headquartered

> *The most immediate and profound change wrought by Europeans was caused by the introduction of the horse. Suddenly, people who had traveled only on foot could traverse vast distances with greater speed and freedom than ever before.*

in a remote canyon in the center of the 25,000 sq mile (65,000 sq km) San Juan Basin, rose to prominence c. AD 1000. Chaco seems to have served as a ceremonial center for Ancestral Puebloan peoples. It may have succeeded by redistributing trade goods from as far away as the Pacific, the Mississippi River, and Mexico.

By the mid-1100s, Chaco and its hundreds of satellite villages had become ghost towns and its former wealth was scattered to the winds. Its leaders may have become straw men in the face of long-running drought, leaving desperate farming families to their own devices. They fled to surrounding highlands, including the Montezuma Valley of southwestern Colorado, just west of Mesa Verde. As newcomers poured into the area and resources dwindled, Mesa Verdeans left their mesa-top villages and moved into hundreds of warm, south-facing villages cleverly concealed in the cliffs.

At its height, Mesa Verde supported 5,000 people. Some 30,000 lived in the adjoining Montezuma Valley. Villages sprang up on every mesa with a stream. Lookout towers were built, perhaps to safeguard communities from outsiders. These enclosed pueblos were hastily constructed, using large stones loosely mortared with mud, and some were built in unusual shapes, such as the oval, circular, square, and D-shaped buildings at Hovenweep and Canyons

Cliff Palace, one of the largest cliff dwellings in North America.

of the Ancients National Monuments on the Colorado–Utah border.

People continued to move north of the San Juan River into the narrow canyons of southeastern Utah, east of the Colorado River, in places such as Horse Canyon in the Needles District of Canyonlands National Park, where they built tiny homesteads big enough for just a single family and bravely continued to farm. The Great Drought of the late 13th century doomed all these efforts.

THE FREMONT

The people who lived in northeastern Utah and northwestern Colorado had much in common with their neighbors immediately to the south. They too made pottery, grew corn, squash, and later beans along washes, and lived together in villages. But for these people the hunter-gatherer lifestyle still beckoned. The Fremont culture (named for their strong presence along the Fremont River in Capitol Reef National Park and adjoining lands) are less obvious in the archaeological record, perhaps because of their fondness for remote places. They developed a hardy dent-style corn that suited the highlands they lived on, fashioned plain, utilitarian pottery, and made moccasins with the dewclaws of deer, for traction.

GREAT BASIN NEWCOMERS

The arrival of Utah's modern Indigenous people in a region already stressed by scarce resources may have tipped the balance. The Utes, Paiutes, Goshutes, and Shoshones all belong to the Uto-Aztecan language family and are part of its Numic-speaking branch, which linguists say originated in Southern California by way of Mexico. These hunter-gatherers seem to have entered the Great Basin area by AD 1000 and spread into Colorado about 1300.

The first view of the Great Salt Lake Valley from a mountain pass.

Long after the Ancestral Pueblo people of the Four Corners were building large stone villages, the Fremont culture found comfort in their pit houses – by far the most practical shelter in the extreme temperatures of the desert. Their rock art, too, echoed that of early Archaic people, with depictions of big-shouldered anthropomorphs, game animals, and enigmatic figures, such as Kokopelli the flute player. Hundreds of Fremont pictographs can be found between the Colorado River and the Great Basin and immediately west of the Green River, in the area of Nine Mile Canyon and Range Creek in central Utah. Like the Ancestral Pueblo, the Fremont culture ceased to exist in an identifiable form around AD 1300, probably due to a combination of drought and overutilization of natural resources.

They were joined soon after by nomadic Athabascans, or Dineh, from northwest Canada, who split into the Navajo and Apache Indigenous groups around the 12th century. The groups jostled for dominance throughout the region which, by the 17th century, had also attracted the attention of Spanish explorers.

Borrowing technologies from the Plains Indigenous people, Utes and Navajos used travois, meaning "horse-drawn sleds," to transport their possessions from place to place. Mounted Utes left their homes in the mountains of northern and eastern Utah to hunt bison on the western plains. Gone for long periods, they left behind their families to gather food, tan bison and deer skins, and make highly prized clothing at encampments of hide-covered tents, or tepees. A man's wealth was measured by the number of horses he owned; his status as a warrior was determined by the number of enslaved people he stole from other Indigenous groups. In addition to longstanding ceremonies such as the Bear Dance, Utes adopted the Sun Dance, a test of endurance in which men pierce their flesh with hooks, abstain from food and drink, and dance to exhaustion. Utes drove the Navajo back into southeastern Utah and the adjoining portions of Arizona and New Mexico, where they remain today. By the early 1700s, both Navajos and Utes raided Goshutes and Paiutes to enslave people to trade to the Spanish in New Mexico. Within a few short years, Goshute and Paiute populations had dropped by 90 percent, creating fear of outsiders among indigenous people that lived together harmoniously..

Petroglyphs, Dinosaur National Monument.

MORMON RELATIONS

The arrival of the Mormons in the Salt Lake Valley in 1847 did little to help matters. Soon after founding Salt Lake City, Mormon farmers began a rapid colonization effort in the surrounding desert lands traditionally used by some 20,000 Native Americans. Settlers monopolized precious water sources and grazed livestock in areas used for hunting and gathering by Native American families, who began to starve and grow dependent on handouts. Mormons referred to Goshutes and Paiutes as "Digger Indians" for their habit of digging up the edible roots of desert plants. Ironically, when crickets and floods destroyed Mormon crops, many farmers were saved from starvation by Native American knowledge of wild foods.

Mormons were "called" by the Church to create missions to convert and teach agriculture to Native Americans, believing they were a fallen indigenous group known as the Lamanites whose dark skin would be reversed by accepting Jesus Christ. Mormon Native American farms later formed the nucleus of several Native American reservations, including the Goshute reservations at Deep Creek and Skull Valley and the Southern Paiute reservation in Cedar City.

But for most settlers living frugally on ranches in remote areas, any charitable feelings toward their impoverished Native American neighbors often evaporated when they felt threatened or lost livestock to theft. Numerous clashes took place between Mormon ranchers and Navajos, Southern Utes, and Paiutes in the mid-to-late 1800s, which shifting alliances among Mormons, the federal government, and Native American indigenous people only served to complicate. These clashes continued well into the 1900s, ending with an armed standoff between white ranchers and Paiute and Ute over stolen livestock in Bluff, Utah, in the late 1920s, known as the Posey War.

SUBJUGATION AND RESISTANCE

After picking up farming, weaving, and pottery from Pueblos and acquiring horses from Spaniards, then systematically raiding both, Navajos were forced to accept American rule in 1868 after a series of devastating military campaigns and a four-year incarceration at Bosque Redondo and Fort Sumner in central New Mexico. They agreed to a reservation spanning portions of Arizona, New Mexico, and Utah, which today encompasses 29,000 sq miles (75,000 sq km) and has the largest tribal population in the country – some 300,000 people.

Utes were also forced onto reservations beginning in 1864, after the 1853 Walker War led by Ute leader Wakara against Mormon settlements ended with a peace treaty requiring the Native Americans to move to the Uintah Basin. Utes along the Wasatch Front, including the Timpanogos, Corn Creek, and Spanish Fork bands, made the move, but the San Pete band, led by Black Hawk, continued to raid settlements until the early 1870s. The Moache Utes were moved to Ignacio, Colorado, where they became known as the Southern Ute Tribe. The Weeminuche settled at Towaoc on the Ute Mountain Ute Reservation, also in Colorado, while some members chose to move to White Mesa, Utah, where they now number 380 people. Finally, in 1880, following the massacre of missionary Nathan Meeker at White River, Colorado, the White River and Uncompahgre/Tabeguache bands were forced to move from their mountain homeland to the desolate Uintah Basin. Today, the million-acre (4,047 sq km) reservation is known as the Uintah and Ouray Reservation.

The fate of Utah's Northwestern Shoshone remains up in the air. Some 350 members of the indigenous group encamped on the Bear River were massacred in 1863 by the US Army, and they lost all their traditional lands in Utah. In the 1960s, the group acquired a 189-acre (76-hectare) patch of land on the Utah–Idaho border from the Mormons, but they still do not have a formal reservation (they also purchased the Bear River Massacre site in 2018).

Even more remarkable is the triumphant story of the Southern Paiutes. After having its tribal status "terminated" by the federal government in 1954, the Paiute Indian Tribe of Utah thankfully had its land restored in 1980 and has made huge strides in health, housing, education, and employment for its members. Every June, the Paiutes hold an annual Restoration Gathering in downtown Cedar City (2022 will mark the group's 42nd gathering) in southern Utah. For all who attend, the message is loud and clear: We are still here and we are thriving.

Anti-Mormon cartoon by Thomas Nast.

⊙ POWWOW HIGHWAY

Tribal gatherings, known as powwows, are held throughout Utah every year. Originally pau-wau, an Algonquin word, meant "medicine man;" as a verb it meant "to perform a healing ceremony." By the 1800s, however, it applied to any gathering of Native Americans, and today it refers to hundreds of public events in which dancers, singers, and other followers of the powwow trail come to celebrate Native American culture.

Among the best-known Utah powwows are the Paiute Restoration Gathering in Cedar City in June, the Northern Ute powwows in Fort Duchesne in July and at Thanksgiving, and the Northern Navajo Fair and White Mesa Ute Bear Dance which are both held in September. Most powwows welcome spectators but keep a few rules in mind. Before pulling out your camera, check to see if photography is allowed or if a permit is required. Always ask permission before snapping the shutter; sometimes a small payment is appropriate. Dress modestly and try to be unobtrusive; avoid asking questions about traditions and customs. Don't join a dance unless invited. Non-Native Americans may be encouraged to participate in the Round Dance, which celebrates the universality of all humankind. For more information, contact the Utah Division of Indian Affairs (tel: 801-538 8803; https://indian.utah.gov).

A traditional pioneer cabin.

TRAILBLAZERS

Explorers and soldiers were the first Europeans to penetrate the Utah hinterland, followed over time by an assortment of others – including a pair of adventurous padres.

Utah was for a long time the "undiscovered country," remote and uninviting. Inevitably, intruders began showing up, arriving from the south, the east, and the west, to penetrate its forbidding terrain. Spaniards came first, up from Mexico, seeking material treasure and/or souls for salvation, while ever keeping a jealous eye out for other interlopers – chiefly French, British, and homegrown Anglo–Americans.

In the vanguard were soldier-explorers, Franciscan friars, traders seeking to do business with the indigenous people, and then a variety of opportunists – fur trappers, gold-diggers, mapmakers, farmers, and land-hungry expansionists. Most of them, early on, were transients passing through and around. But their probes and ramblings succeeded in putting Utah, or what became Utah, on the map as they carved out trails later to be followed by emigrant settlers. Most famous of Utah's settlers would of course be the Mormons, who in the 1840s found their "promised land" in what generally had been thought a most unpromising place. They were pioneers, too, if not exactly trailblazers. The real trailblazing had taken place up to three centuries earlier, starting with Francisco Vázquez Coronado's famous expedition into the region in search of more of the precious metal that was being unearthed elsewhere in New Spain.

Coronado's expedition may have left tracks in present-day Utah when a detachment of his men, under Captain García López de Cárdenas, crossed over into land south of the Colorado River.

Kit Carson (1809-1868) with his horse Apache.

Coronado returned to Mexico in 1541 with little material treasure to speak of, and little effort was expended on going that far north again. There were thrusts here and there, into the farther reaches of New Mexico and beyond to Arizona and Colorado, but not much of lasting impact. People were certainly aware of the Ute bands that roamed western Colorado in the Utah region, from which awareness came the term "Yuta" or "Yutta." It was the Spanish spin on the indigenous self-reference for "people of the mountains." The term seems to have gained currency with the Spanish from about 1610, arising largely out of trading exchanges between Native Americans and the European-descended newcomers in places like Taos, New Mexico. Anglos gave the term their own linguistic twist, spelling it "Utah."

> For help, Domínguez called on the services of the Spanish-born priest Silvestre Vélez de Escalante, who long had ministered to the needs of Native American Christian converts in New Mexico.

EARLY SPANISH EXPLORATION

It was a trading exchange in Taos that helped open a new chapter in Utah history. The exchange occurred in 1765 when an old Ute trader known as Cuero "Wolfskin" de Lobo aroused curiosity in the Taos area by offering to trade an ingot of silver. To find out where more of the precious stuff might be mined, a small expedition headed by Juan Antonio María de Rivera was sent north. Following trails known to Spanish and Ute traders, Rivera's party got as far as the Dolores River in western Colorado before turning back.

A second expedition was immediately mounted, again under Rivera, to search for the source of such a lode of silver and to check on the veracity of the various legends that surrounded the people and the land beyond the Colorado River. This time Rivera made it all the way north into Utah (northeast of present-day Monticello). His group went by the La Sal Mountains, found a good place to cross the Colorado River, observed the lifestyle of the Native people, heard intriguing reports of a far-off "great lake" – which was of course the Great Salt Lake – and left a large inscribed cross claiming Spanish sovereignty before heading home.

Rivera's basic accomplishment was to forge a trade route from Santa Fe north to the Colorado River and into central Utah that was a first step along what became legendary as the Old Spanish Trail. This was a passageway arching up through southeastern Utah and then veering off westward in the direction of California. Following an ancient trail, it developed as a major trade route 1,120 miles (1,800km) long between Santa Fe and Los Angeles, touching six states. It remained "Spanish" in formal identity until 1848 and the American takeover of the West.

THE ESCALANTE–DOMÍNGUEZ EXPEDITION

Even more decisive in opening up Utah's modern history was an exploration that occurred a decade after Rivera's penetration of 1765. This time the protagonists were two Spanish padres named Escalante and Domínguez. They made their move in 1776. Francisco

John Jacob Astor.

John C. Fremont.

Atanasio Domínguez, born in Mexico, had a twofold agenda: Firstly, to inspect the Catholic Church's far-flung outposts in New Mexico, and secondly, to seek a better overland route connecting the old communities centered at Santa Fe with newly established missionary outposts in Monterey and Southern California.

Escalante and Domínguez planned to set forth on July 4, 1776, that most historic of American dates, though they didn't actually leave until July 29 owing to a delay caused by a Comanche assault in the region. The two priests were accompanied

Early snowfall and signs of a harsh impending winter impelled the two priests to abort their planned trip to California, and they headed south for home. They arrived in Santa Fe on January 2, 1777, after a journey of more than 1,700 miles (2,700km). Their search for a more secure route around hostile Native American territory as well as impossibly arid desert and rugged mountains was unfulfilled. But they had succeeded in finding a most hospitable land up north which they depicted in detailed journals and maps. Their published account served as an introduction

The handcart pioneers struggle through a blizzard while crossing the Rocky Mountains on the Mormon Trail.

by eight other Spanish colonials and, eventually, two Native Americans they recruited along the way as guides. Taking a circuitous route, the Escalante–Domínguez expedition proceeded north through western Colorado, then westward into Utah. The Colorado–Utah border (as we know it today) was crossed on September 12, near the present-day Dinosaur National Monument.

Eventually, the 12-member group reached the Utah Valley and found a land rich with water, game, fish, timber, firewood, and other resources. Also encountered were communities of Timpanogos, friendly indigenous people whom the priests deemed likely candidates for religious conversion. Escalante and Domínguez promised to return for that purpose, although they never did.

to the land, however skewed by their imperfect sense of the actual geography involved.

TRAPPERS AND TRADERS

Spaniards never did establish permanent settlements in Utah, although their sovereignty over the land was formally affirmed by the Adams–Onís Treaty of 1819 hammered out by diplomats in Madrid and Washington. When in 1821 Mexico won independence from Spain and declared itself a republic, control over the Utah territory shifted. In fact, however, the distance from Mexico City was too great for any meaningful control to be exerted. Still, Hispanic traders bartered actively in Utah, offering goods such as corn, firearms, and liquor in exchange for furs.

But it was the advent of fur-trapping activity in the north and west, much of it Anglo-inspired, that sowed the seeds for a major change of identity that would be fully realized in 1848 with the American military victory over Mexico. British withdrawal after the War of 1812 had helped open the way to an increase in American private enterprise (as opposed to government-sponsored activity) in pursuit of fur-trading profit by companies operating in the American West. Large-scale trading activity began to develop along such routes as the Old Spanish Trail, and famously as "mountain men," whose dogged pursuit of beaver fur brought them into intimate contact with the land and waterways of Utah and enlarged on such trails as had already been plied by Native peoples, explorers, missionaries, early traders, or whomever else. British tended to come from the northwest, Americans from the east and southwest.

It was a party of Astor's trappers that discovered, in October 1812, a gap in the Central Rockies in Wyoming, just above Utah, that would provide a passageway to an eventual stream of

Ogden Utah Temple.

fur was destined to play a major role in Utah's development. Mexican authorities protested from time to time, to little avail.

Fur became an object of conspicuous consumption early in the 19th century. Suddenly, beaver hats were exceedingly fashionable with the urbane gentlemen of New York, London, and Paris, and the profits to be won from trappers foraging along ponds and streams in the central Rocky Mountain region attracted British and American business interests.

Major players were the American Fur Company, organized by that prototype American millionaire John Jacob Astor; the Hudson's Bay Company; and the Rocky Mountain Fur Company. They employed a force of trappers, known mobile Americans heading west. This strategic gap in the Rockies – that mountain range often called "Uncle Sam's backbone" – was the South Pass. The year 1824 brought another notable contingent of trappers, led by William H. Ashley of the Rocky Mountain Fur Company. These pacesetting mountain men crossed South Pass and established Fort Ashley at Lake Utah. Centered there in the late 1820s was the first Rocky Mountain fur-trading province.

THE RENDEZVOUS SYSTEM

Out of Ashley's pioneering effort came the custom of annual meetings, or rendezvous, starting in 1825. At these prolonged and often raucous gatherings, trappers swapped their stored-up fur caches for supplies brought overland into the mountains from places like Ashley's adopted St Louis. Before the rendezvous series came to an end in 1841 there were 16 such meetings, early ones being held in northern Utah. Among the mountain men involved were such famous names as Jedediah Smith, Jim Bridger, Tom Fitzpatrick, Milton and William Sublette, Étienne Provost, and David Jackson.

A kind of new "national road" was taking shape, with the Utah region lying in its path. The man often considered the greatest of Utah's trailblazing pioneers, Jedediah Smith, crossed Utah in 1826 on route to completing the first overland journey to California by an American. Smith, who had been one of Ashley's trappers, was also the first non-Native to traverse Utah from north to south, and the first to cross the Sierra Nevada and the deserts of the Great Basin. He would die in a skirmish with the Comanche in 1831 on the Santa Fe Trail.

First of these travelers to come upon the Great Salt Lake, or so many historians believe, was another of the legendary mountain men, the young Jim Bridger. At the age of about 20, Bridger spotted the lake while searching for the source of the Bear River in 1824 as a scout for the Ashley expedition. His trek had taken him beyond the Green River valley and down into Utah. Tasting the saline waters of this unexpected natural resource, he mistook it for the deep blue sea. "Hell," he is said to have declared, "we are on the shores of the Pacific." Utah's northwest corner was crossed in 1833 by the Tennessee-born fur trader and explorer Joseph Walker during an arduous journey that took him all the way to California. Walker reported such difficult conditions that no one else even attempted the route for the rest of the decade, but waves of emigrants would follow his trail in later years.

Meanwhile, the fur trade was hitting its peak in the early 1830s, giving rise to the establishment of frontier forts and outposts for collecting the pelts while storing up supplies to sustain the trappers. One of the earliest posts was set

Jim Bridger.

ʘ THE FUR TRAPPER

Utah's prodigious landscape was penetrated by such early voyagers as the Canadian-born fur trader Peter Skene Ogden, who spent his entire career with the Hudson's Bay Company. This scion of loyalist forebears became a chief operative for that Anglo-oriented company, and two of the five "Snake Country" trapping expeditions he led between 1824 and 1829 brought him face to face with Utah.

In the first of the five forays, Ogden and his 131-man brigade pushed south starting in December 1824 along the Bear River and into Utah territory. They trapped the Cache and Ogden Valleys, set up camp as far south as Mountain Green, and ultimately exited after their famous confrontation with dreaded American trappers. Whether Ogden himself entered the area memorialized by his name, or encountered the Great Salt Lake, is uncertain, but the expedition provided the first written account of northern Utah via his journal and that of aide William Kittson.

Four years later Ogden was back, in an 1828–29 expedition that was his last Snake Country venture. Moving along what later became tagged as the Humboldt River, Ogden and his trappers explored the region north of Great Salt Lake before returning home.

Ogden lived out his life in Oregon's Fort Vancouver, founded by the Hudson's Bay Company, and died in 1854.

up by Antoine Robidoux at Uintah Basin in 1832. The annual rendezvous system went into effect whereby trappers would display the furs they had snared. They did the bulk of their trapping in fall and spring, before streams froze over. Then, in the winter, they went into hibernation along with, in many cases, their Native American wives.

The first meeting in the new rendezvous system initiated by Ashley was held at Henry's Fork on the Green River. Utah likewise was the site for some subsequent annual meetings before the venue shifted to other territories in the region.

as super-fast highways for motorized transport. An early contingent in the emigrant wave that began rolling through the territory was that headed by John Bidwell in 1841. Organizer of the Western Emigration Society, he led the first wagon train, with 69 adults and children, through South Pass. It then divided into two groups, one heading north to Oregon Territory and the other making a grueling journey west before reaching Sacramento, California. Included were the first non-Native women known to have traveled overland across the territory into Nevada and all the way to California.

Bluff Fort Pioneer Historic Site.

But by 1840, the year of the 16th and last rendezvous, the fur business had declined sharply. There was much less consumer demand for beaver. But the trappers had played an important role in providing the American public with a sense of the region's geography, a bare-bones knowledge of its land, resources, and opportunities, and thereby facilitated access to the golden lands, fertile valleys, and nourishing waterways of the West, Far West, and Pacific Northwest.

THE PIONEERS

Now would come the wagon trains, or "prairie schooners," creaking along the rough paths and wide-open plains of Utah and adjacent regions, over homely trails that in later times would serve

There could be plenty of bumps along the way. The Bidwell emigrants skirted the edges of the Great Salt Lake and the Great Salt Lake Desert, encountering daunting and often inaccessible twists and turns. Many a wagon broke down and had to be abandoned on such passages. No journey proved as wretchedly unfortunate as that undertaken by the ill-fated Donner-Reed party of 1846 (see page 39). The route taken in that lamentable episode – a so-called short-cut aimed at lopping off 400 miles (640km) from the scheduled passage to California – had already been traversed by the soldier-adventurer John C. Frémont, who, with the famed scout Kit Carson and three others, explored the northern Great Salt Lake in a rubber boat in 1843. Frémont was bound for Oregon and

California in the first of his five famous western expeditions. A year later, in 1844, he and another expeditionary force passed through Utah again, going north to Utah Lake and then east through the Uintah Basin and Browns Hole. And in still another trip in 1845 Frémont circled the southern shore of Great Salt Lake before heading across the Great Salt Lake Desert to California.

By the mid-1840s, thanks to the carving out of these trails and related circumstances, Utah's modern history was unfolding in a full sense. Its first permanent Anglo settlement, for example, was built in 1845 by Miles Goodyear, a Connecticut-born trapper and trader. He called it Fort Buenaventura, out of which arose the town of Ogden. In 1848, Goodyear took a pack train from the Great Salt Lake to Los Angeles, and eventually Mormons turned the western part of the Spanish Trail into a wagon route conveying pioneers to California.

The year 1848 brought the start of one of the most transformative events in American history, the California gold rush. A wave of emigrants and transients succeeded in transforming the public perception of Utah territory as a terra incognita.

Francisco Fort Day festival.

⊙ THE DONNER PARTY TRAGEDY

Rightly or wrongly, the blame for the tragic Donner party disaster of 1846-47 has usually been pinned on Lansford W. Hastings, author of *The Emigrants' Guide to Oregon and California* and propagandist for western expansion. Hastings' 1845 book was read widely, and he gave credence to a short-cut supposedly capable of abbreviating the arduous western passage. Emigrants could bypass the normal route via Fort Hall in eastern Idaho, head south for the Great Salt Lake and then turn due west.

Alas, it proved disastrous for George Donner, age 60, of Springfield, Illinois, his wife and children, and many others. Of the original group of 87, only 48 survived. They had opted in July 1846 for Hastings' Cut-off, failed to connect with Hastings himself at Fort Bridger in Wyoming, and embarked on a hellish ordeal.

The party traveled through the Wasatch Mountains and around the southern end of the Great Salt Lake before striking out across the Bonneville Flats. Mud beneath the salt crust soon bogged down the emigrants, who abandoned several wagons, livestock, and equipment. They dashed across Nevada but, exhausted by their ordeal in Utah, couldn't make up for lost time. Trapped by early snow in the Sierra Nevada, the famished emigrants resorted to cannibalism for sustenance.

BUTCH CASSIDY AND THE SUNDANCE KID

Thanks in large part to the 1969 movie (starring Paul Newman and Robert Redford), Butch Cassidy and the Sundance Kid remain legends not only of the Old West, but of a romantic outlaw existence in which breaking the law became an expression of personal freedom.

BIRTH OF A LEGEND

Butch Cassidy was born Robert LeRoy Parker in Beaver, Utah, on 6 April, 1866. Taught the art of cattle rustling by ranch hand Mike Cassidy, he borrowed his mentor's last name, and picked up the handle "Butch" while working as a butcher in Rock Springs, Wyoming. Having pulled his first bank job in Telluride, Colorado, in 1889, he threw in his lot with a group of outlaws known as the Wild Bunch. Among them was one Harry Longabaugh – the Sundance Kid – who picked up his nickname following a jail stint in Sundance, Wyoming. Eclectic in their criminal pursuits, the Wild Bunch's resumé would include horse rustling as well as the robbing of trains, banks, and mine payrolls; between them, they gave away a fortune in gold to friends and even strangers in need. The spent winters in Brown's Hole, a broad river valley in remote northwest Colorado near Utah, but were also known to visit the nearby towns. Their saloon excesses were tolerated, however, because at the end of a spree they would meticulously account for every broken chair and bullet hole, making generous restitution in gold.

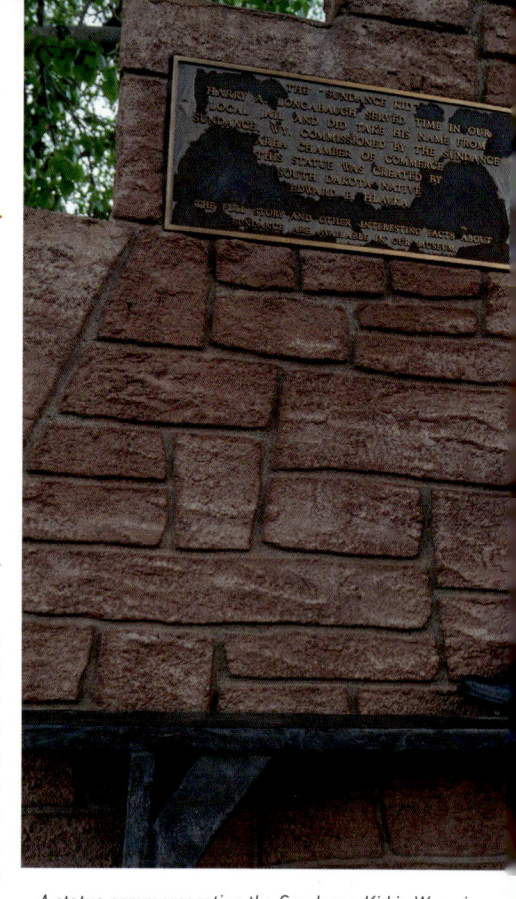

A statue commemorating the Sundance Kid in Wyoming.

Wax model of Paul Newman and Robert Redford from the movie Butch Cassidy and the Sundance Kid.

Wanted poster for Robert Leroy Parker known as Butch Cassidy.

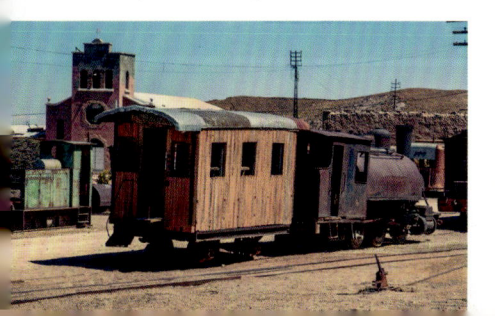

Butch Cassidy.

The end?

The gang, however, was eventually undone by their own vanity: during a visit to Fort Worth, Texas, five of the men posed for a photo in smart suits and derby hats, looking so dapper that the photographer proudly placed the photo in his shop window, where it was seen the following day by a detective from the famous Pinkerton agency.

Wearying of life on the run, Butch and Sundance sailed for South America in 1902, and were soon trying their hand at gold mining, while robbing the occasional bank or train. The Hollywood version was true enough to this point, but legend has it that Butch Cassidy did not die in a hail of bullets at the hands of Bolivian soldiers in 1909 as depicted in the film – although it seems that Harry Longabaugh did. The last say belongs to Josie Morris, an old girlfriend from Butch's Brown's Hole days, who insisted that he came to see her on his return from South America and claimed furthermore that he died an old man in Johnny, Nevada, sometime in the 1940s.

Butch Cassidy's cabin in Fruita.

The cabin where Butch Cassidy and the Sundance Kid hid.

The wooden wagon at this abandoned silver mine is the last one robbed by Butch Cassidy and the Sundance Kid.

A Mormon preacher, purported to be Brigham Young.

PROMISED LAND

"This is the place" where the Mormons under Brigham Young left an indelible mark on an arid land they transformed into a bountiful "Zion."

If 1848 was a golden time for America, equally imposing was 1846. That latter year encapsulates the great leap forward a young nation was making toward the middle of the 19th century. Americans were on the move, by land and by sea, and usually westward. "Go west!" young men were admonished. Most fatefully, 1846 marked the start of a war by which Mexico would be supplanted as landlord over a big chunk of territory, transforming the US from developing nation to continental colossus.

It was an important moment, too, for an incipient Utah, that remote territory hard by the Rockies that was long disdained as a bleak netherworld somewhere between East and West. One early visitor dismissed it as a "Great American Desert." Anybody heading that way was, likely as not, a passerby on route to some more rewarding place, like the greener pastures of Oregon and California.

Wagon trains were rolling in the 1840s, conveying emigrants over frontier routes like the Oregon Trail and into such hinterlands as the Utah region. It was a time when Americans were picking up and starting over, and why not? As the boosters of Manifest Destiny were proclaiming, this land is your land.

Out of such expansionist striving did Utah take shape, first as a territory in 1850, finally as a state in 1896. Other states would emerge, too, but none in quite the way Utah did. In her case the driving force was what we nowadays call a faith-based initiative. It impelled a new breed of reformist Christians who called themselves Mormons – formally, the Church of Jesus Christ of Latter-day Saints, or LDS – to establish a sanctuary in the far-off western hills and desert after the most famous mass migration in

Joseph Smith, Mormon leader and prophet.

American history. For the "Saints," 1846 was the central year of passage in a quest for a promised land, a new Zion, far from the madding crowds of eastern unfriendliness.

JOSEPH SMITH AND THE EARLY MORMONS

The "Church of Christ" was founded in the 1830 in upstate New York by a young farmer named Joseph Smith. Revered by Mormons as their original "Prophet," Smith was reputedly directed to unearthing a cache of inscribed golden plates in upstate New York. They provided, along with his revelations and the Holy Bible, the basis for a renewed Christian faith whose tenets he set forth in *The Book of Mormon*. Its millennialist

> *This practice of plural marriage, known in Mormon parlance as "celestial marriage" and "spiritual wifery," came to be the sorest point in the sect's long troubled relationship with the outside world.*

message – the Second Coming was expected imminently – attracted followers from the outset. Non-believers, on the other hand, were repelled by the doctrinaire claim to religious truth and the Mormon rejection of much traditional theology. To many of them, Smith was a charlatan, while to the Mormons, non-believers were disdained as "Gentiles."

In 1831, one of Smith's early revelations caused him and his followers to relocate to Kirtland, Ohio, in search of a peaceable religious haven. But the newcomers' radical Christian doctrines and "evangelical socialism" aroused resentment, and the Mormons made subsequent moves. In western Missouri, with its strong pro-slavery sentiment, the newcomers were widely detested as trouble-making "Yankee invaders." Tension there reached fever pitch by October 1838, when an attack by the Missouri Militia on a Mormon settlement at Haun's Mill caused 18 deaths. Joseph Smith, his brother Hyrum and five of their co-religionists were convicted of treason. They escaped death by fleeing to Illinois.

There, at a village on the Mississippi River called Nauvoo, the Saints built a bustling community that grew to be one of the most prosperous in the state. It was dominated by a great hilltop Mormon temple – until the building was burned down by non-Mormons. Hostility to the Mormons became sorely aggravated by reports that polygamy was being widely practiced.

Joseph Smith's vision.

Joseph Smith murdered at the Carthage Jail. The mob propped Smith's body against a well and ordered Colonel Levi Williams to "Shoot the damned rascal."

The practice was at first denied outright, then kept under wraps. Joseph Smith first spoke of it publicly in 1843, as an approved doctrine, and in 1852 the practice of plural marriage received the church's official blessing.

Meanwhile, the tense situation in Illinois that was developing came to a murderous climax in June 1844. Provoked by an editorial attack on the Mormon message, Smith's fulmination incited some of his co-religionists to smash the offending newspaper's printing press. Accused of causing a riot, Joseph and his brother Hyrum were confined to a jail at Carthage, Illinois, while charges of treason were drawn up. An anti-Mormon mob, enraged, broke into the jail and shot both fatally.

BRIGHAM YOUNG

Once again, Mormons decided to leave all behind and move on, this time to some far-off land out west for a hoped-for permanent haven. Smith as early as 1842 had envisioned such a long-distance remove, telling associates to seek "a place of refuge" for a "government of our own." But plans were sidetracked when he turned his attention to making a run for the US presidency in 1844.

After his death, the planning was carried forward chiefly by Brigham Young, who survived a schism in Mormon ranks to emerge as Smith's successor. Though less charismatic than his predecessor, Young was a practical genius who would guide the Church's affairs ably over the next three decades. With military-like precision, he charted the great 1,200-mile (1,900km) exodus of 1846–47 that brought the Mormon vanguard to Utah, followed by waves of others in the following years that numbered some 16,000. Once there, Brigham Young supervised the settlements that overcame harsh conditions to flourish in the Great Salt Lake Basin and beyond, up into the north and down below to the south. He dealt as best he could with the vexing problem of Indigenous people whose land and resources were rudely encroached on, and with a federal government that often felt sorely tested by this idiosyncratic group of believers who seemed somehow to hold themselves above and beyond the rules of normal civic and Christian conduct.

Young had also been raised in an upstate New York region rife with revivalist fervor. He had joined the fledgling Mormon movement in 1832 and three years later was named by Smith as one of the Church's original Twelve Apostles.

Brigham Young officiating at a plural marriage.

Young was in England from 1839 to 1841 helping to recruit some of the many European converts who would join the diaspora to Utah.

CHOOSING UTAH

Brigham Young sent forth a preliminary expedition in 1845 to seek out suitable areas for settlement in places that "nobody else wanted," with special consideration given to Texas, California, Oregon, and Vancouver Island. And he studied with great interest published reports in newspapers and best-selling books that were stirring wide interest in the West's vast terrain. These reports represented the findings of the soldier-adventurer John Charles Frémont, who had surveyed on behalf of the U.S. Army's Topographical Corps.

HISTORY & FEATURES

Frémont, celebrated as "the Pathfinder," undertook three major western expeditions, in 1842, 1843–44, and 1845–47. His vivid descriptions of the rich landscape were firing the imagination of readers around the country, including such literary luminaries as Longfellow, Emerson, and Thoreau, who were enchanted by glimpses of the grand western vistas.

Young, too, was absorbed by the descriptions. He focused on the Great Basin, situated 1,000 miles (1,600km) from the Pacific Coast and accommodating no people beyond those native to the region. Even the Ute presence was tenuous, their settlements being less permanent in nature than those of the Pueblo peoples to the south. Frémont had written approvingly of the area's soil and grazing land, sheltered by the Wasatch Range. The desert chosen for settlement by Young, part of the Great Basin, was marked by dry lake beds, but there were sufficient mountain streams from which to draw water for irrigation.

By the summer of 1845 Young was decided on the region as a likely promised land. He envisioned as his new haven for Mormons an immense expanse of land far exceeding present-day Utah. It also included most of Nevada and Arizona plus parts of Oregon, Idaho, Wyoming, Colorado, New Mexico, and even California. For the most part he kept the destination a secret, though he did divulge it in a letter to President James K. Polk.

THE GREAT TREK

Preparations were undertaken in Nauvoo for the construction of large numbers of wagons and the amassing of necessary supplies and equipment. Some of the Mormon men took on additional wives – Young himself contracted marriage with 19 additional partners. Many of the marriages were pro forma, undertaken not for conjugal purposes but to assure a degree of security for women who were leaving everything behind for an uncertain future.

The great trek from Nauvoo to Utah began in February 1846. Wagon trains left at regular intervals in separate caravans, inching their way along Iowa day by day, then season by season, into Nebraska, Wyoming, and finally south to the Great Salt Lake Valley. The first arrival occurred in July 1847. Some 3,000 pioneers were involved in the earliest encampments in Iowa, and the number would swell to about 16,000 assembled at a site near present-day Omaha, Nebraska, that was designated as Winter Quarters.

Mormon pioneers on the 'Mormon Trail' from Nauvoo.

The routine grew familiar. A bugle would sound at five o'clock in the morning, followed by prayers and breakfast, and the wagons would start rolling again. It was slow going, with many roads resisting passage.

There was much hardship along the way for the Mormon pioneers. Most costly was the encampment at Winter Quarters for the 1846–47 season. The camp had nearly a thousand log cabins built by the pioneers. Some 600 deaths occurred here due to cholera, malaria, bitter cold weather, and conditions of near-starvation. On the last leg of the trek, Young in April 1847 was part of a separate "Pioneer Band" of 143 men, plus a handful of women and children, that forged a route to the Great Salt Lake Valley. This so-called Mormon Trail coincided with the Oregon Trail as far as Fort Bridger before diverging to the southwest toward Utah.

Young met up with frontier experts, including the famed scout Jim Bridger, who advised that Utah was inhospitable for farm settlement. Disregarding the counsel, Young ordered the party to press on. And on July 24, 1847, he got his first look at the Great Salt Lake Valley from the mouth of Emigration Canyon. The Mormon leader, recovering from a fever that caused him to abandon his horse for the relative comfort of a carriage, lifted his weakened frame, gazed out over the arid land and uttered his memorable approval, "It is enough. This is the right place. Drive on."

> During the great trek west, some 500 volunteers were signed up by US Army recruiters in Iowa for a Mormon Battalion to assist in the war with Mexico – they made their own remarkable overland march to California.

Salt Lake City, 1891.

SETTLING THE UTAH VALLEY

The newcomers wasted no time in putting down roots. They developed a network of ditches for irrigation and planting crops. Water, the crucial natural resource, was commonly owned. It was diverted from mountain streams via dams and canals and efficiently delivered to serve the needs of homes and gardens, livestock, and orchards.

Lots were equitably assigned. Young went forth the day after arrival to mark off streets and configure whatever traffic patterns would be necessary for the central village that became

> *Skeptical mountain man Jim Bridger offered to pay "$1,000 for a bushel of corn grown in the Great Salt Basin." Ironically, by the early 1900s, northern Utah was among the most productive agricultural areas on the Union Pacific line.*

Utah's great metropolis. It was first called Great Salt Lake City, then (in 1868) simply Salt Lake City. Situated at its heart would be Tem-

Salt Lake City scene in 1849-50 as depicted in the Army Survey of the lands around the new Mormon settlement.

ple Square, accommodating the great religious structure that began to arise in the 1850s and would not be dedicated until 1893.

The rate of growth was phenomenal. The original 300 pioneers who reached the valley in 1847 swelled a year later to 5,000, plus a battery of houses, stores, bridges, mills, and in 1850, the first newspaper of its kind west of the Mississippi River, the Deseret News. Colonization was extended beyond Salt Lake Valley, first to southern Utah, then to other areas. By 1857 there were 96 separate communities in the Territory of Utah.

A thousand acres (405 hectares) of farmland were brought under cultivation in that brief period, but in the summer of 1848 hordes of giant crickets attacked, devouring nearly everything in sight. The settlers were in despair, expecting a total blight, when flocks of seagulls from the Great Salt Lake suddenly appeared, swooping in to rid the landscape of the pests. It was in the nature of a miracle, but there would be recurring plagues of crickets and grasshoppers for years to come, sometimes causing near-famine.

UTAH TERRITORY

With the Mexican surrender of 1848, the vast chunk of western territory that included the Mormons' new homeland came formally under American sovereignty. A provisional State of Deseret was established in 1849, and Brigham Young and associates asked Congress for full admission within the Union. They proposed the name "Deseret," a Mormon scriptural reference for "honey bee," suggesting industriousness. Congress rejected the idea of putting Utah on a fast track to statehood. The land mass proposed was huge, encompassing not only present-day Utah but also most of Nevada and Arizona and parts of six other states – including California and its highly prized seaports. This was scaled back in size by Congress to something more like today's combined Utah and Nevada plus adjacent land in Colorado and Wyoming. When in the 1860s land was carved out to create the Nevada, Colorado, and Wyoming territories, Utah assumed her present size.

The name "Deseret" was also rejected by the Congressmen as bleakly uninviting. They opted instead for "Utah" as more fittingly representative of the region's people – the Utes, Paiutes, Goshutes, and others.

Utah Territory was crafted as part of the intense jockeying between North and South that resulted in the Compromise of 1850 – the attempt to maintain a delicate balance between the admission of free states versus slave states. Mormon leaders tried to keep their distance from the searing issue – Utah was largely a neutral place during the Civil War – but this sense of apartness stirred federal suspicion about the allegiances of the LDS Church and its people.

Rumors were rife that an attitude suggesting sedition was prevalent in the territory. Worse still, in public estimation, was the practice of polygamy, affirmed in 1851 and made official

Church doctrine a year later. Mormons were denounced as "a pack of outlaws" by President Zachary Taylor, who deemed them "not fit for self-government." More sympathetic was his successor, Millard Fillmore. He made Brigham Young the first governor of the Utah Territory, in 1851, and Mormon leaders reciprocated by naming the site of its first capital Fillmore (later it was returned to Salt Lake City).

The territorial legislature met for the first time in 1851, moving to establish a militia and a prison, build roads, bridges, and canals, and bring towns into legal existence. And to meet the threat posed by an increasing influx of non-Mormons into the region, Young encouraged the practice of plural marriage to bring more children into the faith.

Mormon numbers were greatly augmented by a steady flow of immigrants in the 1850s, many from abroad – British, Dutch, Scandinavians, Germans, and others. Utah's population rose from about 10,000 to 60,000 in that period. To cut costs, Young initiated a Handcart Brigade scheme whereby emigrants made the trek on foot tugging only two-wheeled carts. More than 3,000 Mormons traveled that way to the Great Basin, hundreds becoming bogged down in early snowfalls and marooned in the mountains. Many perished along the way.

CONFLICT WITH NATIVE AMERICANS

Inevitably, there was conflict growing out of settlers' encroachment on Native grounds. Mormons liked to think they were more sympathetic than most to Native Americans, who they regarded as, in a sense, fellow outcasts, and whom the Book of Mormon identified as "Lamanites" of old Israelite origins. Brigham Young famously advised that "it is better to feed them than to fight them."

In 1849, Young sought out the Ute leader known as Chief Walker to seek permission to settle the Sanpete Valley of central Utah. Permission was granted, but the chief was not always able to rein in younger Ute militants angered by the constant influx of settlers, and the Walker War of 1853–54 followed. A series of

The Deseret costume in the 1850s.

⊘ SIZING UP THE PROPHET

Richard Francis Burton was big on exotica, not to mention erotica, so it was perhaps natural that this much-traveled English adventurer should find himself in Salt Lake City in 1860 to examine Mormon peculiarities, like polygamy, and take personal measure of the prophet himself, Brigham Young.

A man for all seasons – linguist, explorer, mystic, orientalist, bon vivant – Burton spent three weeks in the Utah capital after a 19-day stagecoach trek from Missouri during which he filled his notebooks with observations on Western ways. He was much taken with Young, whom he judged to be "no common man" and whom he described in fastidious detail in a published memoir. "He shows no signs of dogmatism, bigotry or fanaticism," Burton wrote of his personal encounter with the Mormon leader, "and never once entered – with me at least – upon the subject of religion."

Burton, equally famous for his African explorations and his 16-volume translation of the sensual Arabian Nights text, capped off his American visit in San Francisco before returning home to England to marry his beloved, Isabel Arundel, publish his account of the New World in The City of the Saints and *Across the Rocky Mountains to California* (1861), and be awarded a knighthood.

Ute raids took several Mormon lives and caused the loss of about 400 head of livestock.

Relations were seriously set back when a team of US Army engineers under the command of Captain John W. Gunnison was attacked by Paiute in 1853 while surveying sites for a transcontinental railroad route. The massacre of Gunnison and seven others in Utah raised suspicions that Mormons were somehow at fault, and President Franklin Pierce sent an army force to investigate and oust Brigham Young as governor. Young remained in office.

and cattle. Mormons had to rely for protection on their own Nauvoo Legion, the federal government refusing to send Army troops, and the conflict dragged on until 1872. Several hundred Native Americans were killed during the seven-year war.

CONFLICT WITH THE FEDERAL GOVERNMENT

Tension between Mormons and federal officials over the doctrines and lifestyle of a Church-dominated Utah Territory that hoped to be fully accepted into the Union erupted in the Utah War of 1857–58. It

The Mountain Meadows Massacre, 1857.

In 1863, as the Civil War raged between North and South, a large force of federal troops commanded by Colonel Patrick E. Connor killed over 300 Shoshone at the Bear River Massacre in southern Idaho. It put an end to hostilities involving Native Americans in northern Utah and led to the creation of the Uintah Reservation for the Ute in 1864.

One more major uprising occurred in 1865 with the start of the Black Hawk War in central Utah. It was brought on when Native Americans averse to Mormons encroaching on traditional hunting grounds launched a guerrilla action under the young Ute war chief Black Hawk that cost the lives of 75 Mormon settlers, the abandonment of 25 settlements, and the loss of thousands of horses

started when President James Buchanan, reacting to widespread public antipathy to Mormons and their "barbaric" practice of polygamy, moved to quell the perceived "rebellion" brewing there and replace Brigham Young with a non-Mormon governor.

Escorting the appointee was a 1,500-man force of federal troops commanded by Colonel Albert Sidney Johnston. Young denounced the action as religious persecution. "My power will not be diminished," he declared as he imposed martial law and ordered Mormon militiamen and the Nauvoo Legion to undertake guerrilla operations. They burned Fort Bridger, then a Mormon possession, for defensive reasons, and set afire US Army supply trains. Government cattle were driven off, and Salt Lake City was evacuated.

Amid this conflict occurred one of the most heinous acts of civilian slaughter in western annals. It involved the Baker-Fancher party, a wagon train bearing Arkansas emigrants through southwestern Utah on route to California. In the hysteria of the moment, when Mormons feeling beleaguered were espousing "blood atonement" as righteous retribution, the intrusion of non-Mormons was seen as a dire threat. At a place called Mountain Meadows, the emigrants were ambushed by an unholy alliance of Mormon militiamen led by John D. Lee, and a Paiute war band. The emigrants were deceived, then mercilessly slaughtered, women, children, and men. About 120 deaths occurred, only 17 children surviving. Twenty years later, in 1877, justice was finally meted out to one perpetrator – Lee was executed by firing squad at the site of the massacre.

The Utah War came to an end when a deal was worked out that provided pardons for alleged Mormon offenses. Young accepted it, as well as his replacement, and a force of federal troops paraded through a nearly deserted Salt Lake City. Later, Mormons returned to their abandoned homes. In 1861, the last of Johnston's troops left Utah.

CONFRONTING POLYGAMY

Polygamy as an issue continued to divide Utah from the rest of the nation, and to keep the territory from becoming a state. Utah was the target of the Morrill Anti-Bigamy Act passed in 1862 that outlawed plural marriage in any US territory. The measure permitted Young and others to be tried in 1871 on charges of "lascivious cohabitation," but legal appeals blocked successful prosecution.

In 1877, two years after Young's death in Salt Lake City, anti-polygamy laws were upheld by the US Supreme Court. Congress made polygamy a federal crime in 1882, and many of the Mormon leaders went into hiding. They included the church president, John Taylor, who was still a fugitive at the time of his death in 1887. Arrests and imprisonment for unlawful cohabitation were becoming frequent – in all, some 1,300 polygamists were locked up. Congress passed an even harsher law in 1887 that disincorporated the Church and seized its property.

Church sanctioning of plural marriage ended abruptly in 1890 when its new president, Wilford Woodruff, issued a manifesto urging full compliance with federal laws dealing with marriage. He attributed his action to a divine revelation. It effectively brought closure to the long-simmering "Mormon problem."

In 1893, President Benjamin Harrison granted amnesty to all who engaged in the practice of polygamy, and the following year their civil rights were restored by his successor, Grover Cleveland. Finally, on January 4, 1896, after being turned down five times between 1856 and 1887, the Territory of Utah was admitted to the Union as the nation's 45th state.

Brigham Young with a large group of wives and children.

⊘ BRIGHAM YOUNG'S WIVES

Brigham Young is thought to have had 56 wives in all, from Miriam Works in 1824 to Hannah Tapfield in 1872. Many of the "sealings" were expedient in nature rather than conjugal. Nonetheless, Young was presented with 57 children by 16 of his wives. Ten of his wives divorced him. The most notorious divorce was that involving Ann Eliza Webb, who was married to Young in 1868 – she was 23, he 66 – only to flee her polygamous coop to pen a best-selling exposé. The public was titillated, and Ann Eliza excommunicated. She charged cruelty and neglect but got little legal satisfaction – a meager $100 a month – years later.

THE ORIGINS OF MORMONISM

The Church of Jesus Christ of Latter-day Saints (LDS) was created in 1830 by Joseph Smith in upstate New York, when he published the Book of Mormon, the founding text of the LDS.

ROOTS

Born in Vermont in 1805, Joseph Smith grew up poor in a period of intense religiosity and Christian revivalism known as the "Second Great Awakening." As a boy, he was given to attempting to "divine" where precious old relics or treasure might be buried, and while still a teenager he experienced the first in a series of supernatural revelations of long-lost Christian principles.

MORONI

Smith claimed to have been visited by an angel in 1823 while he was living in Palmyra, New York. The angel, named Moroni, led Smith to a buried set of inscribed golden plates, which, after four years of visits, Smith retrieved and translated into what would become the Book of Mormon. Joseph Smith kept the plates concealed behind a curtain in his house while he worked through his translations, using a pair of seer stones he said had been buried with the plates. He supposedly did show the plates to a limited number of his followers: the "Three Witnesses," and the "Eight Witnesses," before Moroni took them back.

Interior of Joseph Smith's home.

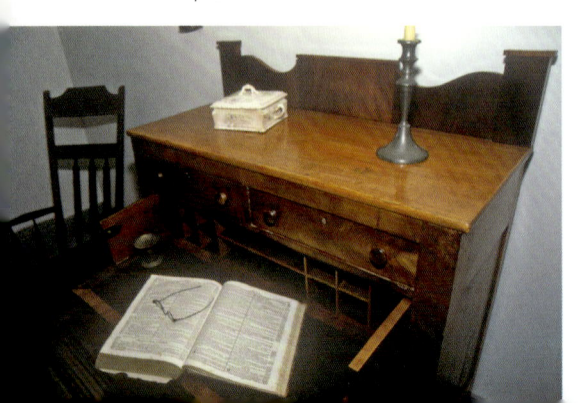

Joseph Smith brings a corpse back to life. This incident was reported in Maria Ward's The Mormon Wife, 1872.

Mormon Prophet Joseph Smith as Lieutenant General of the Nauvoo Legion.

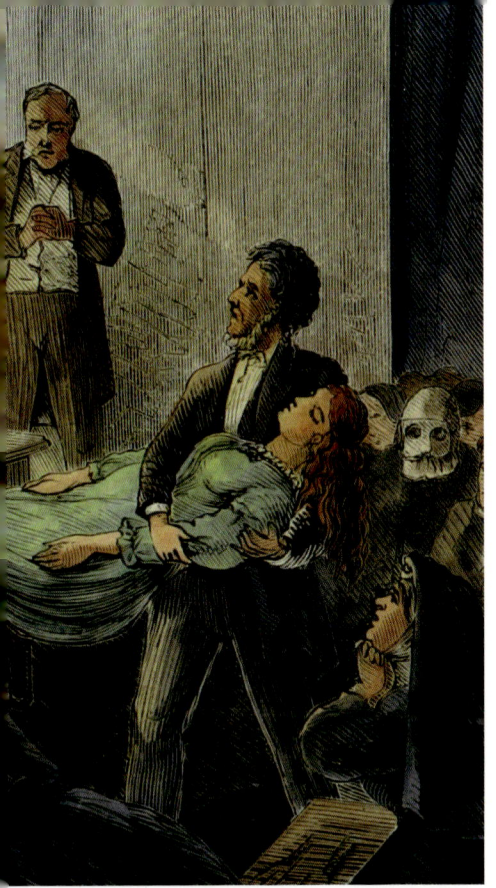

The Joseph Smith Memorial Building and the Mormon Temple.

The Book of Mormon

The Book of Mormon: An account written by the hand of Mormon upon plates taken from the plates of Nephi tells the history of an Israelite family that fled Jerusalem c. 600 BC for a new "Promised Land." The patriarch, Lehi, had six sons, Laman, Lemuel, Sam, Nephi (chosen by God to lead the family), Jacob, and Joseph. Laman and Lemuel eventually rebel, and the colony splinters. The ensuing war between the Lamanites – supposed ancestors of Native Americans – and the Nephites (waged for a thousand years) concludes with the genocide of the Nephites. Mormon's son, Moroni, completes the plates and buries them.

The book was published in Palmyra in 1830, and Smith organized the Church of Christ a few days later. He and his followers ran into local opposition, and they moved to Kirtland, Ohio, in 1831 – he would later flee to Missouri and then Illinois in 1839, enduring beatings and periods of imprisonment.

He also seems to have begun practicing polygamy in the 1830s. His luck finally ran out in 1844, when he was shot by a mob at Carthage Jail.

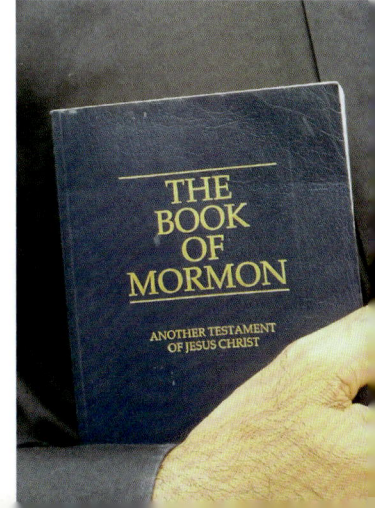

Joseph and Hyrum Smith murdered in the Carthage Jail.

Joseph Smith visited at night by the Angel Moroni.

The Book of Mormon, first published in 1830.

Main Street, Salt Lake City, c. 1908.

HISTORY & FEATURES | 55

UTAH IN THE MODERN AGE

Beyond the spiritually determined Mormon pioneers came waves of opportunists who helped reshape Utah's latter-day history well into the 21st century.

For the Mormons, Utah was a regular utopia wherein was founded a peaceable kingdom complete with self-sufficient economy. The only trouble was, others inevitably began showing up as well. By 1880 the percentage of the population that was Mormon had shrunk to 85 percent. In the Ogden municipal election of 1889, non-Mormons won every seat on the city council. A year later the Church of Jesus Christ of Latter-day Saints ceased trying to defend the practice of polygamy. Little by little, Utah was becoming "Americanized."

The Ogden case was instructive. This northern outpost, destined to become Utah's second-ranking city, had been founded in 1846 as Fort Buenaventura. It was sold a year later to the Mormons, who renamed it for the early fur trapper Peter Skene Ogden. In 1869 it was transformed from an agriculture-based community to an important western rail center. This occurred because America's long-awaited transcontinental railroad, which became a reality that year, was nearby, and Ogden became a "junction city."

Work on the cross-country railroad sped up once the Civil War ended in 1865, and its coming transformed the Utah region. A horde of jobseekers and opportunists, mostly non-Mormons, was attracted and places like Ogden prospered. There was disappointment on the part of Salt Lake City that the rail line didn't go directly through their

"The coming of the railroad unlocked Utah," historian Charles S. Peterson observed, "changing a desert fastness to a national highway and a burgeoning economic region."

Utah State Railroad Museum at Ogden Union Station.

locale, but plenty of Utahans prospered anyway. Some 4,000 were involved in grading and various other related projects.

THE TRANSCONTINENTAL RAILROAD

For the nation at large, the historic hookup that took place on May 10, 1869, at Promontory Summit in northern Utah linking the Central Pacific and the Union Pacific signaled the fading of the frontier as a most decisive factor. A large crowd was on hand at Promontory Summit, 56 miles (90km) northwest of Ogden, on that memorable day when Leland Stanford of the Central Pacific drove home a golden spike to connect the two rail lines after years of track-laying from east and west. News of the deed was sent by telegraph to a waiting crowd in Washington, DC. It was also in Washington, several years earlier, that another signal event involving Utah – hooking up the transcontinental telegraph system in Salt Lake City – became history when a wired dispatch was received by President Abraham Lincoln. The telegraph superseded yet another innovation that had a Utah link – the Pony Express.

Salt Lake City was brought into contact with the transcontinental rail system in 1870 when the Utah Central Railroad was linked with Ogden – Brigham Young and sons, among others, profiting through construction-related contracts. Still another major connection, in 1880, made Salt Lake City a station for the Denver & Rio Grande Railway.

Utah, meanwhile, became a more diverse place as its isolation was lessened. One result was a widened gulf between Mormons and others, another was industrial development, mining being a case in point. The railroads also opened marketing possibilities for farmers, sheep herders, cattle raisers, and a growing merchant class, undermining the Mormon attachment to agriculture as a more wholesome way for Saints to raise families, let the desert bloom, and make of their western sanctuary a heaven-bent commonwealth. Many LDS Church leaders, including Brigham Young, were not comfortable with the prospect of breadwinners being distracted by the chancy pursuit of trying to divine where precious metals might be buried in Utah's hills and ranges.

In addition to farming, the Mormon pioneers had engaged in handicrafts, some small industry, and whatever opportunities presented themselves – for example, catering to the needs of all those California-bound prospectors who were passing through in the early years of the gold rush. There were thousands of them, and they needed lots of goods and services, which Utahans were pleased to supply for the right price. Some of the original gold dust was brought back to Utah, in fact, by former members of the Mormon Battalion who had been at the scene of the original California strike, and it was utilized in minting Utah money.

THE MINING BOOM

Although the early emphasis was on agriculture, Church leaders in Salt Lake City had been enticed by reports of rich deposits of iron ore in southern Utah. They called on their co-religionists to go forth and establish missions beyond the Great Basin and unearth the much-needed iron. Many did, and the first smelting of Utah-produced iron occurred in 1852 in Cedar City. But the great leap forward for Utah mining came following the arrival in 1862 of Colonel Patrick E. Connor and his California Volunteers, a military force dispatched to protect the overland mail and telegraph systems from Native American raids. Connor regarded Mormons as out-and-out "rebels" and encouraged his ex-prospector soldiers to search the hills for precious metals to attract the eventual wave of non-Mormon fortune-seekers that he knew would follow – and thereby undermine the Church's dominance in Utah's public affairs.

Nevertheless, Utah's poor roads had impeded the transportation of ore, and the territory suffered for that reason by comparison, for example, with next-door Colorado, where mining camps boomed. When the railroads provided easier access to markets, Utah underwent a boom of its own, miners unearthing riches in the form of copper, gold, silver, coal, tin, lead, uranium, and a trove of mineral deposits.

Silver-bearing ores were discovered, and the 1870s saw bustling mines along the Wasatch

Bingham Copper Mine.

Front, on the Oquirrh mountain range to the west and south of Salt Lake City, in central and southern Utah, and in other districts. Non-Mormons and interlopers of various ethnicities were numerous in the industry as entrepreneurs and laborers. Fortunes were made by such well-known speculators as George Hearst, with holdings in the richly endowed Park City District, and banker Jay Cooke, who had mining interests in southern Utah.

There were losses, too, none more spectacular than in the case of Emma, a mine in Little Cottonwood Canyon east of Salt Lake City. Stock manipulation and fraudulent claims made the Emma Mine an infamous case involving fleeced investors both at home and in Europe, the resulting financial debacle aggravated by the economic Panic of 1873.

"THE RICHEST HOLE ON EARTH"

Copper emerged as Utah's most lucrative mining treasure late in the 19th century. One young metallurgist, Daniel Jackling, made a fortune by figuring out a system of efficiently extracting valuable ore from daunting hunks of low-grade copper deposits. In 1903 he formed the Utah Copper Company – ultimately to be acquired by the giant Kennecott enterprise – to work a huge deposit at Bingham Canyon south of Salt Lake City. Drawing on assets of the well-heeled Guggenheim family, Jackling assembled an array of super-sized steam shovels plus dump cars, locomotives, and miles of railroad track to build a humongous copper-reducing facility. From an excavation known as "the richest hole on earth," millions of tons of copper would be retrieved. The Bingham operation alone would account for about one-third of the nation's output of copper in the 20th century.

LABOR UNREST

Inevitably, labor-management troubles emerged over pay and working conditions, intensifying in the 1890s amid economic downsizing and social unrest. Radical groups agitated for reform, and such unions as the United Mine Workers fought bitterly for bargaining power in clashes with recalcitrant owners. Making things worse were hazardous workplace conditions of often lethal severity, the worst example of which came on May 1, 1900, when an explosion in a Scofield coal mine killed 200 men and boy laborers. Many would-be rescuers succumbed to lethal gas in the poorly ventilated tunnels.

A strike at Bingham Canyon in 1912 involved some 5,000 workers from among Utah's growing labor force. Most famous of the militant unions was the International Workers of the World – the "Wobblies" – and from them emerged the legendary Joe Hill, a Swede with a talent for poetry and song. Convicted of the fatal shooting of two persons at a Salt Lake City store in 1914, he was sentenced to death by firing squad. Neither a personal appeal by President Woodrow Wilson nor a barrage of international protest failed to stop the penalty from being carried out, and Joe Hill became an enduring martyr of the working class.

Reed Smoot (1862-1941) the first Mormon U.S. Senator.

MORMONS AND POLITICS

As for the old issue of Mormonism and divided loyalties, it resurfaced only periodically. One notable instance was the protracted campaign to bar Reed Smoot, a Church official, from taking his seat in the US Senate following his election in 1902. Smoot had to endure a protracted inquiry that was malevolently directed as much at LDS Church policy as at his own allegiance to the public order. He was finally accepted by the

Senate in 1907, a colleague quipping that Smoot was adjudged "a polygamist who doesn't polyg."

In a sense, this was an acceptance of Mormons and their Church into the American community after a long history of suspicion and outright hostility. Mormons became paradoxically aligned with the establishment worldview of their old Republican antagonists – as exemplified by Smoot himself. A protectionist in trade matters, he achieved notoriety as an architect of the Smoot-Hawley Tariff Act that sought to protect American firms in competition with foreign interests – thereby, as many believe, helping to bring on the Great Depression.

AGRICULTURE IN UTAH

In the realm of agricultural development, water supply was crucial in dealing with Utah's abundance of arid landscape, hence the necessity of installing irrigation systems from early on. The huge Strawberry Reservoir Project, federally funded and completed in 1913, diverted water to the Great Basin and thereby increased the extent of Utah's irrigated farmland. Irrigation projects sustained a bustling dairy industry, fruit orchards, and grain and hay production. Sheep, introduced in 1870, grazed the uplands and mountain meadows.

Sugar beets became a major product with construction of a Mormon-sponsored factory at Lehi in the early 1890s that was the first of its kind in Utah. Thousands of farms cultivated beets, and sugar came to rank as a major manufacturing enterprise.

There was a downside after World War I, however, as cutbacks in government orders reduced mining profits, and farmers were hurt as well by a drop in crop prices. Even harder times followed with the financial crash of 1929 and the Depression it engendered. By 1932, fully a third of Utah's labor force was unemployed. Residents left the state in heavy numbers, and for the first time the rural population fell behind its urban counterpart. More than 60,000 residents moved away between 1920 and 1940, and severe droughts and dust

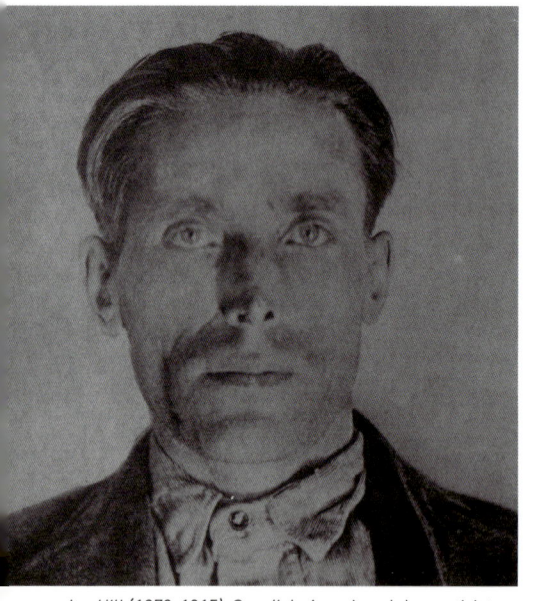

Joe Hill (1879-1915), Swedish-American labor activist.

⊘ THE LEGEND OF JOE HILL

Born in Sweden in 1879, Joe Hill (also known as Joseph Hillström and Joel Hägglund) was an itinerant laborer, songwriter, and sometime hobo, who organized on behalf of the Industrial Workers of the World (IWW), or Wobblies. He came to Utah in 1913 and worked in the Park City mines before being executed by firing squad in Salt Lake City on November 19, 1915, after being found guilty of murdering two men – a father and son – in a grocery store. Some believe the criminal charges against him were fabricated by the "copper bosses" of Utah, an anti-union state, although nothing has ever been proven conclusively.

Since his death, Hill has become a folk hero. Among his well-known songs about the life of ordinary working men, collected in the IWW's Little Red Song Book, were "Casey Jones," "Rebel Girl," and "The Preacher and the Slave." He is also known for two famous statements: "Don't mourn, organize!" and "I don't want to be found dead in Utah," a sentiment poignantly expressed shortly before his execution. Several books, films, plays, and songs have been written about Joe Hill, including the American folk song "I Dreamed I Saw Joe Hill Last Night" by Alfred Hayes and Earl Robinson, which captured the continuing struggle for labor rights after Hill's death.

storms in the 1930s wreaked havoc on irrigation-dependent Utah.

Mormons commiserated by pulling together and establishing storehouses of goods for distribution to the needy. Out of the experience came a permanent welfare program, established in 1936, which gave rise to farms and canneries. Federal relief programs helped Utah combat the Depression and inspired conservation and reclamation projects. Work began in 1967 on an ambitious effort – the Central Utah Project – to divert water from other areas of the state to help places sorely in need of it. Today, farm income derives largely from livestock products, and commercial agriculture is the major enterprise.

THE WORLD WAR II BOOM

Utah was transformed by World War II, socially and materially. The federal government pumped millions of dollars into the local economy through new and expanded programs, especially for military training and defense. Uncle Sam had already lent a hand, via relief programs, to help lift the state out of the Depression. Now the gathering storm in Europe climaxed by the devastating attack at Pearl Harbor in late 1941 intensified the recovery and changed Utah from backward hinterland into cultural mainstream.

In a state in which the federal government owns nearly two-thirds of the land, there were more than a dozen military installations operating, and they provided thousands of jobs. Hill Field near Salt Lake City was a major repair and supply depot for the Army Air Force.

The Ogden Arsenal was a storehouse for arms bound for the West Coast. The old Fort Douglas near Salt Lake City was used as a process center for recruits. Wendover's flatland on the Nevada border was ideal for year-round navigational and bomber training.

Utah also lent itself handily to an experimental platform for deadly warfare, as with the chemical weapons tested at remote Dugway Proving Ground in Tooele County.

Utah contributed about 65,000 of its own men and women for military service during the war. On the negative side, the prevailing anti-Japanese hysteria following the Pearl Harbor attack resulted in the establishment of an internment camp, which began operations on September 11, 1942. This was the Topaz "Relocation Center"

near Delta in Millard County, ultimately taking in 8,000 Japanese Americans. It was phased out soon after the Japanese surrender at Tokyo Bay in September 1945, and many of the former internees opted to settle in Utah.

They and the large numbers of Hispanics, Black Americans, and other "outsiders" attracted by wartime economic opportunity added a degree of cultural diversity to the state's population, resurgent after years of stagnancy. Totaling half a million in 1940, the population doubled by 1970 and quadrupled by 2000.

Hill Aerospace Museum.

POSTWAR UTAH

After World War II, the military-defense buildup continued as the state became a missile center, with plants at Ogden, Salt Lake, and Brigham City. By 1960 the federal government was Utah's largest employer, and the state's economic emphasis had shifted from agricultural enterprises to industry and manufacturing. There was strong activity in food processing, petroleum refining, and manufacturing of computer software. Many steam and hydroelectric plants were built, and there was a major resurgence in uranium mining following the 1952 discovery of a rich deposit in desert land near Moab. The discovery set off a latter-day "uranium fever" that rewarded investors and prospectors handsomely.

Industrial growth was fueled in the 1960s by the construction of dams, most notably Flaming Gorge and Glen Canyon. Copper production fell off following a price decline in the 1980s. Utah nonetheless leads the world in the output of beryllium, it is a major producer of coal, and it is the only state that turns out Gilsonite, an adhesive agent used in road and asphalt paving.

Postwar affluence combined with Utah's abundance of natural resources also made tourism an important sector of the economy. Visitors were attracted by recreational opportunities in skiing, hunting, fishing, hiking, camping, and snowmobiling. Skiing has become an especially important industry, furthered by a steady upgrading of facilities. The state is blessed with a trove of national forests, parks, and monuments in addition to nearly four dozen state parks. Zion National Monument was the first of the major federal preserves, designated in 1909 by the administration of President William Howard Taft – the latest was Bears Ears National Monument, established by President Barack Obama in 2016.

A cowboy with his cattle, La Sal.

THE LAST GUNFIGHT

The so-called Posey War – a short-lived violent conflict pitting Utes and Paiutes against white ranchers – took place near Blanding in March 1923. It was sparked by the escape of two young Utes who had been arrested for robbing a sheep camp, killing a calf, and burning a bridge. Forty years of friction between Native Americans and ranchers rapidly erupted into all-out confrontation. A large posse of angry, trigger-happy men rounded up Ute men, women and children in the nearby community of Westwater and held them in a barbed-wire stockade in Blanding. They then tracked down a 60-year-old Paiute named Posey who had married into the Ute band in Allen Canyon and gained a reputation for arrogance and thievery. A gunfight between Posey and his followers and the posse ensued. The Utes killed a horse, just missed three passengers in a Model T Ford, and made headlines in national newspapers.

Unknown to the sheriff, Posey was fatally wounded in the gunfight, but his body was not recovered for a week, during which time innocent Utes remained in captivity. Upon their release, these Utes were given individual land allotments in Allen Canyon by the federal government and their children were sent to school at Towaoc, the Ute Mountain Ute Agency in Colorado. The last major gunfight in the West was over.

Perhaps no institution is more identified with growth than the Church of Jesus Christ of Latter-day Saints, which has slipped the bonds of regional containment to spread its message around the world through an army of missionaries. For both church and state, diversity is emphasized. Public facilities like swimming pools long ago ceased invidious racial practices, and in 1978 the LDS Church declared the priesthood open to all worthy males. The following year brought professional basketball to Salt Lake City, via the improbably named Utah Jazz.

When dealing with the Covid-19 pandemic (2020–22), like much of conservative America, Utah responded first with a degree of cynicism then a patchwork of moderate restrictions on its citizens, keen to avoid criticism of government over-reach. With its primarily rural population, Utah fared much better than urban America, but the statistics remain grim. By 2022 over 36,000 had been hospitalized and almost 5,000 people had died (only around 350 people die annually in Utah from flu or pneumonia).

Bobsledding at 2002 Winter Olympics.

UTAH IN THE 21ST CENTURY

Today Utah's economy remains one of the nation's most dynamic, driven by cattle ranching, coal mining, salt production, and tourism, with farming and oil production also important. Utah has also become a bastion of the Republican party in the 21st century, voting reliably for Republicans in presidential elections, and for the state legislature. The only exception is Salt Lake City, the so-called "blue dot in a red sea." Utah hasn't elected a Democratic governor since 1980; a Democratic senator since 1970; or voted for a Democratic presidential candidate since 1964. The vast majority of culturally conservative Mormons vote Republican despite the LDS Church officially remaining politically neutral.

⊘ THE 2002 WINTER GAMES

Utah gained huge exposure in 2002 when Salt Lake City hosted the XIX Olympic Winter Games (commonly known as Salt Lake 2002), only the second American site to be thus selected (the winter games were held at Lake Placid in both 1932 and 1980). Future Utah senator Mitt Romney was president of the Organizing Committee. A worldwide audience of more than 2 billion viewers watched the televised broadcast emanating from Utah over 16 days and involving 2,400 athletes from 78 nations. Norway swept the medal table, with 13 gold and 25 medals overall. The games are widely regarded as a major success, ending with a surplus of $40 million.

Happy family life in South Jordan, Utah.

...use two people fell in Love

"Grief never ends...
but it changes.
It's a passage, not a place to stay.
Grief is not a sign of weakness, nor a
lack of Faith...
It is the price of Love."

"I have no greater
joy than to hear that
my children walk in truth"

THE CULTURAL LANDSCAPE

Though around 60 to 70 percent Mormon, Utah's population is unexpectedly diverse, with Native Americans, Hispanic immigrants, and LDS converts from around the world.

In February 2002, thousands of international sports enthusiasts flocked to Salt Lake City to attend the Olympic Winter Games. Many had prepared themselves to endure what some dubbed the "Mormon Games," dominated by dour followers of the Church of Jesus Christ of Latter-day Saints who would try to convert everyone they met. The reality was, of course, completely different. Almost overnight, it seemed (though not to the residents who had spent a decade enthusiastically laying the groundwork to host the Games), Utah had morphed into the sixth most urban state in the Union – there were five-star hotels, historic bed-and-breakfasts, nearby ski resorts, gourmet restaurants, nightclubs, bistros, coffeehouses, independent bookstores, high-end shopping, a well-regarded university and medical research center, museums, and world-class arts and music. The Games themselves went off without a hitch. What most visitors remembered, instead, were the huge number of polite and welcoming Utah residents and the surprising ethnic diversity of the people they met.

Since the Games, Utah's population has soared by around 30 percent to over 3.3 million, one of the fastest growing of any US state, and its diversity has similarly increased. Though it remains small compared to the likes of New York, Texas, and California, around 80 percent of the population is concentrated in the Utah Valley/Wasatch Front, in and around Salt Lake City, making a densely populated urban corridor. The Hispanic population (predominantly Mexican) is now around 13 percent, with smaller Asian, Black, and Native American communities. Today, over 90 different cultural groups have made Salt Lake City their home. As a result of

Navajo woman weaving a rug at Monument Valley.

the influx of new arrivals from outside the state, the percentage of Utah residents who are Mormon has declined, though it's become difficult – and controversial – to put a definitive figure on the decrease. And contrary to its conservative reputation, there's now a dynamic LGBTQ+ community in Salt Lake City.

Ever since its founding as a Mormon sanctuary for converts from around the world, Utah has had a strong international makeup. When the Mormons arrived, the territory was nominally under Spanish rule. It had been home to Indigenous cultures dating back thousands of years, then members of the Ute, Paiute, Goshute, Shoshone, and Navajo indigenous people who now make up over 33,000 of the state's residents. Mormon proselytizing in Britain and Scandinavia attracted thousands of immigrants to settle in Brigham Young's new State of Deseret. They were joined by migrant cowboys, farm workers, and poor laborers from Greece, Italy, Russia, Finland, Ireland, China, and elsewhere, who arrived in Utah with the railroads and mines. Today, new immigrants are increasingly Mormons from Polynesia, Latin America, and Africa, as well as refugees from trouble spots throughout the world.

NATIVE AMERICAN UTAH

The state's Native American Indigenous people remain deeply attached to traditional lifeways, particularly in southern Utah, where ancient and modern Native American cultures sit side by side on the Ute, Paiute, and Navajo reservations. Native American residents account for more than half of San Juan County's population of around 15,000. The county encompasses the Four Corners region, which was once the homeland of the Ancestral Pueblo people, whose descendants now reside in villages in New Mexico and Arizona.

The Book of Mormon.

⊘ IOSEPA AND THE HAWAIIAN CONVERTS

Unknown to many, a farming community of several hundred Hawaiian converts to the LDS faith under the leadership of I. W. Kauleinamoku was established in Tooele County's Skull Valley in 1889, close to the Mormon farm that eventually became the Skull Valley Goshute Indian Reservation. Iosepa (yo-see-pa), or "Joseph" in the Hawaiian language, was named after the LDS Church's founder, Joseph Smith, and a later missionary of the same name who visited the Hawaiian Islands in 1854.

In true Hawaiian style, Iosepa's residents raised pigs and fished for carp in ponds in addition to growing crops. When their crops failed, many residents began to work in local gold and silver mines during the late 1890s. The community was never self-sustaining and was largely supported by funds from the LDS Church, which had also paid the travel expenses of the new converts.

A combination of the harsh, dry environment and several cases of leprosy, a disease to which Hawaiians were particularly susceptible, doomed Iosepa. In 1917, Hawaiian Mormons returned to Laie on the island of Oahu, to live next to the newly constructed Hawaiian LDS Temple. The old Iosepa cemetery is now included on the National Register of Historic Places.

Near the San Juan River, residents of the Navajo Nation and Southern Ute reservation live in family compounds next to empty stone pueblos left behind by departing Ancestral Puebloans in AD 1300, while the people of the Uintah and Ouray Ute Reservation near Vernal and the Southern Paiutes headquartered in Cedar City still use lands once inhabited by the lesser-known Fremont culture. In places with good hunting or plenty of water, such as the Green River canyons, images painted or incised on rock have been left behind by hundreds of generations of Indigenous peoples, signifying their passage.

The once nomadic Great Basin Indigenous people share a number of material traditions, including basketry, leatherworking, drum making, and beading. Mythology centers on the culture hero Wolf, who made heaven and earth, and Coyote, the creative trickster responsible for fire, arts and crafts, and the origin of many plants, animals, and natural features, also celebrated in Navajo winter tales. Contact with Pueblos and Spaniards led the Navajo to develop distinctive crafts, such as silversmithing, pitch-glazed pottery, basketry, and rug weaving. Paiutes and Navajos both make ceremonial baskets in the Navajo Mountain area, after centuries of living next to one another. Intermarriage and pan-Native American powwows bring all of Utah's Indigenous people together at seasonal events like the Ute Bear Dance, a shuffling round dance held in spring to signal the rejuvenation of the natural world, symbolized by a bear awakening from hibernation.

Native Americans hold special significance for Utah's Mormons. The Church teaches that Native Americans are descendants of the Lamanites, one of the fallen Indigenous groups of Israel documented in the Book of Mormon. According to Mormon doctrine, special efforts must be made to bring these "fallen" angels back into the Christian fold. Missionaries have worked among Native Americans since the LDS Church arrived in 1847, and the Church oversees an active adoption and mentoring program with Indigenous people.

A mixture of paternal concern and outright hostility has frequently characterized the relationship of Native Americans and Mormons in Utah's history. At the political level, these conflicting attitudes have led to tragic outcomes at times, such as the ill-fated termination policy sponsored by Senator Watkins in the 1950s that ended federal recognition of the Southern Paiute Tribe until 1980. Still other Mormons,

A family in Manti, Utah.

HISTORY & FEATURES

> Salt Lake City's Living Traditions Festival is a three-day celebration of cultural diversity, featuring artists, dancers, musicians, craftspeople, and food vendors representing numerous ethnic communities. The event is held in May.

such as William Palmer, a leading citizen of Cedar City, became passionately interested in the ethnography of the Paiutes, interviewing families and amassing an extraordinary collection of Paiute-made baskets, now on display at Southern Utah University and Iron Mission State Park.

After 170 years of contact, many of Utah's Native American people have been baptized into the Mormon faith. Many participate in the Church regularly while still keeping alive traditional Native American ceremonies – a duality that comes naturally for any minority forced to walk in more than one world. This same pragmatic pan-traditional approach can be seen throughout the Native American world today and allows tribal people to draw from a variety of influences that has strengthened tribal ties rather than weakened them.

THE BRITISH INFLUX

The same can be said for the many thousands of people from all over the world who have left their homelands to come to Utah, whether as converts to the Mormon faith or as immigrants seeking a better life. The British Mormon Mission, organized in 1837, was among the most successful in drawing new converts to the Mormon city of Nauvoo, Illinois. When the word went out for a "gathering of Zion" in the Salt Lake Valley, thousands more made the sea crossing from England, Wales,

Sisters on a hike in Manti, Utah.

Scotland, Ireland, and elsewhere in Europe, paid for by the Mormon Perpetual Emigrating Fund, which between 1852 and 1887 directly assisted some 26,000 immigrants. They prayed and sang hymns on the long sea voyage, then pulled their belongings 1,000 miles (1,600km) by handcart to Utah.

Mormon history holds a special place for these hardy "handcart pioneers," whose faith was tested by many hardships as they crossed the prairie. Handcarts, wagon wheels, and other pioneer paraphernalia are proudly displayed in front yards all across Utah. Every year, young people reenact portions of the epic voyage at Pioneer Day pageants. And Dutch oven cooking over a campfire is a tradition at thousands of family and church picnics, not just for its sentimental connections to cowboys and trail rides but for the larger connection to pioneer roots that inspires so many Utahans.

By the beginning of the 20th century, 50,000 British converts had made the journey to Utah, and a quarter of Salt Lake City's population was British-born. Brits could be found in positions of political power, business, the media, the arts, and the trades. Leading businessmen included banker David Eccles (for whom Rice–Eccles Stadium in Salt Lake City is named) and Charles Nibley in lumber and sugar. Among the Brits who became editors of leading periodicals was George S. Godbe, founder of *Utah Magazine,* forerunner of the *Salt Lake Tribune,* who, along with Welsh immigrant Joseph Morris, founded the Godbeite Movement, dissenting from Mormonism in the late 1860s and 1870s.

Scottish-born Ebenezer Bryce, a shipbuilder, erected the state's oldest church in Pine Valley in southwestern Utah and went on to pioneer a ranch at Bryce Canyon in southern Utah, in the national park that now bears his name.

A British woman, May Anderson, founded what would become Primary Children's Hospital in Salt Lake City and also established kindergartens. British women sometimes also became polygamous wives in remote desert areas such as southern Utah's Arizona Strip, where one unsuspecting woman married a Cane Beds rancher. There is something forlorn about the accounts of such women, far from Britain's milder climate and not even allowed to indulge in a cup of tea or other simple comforts.

The thousands of quaint cottage gardens sporting hollyhocks, roses, and other English country flowers, even in Utah's driest deserts, are a reminder of the state's strong British heritage. Also prevalent are numerous cultural organizations such as the Caledonia Society, founded in 1884, that organizes Scottish dancing, bagpipe bands, and other highland pastimes at festivals throughout the state.

THE SCANDINAVIANS

Scandinavians, who with 30,000 immigrants by 1900 became the second most numerous group of Mormon converts, have also put their stamp on the state. Danish farmers and artisans were especially prominent in Box Elder and Cache counties north of Salt Lake City and Sanpete County to the south (which was one-third Danish by 1870), and in towns like

Horseback riding in Utah.

HISTORY & FEATURES

> In Sanpete dialect, transportation is in "cores" (cars) and "courts" (carts), and folks eat "carn" (corn) for dinner. When bothered, folks are known to utter the expletive, "oh, my heck."

Mantua, which was nicknamed "Little Copenhagen." One Danish immigrant, Anthony Lund, settled in Sanpete County in 1862 and later served in the territorial legislature and became a Church historian.

Today, Sanpete retains a strong Scandinavian influence. Highway 89 between Nephi and Salinas offers numerous glimpses of small pioneer towns with strong Danish roots, visible in the traditional farm buildings and workshops where musical instruments and other "Old World goods" are produced. Particularly interesting for visitors is the quaint, turned-about dialect heard throughout southern Utah – a combination of Scandinavian, British, and American accents. You may hear jokes about people being "barn in a born" (born in a barn) and be asked how you enjoyed your visit to the national "porks" (parks).

NON-MORMON ARRIVALS

A more typical western influence on Utah's cultural landscape are the many immigrant groups who came to Utah to work the mines, railroads, farms, and ranches. Early Mormons were encouraged to establish agricultural enterprises, so mining fell to non-Mormon immigrants from Europe and Asia, many of whom were part of the westward migration to the California goldfields. Irish, Italians, Greeks, Slavs, Japanese, Chinese, and others worked in the coal mines of Carbon and Emory counties, the hard rock mines of Summit, Salt Lake, Tooele, and Juab counties, and in railroad construction.

While Mormon immigrants were assisted by the LDS Church and encouraged to integrate, non-Mormons immigrants tended to congregate in ethnic communities that sprang up near industrial areas. Many were paid lower wages than Americans and were assigned more dangerous work; discrimination of various sorts was all too common.

Nevertheless, many of these temporary workers ended up putting down roots in Utah, marrying "picture brides" from back home and building strong civic institutions. Their influence can be detected throughout the state. Greek

Family hike in the Rocky Mountains.

Orthodox churches, traditional Mediterranean foods, and colorful celebrations have become a key part of Utah's cultural makeup.

HISPANIC HERITAGE

Today, the fastest growing immigrant group, as elsewhere in America, is Hispanics from Mexico and other Latin American countries. They now number an estimated 450,000, 13 percent of the population, and are the largest minority group in the state.

The Spanish were absentee landowners in Utah when the Mormons arrived in 1847. In the 18th century, Spanish explorers named the Abajo and La Sal ranges and other landmarks in southern Utah, and the Old Spanish Trail was well established by the early 1800s. Spanish mining and ranching practices were important to the founding of those industries in Utah. By 1900, Hispanic settlers from neighboring New Mexico and Colorado were working as sheepherders and cowboys, and later as miners in the Monticello area. At the same time, Mexican immigrants were settling in Salt Lake City and Ogden, where they worked on the railroad and in the mines. During World War II, Hispanics were recruited in their droves to work in defense industries.

During the last 30 years, ever-increasing numbers of Hispanics have arrived from Central and South America. Hard-working people from those countries fill low-paid service jobs other Utahans refuse to do, including processing turkeys in factories in Moroni in the Sanpete Valley, cleaning office buildings in Salt Lake City, and working construction and day labor jobs. Determined to escape the poverty of their own countries and create a better life in Utah, men often take several jobs at once, live together to save money and, after gaining citizenship, send for their families. An increasing number are entrepreneurs who start their own streetside food stands, restaurants, and other businesses, where their strong work ethic has led to numerous successes.

Hispanics have much in common with Mormons – strong families, an emphasis on home life, hard work, and personal ambition, and close connections with their church – yet the sheer exuberance of the culture and its celebrations, as well as religious differences, often collide with conservative Mormon culture. Although some Hispanics have converted to Mormonism, many congregate in their own Spanish-speaking neighborhoods, or *colonias*, on Salt Lake City's largely immigrant West Side, where they attend Catholic churches and are served by Spanish newspapers, television and radio stations, and businesses.

Salt Lake City's Hispanics make up about 22 percent of the population, and their political and purchasing power is growing. Although Utah is far behind other states in representa-

Horse riding in the Monument Valley.

tion, the state does have an Office of Hispanic Affairs and one Hispanic state senator, Luz Escamilla, who is working hard to improve race relations.

In Sanpete Valley, the LDS and Catholic churches have come together to create Friendship Days to promote mutual understanding and tolerance. Fiestas and Hispanic community celebrations, such as *folklorico* dancing and mariachi music, are also popular throughout the state. "When we create a sense of celebrating, we tear down walls that divide us," commented forward-thinking Salt Lake City mayor Rocky Anderson in 2000. "Unfamiliarity is eliminated when we come together."

UTAH FESTIVALS

For the lover of sports or art, nature or culture, summer in Utah is a parade of festivals, concerts, special events, and happenings, though there are also plenty of events in the winter. Lists of happenings in most areas, from environmental and cultural to athletic activities, are available from chambers of commerce and visitor center websites.

SPRING AND SUMMER

The West's biggest Scandinavian Festival takes place in tiny Ephraim in late May, while Cedar City is justly proud of its line-up of annual events, with the pick of the bunch the Utah Shakespeare Festival (late June–early Oct) featuring a seven-show repertory of plays. In Salt Lake City, the Utah Pride Parade & Festival celebrates the LGBTQ+ community the first Sunday of June; the Utah Blues Festival is also in early June, and Utah Arts Festival takes place at the end of the month. Salt Lake City Jazz Festival is usually in July.

Price organizes a fun Greek Festival in early July, with plenty of Greek food, dancing, and music. Park City's roster of summer events includes the Beethoven Festival Park City (mid-July–mid-Aug), a month-long run of classical concerts. Utah's Pioneer Day (July 24) is celebrated in Salt Lake City with the grand Days of 47' Parade. In August, Garden City's Raspberry Days Festival celebrates the harvest of Bear Lake's celebrated raspberry crop.

Ceremonial parade at a rodeo held on Independence Day

Daniel Craig arrives for the 2005 Sundance Film Festival premiere of The Jacket at the Eccles Center Theatre.

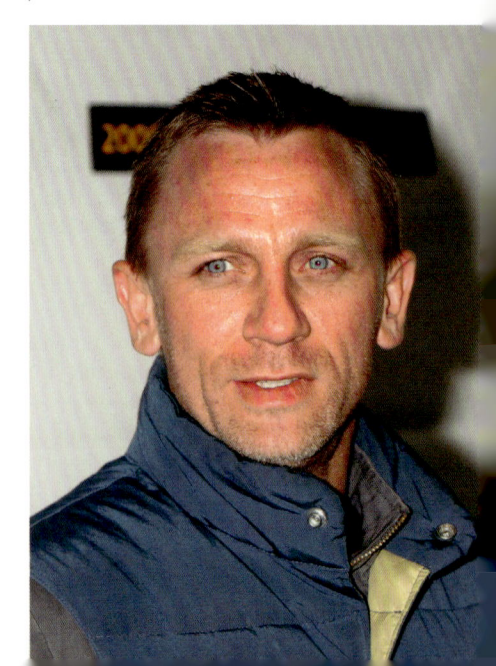

Residents of Utah celebrate Pride Month.

Sundance Film Festival at the Egyptian Theater.

Fall and winter festivals

The Utah State Fair (mid-September) is the biggest annual celebration of all things Utah, held in Salt Lake City. In late September, the place to be is Green River, where the annual watermelon crop is celebrated at Melon Days. The biggest event in winter – and arguably the year – is the Sundance Film Festival at Park City in January, where the year's best independent and foreign films are screened. Not quite as feted, the Hof German Fest in Ogden showcases German food, beer, and lots of polka.

Powwows

Powwows are Native American festivals, where there's dancing, singing, eating, and craft and cultural demonstrations – outsiders are usually welcome, but it's always good to check in advance. Instead of the glamour that some of the other Utah festivals demonstrate, a sincerity and simple, earthy feeling unite all the participants here. Powwows are held throughout the year. Among the most popular in Utah are the Indigenous Voices Pow Wow in Ogden (March), the Goshute Tribe Annual Pow Wow, the Paiute Restoration Gathering and Pow Wow in August, and the Red Canyon Pow Wow in October (featuring Indigenous groups from all over the United States and Canada).

Utah State Fair Park.

ride Parade, Salt Lake City.

Traditional tents at a Powwow.

Bountiful Utah Temple.

HISTORY & FEATURES | 73

EMPIRE OF SAINTS

Noted for tight-knit communities and missionary zeal, the Church of Jesus Christ of Latter-day Saints is one of the world's fastest-growing religions.

It's 8.45am on a warm Sunday in August in Santa Clara, near St George. In every neighborhood of this historic community in southwestern Utah, parents shepherding large families of scrubbed children in their Sunday best climb into equally large cars and head to church. Already the temperature is climbing into the nineties, and the bright Mojave sun is beating down on the black mesa above the town. Newer ranch-style houses sprawl above the sturdy brick homes and cottage gardens of the old town. Dogs bark and cicadas hum on this sleepy morning in rural America. A stream of polished vans and cars winds along wide city streets on either side of the highway, past the irrigation ditch that brings water from Santa Clara Creek to fruit orchards and gardens. They pull into the parking lot of a large, modest building, which sports no spires, crosses, or stained-glass windows. The occupants park and call out an affectionate hello to their brethren as they enter the meeting house.

An organist in the Mormon temple.

WORLDWIDE GROWTH

It's a scene that plays out across the Christian world every Sunday. But this group stands out. They are members of the Church of Jesus Christ of Latter-day Saints, commonly called Mormons. And since their church's founding, in 1830, they have proved themselves far from ordinary. The LDS Church, as it is known to its members, is the most successful religion ever founded on American soil. It now numbers almost 17 million members worldwide, almost doubling since 1994, with most new members from Latin America and Africa. Utah, however, remains home base. It was here, in 1847, that second Church president Brigham Young led his weary followers to safety after the murder of Church founder Joseph Smith and his brother Hyrum in Carthage, Illinois, by an angry mob of "Gentiles." Inspired by Young's canny leadership and vision for a new life in an American Zion, poor converts from Great Britain, Scandinavia, and across Europe flocked to Utah by wagon,

> *Here, the LDS Church came into full flower, making the "desert bloom like a rose." No matter your station in life, if you lived a blameless life according to the tenets of LDS belief, you were assured of success.*

handcart, and later trains and automobiles, founding small, preplanned agricultural communities throughout the Salt Lake Valley.

Eager and hardworking converts from the poorest neighborhoods in Europe embraced their new life in the desert, sharing in the community's wealth and ranching, farming, practicing trades, opening successful businesses, and looking forward eagerly to Jesus Christ's second coming on American soil in the Latter Days, or End Times, thought to be imminent at the beginning of the 20th century.

floods, crop failures due to insect infestation, malaria, and Native American resistance, they endured, becoming self-supporting by raising fruit, vegetables, cotton, and, for a time, silk.

Today, in common with the majority of small communities all across Utah, 70 percent of Santa Clara's 7,500 or so residents are active members of the LDS Church. As ever more people move into the St George area, attracted by its warm climate, economic and recreational opportunities, and proximity to Las Vegas, Nevada, the population continues to climb –

The Church of Jesus Christ of Latter Day Saints Conference Center in Salt Lake City.

By the early 1850s, the most successful of the first wave of converts had been "called" to colonize the remote canyon country of southern Utah. Pushing farther into the Great Basin, they built communities in northern Arizona, Nevada, Idaho, Southern California, and Mexico, fired up by Young's vision of a Mormon homeland, ever-after known as Deseret, where they could live away from others and practice their faith in peace. Santa Clara was founded in 1854 by elder Jacob Hamblin, a missionary to the Paiute. By 1861, he had been joined by 30 families of new Swiss converts, as the Church established the Cotton Mission in a warm, irrigated desert area that came to be known, on the eve of the US Civil War, as Utah's Dixie. Despite famine, drought,

since many of these newcomers are not Mormons, the overall percentage of LDS members in the population is likely to decline. Nevertheless, the church remains the dominant cultural force here, and throughout rural Utah.

SOCIAL LIFE

Meetinghouses are a hive of activity most days of the week. On Sunday, each ward offers three-hour services. On Wednesday evening, youngsters return for Church-sponsored sports and other activities; and throughout the week, adult members of the Church hold meetings of various LDS organizations, such as the Women's Relief Society, the longest-running charity in the country, which sees to it that all Church members in need are taken care of within each ward. The one night of the week when you can expect to find LDS faithful at home is Monday evening, when devout Mormons observe Family Home Evening, a two-hour period when parents join their children to study scripture and share quality time together. Unlike most LDS activities, which are little changed since the Mormons arrived in Utah, Family Home Evening was introduced in the late 1960s as a way of strengthening family values during a period of social unrest.

Today, devout Mormons must commit to at least 14 hours of Church-associated activities, many more if they serve as lay clergy. This commitment to the Church is often cited as the main reason it is so difficult for non-Mormons to connect with residents in LDS strongholds. For casual visitors, encounters with Mormons frequently take place in Utah's tourist businesses: souvenir shops, art galleries, and bed-and-breakfasts, as well as tours of Church-run historic sites, temple visitor centers and tabernacles such as those in St George and Salt Lake City.

During off-hours, you're most likely to meet Mormons on the 75 percent of the state set aside as public lands, including the many national parks in southern Utah. Visitors who time their visit to coincide with a community celebration, such as the weeklong Swiss Days celebration held in Santa Clara in September, get a unique opportunity to meet local residents. July 24 is Pioneer Day throughout Utah, commemorating the day Brigham Young and his followers arrived in the Salt Lake Valley in 1847. Most towns observe the day with a variety of events, from parades, floats, and cookouts to family reunions and historic reenactments. Communities like Huntington in Carbon County put on spectacular pageants that rank among the most photogenic events in Mormon Country.

CHURCH HIERARCHY

Church affairs are administered locally by the bishop of an individual stake, consisting of 8 to 12 individual wards, each of which has its own bishop and counselors. In a typical ward, some 200 lay members are "called" to specific assignments, all on a volunteer basis. Children are indoctrinated into the Church through Primary Association lessons aimed at kindergarteners and Sunday school, which all church members attend. Only males may be ordained as priests

> Under the patriarchal authority of the LDS Church, decisions on both religious and temporal matters are made by the Church President, or Prophet, and his two counselors; a Quorum of Twelve Apostles; and Presidency of the Seventy.

and hold positions of power. They begin training early. Between 12 and 14 years of age boys become Deacons, from 14 to 16 they become

Brigham Young statue, Salt Lake City.

Teachers, and between 16 and 19, Priests, responsible for collecting monthly "fast offerings" from member households, working as a Home Teacher with a senior male, and administering the sacraments during communion.

MORMON MISSIONARIES

At 18, many Mormon young men prepare for a two-year, self-financed Mission, where they are "called" to spread LDS doctrine worldwide and bring converts into the Church (men between the ages of 18 and 25 are encouraged to serve – some 30 percent do so). Women over the age of 19 can also be missionaries, but can only serve 18 months. The mission, carried out by passionate young believers, is at the heart of the success of the LDS Church. Presently, more than 55,000 missionaries serve in countries throughout the world. Foreign missionaries undergo training in 50 different languages at one of 10 church Missionary Training Centers (MTCs) worldwide (the largest is in Provo, next to Brigham Young University). They are given two handbooks to guide them: *Missionary Standards for Disciples of Jesus Christ* and *Missionary Standards for Disciples of Jesus Christ: Supplemental Information*.

Proselytizing missions are the most visible sign of the Church in neighborhoods the world over. Carried out 12 hours a day by pairs of clean-cut young men or women living frugally away from home for the first time, the mission is considered excellent training for future leadership roles in business, politics, and the Church. Among those who have taken advantage of this Mormon training ground have been the hotelier J. W. Marriott, who went on to start his expansive hotel chain with funds from fellow Mormons, as well as politicians like Senator Mitt Romney and movie stars like Aaron Eckhart.

WOMEN AND FAMILY

Mormon women, by contrast, remain subordinate to males in the LDS hierarchy but are essential to the day-to-day running of the Church. If men are the generals planning every move and communicating it to the faithful via sermons, conferences, letters, satellite links, and the Church's vast media holdings, women are the foot soldiers carrying out the on-the-ground ward activities. Today, although more than a third of Mormon women work outside the home, the number of daily activities required of devout LDS members and an impressive family-first mentality often make it expedient for one parent to stay home.

Under LDS doctrine, women are the equals of men. In practice, their lives are circumscribed by their primary sacred task to marry and bear children who will become mortal vessels for "preexistent" souls waiting to be saved in the LDS Church. This is no minor role. Central to the Mormon faith is a belief that the family bond is sacred and eternal, and the devout will be reunited in heaven, at the side of God and His Heavenly Wife.

Devout Mormons visit a temple whenever possible to make the appropriate preparations for the afterlife. Here, they don special clothing and receive secret "endowments" in church teachings, undergo baptism, and "seal" their marriages. Of special importance are the legions of volunteers who carry out genealogical research by searching records, databases, and cemeteries worldwide and creating family trees of ancestors. Once the names have been collected, these ancestors are then baptized by proxy in the temple by young people who consider it an honor to be chosen for a task that will ensure families can be reunited in heaven.

CODE OF CONDUCT

Only those LDS members who are deemed "worthy" by their bishop may enter a temple. A worthy life is central to Mormon belief and requires the faithful to adhere to what is called the Word of Wisdom, formulated by first Church president Joseph Smith. Mormons, he taught, should live a busy, productive, and blameless life, improve their minds, serve others, participate in their local ward, attend weekly meetings, study the Bible and accompanying Book of Mormon and Pearl of Great Price daily, tithe 10 percent of earnings to the Church, and fast one Sunday a month and donate the money that would have

Brigham Young surrounded by portraits of 21 of his 27 wives.

been spent on meals to the poor. Best known to outsiders is the requirement that a Mormon shun sexual relations outside marriage, exercise regularly, and avoid alcohol, tobacco, coffee, and tea – a lifestyle that has made Mormons among the healthiest and longest-lived people in the world. People in the LDS faith who find that they cannot follow the Word of Wisdom completely are frequently called Jack Mormons. Most families can count at least one Jack Mormon in their ranks, and Jack Mormons tend to be the most visible members of the Church in Utah, frequenting bars and cafés and other non-Mormon meeting places that devout Mormons shun.

Falling at the other end of the spectrum are breakaway sects of the LDS Church whose adherents attempt to restore what they consider to be the Church's original teachings. One such teaching is polygamy, which was abandoned by the Church in 1890. Polygamy has continued openly in Colorado City and Hildale, remote desert communities on either side of the Utah–Arizona border, where reports of forced marriages of young girls have sparked anger in the mainstream LDS Church as well as among non-Mormons. Fundamentalist leader Warren Jeffs was arrested in 2006 and convicted of child sexual assault in 2011 – he's serving a life sentence.

SECRECY IN THE CHURCH

One aspect of the LDS Church that sometimes disturbs non-Mormons is that, despite its ubiquitous presence in every walk of life, the Church remains shrouded in secrecy. Even devout Mormons, such as former Church historian Leonard Arrington, who attempted to gain access to documents held in vaults for a multivolume history, encounter problems. Arrington, widely respected as a historian inside and beyond the LDS Church, was reprimanded by the Governing Authority and demoted from Church life. Others, less lucky, are excommunicated completely if they speak out against the Church's positions. From the beginning, though, Mormons have been encouraged to keep daily journals, which is one reason there exists a growing Mormon literature, much of it written by those still within the Church. Santa Clara's Lyman Hafen, a longtime journalist and former editor of St George Magazine, writes regularly about the people and history of southern Utah, offering a

One of Jeffs' victims, Elissa Wall, was just 14 when he married her to a 19-year-old man. She later wrote Stolen Innocence: My Story of Growing Up in a Polygamous Sect, Becoming a Teenage Bride, and Breaking Free of Warren Jeffs.

uniquely modern yet devout Mormon perspective on his corner of the state. And one Mormon writer – passionate political activist and nature

A Mormon missionary.

writer Terry Tempest Williams – has succeeded in reaching an international audience with her books. Williams' thoughtful essays on people and place, sparked by a deep love for her Mormon roots and Utah's extraordinary environment, offer a window into what it means to be female and Mormon as well as a Westerner, an American, and a citizen of the world.

In fact, Mormons living in Utah have been atypical Westerners from the start. With their tight-knit communities, emphasis on family and faith, and attractively laid-out, prosperous towns, they are the antithesis of the rugged individualism that has always been part of the Western myth. For those living in Utah, the dream of Deseret is not dead. It is still unfolding.

Cedar Breaks National Monument.

… HISTORY & FEATURES | 79

THE NAKED EARTH

A labyrinth of canyons, arches, and soaring cliffs sprawls across Utah's spectacular landscape, products of millions of years of weathering and volcanic activity.

The mile-high Colorado Plateau, a 130,000 sq mile (340,000km) uplift that covers half of Utah as well as parts of New Mexico, Arizona and Colorado, is geology for the masses: A place where even the most casual visitor is forced, through sheer awe, to look more closely and ask why rocks behave in such incredible ways. Canyonlands. Arches. Capitol Reef. Bryce Canyon. Zion. All of Utah's national parks preserve different aspects of the geology of this colorful and spectacular region, where heat, aridity, uplift, and erosion have laid bare the bones of the earth.

ANCIENT ROCKS

Although you can see ancient metamorphic gneisses and schists dating back to the Precambrian Era at Arizona's Grand Canyon and east of Moab in Westwater Canyon, these much older rocks are most visible in the northern part of the state, where recent volcanism and erosion in the Uinta and Wasatch mountains have exposed deeply buried strata. Northern Utah's mountains are on the fringe of the Southern Rockies and have a consistently alpine look, more akin to Switzerland than the Desert Southwest. In Dinosaur National Monument, which straddles the Utah–Colorado border and contains the converging Yampa and Green Rivers and an important dinosaur quarry, the geological story is even more complete than the Grand Canyon, with 19 different rock formations spanning 2.5 billion years visible in the deep river canyons and Uinta Mountains. The Wasatch Range forms the backbone of the Beehive State, giving way in southwestern Utah to a subdivision of the Colorado Plateau, known as the High Plateaus. This transition

Dinosaur National Monument.

zone, pushed up by the major Hurricane and Sevier faults, includes parks like Zion and Bryce Canyon and has the highest plateaus in North America. One of the highest and most visible is 11,000ft (3,400-meter) Markagunt Plateau, which drops off abruptly on the west parallel to I-15, with the High Plateaus on the east and the searingly hot Basin and Range province on the west. Significantly younger than other geophysical provinces and still highly active, the north-south trending mountains and vast basins of the Basin and Range stretch as far as the eye can see through Nevada to California, the result of the earth's crust thinning between the Wasatch Fault on the east and the San Andreas Fault on the west.

> About 3.5 billion years ago, the first life on earth evolved in the form of bacteria and blue-green algae.

MARINE ORIGINS

The Precambrian Era encompassed about 88 percent of our planet's 4.5-billion-year history. Throughout the Precambrian and subsequent Paleozoic Eras, the great laboratory of life was still in the early experimental stages, out of sight, beneath an ebbing and flowing ocean.

The Three Sisters at La Sal Mountains.

North America was part of a vast global supercontinent that tilted down at its western edge, allowing the sea to encroach. Lime deposits from early calcareous algae and other marine life-forms mingled with the coastal sands. As these deposits settled, they were compressed and hardened into horizontal strata cemented by calcium, manganese, and iron. The Southwest's first sedimentary rocks – limestone, sandstone, and shale – formed during this time. The earliest fossils, algae known as stromatolites, are found in these formations. By 750 to 700 million years ago, marine invertebrates had begun to appear.

Utah lay at the edge of the Pacific Ocean; Nevada and California had not yet emerged from the sea. Late in the Precambrian, western Utah subsided and sediment deposition increased. Brief episodes of mountain building and volcanic activity alternated with long periods of erosion and sedimentation. Movements in areas of weakness, known as faults, provided a conduit for heat to escape from the earth's mantle. Molten rock, or magma, was injected into sedimentary rocks, uplifting and folding them into tall mountain chains with a core of metamorphic gneiss, schist and granite. Attacked by water and wind, they eventually wore down into sediments again, which redeposited, hardened, uplifted, and folded several more times.

The ocean continued to cover western Utah into the Cambrian Period (570 to 505 million years ago) at the start of the Paleozoic Era, or Era of Ancient Life. The sea was now filled with trilobites, brachiopods, and other marine invertebrates whose shells built up at the bottom of the ocean when they died. Calcium in the shells of these dead creatures precipitated into the ocean and cemented sand and other sediments into limestone embedded with marine fossils. For the next 100 million years, western Utah lay under water even as eastern Utah remained a featureless plain above sea level. New life-forms appeared, including the first vertebrates, a kind of primitive fish, that swam in warm, tropical, shallow seas amid coral reefs, which hardened into dolomite as they died.

All of Utah was under water by 400 million years ago. The Stansbury uplift in north-central Utah developed into a prominent ridge above sea level late in the Devonian Period, and the first amphibians split their time between the sea and dry land. Throughout the Mississippian and Pennsylvanian periods (360 to 300 million years ago), fusulinids, brachiopods, and conodonts were among the abundant lifeforms in cyclical seas. Large quantities of limestone were laid down in the Oquirrh Basin in northwestern Utah, trapping organic matter that would yield massive quantities of oil and gas in the 20th century.

As the Pennsylvanian Era gave way to the Permian Era (290 to 245 million years ago), the basement rocks beneath Canyon Country in southeastern Utah were laid down. Uplift along the Ancestral Rockies in present-day Colorado pushed up the Uncompahgre Uplift and adjoining Paradox Basin near present-day Moab. As the sea ebbed and flowed, thousands of feet of salt, potash, and organic-rich sediments from the highlands filled the shallow mountain basin, also trapping oil and gas. When the ocean withdrew and land appeared in the late Permian Period, large reptiles began to dominate the area.

DESERT INVASION

A drastic drying of the climate and withdrawal of the western ocean allowed enormous reptiles known as dinosaurs to dominate at the dawn of the Mesozoic (or Middle Life) Era. Wind-blown sand dunes from the north covered the shoreline of the Paradox Basin in southeastern Utah beginning in the Triassic Period (245–208 million years ago). The dunes alternated with thick layers of red silt and mud washed down from the adjoining Uncompahgre Uplift. The interfingered red-and-white rocks of the Cutler Group – consisting of the White Rim Sandstone, Organ Rock Shale, Cedar Mesa Sandstone and Elephant Canyon Formation/Halgaito Shale – have eroded beautifully into banded spires in the Needles District of Canyonlands National Park above the San Juan River. Below the river, in Monument Valley Navajo Tribal Park, Organ Rock shale forms the pedestals of enormous, highly eroded formations sculpted by the wind from swirling De Chelly Sandstone.

Volcanoes rimmed the western and northwestern margins of Utah and spewed ash across large areas of the Southwest. Silica in the ash mingled with groundwater and entered the woody core of huge conifers that had toppled from riverbanks into swamps. Over time, these silicates changed the woody core of the trees into quartz and other colorful minerals. Petrified wood is common in the multicolored layers of the Chinle Formation and can be seen at Escalante Forest State Park and adjoining Grand Staircase–Escalante National Monument in southeastern Utah.

The crumbly Chinle and younger Morrison formations have also yielded large deposits of uranium. Moab boomed as the Uranium Capital of the World in the 1950s, and uranium exploration on the Colorado Plateau became widespread. Large caches of dinosaur bones in these formations have been unearthed in the Cleveland–Lloyd Quarry near Price, Utah, and in the famous Dinosaur Quarry in northeastern Utah's Dinosaur National Monument, part of a region dubbed the Dinosaur Diamond.

Aridity continued to affect the whole of Utah throughout the Jurassic Period (208 to 144 million years ago), allowing an enormous Sahara-like desert to form dunes up to 3,000ft (90 meters) in height. Swamps between the dunes were haunted by huge Allosaursus, Camptosau-

The Wasatch Mountains.

rus, and other dinosaurs, who left behind footprints in mud that hardened into the Kayenta Formation, a red shale found below sheer cliffs of Navajo Sandstone.

The Navajo desert that spread across the West during the Jurassic lasted a long time, but eventually the climate changed again and became moister. The sea returned, laying down marine and seashore sediments that lithified into Dakota Sandstone, Mancos Shale, and the Mesa Verde Group of the Four Corners. Below them, Wingate and Navajo sand dunes thousands of feet thick petrified so perfectly you can see which direction the wind was blowing when they formed. Calcium cemented the large quartz grains into sandstone. Hematite, derived from iron, tinted it a range of reds, pinks, and oranges. Iron in Zion's Navajo Sandstone creates rust, which changes hue as it washes down through the sandstone. Iron and manganese tinted Bryce Canyon and Cedar Breaks into rainbow hues and are also responsible in part for "desert varnish," the distinctive shiny red, brown, and black streaks that spill down sandstone walls and served as blackboards for ancient Native American rock art. Desert varnish is caused by a combination of minerals, blowing clay, and dust that is fixed on the dripping cliff faces by resident bacteria and microfungi.

SEA AND SAND

Today, sandstone is the most recognizable formation in the West. Throughout Utah, it is found in exposures of Wingate, Navajo, and Entrada sandstones. The Wingate forms the golden cliffs along the Fremont River in Capitol Reef National Park, the Circle Cliffs in the Escalante Canyons district of Grand Staircase–Escalante National Monument, and the soaring headland

La Sal Mountains.

⊘ THE BIG ROCK CANDY MOUNTAIN

One of the most famous geological landmarks in Utah is a taffy-hued mountain beside the Sevier River named Big Rock Candy Mountain. It is made from Bullion Canyon volcanic rocks deposited 35 to 22 million years ago by a cluster of nearby stratovolcanoes, like the one that built Mount St Helens. The distinctive yellow, orange, and red colors derive from iron oxides mixed with creamy alunite and kaolinite, rich in potassium.

The mountain is named after a well-known folk song recorded by Burl Ives, describing a hobo's colorful fantasy of a life of ease, originally penned by a railroad brakeman named "Haywire Mac" McClintock.

The song depicts a fanciful place with "lemonade springs, where the bluebird sings."

The story has it that soon after the song was released in 1928, local boosters placed a sign at the base of the mountain christening it the "Big Rock Candy Mountain" and the nearby cold springs, the "Lemonade Springs." For thousands, the song's evocative lyrics symbolize the escapist frame of mind found throughout the American West. The late writer Wallace Stegner, who grew up in Salt Lake City, certainly thought so. He titled his first book, a biography of his restless father, after the Utah mountain.

that makes up Island in the Sky in Canyonlands. Differential erosion of the brick-red Dewey Bridge siltstone, the lowest of three different "members" of Entrada Sandstone, is responsible for the "hoodoos" in northern Capitol Reef and nearby Goblin Valley State Park. On the other side of the Colorado River, the Entrada's younger two members – the pink Slick Rock sandstone and hard white Moab Tongue limestone, laid down in a seashore environment – offer perfect rock for arches to form.

Late in the Jurassic, shallow seaways from the north invaded Utah. In central Utah, the Arapien Basin developed, trapping more than 6,000ft (2,000 meters) of gypsum and other sediments. The first birds evolved at this time. During the Cretaceous Period (144 to 66 million years ago), lake and river systems gradually declined. In eastern Utah, the sea invaded from the east and southeast, forming an inland seaway from Mexico to the Arctic. This inland seaway was filled with strange creatures, including plesiosaurs, a fearsome marine reptile whose fossilized remains have been unearthed on the Kaiparowits Plateau near Lake Powell. Land-based dinosaurs and other reptiles wandered through major coal-forming barrier islands in swamps and marshes near the coastline, which gradually retreated east from central Utah.

In western Utah, the Sevier Mountains rose due to thrust faulting. Paleozoic rocks folded over younger rocks, and Utah rose. The highlands were attacked by the elements, and coarse sediments began to shed eastward into what is now the Great Basin.

BULGES, WARPS AND MEANDERS

For the dinosaurs and other living things, the end came when an asteroid collided with the earth at the end of the Cretaceous Period, 65 million years ago, paving the way for other lifeforms – flowers and mammals. This was the beginning of modern Utah. Pangaea broke apart into separate continents. Hot lava from the earth's interior escaped through a trough in the Atlantic Ocean, widening the rift between the plates and forcing the North American continental plate west. Inevitably, the North American Plate collided with the eastern edge of the Pacific Oceanic Crust off present-day California. The reverberations sent seismic shock waves eastward through deep-seated Precambrian faults in the bedrock. The Rocky Mountains, the Uintas, and the Colorado Plateau began to rise.

The Colorado Plateau warped and folded as it rose, creating huge swells, or monoclines, such as the Waterpocket Fold in central Utah as well as anticlines (upwarps) and synclines (downwarps), clearly visible in the Four Corners. This warping also created large basins, such as the Uinta Basin, that filled with freshwater along with organic matter including fish fossils and oil shales.

Blue flax in the Wasatch Mountains.

In the Oligocene and Miocene Epochs (38 million to 5 million years ago), igneous intrusions of hot molten lava along faults beneath heavy layers of sandstone pushed up and deformed much of Utah, creating mountain ranges such as the Henrys, the Abajos, and the La Sals. Magma rose along zones of weakness, spread laterally between sedimentary layers, pushed them up into a dome, and the granite has now been uncovered by erosion.

A San Juan River trip, from Mexican Hat to Clay Hills Crossing, offers a rare opportunity to view these rock strata and float through the Goosenecks of the San Juan, technically an entrenched meander, where uplift of the Colorado Plateau caused an older river to cut down several thousand feet

THERE BE MONSTERS

Ninety million years ago, southeastern Utah was at the edge of an expansive interior seaway that split North America in half.

A dinosaur bone at Dinosaur National Monument.

Within this seaway lived huge crocodile-like reptiles known as plesiosaurs, which fed on sharks and fish. On the shores were the last survivors of dinosaurs that had dominated the region in Triassic and Jurassic times, 200 million years ago. The fossilized skeletons and footprints of these early predecessors now lay buried beneath deep sediments deposited in a succession of sandy deserts, beaches, streams, rivers, and oceans. Small land-based mammals had begun their inexorable rise. Fossil remains from this Late Cretaceous Period are few and far between. That's why discoveries of a hadrosaur skull in 2001 and two intact plesiosaurs in Grand Staircase–Escalante National Monument and neighboring Glen Canyon National Recreation Area in 1999 created so much excitement among paleontologists. "To find one intact is really rare," said Barry Albright, a Museum of Northern Arizona curator. "This is what we live for." After examining the two plesiosaurs and the ammonite rich Tropic Shale in which they were found, Grand Staircase–Escalante National Monument paleontologist Alan Titus had further good news. These plesiosaurs – with 6ft (2-meter-) long skulls and 25ft (8-meter-) long bodies – apparently represent a new genus and may be older than any ever discovered in North America.

AMATEUR PALEONTOLOGISTS

But the real story here is that of young people with a passion for paleontology, scooping the experts with finds of their own. The plesiosaurs were discovered by 15-year-old David Rankin and his friend Wryht Short of Big Water, Utah, while they were hiking in Glen Canyon National Recreation Area. After spotting a piece of bone sticking out from the hillside, they alerted their friend Merle Graffam, an amateur paleontologist, who contacted Albright and colleague David Gillette at the Museum of Northern Arizona. In 2000, a crew including Rankin, Graffam, and others went to the sites and removed the remains.

The hadrosaur skull was also unearthed by young people. Since the 1930s, students from Webb School in Claremont, California, have been participating in paleontology digs under the auspices of the Raymond M. Alf Museum of Paleontology, the only nationally accredited paleontology museum on a high school campus in the world. After working for several seasons on the remote Kaiparowits Plateau, the students struck gold when they unearthed a 400lb (180kg) hadrosaur skull in the 75-million-year-old Kaiparowits Formation. It is the only hadrosaur skull to be found south of Montana and the first intact dinosaur skull ever excavated in southern Utah.

If all these bones get you wondering what the real-life great lizards looked like, you'll enjoy the Dinosaur Museum (754 S 200 West St, Blanding, UT; tel: 435-678 3454; http://dinosaur-museum.org), the brainchild of artists Sylvia and Stephen Czerkas, whose life-like dinosaur recreations grace museums all over North America. Galleries trace the evolution of dinosaurs around the world, and include the real skeletons of an Argentine *Herrerasaurus*, a Mongolian *Tarbosaurus*, and a clawed *Deinocheirus*, as well as the Czerkas' own sculptures. Other exhibits emphasize how recent discoveries have altered scientists' understanding of the appearance of dinosaur skin and reproduction.

into its sandstone course and form hairpin bends. Rivers won't meander for long without seeking a more direct route past obstacles. In this case, the grinding action of the river currents punches a hole in a meander wall, widens it, and eventually leaves behind a natural bridge like those at Rainbow Bridge and Natural Bridges National Monuments. Natural bridges are water formed; arches are formed by erosion along joints in sandstone, creating linear fins and eventually arches.

BASIN AND RANGE

Starting about 20 million years ago, the earth's crust beneath the Great Basin began to extend, thin, overheat, and crack along a roughly north-south trend. Stone blocks of earth started to break and tilt, forcing chunks of land to rise and others to drop. The ones that dropped formed basins and began to fill with sediments washing down in huge alluvial fans. Some basins contain 15,000ft (4,600 meters) of fill. The Great Basin has no outlet to the sea.

The Wasatch Fault, which created the Wasatch Mountains, the dramatic backdrop of Salt Lake City, is second only to the San Andreas Fault for activity. Volcanic action along a northwest-southeast trend within sedimentary rocks, such as limestones, is thought to be the reason why the Bingham Mining District, west of Salt Lake City, has such huge copper deposits.

One theory is that the continent drifted northwest over a hot spot in the earth's mantle. Copper ores may have been the last substances to crystallize out of the magma. Associated minerals such as silver were found in sandstone in 1866 in southwestern Utah's Silver Reef Historic District. Between 1866 and 1881, Silver Reef had 2,000 residents and was southwestern Utah's biggest town. It is now a ghost town just north of St George.

FIRE AND ICE

Uplift along the Wasatch, Hurricane, and Sevier faults in western Utah pushed up the Wasatch Mountains and High Plateaus of southwestern Utah, starting about 15 million years ago. The Colorado, Green, and Yampa rivers and their tributaries cut into their meandering courses, creating deep sandstone canyons. In the Quaternary Period, volcanic activity continued to spew lava flows atop the high plateaus, forming the million-year-old basalts atop the Grand

Western Utah's basin-and-range country is much younger and more mobile than the Colorado Plateau and largely the result of pulling apart, not pushing up.

Staircase, a series of colorful plateaus in southwestern Utah.

During this time, the climate became colder and wetter, ushering in the last Ice Age. In

Escalante Petrified Forest State Park.

Utah, glaciers carved valleys in the northern mountains and could be found as far south as Cedar Breaks National Monument, where glacial till made up of ground-up rock can be seen below Brian Head. Great Salt Lake and its smaller siblings are remnants of much larger Lake Bonneville, which covered the valleys of northern and western Utah during the Ice Age. About 10,000 years ago, Lake Bonneville shrank. Island-dotted Great Salt Lake and two smaller lakes to the south are all that remain of Lake Bonneville. Today, Great Salt Lake is northern Utah's biggest geological attraction. It supports several major industries, including, naturally, salt production, and is important to wildlife as well as people, who use the lake for recreation.

The top of the Alpine Loop in American Fork Canyon.

HISTORY & FEATURES | 87

LIFE IN A DRY LAND

From the forested slopes of the Wasatch Range to the sun-blasted flats of the Great Basin, Utah encompasses a fascinating array of plants and animals.

From Skyline Drive atop Utah's Wasatch Plateau, the surrounding country is a study in contrasts. The 11,000ft (3,350-meter) Wasatch Plateau – one of central Utah's High Plateaus – has been uplifted by volcanism more than a mile above the desert; from the top visitors can take in all of Utah's ecosystems in a unique panorama. From up there, it's easy to imagine the sense of possibility felt by LDS Church president Brigham Young when he gathered his followers above the Salt Lake Valley on July 24, 1847, and declared it "the right place."

Atop the plateau, on either side of a dirt road that follows the mountain spine, are dense forests of hardy conifers threaded with icy mountain streams and grassy alpine basins inhabited by mule deer, elk, marmots, raptors, and other denizens of the high country. At lower elevations, stands of Gambel oak, bigtooth maple, and aspen form a border around the tall evergreens. These deciduous forests are the shape shifters of the mountains: bright green in the warm temperatures of spring, softening into a tapestry of magenta, russet, gold, and ochre in late September, weeks before deep snow claims the highlands for the winter.

THE LAY OF THE LAND

Fall colors compete with the rumpled technicolor rocks of Canyon Country, sprawling to the southeast. Immediately east of the Wasatch Plateau, at the heart of Castle Country, is the 1,000ft (300-meter) San Rafael Swell, the most dramatic of several sandstone monocline uplifts soaring above the canyons carved by the Colorado River and its tributaries on the Colorado Plateau. The rivers spilling west from the Wasatch Front couldn't be more different.

Burrowing owl.

Born in the highlands of the Uinta and Wasatch mountains, water from the highlands sinks unceremoniously into the sere, monochromatic expanse of the Great Basin, a desert spanning western Utah and Nevada with no outlet to the sea. The Bear and other rivers pouring from the highlands form lakes, swamps, and other wetlands at the base of the Wasatch Mountains before disappearing into the salty, sterile waters of the Great Salt Lake.

Birds by the thousands, including 37 species of swans, geese, and ducks, descend on the surrounding wetlands seasonally.

Far to the southwest, the Great Basin Desert and Colorado Plateau are joined by a third desert – the Mojave – creating a major ecosystem where

HISTORY & FEATURES

> A century and a half of damming have helped make the Wasatch Front a productive area for agriculture as well as for migratory and residential waterfowl.

Utah, Arizona, and Nevada meet along the Virgin River. Here, in a pocket-sized corner of Utah populated by Joshua trees, riparian streams, and the craggy Beaver Dam Mountains, two nature

Prairie dog, Bryce Canyon.

preserves – the Lytle Ranch and nearby Red Cliffs Reserve – protect three desert vegetative zones and endangered species such as the Virgin River chub and desert tortoise.

SEA OF DIVERSITY

With an average 13in (33cm) of rainfall a year, Utah is one of the most arid states in the USA; only neighboring Nevada is drier. Happily, though, with a topography that ranges from an elevation of 2,500ft (760 meters) in the south to 13,528ft (4,123 meters) at Kings Peak, precipitation varies greatly, from a low of a few inches to a high of over 30, allowing a wide variety of plants and animals to find a suitable niche. Some 600 vertebrate species and thousands of plant families call Utah home.

Many are endemic, meaning they exist nowhere else, such as species of milkvetch found only in the selenium-rich soil of Zion National Park. With varied topography, soil and climate, Zion is particularly blessed with wildlife. More than 80 percent of the total wildlife found in Utah live within its boundaries, making it an important nature preserve as well as geological landmark in the High Plateaus of southern Utah.

To date, 17 animals in Utah are endangered or threatened, mostly due to habitat loss from rapid development. The list includes major predators such as the gray wolf and California condor; smaller creatures such as the Mexican spotted owl, peregrine falcon, black-footed ferret, burrowing owl, and Utah prairie dog; and tiny natives such as the Kanab ambersnail and Virgin River chub that hang on in a few scattered preserves but have disappeared elsewhere in their range. The Colorado River, which transects southeastern Utah, has more than its fair share of listed species, as damming has altered the natural environment of the river and its canyons. Warm water fish species such as the Colorado pikeminnow, razorback sucker, and bonytail are unable to survive in the icy conditions created by Glen Canyon Dam. Their days seemed numbered until the recent drought along the Colorado River caused Lake Powell's northern reaches to shrink, returning the lake to a river system able to support native species again, albeit temporarily. Even as fish that evolved in the warm waters of the historic Colorado River struggle for survival, those adapted to cold water, such as trout, thrive. Trout fishing below the dam in Flaming Gorge Reservoir in northeastern Utah is some of the best in the state, while the adjoining Uinta Mountains are notable for another seasonal event: the annual return of kokanee salmon, which spawn in Sheep Creek each fall, providing eggs for hatcheries throughout Utah and Wyoming. The southwest willow flycatcher, a neotropical migrant that historically bred in the willows along the Colorado, has also declined after its preferred willow habitat was replaced by water-guzzling tamarisk, or salt cedar, along riverbanks. Tamarisk, an attractive but lethal exotic shrub introduced for erosion control and now out of control throughout the West, has sounded the death knell for native willows and cottonwoods along disturbed waterways. It is not the only non-native plant to wreak havoc. Introduced cheatgrass, a vigorous annual with little nutritional value, has also created problems for protein-rich native grasses such as winter fat, galleta, and ricegrass that have traditionally provided year-round browse for livestock on the Colorado Plateau. Competition from man-made activity remains the greatest danger for native plants. Twenty-five are now listed as endangered (three more are candidates for listing). One endemic species, the pretty little kachina daisy, is found only in "hanging gardens"

Biologists are trying to restore the endangered California condor to the American Southwest. Among the largest flying birds, with 9ft (3-meter) wingspans and bald heads, the scavengers started nesting in southern Utah in 2014.

Such changes piqued the interest of a young naturalist named C. Hart Merriam, who traveled to the Grand Canyon in 1889 to study the land-

Pier on the Great Salt Lake.

created by seeps in the sandstone cliffs above Indian Creek. Three other endangered plants are now protected on The Nature Conservancy's historic Dugout Ranch adjoining the Needles District of Canyonlands National Park.

LIFE ZONES

The Canyon Country of southern Utah is a particularly interesting place to view wildlife due largely to a diversity of topographical features, ranging from the Colorado River to the La Sal Mountains, which soar to 12,000ft (3,660 meters). Broad ecological differences are particularly obvious on the Colorado Plateau, where elevation changes allow a variety of plants and animals to thrive.

scape. In just 60 miles (100km), Merriam noted, one passed through ecosystems similar to those between Mexico and the Canadian Arctic. He named and described a series of "life zones," each corresponding to a particular elevation. Modern scientists have expanded on Merriam's ideas, now recognizing that slope angle, soil type, exposure to sun, wind, moisture, and other variables all contribute to local microclimates.

On the Colorado Plateau, elevations average 4,000 to 6,000ft (1,200–1,800 meters), placing it squarely in the high desert zone but also allowing Great Basin vegetation, such as sagebrush and grasses, to cover large tracts of land used by ranchers. In Canyonlands National Park, the 6,000ft (1,800-meter) elevation supports both grasses and pinyon and juniper. "P-J," as it is known in these parts, is useful in a multitude of ways – for nutritious nuts, berries, and firewood – and is the friendliest of the dwarf forests to camp under, offering views of the stars at night and shelter at noon. Cedar gnats, or "no-see-ums," are active when temperatures warm up. Watch out. They give a mean bite.

Equally entrancing is ponderosa pine forest, which forms lofty stands in Bryce Canyon National Park (elevation 7,000–8,000ft/2,100–2,400 meters), west of the Colorado River. Sheltered by the vanilla-smelling, scaly trunks of ponderosa pine are Gambel oak and toothy maple that flare red and bronze in autumn. Mule deer are often seen here, twitching long ears and jumping away skittishly. The forest is often noisy with disputing Steller's jays and tassel-eared squirrels.

Snow is not uncommon in June on the high plateaus and mountains of Utah, so wildflowers are late bloomers. Cedar Breaks, situated atop the 10,000ft (3,000-meter) Wasatch Plateau, has one of the best wildflower shows in the state. Watch for explosions of bluebells, lupines, columbines,

Columbine bloom at Cedar Breaks National Monument.

⊘ DESERT OASIS

Serious birders will want to visit Fish Springs National Wildlife Refuge (tel: 801-831 5353; www.fws.gov/refuge/fish-springs), an isolated wetland oasis, 78 miles (125km) northwest of Delta in the Great Salt Lake Desert. Five major springs and several lesser seeps flow from a fault line at the base of the eastern front of the craggy Fish Springs Mountains. These mineral-laden, saline springs provide virtually all the water for the refuge's 10,000-acre (4,000-hectare) marsh system. Since they maintain a year-round temperature of between 70°F and 80°F (21°–27°C), they provide a home for 5,000 to 6,000 wintering birds representing more than 250 resident and migratory species. The second largest population of snowy plovers can be found here. The springs have been a vital water source not only for birds but for humans, including local Goshute, early explorers like Jedediah Smith, and Pony Express riders. A well-preserved 133-mile (214km) portion of the Pony Express National Historic Trail (www.nps.gov/poex) can be driven on an unpaved scenic backway through western Utah from Stage Coach Inn State Park, in Fairfield, one of the original Pony Express stations, to Ibapah, near the Utah–Nevada border. This is an extremely remote area, so start out with a full tank of gas, bring food, water, and spare tires, and let someone know your itinerary.

LIFE IN A DRY LAND

Indian paintbrush, penstemons, woolly mullein, and numerous asters and sunflowers thronging disturbed roadsides in August and September. Above 8,000ft (2,400 meters), pioneer deciduous species like quaking aspen take over subalpine meadows in silver profusion, but are eventually overshadowed by spruce, fir, and, at higher elevations, lodgepole, limber, Jeffrey, and gnarled bristlecone pines, the world's oldest trees, often reaching ages of 3,000 to 4,000 years.

RIVER CORRIDORS

Spring runoff demands a fast response from wildflowers, birds and other living things in high-altitude parks like Cedar Breaks, a veritable Monet painting of bright, splashy blooms roused from their snowbound slumber in early June, along with hibernating bears, pikas, and marmots. Townsend's nutcrackers make fast work of seeds as the season rolls on. Rushing mountain streams spilling into the lowlands slow to a trickle and ice up in places as winter arrives. Lack of rainfall and damming of major waterways mean that many smaller rivers – dry arroyos much of the year – are flooded by seasonal runoff and summer rains, a danger for hikers caught there at the wrong time.

But where mighty rivers like the Colorado, Fremont, Yampa, and Green run, they form green corridors of cottonwood, box elder, willow, exotic tamarisk, and other water-loving plants that provide a respite from the heat and a habitat for many creatures. Deep canyons, such as those along the Escalante River and the North Fork of the Virgin River, offer cool, moist microclimates in which a Douglas fir might grow across from a prickly pear cactus. Groundwater here percolates through sandstone, sustaining monkeyflower, columbine, shooting stars, maidenhair fern, and other moisture-loving plants to form luxuriant hanging gardens. Also glorious is the cascading song of the canyon wren: often heard, rarely glimpsed, and truly the top of the hit parade of southwestern crooners.

LIFE IN THE DESERT

Diverse as it is, all life in the Southwest is shaped by aridity. This is primarily a rain shadow region of desert basins trapped between high peaks and plateaus, which capture what little Pacific moisture makes it over the 14,000ft (4,300-meter) barrier of California's Sierra Nevada. It's no exaggeration to say that finding water, trying to hold onto it, and adapting to its absence are the main preoccupations of life.

At the lowest desert elevations in Utah, which include the Mojave and Great Basin, the most successful plants – cacti – take advantage of infrequent but hard rains by employing an extensive root network and conserving water in expandable, gelatinous tissues. Waxy trunks and paddles protected by spines are used for photosynthesis instead of leaves. The cacti lure moth and bat pollinators with

Coyote in Southern Utah.

bright flowers and produce tasty autumn fruits that are eaten and disseminated by many animals. Some trees and shrubs shed their leaves and virtually shut down to conserve water; others close up or tilt fleshy, waxy leaves to keep cool.

The desert seems quiet during the day because three-quarters of the animals are nocturnal. Visit a water hole at dusk or dawn for a glimpse of coyotes, kit foxes, bobcats, badgers, perhaps even rare bighorn sheep, which have been reintroduced in Canyonlands and Arches National Parks. During the day, look skyward to see red-tailed hawks, golden eagles, lightning-fast peregrine falcons and enormous desert ravens. These birds patrol the skies from cliff aeries in search of unsuspecting cottontail rabbits or Uintah ground

SEA MONKEY BUSINESS

You won't find any fish to catch in the Great Salt Lake. What there is to find is the peculiar creature known as brine shrimp.

Artemia plankton.

That's the common name for this member of the crustacean class. Brine shrimp have also become known popularly as "sea monkeys," and therein lies a tale. Although they're of the class that includes the lobster and the crab, brine shrimp are absent from oceans while being prevalent in inland saltwater or wherever salt water evaporates. The species involved here is *Artemia*, and the most familiar example in the United States is *Artemia franciscana*, the name deriving from the San Francisco Bay Area in California. Another chief location is the Great Salt Lake of Utah.

Brine shrimp lack bones. They come equipped with exoskeletons – outer shell-like skeletons that cover their bodies. Starting out as tiny larva, the shrimp reach their adult size of about 1cm in four to six weeks. The eggs can dry out and remain viable for years, and then, under the right conditions, begin to hatch.

Beginning in the 1950s, a big business developed whereby adult shrimp were harvested on the Great Salt Lake for use as fish food for America's aquarium trade. By the 1970s there was a big build-up of commercial demand for brine shrimp eggs.

Hatched in late February and early March, the cysts float on the surface before being hauled in by a horde of commercial fishermen, who descend each October on the Great Salt Lake. The eggs are so tiny that 50 could easily fit on the head of a pin. As seen from planes employed in the harvesting, the cysts take on the appearance of rosy swirls or reddish-brown streaks on the water.

The trade has become highly lucrative, with Artemia cysts selling for upwards of $70 a pound – it's a $70 million-a-year industry. There has been much environmental concern lately centering on the intense commercial harvesting, and wildlife agencies have been monitoring the population of brine shrimp since 1992. A major worry is the effect which a diminished population could have for the millions of shorebirds and waterfowl that depend on the shrimp for sustenance during their migratory journeys. Limits on cyst harvesting have been tried, to the dismay of the commercial shrimp harvesters.

PET SHRIMP?

The term "sea monkeys" arose when a variety of the brine shrimp began to be marketed as pets in the 1960s with great success. A few years earlier, in 1957, an eccentric New Yorker named Harold von Braunhut chanced upon the phenomenon of brine shrimp and their ability to spring to life after a long shelf life. As cysts, they appeared to exist in a state of suspended animation, only to revive when introduced to water.

Braunhut decided to offer the shrimp as pets for children which could be sold through the mail. In 1960, he advertised the packaged shrimp as "Instant Life" in ads he placed in the back of comic books. Legions of youngsters would respond over years to come. Dubbing the shrimp "sea monkeys" after their tail-like appendage once they morphed into life, Braunhut touted their ability to cavort in water – racing and performing acrobatic maneuvers. Braunhut's success in selling billions of the Sea Monkeys was offset by controversy stemming from his political extremism. He was identified in a 1996 Anti-Defamation Report as belonging to the Ku Klux Klan and the Aryan Nations. He died in 2003.

squirrels, which keep themselves cool by holding their feathery tails over their backs as they rush from rock to rock. Smaller birds, such as tits, finches, vireos, tanagers, and hummingbirds, flocks in huge numbers to riparian zones in sheltered canyons. Reptiles keep cool hiding under bushes and rocks, becoming active at twilight and leaving strange slither marks and tracks in sandy soil. Collared lizards and whiptails are often seen in low-elevation regions; if you're lucky, you may even glimpse the huge and colorful Gila monster, North America's only venomous lizard, in the Mojave Desert west of St George. Venomous creatures are plentiful in the desert, using poison to immobilize prey, aid in digestion, or defend themselves. The giant desert hairy scorpion, more than 5in (13cm) long, is less poisonous than the pale, inch-long scorpion, whose sting can be deadly. In addition to rattlesnakes and coral snakes, poisonous desert dwellers include an 8in (20cm) centipede, black widow and brown recluse spiders, cone nose bugs, and tarantulas. On the Colorado Plateau, spadefoot toads simply bide their time throughout the year, waiting in the bottom of dried-up potholes for the drumbeat of rainfall, which signals the time to spawn. Spadefoot toads are only one of many species that inhabit desert potholes. Perhaps the most fascinating are tadpole shrimp, which can withstand desiccation (like packaged "sea monkeys") and come back to life again when it rains. Some animals, such as kangaroo rats, have lost the need to drink water at all, recycling it from seeds.

GREAT SALT LAKE

The Great Salt Lake, as Utah naturalist Terry Tempest Williams writes in her memoir *Refuge: An Unnatural History of Family and Place*, is a "liquid lie" in the desert, a mirage, water that does not support life. This relic of Ice Age Lake Bonneville – now northern Utah's most popular natural attraction – is rendered almost lifeless by extreme salinity, but its seasonal fluctuations have a profound effect on adjoining wetlands, such as Bear River Migratory Bird Refuge, which was set aside in 1928 as the nation's first waterfowl preserve. Today, the lake's greatest threat is the long-term drought that has affected the Southwest for over 20 years; by 2022 the lake had lost almost half its surface area from its historical average. With around 768 sq miles (1,990 sq km) of lakebed exposed, the shrinking lake threatens almost 10 million migratory birds that visit annually.

For now, two species manage to live in the lake's salty environment. Green algae thrive in briny water and multiply so rapidly the lake shallows often take on a green hue. In late summer, green algae form the main diet of brine shrimp, which consume so much of the green algae the water begins to clear. The algae also attract swarms of brine flies. The flies, along with algae, reptiles and small mammals, are the major attraction for hundreds of species of birds

Snowy egret at Bear River Migratory Bird Refuge.

that visit the wetlands surrounding the lake. They include avocets, phalaropes, eared grebes, pintail ducks, white pelicans, and thousands of tundra, or whistling, swans, which migrate through in fall.

Utah Mormons have a special place in their hearts for the 80,000 or so gulls that nest and feed around Great Salt Lake. In 1847, shortly after the Mormons had planted their first crops, an infestation of crickets threatened to destroy what little food the people had managed to grow to get them through the winter. At the last moment, when all seemed lost, a flock of gulls came to their rescue, killing and eating the crickets, and saving the crops. The grateful Mormons never forgot this reprieve. Today, the gull is Utah's state bird.

PUMA COUNTRY

The mountain lion – also referred to as a puma or cougar – roams throughout Utah's desert and mountain country, and are usually quiet and elusive, avoiding human contact. This sleek, handsome animal has perhaps the most accurate Latin name of all – *Felis concolor*, meaning the "one-colored cat."

A THREATENED SPECIES

Mountain lions are so endemic to Utah there is an annual quota to allow hunters to shoot them. In 2021–22, the Utah Wildlife Board voted to allow unlimited cougar hunting in most of the state. A single hunter can kill up to two cougars per year. This is extremely controversial – the idea is that killing mountain lions results in higher mule deer and elk populations, but the statistics from other states like California (where mountain lions are not hunted) doesn't back this up. Hunting also results in juvenile pumas having to fend for themselves, leading to more "encounters" with humans and pets. Estimates of how many mountain lions actually live in Utah vary and are highly unreliable, ranging from 1,600 adults to over 2,700 – in the 2020–21 season, some 702 animals were killed. Animal rights organizations such as the Mountain Lion Foundation (https://mountainlion.org) campaign against hunting, claiming that pumas are likely to be endangered by the annual hunt.

Mountain lion footprints along the Green River in Canyonlands National Park.

A mountain lion on the prowl.

A mountain lion surveys the land looking for prey.

Mountain lion cubs.

Puma safety

Scary encounters (and very rare maulings) receive so much media attention (especially the ones filmed on smartphones), that a somewhat exaggerated impression has been created of mountain lions. Realistically, your biggest irritations while hiking in Utah are likely to be mosquitoes, flies, and gnats. However, mountain lions are unpredictable and can be dangerous, especially when hikers stumble across their cubs playing on trails – mother pumas are aggressively protective.

In general, do not jog or hike alone in mountain lion habitats. Pumas have, very rarely, been known to stalk single hikers or runners when hungry, but they totally avoid groups of humans. Needless to say, always keep children close to you and in sight in wilderness areas. In contrast to bears, the best strategy when confronted by a puma is to appear larger (never crouch down or bend over). Stand and face the animal – never turn your back and run. Finally, fight back if attacked. Throw stones, branches, or whatever you can – you need to convince the mountain lion that you are not prey and that attacking you isn't worth the risk to its safety.

ugars live for around 8 to 10 years in the wild.

ese mammals have great leaping ability which allows em to surprise and catch their prey.

Rather than roaring mountain lions make loud piercing screaming noises.

Devils Garden.

OUTDOOR ADVENTURE

Slot canyons, whitewater rapids, mountain heights, and slickrock trails beckon travelers with an itch to experience the wild side of the Beehive State.

The National Sporting Goods Association regularly conducts state-by-state surveys of how many people participate in a range of sports and fitness activities, from backpacking, mountain biking, and downhill skiing to bowling, darts, and working out at fitness clubs. According to NSGA surveys, Utah ranks among the top five states in every activity except saltwater fishing. In fact, compared to the national average, Utahans are more than twice as likely to participate in sports and fitness activities.

One reason for the high ranking is the Mormon emphasis on physical fitness, a corollary of the belief that the body is a temple. Even in the 19th century, when many churches associated play with idleness and most "outdoor adventures" were a matter of survival, Mormons strongly advocated recreation as part of a wholesome lifestyle. According to historian Rex A. Skidmore, Brigham Young "not only enjoyed recreational pursuits himself, but some of his august religious speeches were on this subject."

There's another reason that outdoor sports are so popular: Utah is built for adventure. This is a land of slickrock canyons, whitewater rapids, sandstone cliffs, alpine meadows, crystalline lakes, and wilderness so rugged that some areas have only been surveyed from the air. Viewing it through a windshield can't come close to truly experiencing it. And that's where the adventure begins.

RAFTING

If you explore the great outdoors in Utah long enough, you're sure to cross paths with the ghost of John Wesley Powell. A geology professor and Civil War veteran, Powell became the spiritual father of adventure travel in 1869,

Kayaking on Lake Powell.

when he ran the rapids of the Colorado River in a wooden boat. Poised with his 10 men and four boats at the upper end of Cataract Canyon, the start of nearly 1,000 miles (1,600km) of whitewater wilderness, Powell declared, "We are now ready to start on our way down the Great Unknown. We have an unknown distance yet to run, an unknown river to explore. What falls there are, we know not; what rocks beset the channel, we know not; what walls ride over the river, we know not. Ah, well!"

Every year some 2,000 people raft through Cataract Canyon in the heart of Canyonlands National Park. Unlike Powell, today's whitewater enthusiasts know what lies ahead: 25 rapids, several of them rated Class IV (the

> When nature calls, answer with a trowel. Dig a hole at least 6in (15cm) deep for human waste and bury or carry out toilet paper. Pick a site at least 200ft (60 meters) from water sources.

KAYAKING AND BOATING

While virtually all rafting in Utah is done on the Colorado and Green rivers, kayaking is different. A kayak opens up more possibilities than any other watercraft. You can rent a kayak at any marina on Lake Powell and spend a weekend or longer paddling and camping along the lake's remote tributaries. Or you can test your mettle against one of the fast, cold rivers that pour down canyons along the Wasatch front. Ogden even has a kayak practice park within its city limits.

second-highest level) in just 37 miles (60km). At the end of the four-day trip, a small plane or van returns them to their starting point. Their

Rafting is a popular way to explore the rivers and lakes of Utah.

spiritual bond with Powell is clear. Each of them has undertaken a journey fraught with danger for the promise of a remarkable, once-in-a-lifetime experience.

Rafting, like other outdoor adventures, comes in all degrees of difficulty and risk. If Cataract Canyon sounds too intimidating, rafting companies in the Moab area offer trips on smooth-as-glass stretches of the Green and Colorado rivers. Farther afield, the Green River flows through Dinosaur National Monument on a trip that is placid one minute and thrilling the next, but always magnificently scenic. Place names like the Gates of Lodore and Rainbow Park lend a Tolkienesque mystique to the multiday, Class-III journey.

You can also kayak on the Great Salt Lake. The lake's extreme salinity corrodes the metal parts of motorized boats, so aside from kayaks and canoes, the only watercraft you're likely to see are a few sailboats. Since kayaking is best when there's no wind, kayakers often find that they have the water all to themselves.

In contrast, Lake Powell – on the Colorado River between Canyonlands and the Arizona state line – is one of the most celebrated boating lakes in the West. More than 100 miles (160km) long and fringed with countless side canyons, the lake is best known for houseboating vacations. Often lasting for a week or longer, the journey unfolds at a leisurely pace, with plenty

OUTDOOR ADVENTURE

of time to investigate remote areas by kayak or canoe and fish for dinner in waters that haven't seen an angler all season. Reservations must be made far in advance; the cost per week is about the same as a posh resort.

Elsewhere in the state, boaters and anglers can explore the waters of alpine reservoirs such as Pineview, Deer Creek, Jordanelle, and Strawberry. There are a number of natural lakes, too, including broad, shallow Utah Lake near Provo and aquamarine Bear Lake, which spills into Idaho. Sailboats, bass boats, windsurfers, and sunbathers share all these waters. So do scuba divers, though by far the top dive areas in the state are the submerged slot canyons of Lake Powell and, even more popular, an underground warm spring called Homestead Crater near Heber City.

HIKING SAFETY

For some, hiking is adventure enough. A slow, steady walk in the wilderness seems relatively harmless, but hiking can be risky for several reasons. First, it is the activity people are most likely to undertake without an experienced guide. Second, it is tempting and far too easy to set out on a hike without equipment that may prove essential. And third, it is more likely than any other activity to leave you at the mercy of the elements without an easy way back to safety.

What gets most people into trouble isn't snakebite, flash floods, or falling off cliffs but the far more mundane risk of dehydration – a critical loss of moisture due to extreme heat and aridity. The condition is particularly insidious because in the desert even mild exertion, like hiking, can cause the body to lose moisture faster than the brain can generate an urge to drink. In other words, you become dehydrated before you feel thirsty.

Make sure to take a hat and drink plenty of water when hiking in Utah.

Prevention is simple enough. Carry plenty of water and drink it at regular intervals, whether or not you feel thirsty. The rule of thumb is one gallon (4.5 liters) per person per day, but it's best to take more than you think you'll need just in case you want to extend your trip or you lose your way. Getting lost is notoriously easy to do in the desert, where the absence of trees and other landmarks leaves you with few reference points and the bare ground makes it easy to stray from even a well-marked trail. Coupled with the symptoms of mild dehydration – fatigue, light-headedness, disorientation – losing your way can quickly spiral into a life-threatening situation. Carry a map and compass (or GPS) and know how to use them, and leave a travel plan with someone at home, so they know when and where to start looking if you don't turn up.

Other basics you'll need to take with you are a hat, sunglasses, and sunscreen with a high SPF. The Utah sun is unrelenting, and shade is scarce. Left unprotected, your skin and eyes will be fried in no time.

HORSEBACK RIDING

In the 19th century, Utahans like mountain man Jim Bridger and outlaw Butch Cassidy roamed the mountains and canyons on horseback with a freedom that modern travelers dependent on maintained roads can only envy or, if they wish, emulate. The first step in booking a backcountry riding trip is to find a reputable stable or outfitter. Among the best areas for horseback riding are Bryce Canyon and Capitol Reef national parks, the Escalante Canyons, the San Rafael Swell, and the Uintah Plateaus. For trips of more than one day, most stables require that you arrange a trip through an outfitter who will make sure you and the horses return safely.

Horseback riding in Bryce Canyon.

⊘ FOOT NOTES

As a hiker, you will rely almost entirely on your feet, so keep them in good shape with the best hiking boots you can afford. Modern boots are lightweight but sturdy enough to protect your feet from cactus and thorny underbrush and need little or no breaking in, which helps avoid painful blisters. Wearing polypropylene liner socks under a thick pair of poly-wool outer socks will wick moisture away from your feet and prevent blisters. Avoid cotton socks, which soak up moisture and tend to be rough. If a hot spot develops, cover the area with moleskin (available at most camping supply shops) or white athletic tape and allow yourself extra time to rest.

Overnight trips are naturally more complicated to plan and require a rather daunting list of additional equipment, including a backpack, sleeping bag, tent, water-purifying kit, and camping stove. The design and quality of camping gear has never been better, though choices (and prices) can quickly become overwhelming – go to a reputable camping-supply retailer and work with a salesperson who's willing to take the time you need to make the right decisions. Remember: Comfort is key. The idea is to simplify your life, unload stress, and enjoy the place, people and moment, not aggravate yourself with ill-fitting or poor-quality equipment that leaves you cold, hungry, achy and generally miserable.

Outfitters who guide pack trips in the national parks or forests must be certified by the managing agency.

Horses are an especially appealing alternative in wilderness areas where wheeled vehicles are prohibited. Llamas are a popular alternative, too. Though you can't ride them, llamas can carry as much weight as a human, turning a back-breaking schlep into a comfortable stroll. Llamas make amiable trail companions and getting to know one can be the most memorable part of the trip.

12-mile (19km) route across sloping sandstone surfaces that was first developed by motorcyclists in 1969. Today, Slickrock is said to be the world's most popular mountain bike trail, used by more than 100,000 cyclists each year. The White Rim Trail, a 100-mile (160km) four-wheel drive road around the base of the Island in the Sky district of Canyonlands National Park, makes for a spectacular two- to three-day trip that has enhanced Moab's reputation as a mountain biking hub. Today, Moab's main street has more bike rental shops than restaurants.

Slot canyon in Grand Staircase-Escalante National Park.

MOUNTAIN BIKING

Nothing since the advent of downhill skiing has transformed outdoor recreation in Utah as much as mountain bikes. Invented around 1980 in the ski towns of central Colorado and popularized in the redwood forests of Northern California, this new breed of bicycle with extra-strong frames and heavy-duty tires had been around for a while before cyclists realized that Moab's slickrock country was a mountain biker's paradise. It started when off-road cyclists pioneered the Kokopelli Trail, an ambitious 142-mile (229km) cross-country trek from Loma, Colorado (near Grand Junction), to Moab.

Once there, mountain bikers soon discovered Moab's Slickrock Trail, a technically challenging

Mountain bike rentals and tours can be arranged in towns near all national parks. Unless otherwise posted, cycling in the parks is limited to roads open to motorized vehicles. A notable exception is Zion National Park, where a 3-mile (5km) bikes-only trail offers a shortcut between two scenic drives. Biking is an ideal way to bypass the traffic congestion that often plagues Bryce Canyon National Park, as well as to experience the unpaved scenic routes in and around Capitol Reef National Park.

Visit any bike shop for information on nearby trails, many of which traverse land managed by the National Forest Service or BLM. Some of the biking adventures awaiting discovery are epic in scope, such as a 50-mile (80km) cycling route along the Pony Express National Historic Trail across the Great Salt Lake Desert. If you haven't brought your own bike, you'll find rentals in sizable towns throughout the state, from Price in the northeast, where the 19-mile (30km) Castle Valley Ridge Trail challenges even the most advanced riders, to St George in the southwest, where Snow Canyon State Park, Gooseberry Mesa, and the Green Valley Loop are popular biking destinations.

The most ambitious effort to create a trail network for mountain bikers has taken place around Park City, a popular ski town in the Wasatch Mountains. Here, many ski shops have discovered that bike rentals are an ideal off-season business and hugely popular with visitn tourists. With their support, cycling organizations have established more than 450 miles (724km) of trails designated especially for mountain bikes. Chairlifts equipped with bike racks operate in summer at ski resorts, allowing cyclists to ride to the top of the mountain and spend hours coasting down ski trails. Other relatively effortless trails in the Park City area include the 28-mile (45km) Historic Union Pacific Rail Trail, an old railroad grade stripped of its tracks and ties. The Park City trail system also includes short, technical routes like the Round Valley Trail that challenges bikers of all different skill levels.

Elsewhere in Utah, cyclists enjoy excellent opportunities for road touring. Bike routes separated from traffic lanes have been established along a number of scenic drives in the Wasatch Mountains, such as Ogden and Provo Canyons. Perhaps the most memorable spot is Antelope Island State Park, set on an island in the Great Salt Lake. A 7-mile (11km) causeway connects the island to Syracuse, near Ogden, and an 8-mile loop road leads

Mountain biking on the Jem Trail.

through the park, home of a free-ranging bison herd.

CLIMBING AND CANYONEERING

For a uniquely Utahan experience, consider canyoneering, a hybrid sport that involves hiking, boating, and rock-climbing techniques such as rappelling and "chimneying" as well as navigation and survival skills. The sport is ideal for guide services, which offer a wide range of adventures depending on the participants' particular skill level. Rock climbing can be the focus of advanced canyoneering, or it can be a passion all its own. From the tortured rock faces of Zion National Park to the granite cliffs of the Wasatch Range, those in search of a vertical vacation will find an inviting menu of possibilities.

Though technically demanding, rock climbing has become much easier for novices to try. Guides in popular rock-climbing areas like Moab tailor their services to the needs of beginners, offering supervised ascents on short, clearly blazed climbing routes and rappels down cliff faces that are more thrilling than hazardous. Advanced climbers, on the other hand, can take advantage of year-round opportunities, tackling the cool canyons of the Wasatch Range in summer and shifting to desert areas in spring and fall. On those rare days when the weather is miserable, there are indoor climbing walls where residents and visitors alike hone their skills.

For information on guides and climbing routes, contact the Salt Lake Climbers Alliance (www.saltlakeclimbers.org). Also helpful is the American Canyoneering Association (ACA), based in Cedar City (www.canyoneering.net). The association trains canyoneering guides, search and rescue teams, backcountry rangers, and law enforcement officials. When undertaking any canyoneering adventure, it's prudent to select an ACA-certified guide.

At least as important as the guide's qualifications are your own. Each traveler bound for Utah's backcountry should evaluate honestly his or her tolerance for adventure. This is especially true in the realm of climbing and canyoneering, where the array of trips can range from mild to death-defying. Guides will usually interview you to ascertain your experience so they can help you select the most suitable trip. Avoid hubris or exaggeration; your objective is not to impress your guide. With that word of caution in mind, seize the opportunity to go boldly into the Utah backcountry. Whether by water or land, you'll discover landscapes so wild and strange they might as well be on a distant planet. You may discover something about yourself, too – hidden reserves of strength, courage and wonder that will change forever the way you relate to the natural environment.

Climbing in Utah.

SKY HIGH

Topping the list of thrills in Utah is hot-air ballooning, which lets you experience the freedom of drifting high on the wind to the dragon-like roar of a propane burner, lifting you a world away from the terrain far below – whether it be the wilds of Canyonlands National Park, the rugged Wasatch Mountains or the Great Salt Lake. Balloon trips usually take off early in the morning, when the cool air provides the best lift. Balloon companies operate out of Moab, Park City, Provo, and Ogden.

Other sky-high adventures include paragliding and hang gliding at Point of the Mountain Flight Park (https://stateparks.utah.gov/parks/flight-park), about 13 miles (21km) south of Salt Lake City. Tandem flights, which team a "passenger" with a seasoned flier, allow even rank beginners to get airborne on their first outing. An airport near the flight park was Utah's main skydiving zone for more than 30 years until the area became too developed for safe landings. Now skydiving has moved to the Tooele Valley Airport in Erda, a desert location 20 minutes west of Salt Lake City.

Travelers who dream of soaring can do so in a fixed-wing glider at Heber Valley Airport (www.hebervalleyairport.com). If you prefer a vehicle with a motor, several companies offer helicopter and airplane tours over some of the most spectacular terrain in all the West.

Skiers and snowboarders on top of Hidden Peak at Snowbird Ski Resort.

SNOW SPORTS

Huge vertical drops and tons of light, dry powder lure skiers and snowboarders to this Olympic-quality kingdom of snow.

In winter, a chill wind out of the west howls across the salt flats most of the time. As it reaches the Great Salt Lake, churning up choppy waves on the surface of water too saline to freeze, evaporation occurs rapidly, saturating the desert air with humidity. Reaching the other side of the lake, the wind slams into the near-vertical rock faces of the Wasatch Front, creating an updraft that hurls the moisture-laden air upward a mile or more into the sky, where the temperature drops by as much as 50°F (10°C). The water content in the air flash-freezes into tiny crystals that drop in the form of fluffy white powder on the mountain slopes below. The result of this unique phenomenon is an astonishing average of 500in (1,270cm) of snowfall each winter. That's more than 40ft (12 meters) of snow – enough to bury a five-story building. By way of comparison, the most famous ski resorts in neighboring Colorado – Aspen, Vail, and Breckenridge – average only about 300in (760cm) of snow a year.

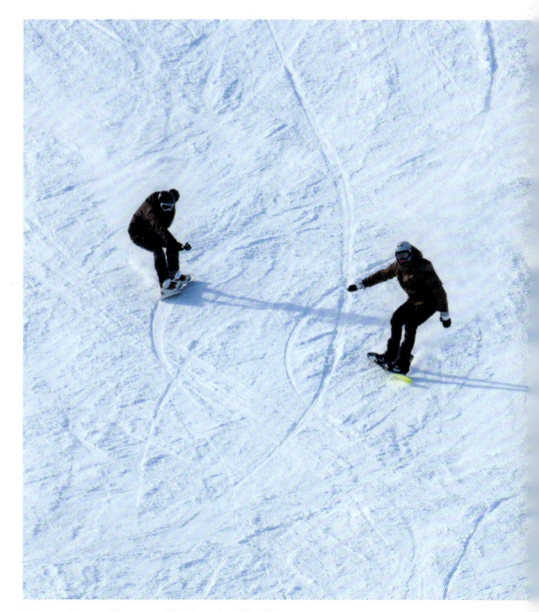

Snowboarding at Solitude Ski Resort.

> From 1985 to 1997, Utah license plates bore the slogan, "Ski Utah! The Greatest Snow on Earth." And yet, Utah's snow remained a local secret.

SKI RESORTS

Of the dozen top downhill ski areas in Utah, 11 are in the Wasatch Mountains within an hour's drive of Salt Lake City, Provo, Ogden, or Logan. Four areas – Solitude (tel: 801-534 1400; www.solitudemountain.com) and Brighton (tel: 801-532 4731; https://brightonresort.com) in Big Cottonwood Canyon and Alta (tel: 801-359 1078; www.alta.com) and Snowbird (tel: 801-742 2222; www.snowbird.com) in parallel Little Cottonwood Canyon – are less than 30 miles (48km) from Salt Lake City International Airport and less than half that distance from I-215, the beltway along the east edge of the city, making them the most accessible major ski areas in the US. These areas have always been popular with local skiers but, until the 2002 Winter Olympics, all but ignored by out-of-towners.

Most of the others, farther from Salt Lake City, were little family-run resorts with one lodge and two or three chairlifts. They include places like historic Beaver Mountain (tel: 435-753 0921; www.skithebeav.com) in Logan Canyon, Utah's first ski resort, built in 1939, and Sundance (tel: 801-225 4107; www.sundanceresort.com) in Provo Canyon, formerly owned by actor Robert Redford and better known for its namesake film festival than for its easygoing elegance, uncrowded slopes, and the last tow rope in the West.

The largest ski area in Utah, Powder Mountain (tel: 801-745 3772; www.powdermountain.com) near Ogden, has expanded to 8,464 skiable acres (34 sq km) including 3,000 acres (12 sq km) of backcountry skiing accessible by Snow Cat, and 2,800 acres (11 sq km) served by lift. The sprawling slopes also offer night skiing until 9pm. On the opposite side of Pineview Reservoir, Snowbasin (tel: 801-620 1000; www.snowbasin.com) is smaller but features spectacular slopes and trails, including racecourses and two terrain parks. It features two gondolas and a tram in addition to 11 lifts.

Park City has become Utah's premier resort town. Before the Olympic Games came to Utah in 2002, the state's only slopes adjacent to a real ski town was Park City Mountain Resort (tel: 435-649 8111; www.parkcitymountain.com), which got its start in 1963 as a small day-use area. In those days, Park City Mountain used a train and elevator to carry skiers through an old mine shaft – a far cry from the present-day megaresort, with its 7,300 skiable acres (30 sq km), 330 runs, and 43 lifts. Not only has Park City Mountain Resort expanded (and absorbed the former Canyons Resort), but another prestigious resort – Deer Valley (tel: 435-649 1000; www.deervalley.com) – has added more downhill skiing options with 2,026 skiable acres (8 sq km) served by 21 chairlifts. That's over 9,300 skiable acres (38 sq km) all within easy shuttle distance of the cafés and boutiques that line the town's historic main street.

Finally, no survey of Utah ski areas would be complete without the only ski resort outside the Salt Lake City vicinity. Brian Head (tel: 435-677 2035; www.brianhead.com) is situated in Dixie National Forest just north of Cedar Breaks National Monument. With just over 650 skiable acres (3 sq km) and eight lifts, it's tiny compared to the behemoths of the Wasatch Front, but it holds a reliable snow base despite its southerly location due to an 11,307ft (3,446-meter) elevation. In fact, its base elevation is higher than the summits of most Salt Lake City ski resorts.

2002 WINTER OLYMPIC GAMES

When Salt Lake City was nominated to host the 2002 Winter Olympic Games, the skiing world immediately took notice. Articles about Utah's little-known ski resorts flooded the ski magazines. Soon, allegations began to emerge about bribery, fraud and corruption on the part of the original organizers of the Salt Lake City Games. Although some officials were forced to resign, the scandal created an avalanche of publicity for Utah skiing. Before ground was broken for the Olympic facilities, Utah's snow became an instant legend among skiers. One question remained: Could Salt Lake City deliver on the massive preparations required of an Olympic host?

The results astonished everyone. Within less than two years, the city and state built an array of special-use facilities including ski jumps, bobsled runs, Nordic ski courses, snowboard pipes, a skating rink, and a ceremonial stadium, but also widened highways in several canyons and met stringent demands for security. Making it one of the best organized games in Olympic history

The legacy of the 2002 Olympics has been an expansion of Utah's ski industry beyond all expectations. Alta, for instance, replaced its main chairlifts with a detachable quad that offers summit-to-base skiing with a single lift. It established a lift-served connection with nearby Snowbird for a combined 5,000 plus skiable acres (20 sq km) – the third-largest ski area in Utah – for the price of a premium lift ticket.

Skiing on the slopes.

SNOWBOARDING

The 2002 Winter Games also gave a new air of respectability to snowboarding. Snowboarding's Olympic debut, four years earlier at the Winter Games in Nagano, Japan, had been marred by scandal when Canadian Ross Rebagliati, the first-ever gold medalist in snowboarding, was stripped of his title after testing positive for marijuana. In 2002, the Americans topped the snowboarding table with five medals (including two golds) – they've since dominated the sport, with boarders like Shaun White and Chloe Kim emerging as global superstars.

Once again, Utah's ski resorts capitalized on the 2002 Games, this time by developing world-class "terrain parks" – special areas with halfpipes, jumps, and other features designed to provide maximum thrills. Park City Mountain Resort, home of the world's first competition superpipe, now has eight terrain parks with numerous rails, jumps and "funboxes".

Other ski areas that emphasize snowboarding include Snowbird, with its Big Emma Terrain Park for boarders of varying skill. Brighton has four interconnected terrain parks that let boarders ride hips, tabletops, and jumps from the top of the highest chairlift to the base of the mountain. Beaver Mountain (two), Eagle Point (one), Nordic Valley (one), Powder Mountain (two), Snowbasin (three), Sundance (one), and Solitude (one) have also added terrain parks, as has Brian Head (two) in southwestern Utah, leaving Alta and Deer Valley as the only ski resorts in Utah that do not allow snowboarding.

CROSS-COUNTRY SKIING

Of course, you don't need a ski slope to ski. Utahans have been doing it ever since the 1870s, when snowbound miners in the Wasatch Range got around by strapping on 12ft (4-meter) skis made from lumber. By 1912, the Wasatch Mountain Club was taking recreational cross-country ski treks into the wilderness. Before the Olympic Games came to town, skiers were flocking to trails groomed by resorts and Nordic ski clubs, while others skied into the national forests of the Wasatch and High Uintas Mountains.

The 2002 Winter Olympics included 12 cross-country ski competitions ranging from sprints to 30km endurance races. The site chosen for the Nordic ski course was Soldier's Hollow, an area of Wasatch Mountain State Park in the Heber Valley south of Park City. Unlike most other Olympic facilities, cross-country ski courses need not be permanent; the groomed trails melt away in the spring. Soldier Hollow, however, has proved so popular with local skiers that the Olympic course is regroomed annually and set aside for cross-country skiing in winter. It's the largest groomed Nordic ski park in Utah. Ruby's Inn near the entrance of Bryce Canyon National Park is similar, with 19 miles (30km) of trails; all trails within the national park are open for cross-country skiing in winter.

Deer Valley.

⊘ SPEED DEMONS

The Olympics are long gone, but the Utah Olympic Park in Park City is busier than ever. Not only do US Olympic contenders train there, but the facilities are open to teams from other countries to practice bobsledding, luge, and skeleton. If watching isn't thrilling enough, you can ride a bobsled yourself. The Park provides the pilot and brakeman; two passengers ride in between. It costs about $175 per person, and the ride is over quickly (the course record is 48 seconds), though it may seem to last forever. You can also take a half-day introductory course in ski jumping or ride a luge or skeleton with a protective shell.

The Fisher Towers Trail.

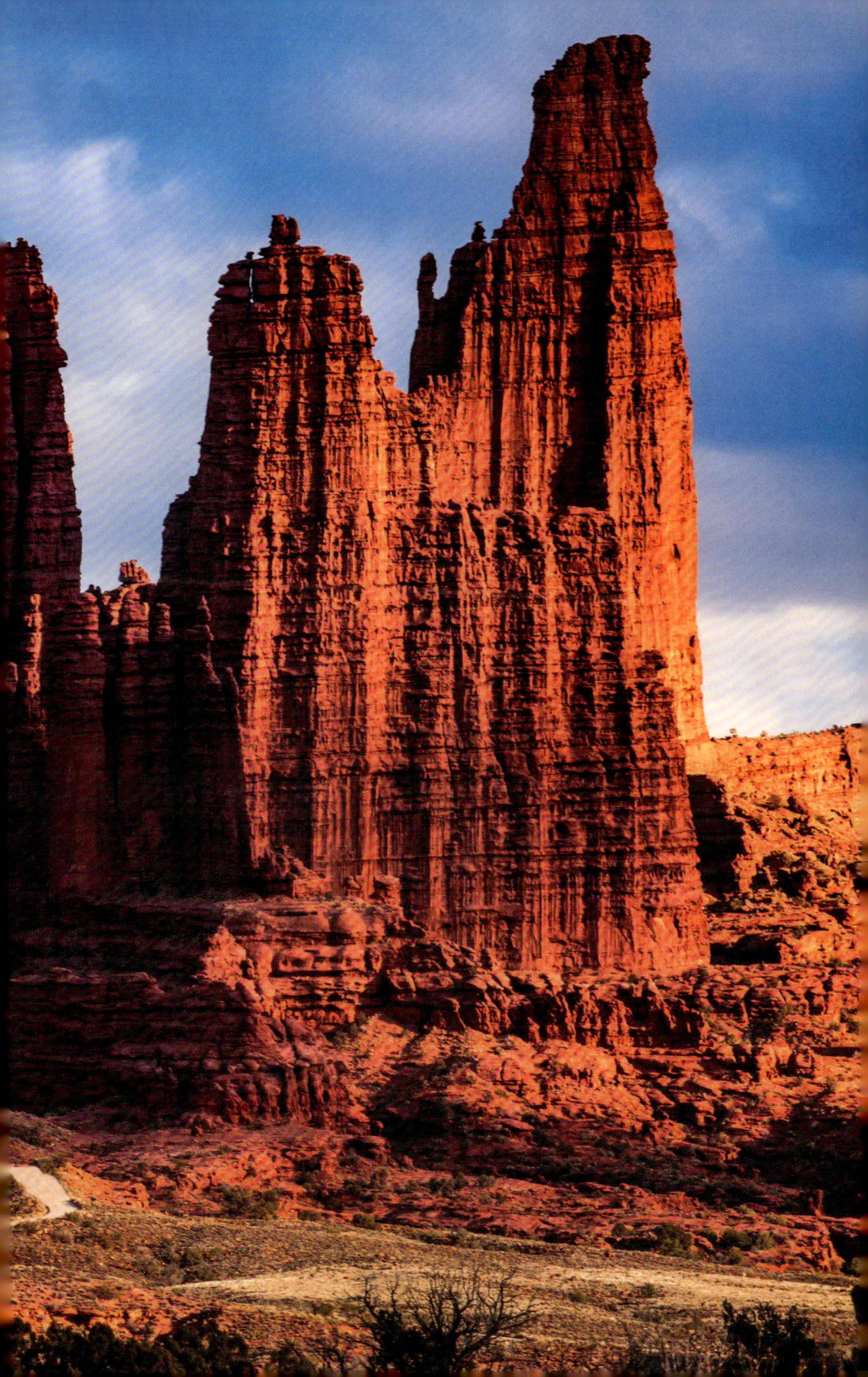

The Wasatch Mountains in fall.

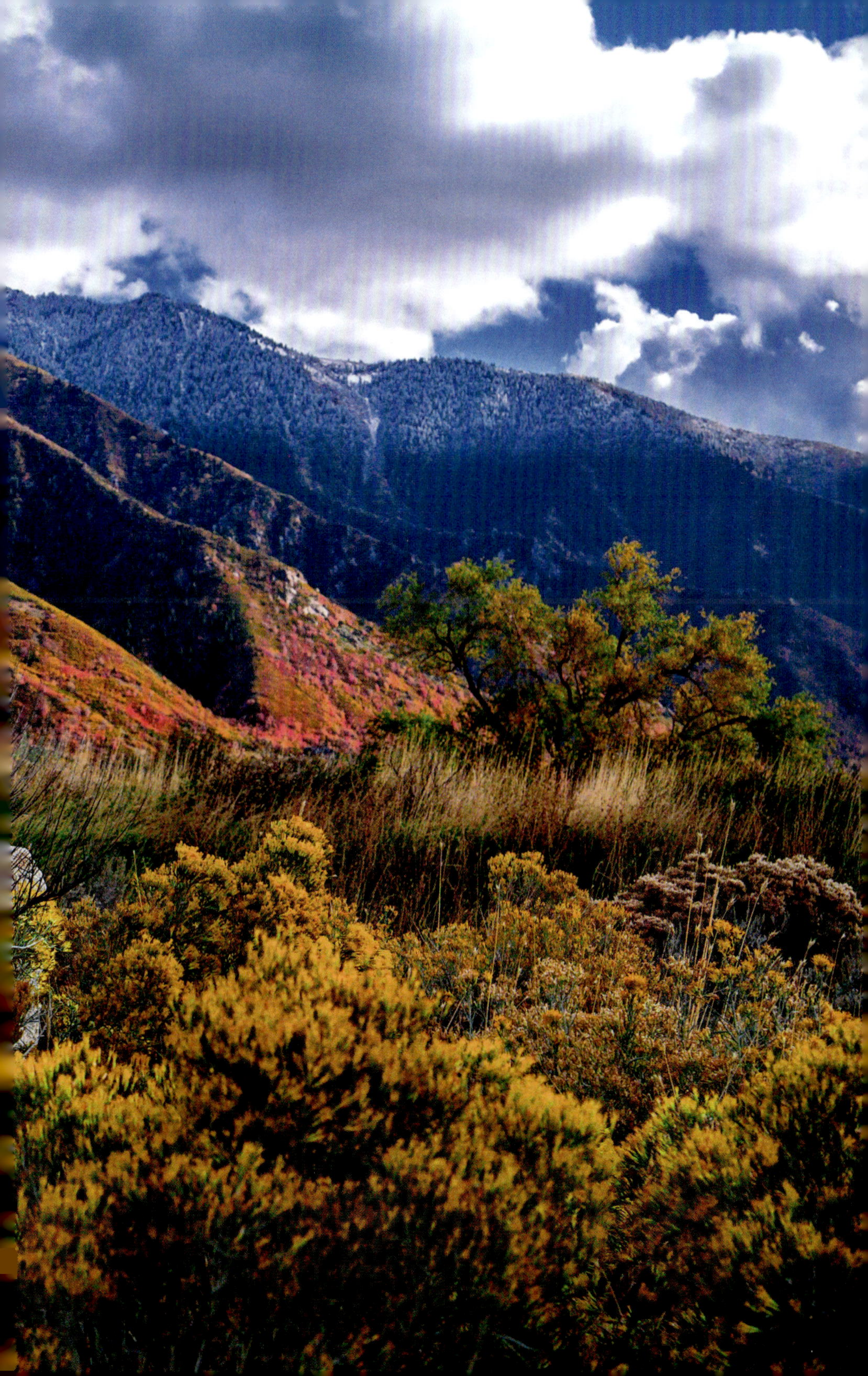

Bryce Canyon National Park in winter.

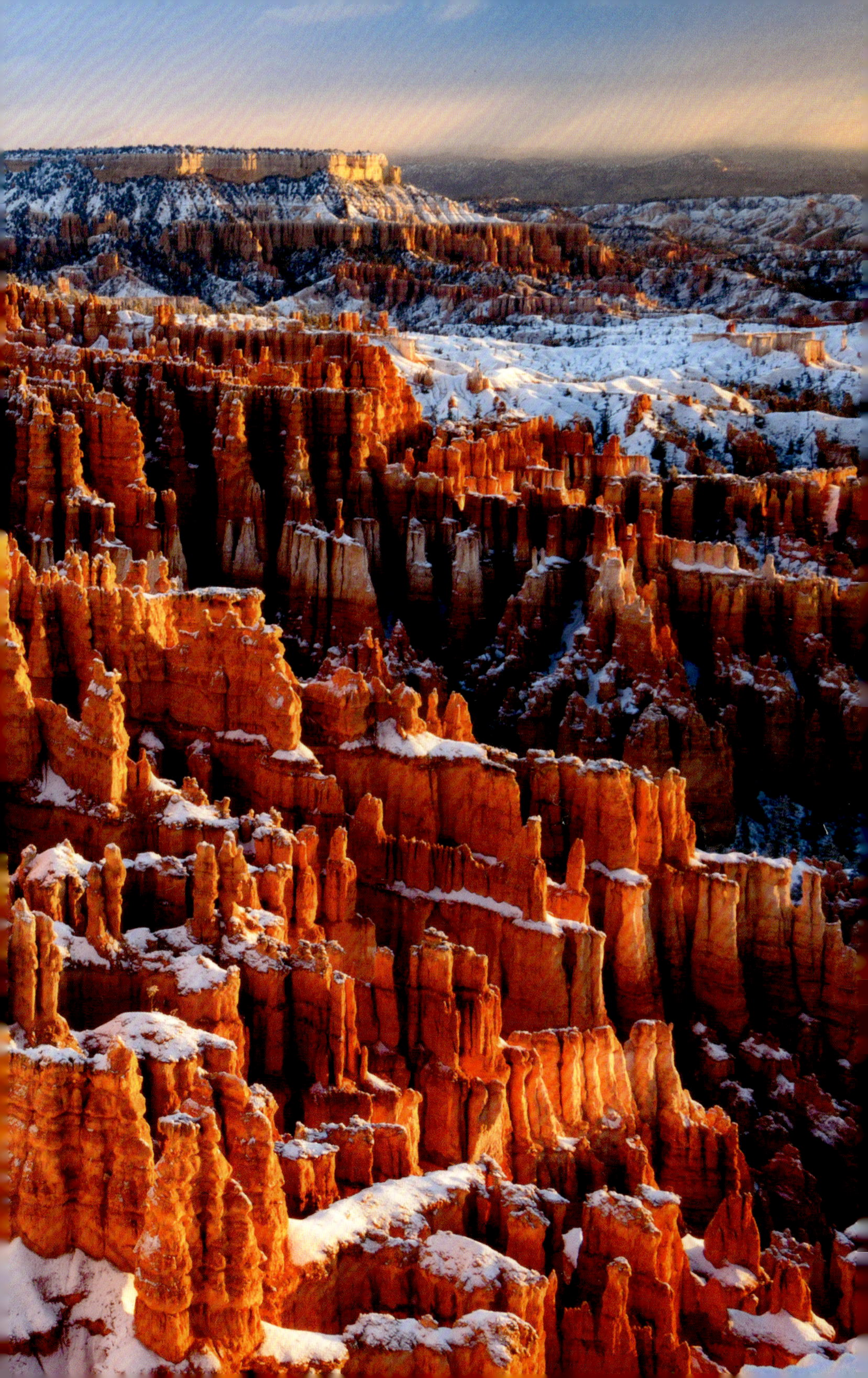

Arches National Park.

INTRODUCTION

A detailed guide to the entire state, with principal sites clearly cross-referenced by number to the maps.

Buffalo, Great Salt Lake.

Utah is home to the biggest and most beautiful landscapes in North America. In southern Utah, especially, the scenery is stupendous, a stunning geological freak show where the earth is ripped bare to expose cliffs and canyons of every imaginable hue. The most accessible national parks – such as Arches (a quick drive from hip Moab, the "mountain bike capital of the world" and a hub for all stripes of outdoor adventurers), Zion, and Bryce Canyon – are by far the most visited. But lesser-known parks like Canyonlands, Capitol Reef, and the Grand Staircase–Escalante National Monument, as well as the forested ramparts of the La Sal Mountains, are every bit as dramatic. Huge tracts of this empty desert, in which fascinating pre-Columbian petroglyphs and Ancestral Puebloan ruins like Hovenweep National Monument lie hidden, are all but unexplored. Monument Valley, part of the Navajo Nation, is perhaps the most iconic landscape of all, with its towering buttes and jagged fingers of rock.

Northern Utah is anchored by the state capital, Salt Lake City, home of the headquarters of the LDS Church, first-class theater, bustling farmers markets, gourmet restaurants, and a cluster of absorbing museums. About 30 miles (50km) west of Salt Lake City is Park City, a busted-out mining town that has been reborn as a winter sports center and hub of the prestigious Sundance Film Festival. The Wasatch Range is actually laced with top ski resorts, and scenic byways that cut through the canyons to the smaller hubs of Ogden and Provo. To the west lies shimmering Great Salt Lake and the otherworldly Bonneville Salt Flats; to the east, the isolated Dinosaur National Monument, Bear Lake, and the beautiful Flaming Gorge National Recreation Area.

Poppy field near Mantua.

In central Utah, in a lightly traveled region known as Castle Country, you'll discover a former mining town transformed into an artist haven, the hideout of outlaw Butch Cassidy, and a dinosaur museum across from 6,000-year-old Native American rock art. There is Scandinavian culture in the Sanpete Valley, hiking in Goblin Valley State Park, cowboys and ranchers on vast expanses of rangeland, and, of course, tight-knit Mormon communities throughout the state. Utah is truly a national treasure. So come share in the adventure.

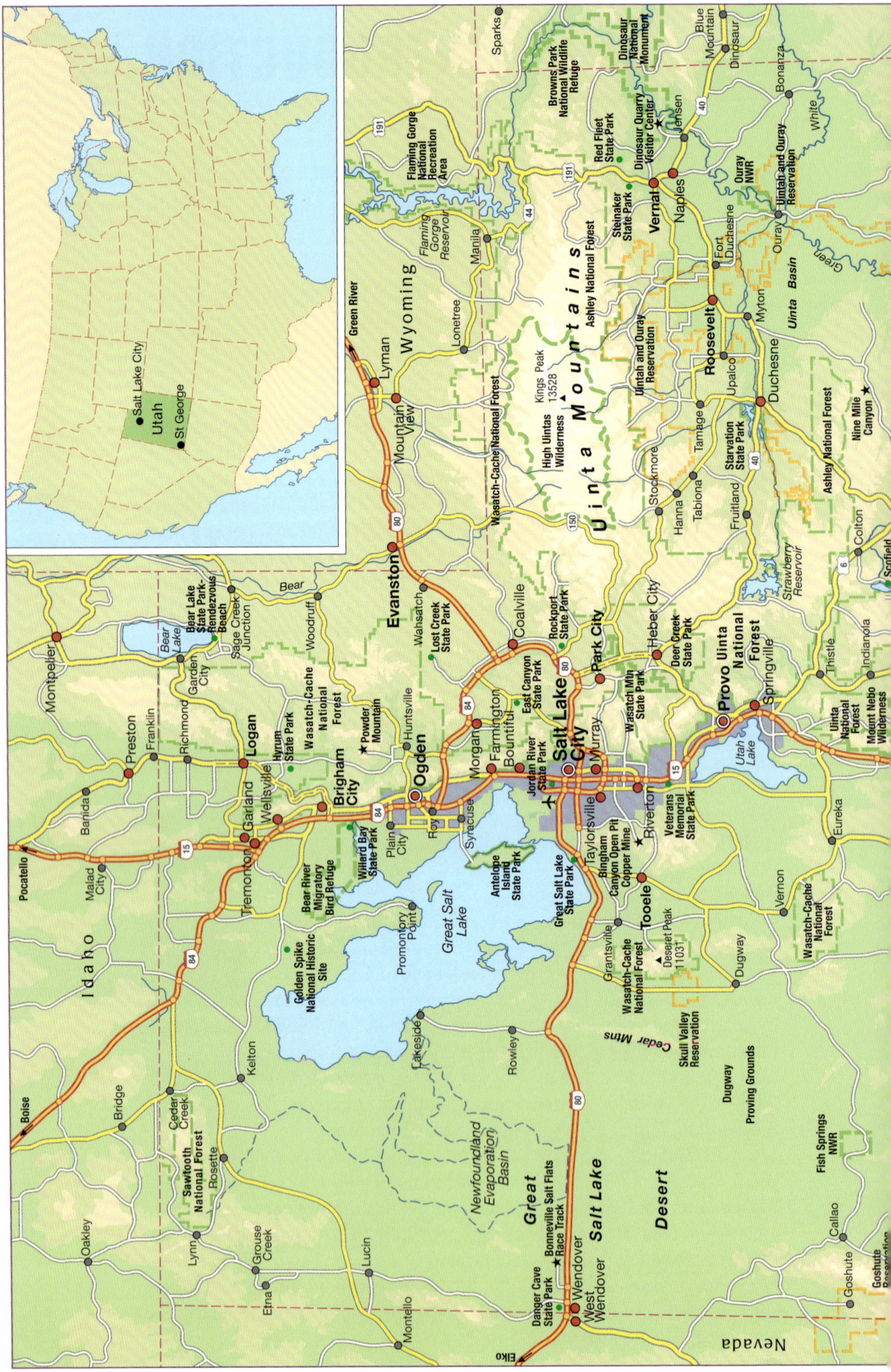
Utah
Salt Lake City
St George
Idaho
Wyoming
Nevada
Great Salt Lake
Utah Lake
Bear Lake
Great Salt Lake Desert
Uinta Mountains
Uinta Basin
Salt Lake City
Ogden
Logan
Provo
Brigham City
Evanston
Tooele
Park City
Heber City
Vernal
Roosevelt
Duchesne
Wendover
West Wendover
Pocatello
Boise
Elko
Green River
Preston
Montpelier
Tremonton
Garland
Wellsville
Morgan
Farmington
Bountiful
Murray
Taylorsville
Riverton
Springville
Coalville
Lyman
Mountain View
Manila
Lonetree
Naples
Jensen
Dinosaur
Ouray
Myton
Fort Duchesne
Kings Peak 13528
Deseret Peak 11031
Flaming Gorge Reservoir
Flaming Gorge National Recreation Area
Wasatch-Cache National Forest
Ashley National Forest
Uinta National Forest
High Uintas Wilderness
Uintah and Ouray Reservation
Dinosaur National Monument
Golden Spike National Historic Site
Bear River Migratory Bird Refuge
Antelope Island State Park
Bingham Canyon Open Pit Copper Mine
Bonneville Salt Flats Race Track
Newfoundland Evaporation Basin
Dugway Proving Grounds
Skull Valley Reservation
Fish Springs NWR
Goshute Reservation
Cedar Mtns
Strawberry Reservoir
Mount Nebo Wilderness
Nine Mile Canyon
Browns Park National Wildlife Refuge

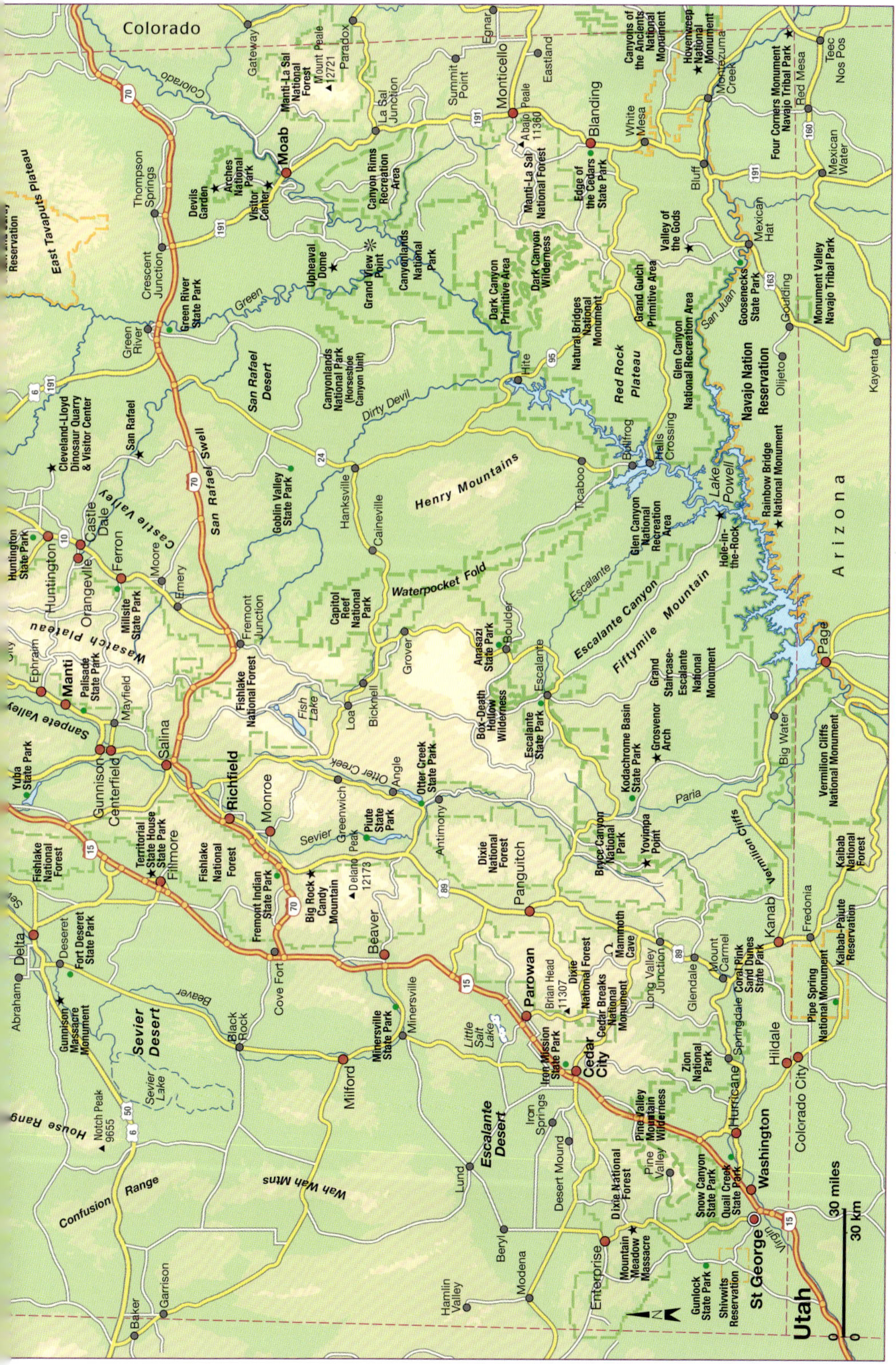
Utah
Colorado
Arizona
East Tavaputs Plateau
Moab
Monticello
Blanding
Bluff
Mexican Hat
Green River
Thompson Springs
Crescent Junction
Arches National Park
Canyonlands National Park
Manti-La Sal National Forest
Natural Bridges National Monument
Hite
Lake Powell
Bullfrog
Halls Crossing
Glen Canyon National Recreation Area
Navajo Nation Reservation
Monument Valley Navajo Tribal Park
Four Corners Monument Navajo Tribal Park
Hovenweep National Monument
Henry Mountains
Hanksville
Caineville
Capitol Reef National Park
Waterpocket Fold
Goblin Valley State Park
San Rafael Swell
San Rafael Desert
Castle Dale
Huntington
Ferron
Emery
Fremont Junction
Wasatch Plateau
Manti
Ephraim
Sanpete Valley
Gunnison
Salina
Richfield
Monroe
Fishlake National Forest
Fish Lake
Loa
Boulder
Escalante
Escalante Canyon
Fiftymile Mountain
Grand Staircase-Escalante National Monument
Page
Big Water
Kanab
Fredonia
Vermilion Cliffs
Bryce Canyon National Park
Panguitch
Dixie National Forest
Parowan
Cedar City
Cedar Breaks National Monument
Zion National Park
Hurricane
Washington
St George
Hildale
Colorado City
Enterprise
Escalante Desert
Milford
Beaver
Minersville
Cove Fort
Fillmore
Delta
Sevier Desert
Sevier Lake
House Range
Confusion Range
Wah Wah Mtns
Notch Peak 9655
Baker
Garrison
Modena
Beryl
Lund
Iron Springs
Desert Mound
30 miles
30 km

Bonneville Salt Flats.

NORTHERN UTAH

Utah's largest metropolitan area is snugged between the Great Salt Lake Desert and Wasatch Mountains, anchored by the capital, Salt Lake City.

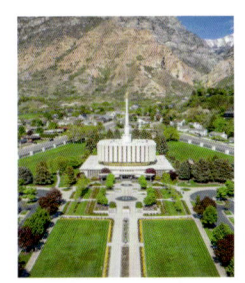

Provo Utah Temple.

From the summit of Mount Olympus, you can see northern Utah laid out before you in all its dramatic contrasts. On the hazy western horizon lies the Great Salt Lake Desert, one of the most desolate places in North America, utterly devoid of the essentials to sustain life. Closer, the Great Salt Lake is nearly as lifeless, sustaining only tiny brine shrimp and brine flies. In the middle of the lake, mountainous Antelope Island hosts an abundance of improbable creatures, from sea gulls and pelicans to free-roaming herds of bison, but no human inhabitants.

Along the eastern lakeshore, ragged with marshes and salt evaporation ponds, the urban corridor encompassing Ogden, Salt Lake City, Provo, and their many suburbs stretches unbroken for 100 miles (160km) north to south. In this hazy strand of skyscrapers, sprawling neighborhoods, and strip malls live over 2 million people – over two-thirds of the entire population of Utah. Mount Olympus is surrounded by other granite and limestone crags of the Wasatch Front – Twin Peaks, Gobbler's Knob, Grandeur Peak, Mount Timpanogos, and many others – along with equally dramatic gorges such as Big and Little Cottonwood canyons and American Fork Canyon. What is most striking about these mountains is the abruptness with which they rise out of the urban sprawl. The climb up Mount Olympus begins within the town limits of Salt Lake City and rises more than 4,200ft (1,280 meters) in elevation in less than 4 miles (6.5km) of climbing, so that from the summit you feel like you're looking straight down into suburban backyards.

Wildflowers on Dromedary Peak.

As impressive as the bird's-eye view of northern Utah is, there's more to be discovered by exploring at ground level. Within this region you'll find such marvels as the center of the Mormon faith at Temple Square. You'll find farms that still operate just as they did at the end of the 19th century, and bobsled runs and ski jumps where future Olympic contenders train. You'll find parks where life-size dinosaur sculptures lurk in the woods and kayakers practice whitewater paddling within blocks of downtown.

This is northern Utah, and there's no other place on earth quite like it. See for yourself.

Logan Tabernacle.

… PLACES | 121

OGDEN AND ENVIRONS

Utah's second-largest urban cluster is home to the state's oldest settlement and is a gateway to its remote northern corner and the Great Salt Lake.

The northern end of Wasatch Front, the narrow, heavily populated strip between the Great Salt Lake and the towering Wasatch Range, contains the historic cities of Ogden and Logan, Wellsville and the American West Heritage Center, and Brigham City's Bear River Migratory Bird Refuge. The main highlights along this stretch, however, are the wonderful hiking, fishing, and exploring to be had in the Logan and Ogden canyons through the mountains, as well as some fine swimming in the impossibly blue waters of Bear Lake, which straddles the Utah–Idaho border – accessible by two spectacular scenic byways.

GREAT SALT LAKE – ANTELOPE ISLAND

Most travelers are drawn to Utah's northernmost tier by the **Great Salt Lake**. For a close-up view, drive the 7-mile (11km) causeway from **Syracuse**, a small bedroom community just southeast of Ogden, to **Antelope Island State Park** ❶ (tel: 801-725 9263; daily 6am–10pm). Encompassing around 42 sq miles (109 sq km), it is the lake's largest island and Utah's largest state park (though the ongoing drought has meant the island is now attached to the mainland for much of the year). Hikers who reach the summit of **Frary Peak**, the island's high point half a mile above water level, can see the entire Great Salt Lake spread out before them. Sunbathers bob like corks in the salt-saturated water of two bays near the island's north end (where there are also campgrounds), and mountain bikers cycle among hundreds of free-ranging bison. The island also lures birders, who spot species as diverse as bald eagles, pelicans, and burrowing owls.

Named for the antelope-like pronghorn explorers found grazing there, Antelope Island served for much of

◉ Main attractions
American West Heritage Center
Antelope Island
Bear Lake
Golden Spike National Historical Park
Great Salt Lake
Lagoon
Logan Canyon Scenic Byway
Maddox Ranch House
Ogden River Scenic Byway
Shooting Star Saloon

Map on page 122

Antelope Island State Park.

the 19th century as a private hunting preserve for Mormon elders, who introduced game species such as bison and elk. In 1969, the island opened as a park, the causeway was completed that same year, although an unexpected rise in water level in the 1980s destroyed the road and left the island isolated for more than a decade. Completion of the present causeway in 1992 allowed the island to be reopened in 1993 to the public. By that time, the original herd of 12 bison introduced in 1893 had multiplied to 500 to 700, grazing on the golden grass and drinking from freshwater springs along the east shore. Near the south end of the island, the **Garr Ranch** is also part of the state park. The ranch house, which now serves as a museum, is the oldest building in Utah in its original location, dating back to a small log cabin built in 1848 by Mormon settler Fielding Garr.

OGDEN

Ogden ❷ claims to be the oldest settlement in Utah because mountain man Miles Goodyear built a trading post there in 1845, then sold out to the Mormons two years later. A reconstruction of Goodyear's stockade and cabin can be seen today at **Fort Buenaventura Park** (2450 Ave; tel: 801-621 4808; daily 7am–9pm; free), a wooded site on the Weber River. Brigham Young renamed the burgeoning community after Peter Skene Ogden, a fur trapper who led the first Hudson's Bay Company expedition into the Wasatch Range in 1825. Many of Ogden's men deserted him and joined another fur expedition led by John Weber, for whom the county is named, taking Ogden's beaver pelts with them. Ogden left empty-handed and never returned to Utah or saw the town named after him.

The completion of the transcontinental railroad in 1869 transformed the quiet farming community almost overnight. Ogden became the largest railroad hub between Denver and Sacramento, with up to 120 trains coming and going every day. The commercial center of town shifted several blocks south of the Mormon Temple to 25th Street, where the passenger terminal was situated.

Today, no passenger train services Ogden, and the refurbished **Ogden Union Station** houses the **Museums at Union Station** (2501 Wall Ave; tel: 801-629 8000; https://ogdencity.com; Wed–Sat 11am–4pm), with various collections of prints, photographs, decorative arts, costumes, paintings, sculpture, toys, and railroad ephemera, including the Utah State Railroad Museum/Eccles Rail Center and the John M. Browning Firearms Museum. The latter chronicles the accomplishments of Ogden native John M. Browning, who designed weapons for Colt, Remington, and Winchester.

During the railroad era, 25th Street became notorious for its opium dens and houses of ill repute – an oasis of vice amid Utah's clean-living Mormon settlements. With the decline of passenger trains, 25th Street was in danger of being razed. A citizen movement succeeded in gaining recognition for the **25th Street Historic District**, opening the way to gentrification in the form of galleries, boutiques, restaurants, and "private clubs" (that is, bars). Anchoring the east end of the district, **Peery's Egyptian Theater** (2415 Washington Blvd; tel: 801-689 8700; www.ogdenpet.com) is one of the last survivors among the grand old movie palaces of the 1920s. Its lavish decor features towering columns covered with hieroglyphs, as well as mummies and a golden "sun" that moves across the lofty ceiling. It now serves as an overflow venue for the Sundance Film Festival and presents community theater.

The Ogden of a century ago may have been a den of iniquity, but today it's a scrubbed and wholesome community with an abundance of attractions designed for kids. The **Treehouse Museum** (347 22nd St; tel: 801-394 9663; www.treehousemuseum.org; Tue–Sat 10am–4.30pm) is packed with play exhibits that encourage literacy, artistic expression and an interest in history – like a replica of the president's desk in the White House. The museum isn't really in a treehouse, but it does have two-story playhouses shaped like castles and mountains.

Kids also love the **Ogden Nature Center** (966 W 12th Ave; tel: 801-621 7595; www.ogdennaturecenter.org; Mon–Fri 9am–5pm, Sat 9am–4pm), a 152-acre (62-hectare) park where you can spot birds and deer, plus gardens

The Ogden Utah Temple.

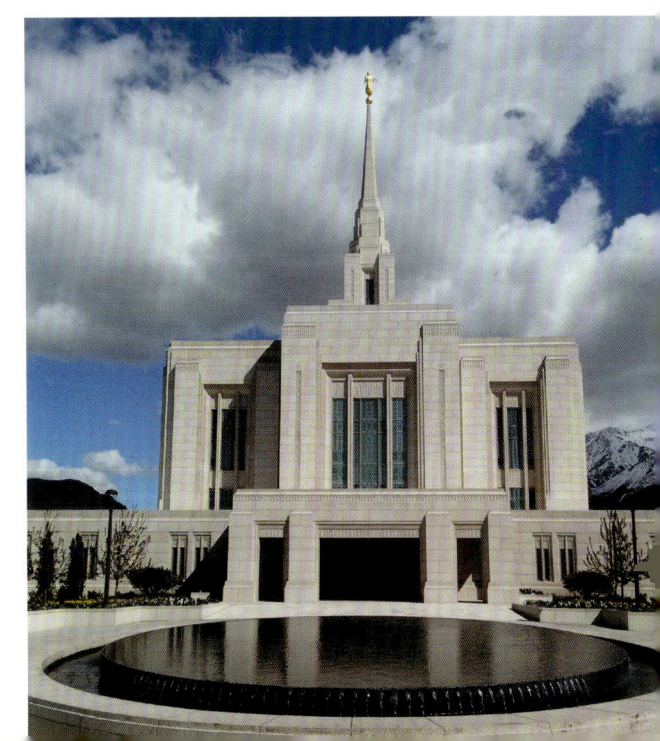

and mews (homes for hawks and other birds of prey). The center cares for hundreds of rescued wild birds, and visitors can meet many of them up close.

Most kids agree that the coolest place in town is **Ogden's George S. Eccles Dinosaur Park and Museum** (1544 E. Park Blvd; tel: 801-393 3466; www.dinosaurpark.org; early Sept–Oct Tue–Sat 10am–5pm, Sun noon–5pm; check website for seasonal hours; charge), near the mouth of Ogden Canyon. Full-size replicas of more than 100 dinosaurs lurk behind trees and underbrush waiting for you to find them. In the park museum, visitors can watch scientists carefully preserve real dinosaur bones.

A unique attraction for whitewater enthusiasts right in metropolitan Ogden, the **Kayak Park** (24th Street at Exchange Road) was born when the city asked for ideas to beautify city parks. One artist, who was also a kayaking fanatic, proposed moving boulders to strategic locations in the Weber River to create a series of holes and eddies. When the mayor cut the ribbon across the river in 2002, the course of perfect rapids – and eager hordes of college students – made Ogden the kayaking capital of Utah overnight.

SOUTH OGDEN

There are a couple of enticing attractions to the south of central Ogden, just off the main I-15 corridor. You can learn about military history and see retired jet fighters at the **Hill Aerospace Museum** (7961 Cottonwood St, Hill AFB, I-15 Exit 338; tel: 801-777 6818; www.aerospaceutah.org; Tue–Sat 9am–4pm; free).

Lovers of old-fashioned amusement parks will be thrilled at **Lagoon** (off I-15, 375 North Lagoon Drive, Farmington; tel: 801-451 8000; www.lagoonpark.com; June–mid-Aug Sun–Thu 10am–9pm, Fri and Sat until 10pm; see website for spring and fall schedule; charge), set near the lakeshore 17 miles (27km) southeast of Ogden. Opened in 1886, Lagoon retains a nostalgic cotton-candy flavor with a vintage roller coaster and log flume and a huge Ferris wheel with spectacular views of the Great Salt Lake. There are also newer gravity-defying thrill rides and Pioneer Village, a restoration of a 19th-century Utah town with carriage and gun collections. Live entertainment is presented at Lagoon throughout the summer season, primarily in its Carousel Theatre. Family-friendly shows (free with admission) can include music, dance, magic, and plays.

OGDEN RIVER SCENIC BYWAY

Ask Ogden residents about the key to the quality of life, and most will tell you it's outdoor recreation. The mouth of **Ogden Canyon**, which provides access for hiking, skiing, camping, boating, and fishing in the Wasatch Mountains, is a five-minute drive from downtown via East 12th Street or a gentle walk or bike ride along the paved, 17-mile (27km) **Ogden River Parkway**. Within the canyon, UT 39 – officially designated the **Ogden River Scenic Byway**

George S. Eccles Dinosaur Park.

OGDEN AND ENVIRONS | 125

– winds between sheer limestone and shale cliffs. Along the way are parking areas for anglers hoping to catch brown trout or wild cutthroat trout, as well as trailheads for several hiking and mountain biking trails. Among the most popular are the edgy, hikers-only **Indian Trail**, which runs up the canyon 4-miles (6.5km) high above the river, and the challenging **Beus Canyon Trail**, which takes hikers, bikers, and equestrians to the 9,572ft (2,917-meter) summit of Mount Ogden, a 6-mile (10km) trip with more than 4,000ft (1,200 meters) of altitude gain.

About 12 miles (19km) up the Scenic Byway, the canyon fans out into a broad, green valley surrounded by mountain peaks. In the center of the valley is **Pineview Reservoir** ❸, a favorite of bass fishers, water-skiers, and sailing enthusiasts. Surrounding the lake, a hodgepodge of palatial homes stands side-by-side with older farms, some dating to the 19th century. From Pineview Reservoir, sightseers can follow a paved road that switchbacks up to **Snowbasin** (3925 E Snowbasin Road, Huntsville; tel: 801-620 1000; www.snowbasin.com), a ski resort built in the 1930s by the same developers who built Sun Valley in Idaho. Snowbasin remained a local secret until it was selected as the site for several alpine events in the 2002 Olympics. Some 350in (889cm) of natural snowfall a year plus one of the world's largest computer-controlled snowmaking systems assure ideal skiing conditions. Lodges and restaurants at the foot of the slopes have transformed it into a year-round resort. At **Huntsville**, the little town at the lake's southeast tip, motorists can abbreviate their scenic drive by turning onto UT 167, known locally as **Trappers Loop Road** because it runs between rivers named after the area's most famous old-time mountain men, Peter Ogden and John Weber. The paved road traverses the back side of Mount Ogden for 9 miles (15km), climbing steep grades as it makes its way among hills covered with oak and aspen before joining I-84, which runs through **Weber Canyon**, at the village of **Mountain Green**. From there, motorists can be back in the Ogden metro area in 10 minutes or detour about 18 miles (29km) east on the interstate to see **Devil's Slide**, a unique geological landmark where two 40ft tall (12-meter) reefs of white limestone run down the mountainside a mere 20ft (6 meters) apart.

For a longer scenic drive, continue east from Pineview Reservoir on UT 39. Reentering the **Uinta–Wasatch–Cache National Forest** a few miles east of Huntsville, the two-lane blacktop highway takes you along the South Fork of the Ogden River where eight small campgrounds offer numerous tent and RV sites designed with trout fishermen in mind. As the road veers north into the **Monte Cristo Range**, highway traffic fades away, leaving you alone on the open road. When you reach Monte Cristo Summit (around 9,000ft/2,743m), you can see why

⊙ Drink

The Shooting Star Saloon in Huntsville (7350 E 200 South; tel: 801-745 2002) dates back to around 1879 (making it one of the oldest bars in the West), open most days from around 11am to 9pm. It looks ancient – the building was erected in the 1850s and at first served as a general supply store. Hundreds of dollar bills and currencies from other countries are pasted to the ceiling, there's a mounted head of a giant St Bernard dog, and plenty of cheap beer.

Hill Aerospace Museum.

few people come out here: mountain forests drop away as you make an abrupt descent into the barren foothills that lie in the rain shadow of the Wasatch Range. By the time you turn north on UT 16 in the don't-blink-or-you'll-miss-it town of **Woodruff** near the Wyoming state line, you may find yourself wondering what inspired you to come way out here, almost 90 miles (145km) from Ogden.

But soon, after you turn left onto UT 30, the most dramatic sight in this remote corner of the state comes into view. Surrounded by desert, the startlingly turquoise water of **Bear Lake** ❹ fills a natural basin 8 miles (12km) wide and 20 miles (32km) long, extending across the Idaho state line. The unique color is produced by the sun reflecting from countless tiny limestone particles suspended in the water. Geologists believe the lake is a relict of ancient Lake Bonneville, which filled most of northern Utah 28,000 years ago. As evidence, they point to four unique species of fish – the Bonneville Cisco, Bonneville whitefish, Bear Lake whitefish, and Bear Lake sculpin – that live nowhere else on earth but Bear Lake. Fur trappers exploring the Wasatch Range used Bear Lake as a rendezvous as early as 1819, and **Rendezvous Beach** is still the site of one of America's largest "mountain man" gatherings each summer.

LOGAN CANYON SCENIC BYWAY

Continue your loop drive by turning west on US 89 at lakeside Garden City (celebrated for its fresh raspberry shakes), following the **Logan Canyon Scenic Byway**. The road climbs by switchbacks up the arid hillsides, each view of the lake more spectacular than the last. Cresting the mountains, you'll pass the entrance to **Beaver Mountain Ski Area** (www.skithebeav.com), a family-run operation that began in 1939. The byway continues south along the Logan River through the canyon and the Uinta-Wasatch-Cache National Forest. It's worth spending at least half-a-day walking a trail or two, or simply driving up to **Tony Grove Lake** (halfway along),

Wind Caves, Logan Canyon.

⊙ THE BEAR, WITCH AND TREE

Despite its steep walls, Logan Canyon offers a variety of great hiking and biking trails. Three of the most popular lead to curiosities that can't be reached by car. Near the upper end of the canyon, for example, is a 5.6-mile (9km) trail that leads to the Jardine Juniper. Once believed to be over 3,000 years old, the tree is now thought to be around 1,500 years old, still making it the oldest Rocky Mountain Juniper. Today, only the tip of its lightning-split trunk still bears needles.

At the lower end of the canyon, a steep trail (3 miles/4.8km round-trip) leads to Witch's Castle, also known as Wind Caves. The "castle" is a small cave and three delicate arches; the site offers spectacular views of Logan Canyon.

The 10-mile (16km) trail to Old Ephraim's Grave is a moderate all-day hike or bike trip. A grizzly bear standing 11ft tall (3.5 meters), Ephraim gained notoriety for his voracious appetite for livestock and an uncanny ability to evade hunters. The bear was buried here by the man who killed him, in 1923. A Boy Scout troop later dug up his remains and sent the skull to the Smithsonian Institution, which sent it back. The skull now resides at the Merrill-Cazier Library in Logan. Old Ephraim was the last wild grizzly in Utah.

LOGAN

and unpacking a picnic basket and enjoying the view.

At the mouth of Logan Canyon (at the end of US 89 and Logan Canyon Scenic Byway), the town of **Logan** ❺ seems a world apart from Ogden and the I-15 corridor, just a few miles away on the far side of a roadless wall of granite, the **Wellsville Mountains**. Walking Logan's timeless Main Street is like strolling through a Norman Rockwell painting. Main Street highlights are the **Logan Tabernacle** (50 N Main St; tel: 435-755 5594; tours daily in summer) and nearby **Logan Utah Temple** (175 N 300 East), two of the finest examples of 19th-century Mormon architecture. Construction of the tabernacle began in 1865 but was left half-finished while workmen turned their efforts to building the Temple; it was completed in 1891. The Temple, built to the exact proportions of King Solomon's Temple in Jerusalem as set out in the Bible, is the third-oldest Mormon temple in Utah. The tabernacle is used for religious meetings, lectures, and concerts, and contains a large genealogical library in the basement. Another Main Street sight that's a must for history buffs is the **Cache Daughters of Utah Pioneers Museum** (160 N Main St; tel: 435-752 5139; http://cachedupmuseum.org/index.html; June–Aug Tue–Fri 11am–5pm, Sat 11am–2pm; Sept–May Wed–Thu 11am–5pm; donation) in the former Hall of Justice. Exhibits include old-time musical instruments, weaving equipment, and such curiosities as a hair wreath, which women made from the hair of their relatives and wore like a hat. Logan also has a long tradition of theatrical arts. While exploring the historic district, visit the grand **Ellen Eccles Theater** (43 S Main St; tel: 435-752 0026; www.cachearts.org). Built in 1923 and restored in 1993, it is host to ballet, symphonic music, opera, and musical theater. An even older venue, the 1913 Victorian-style **Caine Lyric Theater** (28 W Center St; tel: 435-797 1500), has also been restored and now hosts the modern Lyric Repertory Company (www.usu.edu/lyricrep). The Art

> **Tip**
>
> Birders flock to the Bear River Migratory Bird Refuge (tel: 435-723 5887; https://www.fws.gov/refuge/bear-river-migratory-bird), where the Bear River flows into the northeast arm of the Great Salt Lake, in late spring (usually May) for an annual bird-watching festival, featuring special tours, photography seminars, and bird identification workshops.

Logan Temple.

PLACES

> **Eat**
>
> On the southern outskirts of Brigham City, the Maddox Ranch House (1900 S Highway 89; tel: 1-435-723 8545, https://maddoxfinefood.com; Tue–Sat 11am–9.30pm) has become a destination in its own right, a drive-in diner that's a genuine Utah institution. Open since 1949, it's best known for buffalo steaks and burgers, as well as its "famous" fried chicken and freshly made rolls with raspberry honey butter.

Deco **Utah Theater** (18 W Center St; tel: 435-752 3072; https://theutahtheatre.org), a reconstruction inspired by the movie palaces of the 1930s, shows first-run films nightly.

Much of Logan's unique character comes from the student population of **Utah State University**. With a student body of 27,000 in a community of only 52,000 year-round residents, it's no wonder that the whole town seems to radiate youthful exuberance. The campus sprawls across the northeast of Logan; 500 North Street takes you directly to the school's hallmark edifice, the **Old Main Building**. The university's **Nora Eccles Harrison Museum of Art** (650 N 1100 East St; tel: 435-797 0163; https://artmuseum.usu.edu; Tue–Fri 11am–6pm, Sat 10am–3pm; free) features a collection of 20th-century paintings, photographs, and ceramics.

South of the city center, **Zootah at Willow Park** (419 W 700 South St; tel: 435-750 9893; https://zootah.org; Mon–Sat 10am–6pm) is a private nonprofit zoo that has invested in new exhibits and animals in recent years. The largest animals are elk, reindeer, and coyotes. Water is diverted from the Logan River for a series of ponds, streams, and water holes that occupy more than half of the zoo's total area, providing habitat for a wide assortment of North American, European, Asian, and Australian waterfowl.

WELLSVILLE

Six miles (10km) southwest of Logan, just off the highway to Brigham City, the little mountain town of **Wellsville** ❻ is home to the **American West Heritage Center** (4025 US 89/91; tel: 435-245 6050; https://www.awhc.org; call for opening hours). The Center is a living-history museum that explores the diverse cultures that shaped the Cache Valley from 1820 to 1920; steam powered tractors, harvesters, wagons, and other antique farm equipment is kept in operation. Costumed interpreters demonstrate such skills as dancing, gunfighting, and woodworking. Shoshone and Mountain Man encampments share the 160-acre (65-hectare) park with a pioneer settlement.

A few miles east of Wellsville is another colorful early Mormon settlement, **Hyrum**. Outside it is Hyrum State Park with boating and camping facilities, and to the east, the **Blacksmith Fork Canyon**, a high walled gorge with good fishing and plenty of picnic sites. Further along Highway 101 is the state-run **Wildlife Education Center at Hardware Wildlife Management Area** (https://wildlife.utah.gov/hardware-visit.html; free); the main attraction here is the annual winter feeding of hundreds of elk.

BRIGHAM CITY AND AROUND

Return to I-15 at **Brigham City**. Fruit stands along the way are filled in summer with locally grown cherries, apricots and peaches. On a steel archway over Main Street is a neon sign that reads, "Welcome to Brigham – Gateway – World's Greatest Bird Sanctuary." The sanctuary is **Bear River Migratory Bird Refuge** ❼ (tel: 435-723 5887; https://

Brigham City Utah Temple.

OGDEN AND ENVIRONS | 129

www.fws.gov/refuge/bear-river-migratory-bird; dawn–dusk; free). Whether it is the "greatest" may be debatable, but it's certainly the oldest, created by a special act of Congress in 1928. The 80,000-acre (324 sq km) refuge is enclosed by a man-made dike that separates the lake's briny water from the fresh water carried down from the mountains by the Bear River. Visitors drive a loop along the top of the dikes and watch for birds. More than 250 species frequent the wetlands. Depending on the time of year, they may include whistling swans, Canada geese, white ibis, and snowy egrets. Even rare and exotic "accidentals" are occasionally spotted here, such as American flamingos and roseate spoonbills. You can drive the one-way 12-mile (19km) Auto Tour, or stroll 1.5 miles (2.4km) of trails near the Wildlife Education Center (I-15, exit 363).

Just to the south, another dike encloses the waters of **Willard Bay State Park** (900 W 650 North, Willard; tel: 435-734 9494; https://stateparks.utah.gov/parks/willard-bay; Mar–Nov daily 6am–10pm), a popular spot for swimming, sunbathing, boating, and fishing.

GOLDEN SPIKE NATIONAL HISTORIC SITE

About 32 miles (52km) northwest of Brigham City lies **Golden Spike National Historic Site** ❽ (tel: 435-471 2209; www.nps.gov/gosp; daily 9am–5pm; with exceptions), where the final spike was driven into the country's first transcontinental railroad in 1869. The job fell to Leland Stanford, a grocer-turned-railroad-mogul who traveled from California for the event. Stanford swung a silver hammer and missed. But a telegraph operator sent out a triumphant message anyway. *Dot. dot. dot. Done.* A Central Pacific locomotive crept forward from the west, a Union Pacific engine from the east. Their cowcatchers kissed. Recently sundered by the Civil War, the United States was now united by rail. The site where the last spike was driven now stands near the modern Visitor Center, and is commemorated by a polished wooden tie with a plaque. Visitors may also wish to follow a partially paved scenic road that runs down to **Promontory Point**, a remote peninsula jutting into the Great Salt Lake.

Union Pacific train arriving at the Golden Spike Historic Site.

⊘ SPIRAL JETTY

Artists in America the late 1960s began shifting their attention from gallery walls to the great outdoors, employing nature to create a new genre called, variously, "earthworks," "land art," or "public art." Down with salon artifice, up with primordial reality.

An exemplar was Robert Smithson. Born in 1938 and trained at New York's Art Students League and the Brooklyn Museum, he never got over his childhood fascination for the objects on display at the American Museum of Natural History, and in 1970 he put his budding sculptural inclination to work in Utah on a monumental scale.

Using a bulldozer, Smithson piled up basalt rocks and mud from around the Great Salt Lake in a symmetrical design, creating a coil at Rozel Point stretching counterclockwise 1,500ft (460 meters) into the water. It is called *Spiral Jetty* and ranks as an earthwork classic. Owing to the whims of Mother Nature, *Spiral Jetty* was mostly submerged in subsequent years, although a protracted Western drought has caused it to be permanently visible since 2002. The site can be accessed via 16 miles (26km) of gravel roads from the Golden Spike National Historic Site Visitor Center, and has been maintained by the Dia Art Foundation since 1999 (www.diaart.org). Visitors must "leave no trace" at the site.

Salt Lake Temple.

SALT LAKE CITY

Salt Lake City, the capital of Utah, is by far the state's largest and most cosmopolitan urban center, with a superb setting in the shadow of the snow-capped Wasatch Front.

Thrust into the spotlight by the 2002 Winter Olympics, Utah's biggest city has matured into a world-class urban center in the subsequent decades. An influx of high-tech and energy-related industries and other corporate interests, as well as the robust growth of the Wasatch ski resorts (a short drive from downtown), have helped transform Salt Lake City into a cultured, contemporary urban center. The city (like much of Utah) is of course primarily associated with the Church of Jesus Christ of Latter-day Saints (or Mormons). This was the site chosen by Brigham Young in 1847 to begin building the Mormons' new Zion. Mormon history provides much of the interest here, but the area around the city also offers great hiking and cycling in summer and autumn and, in winter, superb skiing.

TEMPLE SQUARE

By day, the heart and hub of Salt Lake City is the sandstone and adobe walled grounds of **Temple Square** (tel: 801-240 4446; tours 9am–9pm; free), naturally the place to begin a visit. Shortly after reaching the Salt Lake Valley in 1847, Brigham Young, with cane in hand, consecrated the site between two forks of City Creek for the construction of the **LDS Temple A**. For over 40 years, oxen teams hauled granite blocks from nearby quarries in the Wasatch Mountains until the majestic, six-spired, neo-Gothic structure was complete in 1893. Perched atop the temple is a gold statue of Moroni, the angel who, in Mormon doctrine, appeared to Joseph Smith. The temple itself is used for the holy ordinances of the LDS Church, such as baptisms, weddings, and family "sealing" ceremonies. As with all Mormon temples, only Church members in good standing may enter. The general public may wander about the manicured

Main attractions
City Creek Canyon Trail
Natural History Museum of Utah
Ruth's Diner
Temple Square
This Is the Place Heritage Park
Trolley Square
Utah Museum of Contemporary Art
Utah Museum of Fine Arts
Utah State Capitol

Map on page 132

The Joseph Smith Memorial Building.

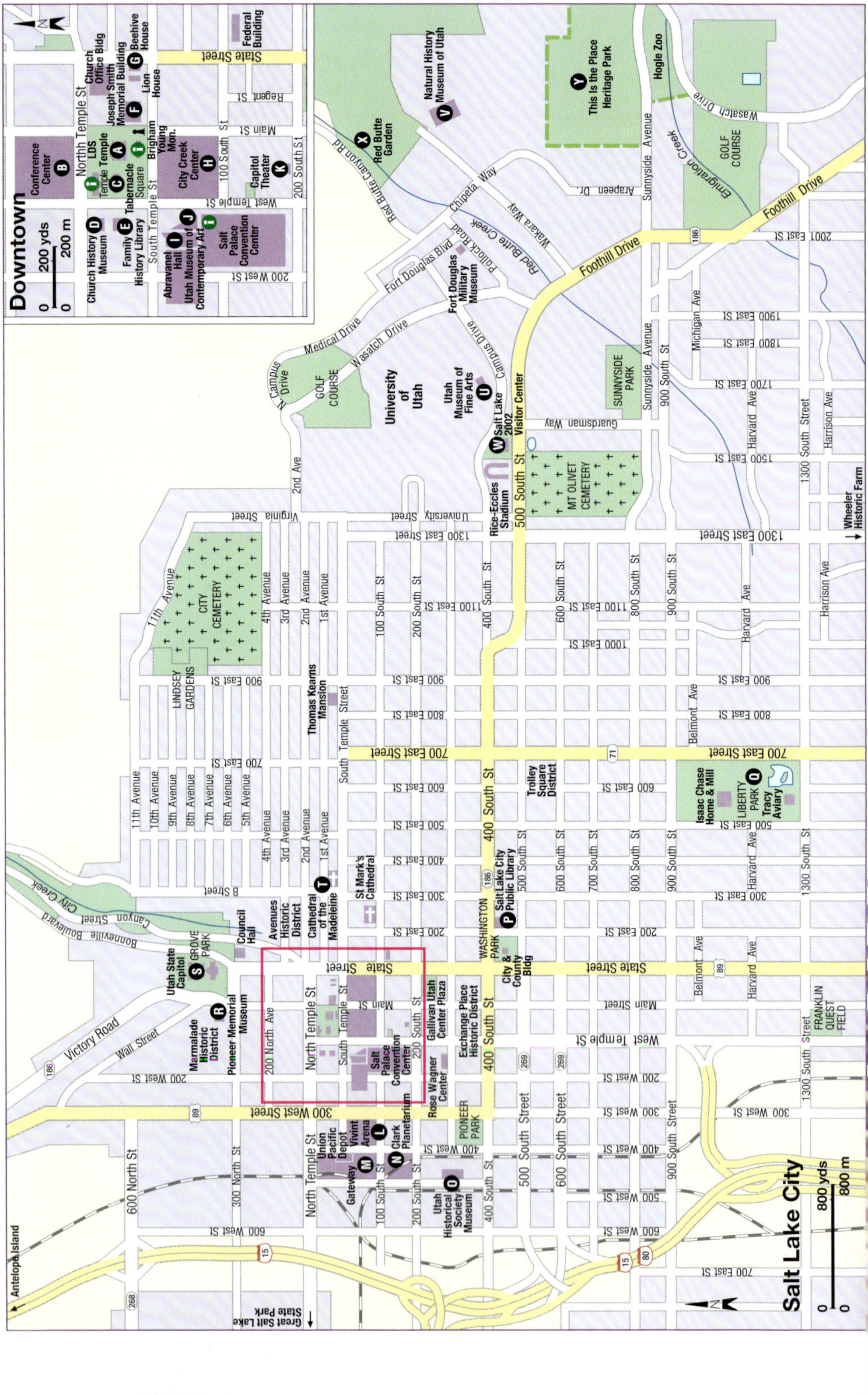
Salt Lake City
0 800 yds
0 800 m
Downtown
0 200 yds
0 200 m
Conference Center B
LDS Temple A
Temple C
Tabernacle
Temple Square
Church Office Bldg
Joseph Smith Memorial Building F
Beehive House G
Lion House
Brigham Young Mon.
City Creek Center H
Capitol Theater K
Church History Museum D
Family History Library E
Abravanel Hall I
Utah Museum of Contemporary Art J
Salt Palace Convention Center
Federal Building
State Street
Regent St
Main St
North Temple St
South Temple St
West Temple St
100 South St
200 South St
200 West St
Red Butte Garden X
Natural History Museum of Utah V
This Is the Place Heritage Park Y
Hogle Zoo
GOLF COURSE
University of Utah
Utah Museum of Fine Arts U
Salt Lake 2002 Visitor Center W
Rice-Eccles Stadium
Fort Douglas Military Museum
MT OLIVET CEMETERY
SUNNYSIDE PARK
CITY CEMETERY
LINDSEY GARDENS
Thomas Kearns Mansion
Trolley Square District
Isaac Chase Home & Mill
LIBERTY PARK
Tracy Aviary O
Cathedral of the Madeleine T
St Mark's Cathedral
Avenues Historic District
Council Hall
Utah State Capitol S
GROVE PARK
Pioneer Memorial Museum R
Marmalade Historic District
Salt Lake City Public Library P
WASHINGTON PARK
City & County Bldg
Gallivan Utah Center Plaza
Exchange Place Historic District
Rose Wagner Center
PIONEER PARK
Vivint Arena L
Clark Planetarium N
Union Pacific Depot M
Gateway
Utah Historical Society Museum Q
FRANKLIN QUEST FIELD
Wheeler Historic Farm
Great Salt Lake State Park
Antelope Island
Foothill Drive
Wasatch Drive
Medical Drive
Fort Douglas Blvd
Red Butte Canyon Rd
Chipeta Way
Wakara Way
Red Butte Creek
Pollock Road
Campus Drive
N Campus Drive
Arapeen Dr
Sunnyside Avenue
Emigration Creek
Guardsman Way
Virginia Street
University Street
1300 East Street
700 East Street
300 West Street
Victory Road
Wall Street
Bonneville Boulevard
Canyon Street
City Creek
B Street
11th Avenue
400 South St
500 South St
900 South St
1300 South Street
North Temple St
600 North St
300 North St
200 North Ave
Harvard Ave
Belmont Ave
Michigan Ave
Harrison Ave

grounds of Temple Square (a delight at Christmas time, when it is aglitter with thousands of lights).

Visits to Temple Square usually begin at the **Conference Center** B (tel: 801-240 8945; www.churchofjesuschrist.org; daily 9am–9pm; free), where there are exhibits, a 17-minute orientation film, and a replica of Christus, a 19th-century statue of Christ by Danish sculptor Bertel Thorvaldsen. The rooftop gardens and observation deck have glorious views of the city. Other notable sights are the **Assembly Hall** (tel: 801-240 4872; daily 9am–9pm; free) completed in 1882, and the **Seagull Monument** commemorating the 1848 "miracle of the gulls" that saved the first Mormon pioneers from a swarm of crickets.

Don't pass up an opportunity to visit the **Tabernacle** C (tel: 801-240 2534; daily 9am–9pm; free), completed in 1867 as a place for church members to gather and hear their leaders. Today, it's the home of the Mormon Tabernacle Choir. The choir offers free admission to its rehearsal on Thursday evenings (7.30–9.30pm) and its broadcast on Sunday mornings (9.30am), the oldest continuous broadcast in the world (in summer performances take place at the Conference Center). Organ recitals take place Monday through Saturday at noon and Sundays at 2pm.

From Temple Square it is only a short walk in several directions to other note-worthy Church sites. Exiting the west gate, you can't miss the **Church History Museum** D (tel: 801-240 3310; Mon, Fri, and Sat 10am–6pm, Tue–Thu until 8pm; free), where exhibits on Church leaders, the Mormon migration and other topics chronicle the evolution of the faith.

Next to the Museum, the **Family History Library** E (tel: 801-240 6996; Mon, Fri, and Sat 9am–6pm, Tue–Thu until 8pm; free) houses the Mormon genealogical library, the largest institution of its kind in the world. Millions of birth, baptism, and death certificates from around the world are stored in its archival collection, and a staff of librarians speaking some 40 languages is on hand to help you dig up the roots of your family tree.

Directly east of Temple Square is a full block of Church-related buildings. Exit through the south gate of Temple Square, near the **Brigham Young Monument**, and walk east toward the historic **Hotel Utah**, which is now the **Joseph Smith Memorial Building** F (tel: 801-240 8945; Mon–Fri 9am–5pm; free), housing the Nauvoo Café and Legacy Theater, which shows films throughout the day that explore the Mormon church and its history.

BEEHIVE HOUSE AND LION HOUSE

Across the plaza are the former residences of Brigham Young and many of his 27 wives. Built in 1854, the **Beehive House** G (67 E South Temple St; tel: 801-240 2681; Mon–Sat 10am–6pm; with exceptions; free) was the official

Brigham Young Monument.

> **Tip**
>
> Salt Lake's bike share program is GREENbike (www.greenbikeutah.org), with stations all over downtown; 24-hour passes are $7 (unlimited 30min rides; $5 for each additional 30min thereafter).

residence of Brigham Young who, as Church president and territorial governor, received President Ulysses S. Grant, Samuel Clemens (aka Mark Twain), General William T. Sherman, and other prominent visitors in the Long Room. Now restored as a small museum of Young's life, the Federal-style residence is named for the carved beehive, a symbol of Mormon industry, atop the cupola.

Next door is the **Lion House** (1855), a "supplementary" domestic residence used by some of Young's wives and 56 children. An impressive stone lion stands guard at the entrance. The women were lodged on the main floor while the children stayed in the upstairs rooms with their 20 gabled dormer windows.

DOWNTOWN

Commercial Salt Lake City lies immediately south of Temple Street, with a spate of shopping malls, skyscrapers, and secular attractions. Just across South Temple Street lies the sprawling **City Creek Center** ❶ (https://shopcitycreekcenter.com; Mon–Sat 10am–9pm), an enclosed shopping mall operated by the LDS Church, with over 100 stores and restaurants. The handsome facade of the section now occupied by Macy's on South Temple is from the original Zion's Co-operative Mercantile Institution, which was established by Brigham Young in 1868 to distribute goods to Church members. Drifting a couple of blocks south on State Street, you come to the **Gallivan Center** (https://thegallivancenter.com) an outdoor plaza with an intriguing design, featuring an ice-skating rink, a giant chess board, and space for concerts, a farmers market, and other social events.

Large civic structures dominate the western edge of the downtown area, including the sprawling **Salt Palace Convention Center** (90 S West Temple St; tel: 801-521 2822), which has a visitor information area, and **Abravanel Hall** ❶ (123 W South Temple St; tel: 801-355 2787), an architectural gem and home of the Utah Symphony. Next door, the **Utah Museum of Contemporary Art** ❶ (20 S West Temple St; tel: 801-328 4201; https://utahmoca.org; Wed, Thu, and Sat 11am–6pm, Fri until 9pm; donation) offers a break from all things Mormon, with carefully curated changing exhibits of contemporary art in all mediums.

The Utah Opera Company and Ballet West perform several blocks away at the historic **Capitol Theater** ❶ (50 W 200 South St; tel: 801-355 2787), which also stages Broadway roadshows and concerts. The largest venue in the downtown area is the **Vivint Arena** ❶ (300 W South Temple St; tel: 801-325 7328; www.vivintarena.com), a 20,000-seat arena where basketball fans cheer on the NBA's Utah Jazz. It is also used for rodeos, concerts, and other large-scale events.

Utah Museum of Contemporary Art.

SALT LAKE CITY | 135

THE GATEWAY
Just beyond the Vivint Arena is the imposing **Union Pacific Depot** (400 W 100 South St), built in 1909 as the city's main railroad terminal. Western scenes are depicted on murals and stained glass in the interior. The building now serves as a portal to the **Gateway** Ⓜ (tel: 801-456 0000; https://atthegateway.com; Mon–Thu 10am–9pm, Fri and Sat until 10pm, Sun noon–6pm), a 30-acre (12-hectare), two-level, outdoor complex of shops, restaurants, movie theaters, and offices built around numerous plazas and performance spaces. Kids love to splash around in the Olympic Snowflake Fountain at **Olympic Plaza**. Anchoring the south end of the complex is the **Clark Planetarium** Ⓝ (110 S 400 West St; tel: 801-456 7827; https://slco.org/clark-planetarium; daily 10am–7pm), which features state-of-the-art astronomy shows and an IMAX theater. Another family-friendly attraction here is the **Discovery Gateway Children's Museum** (444 W 100 South St; tel: 801-456 5437; www.discoverygateway.org; Mon, Wed, Thu, Fri and Sat 10am–6pm, Sun noon–6pm), which offers over 60,000 sq ft (5,574 sq meters) of interactive, hands-on exhibits and games designed to encourage learning.

Another railroad-related landmark, the **Rio Grande Depot**, just south of the Gateway, houses the **Utah Historical Society Museum** Ⓞ (300 S Rio Grande St, 801-533 3500; https://history.utah.gov/utah-state-historical-society; free), which interprets the state's rich and varied past (the museum should reopen in 2023 after a long seismic retrofit, but check the website for updates). Nearby **Pioneer Park** is the scene of a lively farmers market on Saturday mornings (www.slcfarmersmarket.org; June–Oct 8am–2pm).

WASHINGTON PARK
Four blocks east from Pioneer Park, on the edge of **Washington Park**, is the **Salt Lake City Public Library** Ⓟ (210 E 400 South St; tel: 801-524 8200; https://services.slcpl.org; Mon–Thu 10am–8pm, Fri-Sat 10am–6pm, Sun 11am–5pm), which features an eye-catching six-story, crescent-shaped glass wall and rooftop garden. Next door, **The Leonardo** (209 E 500 South St; tel: 801-531 9800; https://theleonardo.org; Wed-Fri 10am–7pm, Sat and Sun noon–7pm) is a family-friendly art and science museum with immersive exhibits inspired by the work of Leonardo da Vinci. The elegant Romanesque Revival building across Washington Park is the **City and County Building**, completed in 1894 and the seat of municipal government.

CENTRAL CITY
Salt Lake City's hip Central City district is anchored by **Trolley Square** (602 E 500 South St; https://www.trolleysquare.com), which encompasses a series of renovated 1908 trolley barns converted into a bustling, brick-paved shopping, dining and theater complex. A few blocks

Salt Lake City and County Building.

south on Seventh East is **Liberty Park** ⓠ, a popular spot for roller blading, riding paddle boats, catching a concert, and strolling the landscaped grounds. Visit the historic adobe **Isaac Chase Home and Mill**, then take a leisurely walk and listen to the trumpeter swans, rare Andean condors, and hundreds of other bird species at the **Tracy Aviary & Botanical Garden** (589 E 1300 South St; tel: 801-596 0900; https://tracyaviary.org; daily 9am–5pm, with exceptions), one of the world's oldest public aviaries.

CAPITOL HILL

Return to Temple Square and head north on Main Street past the elegant **McCune Mansion** (former home of mining mogul Alfred McCune and now an event venue; https://mccunemansion.com), to the **Pioneer Memorial Museum** ⓡ (300 N Main St; tel: 801-538 1050; www.dupinternational.org; Mon–Sat 9am–4.30pm). Operated by the Daughters of Utah Pioneers, there's a warren of chambers and glass-enclosed exhibits stuffed with thousands of artifacts, from period furniture to military paraphernalia.

Across the street from the museum, the copper-domed, Renaissance Revival **Utah State Capitol** ⓢ (350 N State St; tel: 801-538 3000; https://utahstatecapitol.utah.gov; Mon–Thu 7am–8pm, Fri–Sun 7am–6pm; free), the temporal seat of power in Utah, overlooks Temple Square from **Capitol Hill**. On a clear day or night, from the steps beneath its Corinthian marble columns, there is a panoramic view of the Wasatch Mountains and the platted streets below.

Inside the capitol a 165ft (50-meter) rotunda rises above the building's main features: the 23-karat gold-leaf reception room, an exhibition hall with displays on Utah history, and marble staircases. Outside there is a 40-acre (16-hectare) park with strolling gardens and other sites to visit, such as the Gothic Revival **White Memorial Chapel** and **Council Hall**, which was constructed in 1866, moved to this spot in 1963, and now houses a visitor center and bookstore.

Adjacent to Capitol Hill are two historic neighborhoods. West of the Capitol is the **Marmalade Historic District** – its streets are named after fruits – where many early English and Scandinavian immigrants resided. East of City Creek Canyon is the **Avenues Historic District**, which features a wide variety of architectural styles, including many restored Victorian houses. A number of buildings in the neighborhood are noteworthy. They include the **Cathedral of the Madeleine** ⓣ (331 E South Temple St; tel: 801-328 8941; www.utcotm.org; daily 8am–6pm; free), a handsome Romanesque-style church. Also notable are the mansions of two prominent Utah silver magnates who owned the Silver King Mine in Park City: the **Keith Brown Mansion** (529 E Temple St), and the **Thomas Kearns Mansion** (603 E Temple St), completed in 1902 and now

Salt Lake Capitol.

the official Governor's Mansion (tel: 801-245 7330; call for tours).

UNIVERSITY-FOOTHILL

Some three miles (4.8km) east of downtown Salt Lake City is the **University-Foothill District**, a scenic triangle of parks and museums situated near the mouth of **Emigration Canyon**. The dominant presence here is the **University of Utah** (www.utah.edu), the state's largest institution of higher learning and the home of two fine museums. The **Utah Museum of Fine Arts** Ⓤ (410 Campus Center Drive; tel: 801-581 7332; www.umfa.utah.edu; Tue–Sun 10am–5pm, Wed until 8pm) presents traveling exhibitions as well as selections from its collection of American and European paintings, classical artifacts, Native American art, Chinese ceramics, and other Asian works. The **Natural History Museum of Utah** Ⓥ (301 Wakara Way; tel: 801-581 6927; https://nhmu.utah.edu; daily 10am–5pm, Wed until 9pm) cares for more than a million objects that trace the biological and cultural diversity of Utah and the intermountain region. Exhibits cover natural history and Utah's Indigenous peoples. Most impressive is the dinosaur collection, much of it retrieved from the Cleveland–Lloyd quarry (see page 163). Tens of thousands of specimens are housed in the sprawling basement paleontology department, including mounted skeletons of such Jurassic-era monsters as Allosaurus, Ceratosaurus, and Stegosaurus, as well as an extensive collection of Triassic plant fossils.

Also on campus, **Rice–Eccles Stadium** (500 South St at Guardsman Way; tel: 801-581 8314; https://stadium.utah.edu) is the home of the university's football and soccer teams and the site of concerts by big-name performers. The stadium won international recognition (and a $50 million face-lift) when it was selected as the venue for the 2002 Winter Olympics opening and closing ceremonies.

Adjacent to the stadium, **Olympic Cauldron Park** enjoys a hillside vantage overlooking the city. In the park,

Rice-Eccles Stadium.

PLACES

Eat

It's worth driving up scenic Emigration Canyon, on the east side of Salt Lake City, to eat at **Ruth's Diner** (4160 Emigration Canyon Road; tel: 801-582 5807; www.ruthsdiner.com; Mon, Thu, and Sun 8am–9pm, Fri and Sat until 10pm), a quintessential Salt Lake breakfast spot since 1930. With a lovely outdoor patio, set in and around old railroad carriages, Ruth's serves up a wide selection of home-style roasts and chops, great salads, and some of Utah's best breakfast plates. All breakfasts come with Ruth's celebrated fluffy "Mile High biscuits."

This Is The Place Heritage Park.

the **Salt Lake 2002 Visitor Center** (Mon–Fri 10am–6pm) displays Olympic images taken by leading sports photographers, as well as a theater dedicated to a breathtaking multimedia presentation about the Winter Games. The **Hoberman Arch** originally stood over the plaza where Olympic award ceremonies were held; today the 36ft high (11-meter) moving spiral of sandblasted aluminum stands near the Olympic Cauldron, the towering beacon lit by the Olympic Flame. Each winter on the anniversary of the Games, the cauldron burns for 17 nights, sending flames 24ft (7 meters) into the sky. From the stadium it's a short hop to **Fort Douglas Military Museum** (32 Potter St; tel: 801-581 1251; Tue–Sat noon–5pm; free), which preserves parts of a fort built in 1862 to protect stage routes into the city. Just beyond, the **Red Butte Garden** (300 Wakara Way; tel: 801-581 4747; https://redbuttegarden.org; daily May–Aug 9am–9pm; April and Sept 9am–7.30pm; Oct–March 9am–5pm; closes at 5pm on concert days) has 150 acres (60 hectares) of thematic gardens, waterfalls, nature trails, and an outdoor performance space as well as a 1,500-acre (600-hectare) arboretum with trees from around the world.

Both kids and adults will enjoy the modest but appealing **Hogle Zoo** (2600 E Sunnyside Ave; tel: 801-582 1631; https://hoglezoo.org; daily 9am–6pm; with exceptions), which has more than 800 exotic animals in naturalistic "habitats."

THIS IS THE PLACE HERITAGE PARK

Utah's pioneer past comes to life across from Hogle Zoo at **This Is the Place Heritage Park** (2601 Sunnyside Ave South; tel: 801-582 1847; www.thisistheplace.org; daily 9am–5pm, with exceptions), comprising various historic properties salvaged from around the state. The site includes the **Heritage Village**, a recreation of a 19th-century Mormon settlement, including Brigham Young's Forest Farmhouse, built by Young in the 1860s. Costumed interpreters demonstrate period crafts and skills such as blacksmithing, weaving, and carpentry. Nearby, a statue of Young and his councilors, known as the **This is the Place Monument**, stands at the spot where, on July 24, 1847, Young stopped and gazed over the Salt Lake Valley. "It is enough," he declared. "This is the right place."

For another living-history experience, check out the **Wheeler Historic Farm** (tel: 801-264 2241; https://slco.org/wheeler-farm; Mon–Sat Apr–Oct 9am–6pm; Nov–Mar 9am–5pm; free) on the outskirts of the city at South 900 East Street. The site recreates a family dairy farm from the early 20th century. Only manual and animal labor are used. Children are welcome to join the farmers at 11am or 5pm to help milk the cows and gather eggs. Tours of the 1898 farmhouse are offered hourly.

URBAN WILDERNESS

Salt Lake City is only a hop, skip, and hike away from some of the most rugged mountain terrain and trails in Utah.

Get a taster by walking or jogging the much-loved 6-mile (10km) City Creek Canyon Trail, which starts right behind the Utah State Capitol. After a half-mile stroll through grassy Memory Grove, the trail steepens, a dramatic gateway leading from downtown into the forests of the Wasatch Range. The creekside trail shaded with cottonwoods is closed to cyclists, who ride on a paved road winding past picnic areas in oak glens.

City Creek also provides access to the remarkable Bonneville Shoreline Trail (www.bonnevilleshorelinetrail.org), which contours along a terrace notched into the flanks of the mountains by prehistoric Lake Bonneville. A 13-mile (21km) section between City Creek and This is the Place Heritage Park is usually busy with hikers, joggers and mountain bikers in warm weather and snowshoers and skiers in winter. Perched above The Avenues neighborhood and University of Utah, and running right through Red Butte Gardens, the Shoreline Trail provides lovely views over the Salt Lake Valley and the Great Salt Lake. Spur trails lead to rugged mountain bike routes and to the crest of the Wasatch Range.

THE WASATCH CANYONS

For more challenging hikes, head south on I-215 to 3900 South, for Mill Creek Canyon, and to 6200 South, for Big Cottonwood and Little Cottonwood canyons. In all three canyons, steep trails follow drainages into the adjacent Twin Peaks and Mount Olympus wilderness areas. At the south end of the valley, Lone Peak Wilderness Area surrounds its namesake – the first Congressionally designated "urban wilderness," centerpiece of the 1978 Endangered American Wilderness Act.

Though the Cottonwood canyons are best known for winter resorts at Alta, Snowbird, Brighton, and Solitude, their steep granite and limestone walls also attract rock climbers, ice climbers, and geologists. Backcountry skiers take advantage of 500in (1,270cm) of Wasatch powder each winter.

All these canyons start within the city limits and pass into Uinta–Wasatch–Cache National Forest, connecting more than a million people with roadless wilderness that covers half the range along the Wasatch Front. These mountains also serve as the city's watershed, so dogs are not welcome. Mill Creek Canyon is the dog-friendly exception; a small fee is required to drive up to Mill Creek's trailheads.

Fall color in the Wasatch goes beyond the usual yellows and golds of aspen trees to include crimson canyon maple and orange and rust accents from Gambel oak. Mill Creek and Big and Little Cottonwood canyons are good choices for autumn leaf-peeping. A favorite dirt road from Brighton to Deer Valley leads over Guardsman's Pass and through glorious aspen groves.

This rich wilderness experience immediately adjacent to a major city is one of the defining characteristics of Salt Lake City. The city lies between the Wasatch Range and the wild public lands of the Great Basin. This is indeed "the place," for there is no other place quite like it.

Salt Lake City.

Provo City Center Temple.

PROVO, PARK CITY AND THE WASATCH RANGE

Travelers here will find an absorbing palette of mountains, canyons, and rivers as well as an international film festival and some of the finest skiing in the West.

Main attractions
Bridal Veil Falls
Homestead Crater
Museum of Paleontology
Museum of Peoples and Cultures
Park City Mountain Resort
Provo Canyon
Timpanogos Cave National Monument
Utah Olympic Park
Wasatch Mountain State Park

Map on page 142

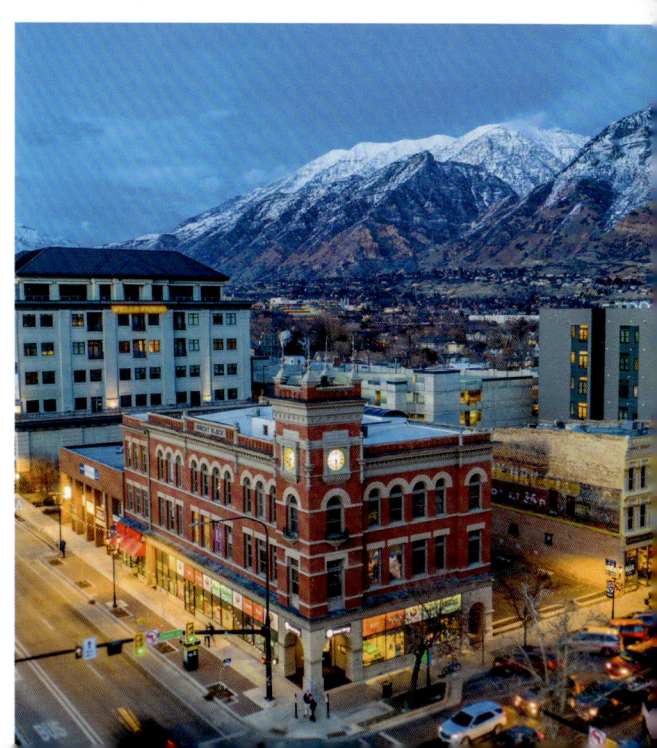

The mountains are a constant presence in **Provo ❶**, where 11,068ft (3,375-meter) **Provo Peak** rises in the east so steeply that its summit is only 4 miles (96 km) as the crow flies from downtown. **Park City**, the winter sports capital of Utah, is a picturesque one-hour drive away. Much of this chapter describes a 116-mile (187km) road trip through the Wasatch Range, with many potential detours and diversions, that motorists can take from Provo. It takes in spectacular Provo Canyon, the lakes and golf links of the Heber Valley and sporty Park City, home of the Sundance Film Festival and the 2002 Winter Olympic Games. Before setting out, though, why not visit nearby Utah Lake or take your pick among Provo's many museums?

PROVO

Unlike many Utah towns, Provo does not wear its history on its sleeve. Redevelopment has long since eliminated most of the old buildings. Nothing remains of the trading post started in 1825 by Quebécois fur trapper Étienne Provot, who gave his name to the river and the settlement on its banks. The T was dropped to encourage correct pronunciation.

Later, in 1849, Brigham Young directed a group of 30 families to establish a fort and farming community here. The Ute of the area, who depended on fish in nearby Utah Lake, allowed the Mormons to stay on condition that they never force Indigenous peoples off their land. But if any trace of the Utes or settlers remains today, it is most likely to be found in the **Provo Daughters of Utah Pioneer Museum** (500 N 500 West St; tel: 801-852 6609; Apr–Oct Wed, Fri, and Sat noon–4pm; free), and the adjacent **Sons of Utah Pioneer Village** (600 N 500 West St; www.provopioneervillage.org; Mon, Wed, and Fri 5–8pm, Sat 11am–3pm, summer only; free). There's not much

Downtown Provo.

to see downtown, though the handsome **Provo City Center Temple** (50 S University Ave) preserves the exterior of the old Provo Tabernacle, dedicated in 1898 but largely destroyed by fire in 2010. A little farther west on Center Street, the **Covey Center for the Arts** (425 W Center St; tel: 801-852 7007) shows art exhibits, performances and theater, while Pioneer Park hosts **Provo Farmers Market** (www.provo-farmersmarket.com; June–Oct Sat 9am–2pm).

BRIGHAM YOUNG UNIVERSITY

Today, LDS-owned Brigham Young University (BYU) has a student body of more than 30,000. About 98 percent of the students are members of the Church of Jesus Christ of Latter-day Saints, including 12 percent "multicultural" students who come from Mormon missions in other parts of the world. To apply, students must submit ecclesiastical recommendations and agree to a strict honor code. The BYU campus has magnificent views of the mountains and 97ft (30-meter) **Centennial Carillon Tower**, which fills the air with the music of 52 bells played by keyboard. You can see the campus on one of the golf cart tours offered by the BYU Hosting Center, located in the former president's residence (tel: 801-422 4678; https://ur.byu.edu/campus-tours; Mon–Fri 9am–3pm; free).

The main attractions on the extensive BYU campus are several free museums. The **Museum of Peoples and Cultures** (2201 N Canyon Road; tel: 801-378 6112; https://mpc.byu.edu; Mon–Fri 9am–5pm) features artifacts from the Great Basin, American Southwest, Mesoamerica, South America, and Polynesia. Among the most striking are the casts of the Stele V "Tree of Life" and the "Tablet of the Cross," both pre-Columbian crosses found in Mexico that were offered in earlier times as proof that Jesus Christ visited ancient America as described in the Book of Mormon.

The **Museum of Art** (N Campus Drive; tel: 801-378 2787; https://moa.byu.edu; Mon–Thu 10am–6pm, Fri 10am–9pm, Sat 10am–4pm) has extensive painting,

⊙ THE ORIGINAL BYU

Provo did not become noteworthy until 1875, when it was chosen as the site of **Brigham Young University**. It started out as the Brigham Young Academy, eventually housed in a stately three-story sandstone building with a mansard roof and bell tower built in 1892 in what is now downtown (550 N University Ave). After the university relocated to its present campus, the academy building became a high school. Abandoned when the school closed in 1968, the structure's date with the wrecking ball was approaching fast when the people of Provo approved a $16.8 million bond issue, and the Brigham Young Academy Foundation kicked in another $5.8 million, to restore the building. After renovation, it became the central **Provo City Library** in 2001.

photography, and sculpture collections. The focus is on works by 19th- and 20th-century American artists, though there are also exhibits of Asian, Egyptian, Greek, and Roman art. The Sacred Subjects collection features traditional biblical themes, scenes from the Book of Mormon, and images of the Mormon migration to Utah.

Exhibits at the **Monte L. Bean Life Science Museum** (645 E 1430 North St; tel: 801-378 5051; https://mlbean.byu.edu; Mon–Fri 10am–9pm; Sat 10am–5pm) include dioramas depicting the wildlife of Utah and Africa.

Finally, the **Museum of Paleontology** (1683 N Canyon Road; tel: 801-378 3680; https://geology.byu.edu/museum; Mon–Fri 9am–5pm) is noted for its collection of dinosaur and prehistoric mammal fossils. Particularly striking is the skeleton of a Utahraptor, a dinosaur found near Moab in 1991. Fast, intelligent, and much larger than the Velociraptors depicted in the film *Jurassic Park*, paleontologists believe it may have been the deadliest dinosaur to have roamed the earth.

UTAH LAKE

Some 4 miles (6.5km) west of downtown Provo, **Utah Lake** ❷, 24 miles (37km) long and 11 miles (18km) wide but only 9ft (2.7 meters) deep, is the state's largest body of fresh water. **Utah Lake State Park** (4400 W Center St; tel: 801-375 0731; https://stateparks.utah.gov/parks/utah-lake; daily Apr–Oct 6am–10pm; Nov–Mar until 8pm) has campsites, picnic areas, a marina, and boat rentals. The park is packed on summer weekends with anglers out to catch channel catfish, bass, walleye, and seven native species of panfish. In winter, part of the lake is roped off for ice-skating; the rest is used by ice fishermen.

SPRINGVILLE

About 7 miles (11km) south of Provo in the suburb of **Springville** ❸ is the **Springville Museum of Art** (126 E 400 South St; tel: 801-489 2727; www.smofa.org; Tue, Thu, Fri, and Sat 10am–5pm, Wed until 8pm; free). Utah's oldest art museum, it was founded in 1903 with paintings donated

> **Tip**
>
> Visitors must purchase a recreation pass to use facilities in the Alpine Loop area (if you don't stop at all, technically you don't need one). A $6 pass is good for three days; a $12 pass is good for seven days (see https://stateparks.utah.gov/resources/passes). The passes are valid along both the Alpine Loop Scenic Drive and the Mirror Lake Highway.

American Fork Canyon.

to the local high school. Today, it presents works by Utah artists of the late 19th and 20th centuries, along with traveling exhibits.

PROVO CANYON

Of all the canyons along the Wasatch Front, perhaps the most dramatic is **Provo Canyon**, northeast of Provo on US 189 (University Avenue). Sadly, the canyon lost much of its seclusion when the formerly narrow, winding road was widened for the 2002 Winter Games in Park City. Still, the towering rock walls have lost none of their majesty. Parking areas along the route give motorists a chance to get out of their vehicles for a close-up look and provide parking space for anglers along one of Utah's most popular trout streams. Cyclists can pedal the 32-mile (52km) climb from Provo to Heber City on a paved bike path partly separated by barriers from highway traffic: some cyclists arrange shuttles to the upper end for the thrill of coasting back down.

A must-see, **Bridal Veil Falls** ❹ is just 4 miles (6.5km) up Provo Canyon. A short trail from the riverside picnic area leads you to the foot of the 607ft (185-meter), two-tiered cataracts, which spill hypnotically down sheer rock faces, filling the air with mist. In winter, the falls attract ice climbers from all over the West.

ALPINE LOOP SCENIC DRIVE

The steep Provo Canyon walls don't allow much in the way of hiking or off-road biking. For that kind of adventure, turn north onto SR 92, clearly marked for "Sundance" and "Alpine Loop." The 20-mile (32km) **Alpine Loop Scenic Drive** (open late May to late October), snakes through the rugged alpine canyons of the Wasatch Range back to Salt Lake City from here. A narrow, paved route that winds through a forest of aspen and Douglas fir, this is one of the most beautiful drives in the Wasatch Mountains.

The road first takes you past **Sundance** ❺, Robert Redford's former resort and film institute (the Hollywood legend sold the resort in 2020), which some critics credit with a

Bridal Veil Falls.

renaissance in American independent filmmaking. In 1980, when the actor bought a small family-run ski resort, his idea was to establish a filmmaking colony outside the influence of the Hollywood mainstream. The Sundance Film Institute, which occupies part of the resort grounds, supports 14–15 projects a year through direct granting or residency labs, out of thousands of submissions. The institute also sponsors the **Sundance Film Festival** (www.sundance.org) every January, where independent filmmakers often gain recognition and financial backing for their work. Among the movies the institute has honored are *Precious*, *Whiplash*, *Minari*, and *CODA*. The weeklong festival is held in Park City, with additional venues in Salt Lake City and Ogden. The event creates around $200 million in economic impact for Utah and attracts a battalion of Hollywood heavyweights, leading some critics to wonder if the festival has become a victim of its own success. Meanwhile, the Sundance Institute carries on quietly in this secluded valley, each year adding new programs such as the Sundance Documentary Film Program and the Film Music Program.

Continue past Sundance into the American Fork Canyon section of **Uinta-Wasatch-Cache National Forest** (you must pay admission at the fee station, unless you only intend to stop at Timpanogos Cave; www.fs.usda.gov/uwcnf). Trailheads along the road lead to the **Mount Timpanogos** and **Lone Peak wilderness areas** as well as mountain bike trails like the 21-mile (34km) **Cascade Springs Loop**. Cascade Springs can also be reached by car, following an unpaved road that forks off to the east. Interpretive nature trails lead visitors around the springs, which pour 7 million gallons (26 million liters) of water a day down a series of pools before vanishing underground.

Farther along the Alpine Loop is **Timpanogos Cave National Monument** ❻ (tel: 801-756 5239; www.nps.gov/tica; tours May–Sept daily 8am–3.30pm), actually a series of three limestone caverns discovered at different times and linked together by man-made tunnels.

Mount Timpanogos.

The caverns have the stalactites, stalagmites, and stone curtains typical of limestone caves but are especially notable for their rare helictites – hollow, gravity-defying calcite formations that grow in unpredictable directions. What many people remember most, however, is the trail to the cave entrance, climbing nearly 1,100ft (335 meters) in 1.5 miles (2.4km).

HEBER VALLEY

Back on US 189, rocky cliffs yield to water views at the upper end of Provo Canyon as you pass **Deer Creek Reservoir** at the south end of the agricultural **Heber Valley**. To the north is the even larger **Jordanelle Reservoir**. The lakeshores are developed for recreational use at **Deer Creek State Park** (tel: 435-654 0171; https://stateparks.utah.gov/parks/deer-creek; daily summer 6am–10pm; winter 8am–5pm) and **Jordanelle State Park** (tel: 435-649 9540; https://stateparks.utah.gov/parks/jordanelle; daily summer 6am–10pm; winter 8am–5pm) Both offer fishing, boating, swimming, and other water sports as well as camping. Deer Creek has a marina with a restaurant and boat rentals and is a favorite of windsurfers and sailors.

Also in the Heber Valley is **Wasatch Mountain State Park** (tel: 435-654 1791; https://stateparks.utah.gov/parks/wasatch-mountain; daily 9am–5pm; with exceptions), Utah's largest, with two manicured 36-hole golf courses, hiking and horseback riding trails, and a Nordic skiing facility called **Soldier Hollow**, which saw Olympic action during the 2002 Winter Games. Nearly 20 miles (32km) of groomed trails are available for cross-country skiing and snowshoeing in winter and mountain biking in summer.

Between the two lakes is **Heber City** ❼, an unpretentious farm and ranch center, and its rustic "suburb," **Midway**. Heber City's top attraction is the **Heber Valley Historic Railroad** (450 S 600 West St; tel: 435-654 5601; www.hebervalleyrr.org; June–Oct Tue–Sat 11am and 3pm), an early 20th-century steam train that chugs past Deer Creek Reservoir and into Provo Canyon.

Scuba diving in the mountains? You'll find it at **Homestead Crater** (Homestead Resort, 700 N Homestead Drive; tel: 435-654 1102; www.utahcrater.com; Mon–Fri 11.30am–8pm, Sat–Sun 9.30am–8pm), just outside Midway in a natural hot spring set inside a 55ft (17-meter) rock dome. The amazingly clear water is 65ft (20 meters) deep and 96°F (37°C). The crater is on the property of the Homestead Resort, which operates a small rental shop with scuba and snorkeling gear. Swimmers are welcome; Utah Crater also offers "scuba experiences" for visitors who don't have their certifications.

PARK CITY

About 20 miles (32km) north of Heber City is **Park City** ❽, a gold rush-era mining town that's been transformed into a major ski resort. Some folks liken it to Aspen, a comparison that

Mount Timpanogos and Heber Valley.

many Park City residents detest. But some similarities are hard to ignore – the multimillion-dollar houses, ski resorts, and frequent sightings of movie stars. Obviously, though, the ritzy shops and restaurants wouldn't exist if not for the town's glorious mountain environment.

Connect with the town's sometimes seamy past at the **Park City Museum** (528 Main St; tel: 435-649 6104; https://parkcityhistory.org; daily 10am–5pm; free), which features vintage photographs and the original town jail. Park City got its start in 1870, when prospectors discovered silver, lead, zinc, and a little gold in the surrounding mountains. Within two years, the town grew to 5,000 people – nearly its present-day population. Most of the mines shut down after the 1893 silver crash, though the population doubled in the next several years as laborers from Colorado came looking for work in the few mines that remained open.

Part of the secret of Park City's survival was illegal liquor. The rough-and-ready boomtown had long held itself apart from the clean-living Mormons who lived on the other side of the mountain. Its 26 saloons thrived thanks to the city folk who occasionally slipped off to the mountains to tie one on. Business was especially good after the enactment of Prohibition in 1921, thanks largely to police officers who looked the other way. But the high times didn't last. The town's alcohol-fueled economy foundered after Prohibition was repealed in 1933. By the 1950s, it was regarded as one of Utah's best-preserved ghost towns. Then in 1963, with the opening of a small ski area, Park City was reborn. At first skiers were carried to the top of the mountain by mine cars that went up the shaft of the old Silver King Mine. When a gondola, chair lift, and two J-bars were installed, Park City quickly became one of the state's most popular winter sports destinations.

History buffs can still find vestiges of the gold-rush days in the four-block-long **Main Street Historic District**, listed on the National Register of Historic Places. A walking-tour brochure is available at the Park City Museum. Don't miss the fully restored **Egyptian Theatre** (328 Main St; tel: 435-649 9731; https://parkcityshows.com), centerpiece of the Sundance Film Festival. Built as an opera house around 1898, it was redesigned in faux-Egyptian style in 1920s.

THE SKI RESORTS

Winter is peak season in Park City, which is blessed annually with 300 to 400in (750cm–1 meter) of some of the world's best snow. **Park City Mountain Resort** (1345 Lowell Ave; tel: 435-649 8111; www.parkcitymountain.com), the town's original ski area, has been improved and expanded. It now encompasses three new terrain parks and has the greatest lift capacity in town. Another standout feature is the Eagle Superpipe, built for Olympic snowboarding competitions and much larger

Homestead Crater.

> **Tip**
>
> Two places with large selections of good rental bikes in Park City are Jans Mountain Outfitters (1600 Park Ave; tel: 800-745 1020; www.jans.com; daily 8am–6pm; with exceptions; also branches at Deer Valley Resort) and Cole Sport (1615 Park Ave; tel: 435-649 4806; www.colesport.com; daily 9am–6pm; also branches at Park City Mountain Village and Deer Valley).

Downtown Park City Mountain Resort.

than regulation halfpipes at other ski areas. **Deer Valley Resort** (2250 Deer Valley Drive; tel: 435-649 1000; www.deervalley.com), the smallest (or as the marketing people put it, "most intimate") of the major ski areas, has dramatic ridgeline runs and a 3,000ft (900-meter) vertical drop. Elegant lodges and four gourmet restaurants make Deer Valley the high-end choice. The final entry is **The Canyons** (4000 The Canyons Resort Drive; now part of Park City Mountain), which has the largest ski and snowboard area in Utah.

Adrenaline junkies might want to forgo the ski slopes for a once-in-a-lifetime ride on a bobsled (late Nov–early Jan) at the **Utah Olympic Park** (3419 Olympic Parkway; tel: 435-658 4200; https://utaholympiclegacy.org/location/utah-olympic-park; daily 9am–5pm). The four-man sleds, under the control of certified drivers, reach 80mph (130 km/h) and 4Gs of force. The price is as steep as the bobsled run – around $175 per person. Slightly less costly are the half-day introductory classes offered in Nordic jumping, slopestyle skiing, luge racing, and skeleton racing. The less adventurous can tour the park and see where US Olympic contenders practice on ski jumps up to 360ft (110 meters), then visit the **Alf Engen Ski Museum** (tel: 435-658 4240; https://engenmuseum.org; daily 9am–6pm; free) and **George Eccles 2002 Winter Olympic Games Museum** (same details) inside the park's Joe Quinney Winter Sports Center.

SUMMER IN PARK CITY

In summer, the sports scene in Park City is dominated by mountain biking. More than 400 miles (644km) of trails have been set aside for non-motorized use (biking, hiking, and horseback riding) in the area. Both the PayDay Express and Crescent Express chair lifts at Park City Mountain Resort, and the Silver Lake Express, and Sterling Express at Deer Valley give hikers and bikers access to trails among the ski runs and clapped out mines high above town. For a moderate ride, the **Historic Union Pacific Rail Trail** ❾, an old railroad bed, runs 28 mostly level miles (45km) from Park City to Echo Reservoir. Or you can put your technical skills to the test on **Sweeney Switchbacks**, a tough 2-mile (3km) trail that climbs to the Park City Mountain Resort trail system. Other summer staples in and around Park City include whitewater rafting and fly-fishing on the nearby Provo and Weber rivers.

With so many bikes whizzing around, hikers may want to seek the relative calm of the **Swaner Preserve & Eco-Center** (1258 Center Drive; tel: 435-649 1867; www.swanerecocenter.org; Wed–Sun 10am–4pm; free), a 1,200-acre (486-hectare) island of rolling alpine meadow. Also available in summer is the **Alpine Slide** (Park City Mountain Resort; tel: 435-649 8111; late May–early Oct daily 10am–7pm; with exceptions), a sled-like contraption that zips down a winding track. Or you can wander over to watch the young and daring at the largest concrete skateboard park in Utah.

HOLLYWOOD IN UTAH

Utah's deserts, towering mountain ranges, and other-worldly landscapes have been the backdrop for hundreds of movies, from *Stagecoach* (1939) and *2001: A Space Odyssey* (1968), to *Con Air* (1997), the *Star Trek* reboot (2009), and many others.

It seems fitting that the state has come to play host to one of the major North American attractions for film lovers and movie moguls: the Sundance Film Festival. Spawned by the Utah Film Commission, the festival began its run in Salt Lake City on a September week in 1978, then shifted in 1981 to Park City about 30 miles (48km) down the road. Its original name was the Utah/US Film Festival, and movies by independent film-makers – "indies" – were encouraged.

By the mid-1980s the festival, now staged during January in a bid to cash in on the ski season, was catching the eye of the media and the imagination of the public at large. The big breakthrough came after 1984, the year that saw the festival fall under the wing of Robert Redford's Sundance Institute. Redford ultimately became board chairman of the Sundance Film Festival, as the annual event was retitled – after his role in *Butch Cassidy and the Sundance Kid*.

NURTURING TALENT

Thanks to Redford and the institute, the festival enjoyed wider contacts and increased prestige, furthered the independent cause in moviemaking, and cast a spotlight on innovative talent. Two early examples from the 1985 festival were the Coen brothers, with *Blood Simple*, and Jim Jarmusch, creator of the offbeat *Stranger Than Paradise*.

The festival has become more ambitious since that opening program in 1978, when three theaters provided showings of classic American films and patrons listened to panel discussions focusing on theory and technique. Also shown were eight feature films made by novice moviemakers.

In the years ahead, competition was opened up to include documentaries, short films, videos and other forms, and as Sundance's prestige as a "happening" has swelled, there has been increased criticism centering on festival hype and commercialization. As the common complaint has it, the streets of Park City are now ubiquitous each January with a gaggle of power brokers and talent scouts manipulating cell phones for, hopefully, lucrative payoffs.

Some notable films were given premieres at Sundance. They include Quentin Tarantino's 1992 entry *Reservoir Dogs* and *American Psycho* (2000). Among others: *Little Miss Sunshine* (2006), *Winter's Bone* (2010), Jordan Peele's *Get Out* (2017), *Promising Young Woman* (2020) and *Judas and the Black Messiah* (2021).

But most significant, by general agreement, was the 1989 showing of a decidedly offbeat film by an erstwhile Sundance volunteer worker, Steven Soderbergh. The movie was entitled *Sex, Lies and Videotape*, and its success at box offices far and wide, to the tune of over $25 million, is widely thought to have turned the corner for Sundance. This Utah event, now showing well over 200 feature films, ranks on a global scale with such distinguished festival venues as Cannes, Venice, Toronto, and Berlin.

The Egyptian Theater.

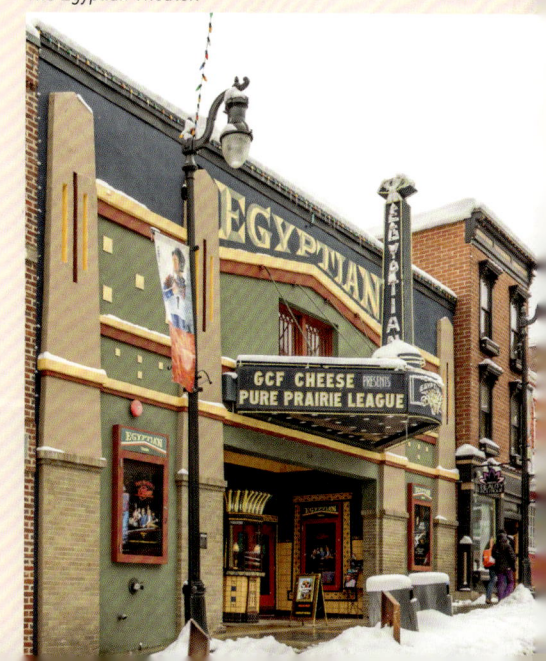

Petroglyphs at Dinosaur National Monument.

PLACES | 151

DINOSAUR, FLAMING GORGE AND THE HIGH UINTAS

Dinosaur quarries, a beautiful lake, scenic drives, and a vast mountain wilderness lure travelers to a region once traversed by mountain men and outlaws.

Natural beauty, wildlife and ancient fossils are the focus of Utah's down-to-earth, rural northeastern corner. You may see everything from raptors and kokanee salmon to moose, black bear, elk, and bighorn sheep. Even more amazing, you'll have the chance to go back in time, geologically speaking. One billion years of earth's history – a more complete record than even the Grand Canyon – is on display here, containing within 23 different strata a remarkable look at the evolution of life on earth. Dinosaurs turn up so regularly in the fossil record here that they have led to the region's nickname: Dinosaurland. Highlights include the Dinosaur National Monument and the Flaming Gorge National Recreation Area, which offers scenic drives, bird-watching, camping, hiking, boating, rustic cabins and lodges, as well as the great wilderness areas of the Uinta Mountains and Ashley National Forest. Access is primarily via incredibly scenic drives such as the Flaming Gorge–Uintas Scenic Byway, Browns Park Scenic Backway, and Spirit Lake Scenic Backway.

DINOSAUR NATIONAL MONUMENT

The **Dinosaur National Monument** ❶ (tel: 435-781 7700), the highlight of any visit to Utah's northeastern corner,

Quarry Exhibit Hall, Dinosaur National Monument.

sprawls across the Utah–Colorado border. But Dinosaur's true locale is the Jurassic period, 140 million years ago, when this arid portion of the Colorado Plateau was home to the largest animals ever to roam the earth. The monument has played an unrivaled role in the history of American paleontology. Among the most important finds here were the first known Brontosaurus (now called Apatosaurus) fossils. But Dinosaur is more than bones. Its dramatic landscape begs to be explored by car, by foot, or by raft.

Main attractions

Browns Park Scenic Backway
Dinosaur National Monument
Flaming Gorge Dam
Flaming Gorge–Uintas Scenic Byway
Flaming Gorge National Recreation Area
Spirit Lake Scenic Backway
Utah Field House of Natural History State Park Museum

Map on page 152

The attraction for which the monument was named – dinosaurs – can only be seen on the Utah side at the **Dinosaur Quarry Visitor Center** ❷ (11625 E 1500 South, Jensen; tel: 435-781 7700), 7 miles (11km) north of **Jensen** on UT 149. The enclosed **Quarry Exhibit Hall** nearby is where a tilted layer of sandstone has been painstakingly exposed to display an incredible three-dimensional jigsaw of fossilized dinosaur bones, left in situ for imaginative visitors to piece together. The "Wall of Bones," as it is known, contains numerous different species of dinosaurs including *Allosaurus*, *Apatosaurus*, *Camarasaurus*, *Diplodocus*, *Stegosaurus*, and *Dryosaurus*, first discovered here in 1909 by Carnegie Museum paleontologist Earl Douglass. Since then, excavations have uncovered more than 2,000 dinosaur bones. This is just a fraction of the dinosaurs that were entombed here when a catastrophic river flood wiped them out 149 million years ago.

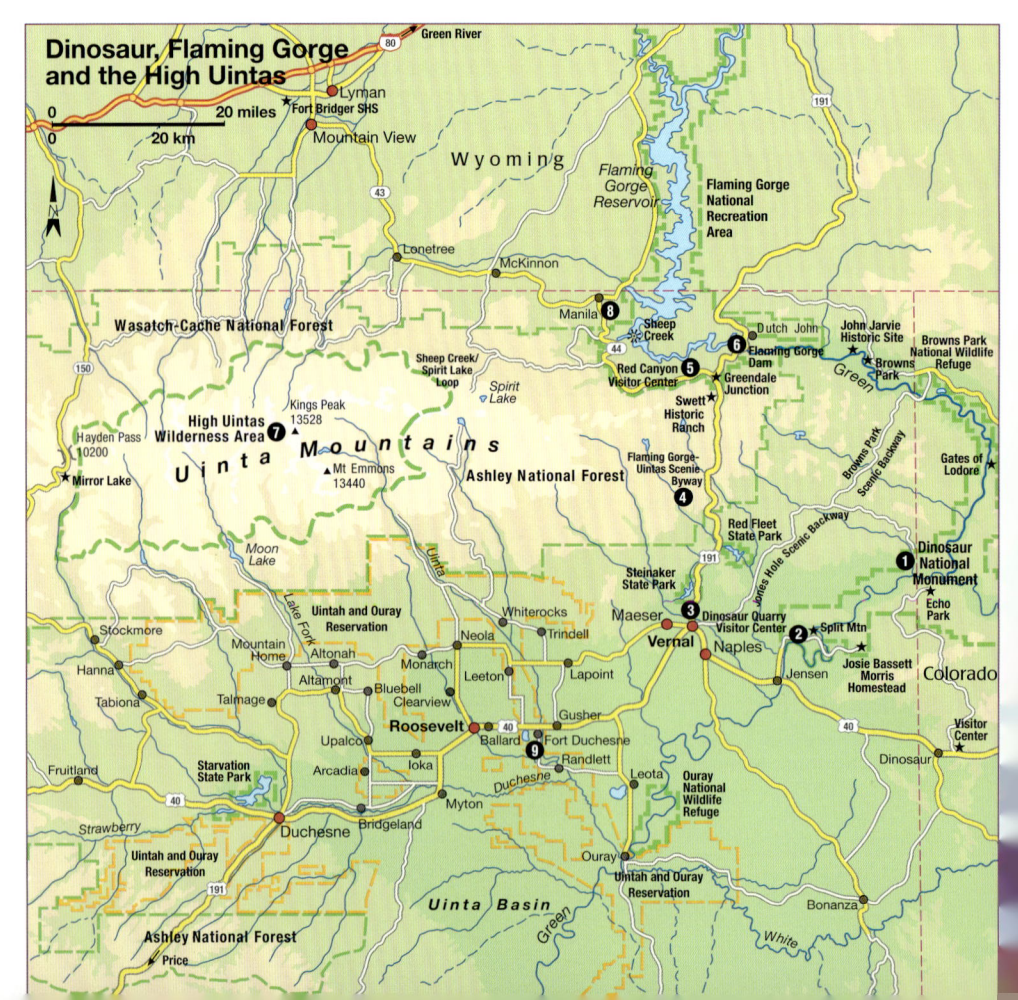

Douglass's discovery triggered a stampede to uncover fossils that threatened to strip the area of dinosaur bones. The quarry was protected as a national monument in 1915. The Green and Yampa river canyons of eastern Dinosaur National Monument were added in 1938. Environmentalists successfully prevented dams from being built at Echo Park and Split Mountain in 1956. Briefly, little-known Dinosaur basked in the national spotlight, only to return to obscurity when more high-profile environmental battles, such as the building of a dam at Glen Canyon, took over the headlines.

In summer a shuttle bus runs from the Quarry Visitor Center to the Exhibit Hall (daily 8am–5pm; every 15min); the rest of the year park rangers lead car caravans to the site.

Overnight visitors will find two developed campgrounds (and five more primitive ones) inside the monument. For motels, your widest range of choices can be found in Vernal, 13 miles (21km) west of Jensen.

You can drive on from the Quarry Visitor Center for the **Tour of the Tilted Rocks**, a 10-mile (16km) scenic drive along the Cub Creek Road (aka Blue Mountain Road), ending at Josie's Cabin (the last 2 miles/3 km are unpaved but maintained). Highlights along the route include petroglyph and pictograph panels (in a rock shelter that was used by Paleo-Indians as long ago as 7000 BC), and the fascinating **Josie Bassett Morris Homestead**. This pioneer woman spent her early years in Browns Park, just north of the area, and knew Butch Cassidy. When she died in 1964, her cabin became part of the park. A short spur road takes you to the Split Mountain Campground and Boat Launch where you can see the Green River (and river rafters) churning out of Split Mountain Canyon.

The Colorado half of the monument lies off US 40, just northeast of the isolated town of **Dinosaur**, the site of the main **Canyon Visitor Center** (4545 E US 40, Dinosaur, CO; tel: 970-374 3000), which has video presentations and exhibits on the fossilized finds (note that there are no fossils in situ on the Colorado side). Take the 31-mile (50km) drive from here on unpaved Harper's Corner Road and then the 2-mile (3km) hike to **Echo Park** overlook and you'll see the meeting of the Green and Yampa rivers 800ft (240 meters) below. If you want to see this view from river level, you have lots of choices. Commercial river runners operate many one- to five-day trips on both rivers.

> **Fact**
> Dinosaur National Monument is officially open daily, 24hr, but check the website (www.nps.gov/dino) for the latest conditions. Entrance is $25 per vehicle. The Quarry Visitor Center operates seasonal hours (late May–mid-Sept daily 8am–6pm; late Sept–Nov and Mar–mid-May 9am–5pm; Dec–Feb 10am–4pm). The Canyon Visitor Center in Colorado is usually open mid-May to late Sept daily 9am–5pm.

Lizard petroglyphs by ancient Fremont people.

⊙ WILD HORSES ROAM FREE

Horses were brought to North America by Spaniards in the early 1500s and quickly became an important means of transportation for Europeans and Native Americans alike. In the West, horses that escaped from farms, ranches, or the US Cavalry headed for the open range and formed large herds. Wild mustangs were rounded up by early pioneers to replenish their stock. By the turn of the 20th century, though, demand had declined, and unscrupulous mustangers rounded up wild horses and sold them for meat and pet food from the 1920s to the 1950s.

Nevada's Velma Bronn Johnson (1912–1977), also known as Wild Horse Annie, and thousands of schoolchildren were instrumental in getting the Wild Free Roaming Horses and Burros Act of 1971 passed, providing for the protection and control of wild horses on public lands. In Utah, approximately 2,000 wild horses and 100 burros roam freely within 19 management areas overseen by the Bureau of Land Management. Regular Adopt-a-Horse auctions allow the public to purchase excess animals, learn how to train them at clinics, and show them in the annual Wild Horse and Burro Festival. Look for wild horses in Hill and Range creeks and Bonanza in the Uinta Basin. For more information, contact the BLM in Vernal at tel: 435-781 4400 (www.blm.gov).

VERNAL

Northeastern Utah is anchored by the friendly little town of **Vernal** ❸, gateway to Flaming Gorge and the eastern Uintas Mountains (see www.dinoland.com). Everything you ever wanted to know about dinosaurs can be found at the **Utah Field House of Natural History State Park Museum** (496 E Main St; tel: 435-789 3799; https://stateparks.utah.gov/parks/utah-field-house; daily 9am–5pm), which contains reconstructed dinosaur skeletons, a regional map chronicling a billion years of geologic history, and exhibits on Native American cultures – life-sized sculptures lurk in their own Dinosaur Garden.

Leave the kids to play among the fake dinosaurs and pick up tour information at the **visitor center** (tel: 435-789 7894), which shares the building. Vernal and neighboring Roosevelt serve as the main commercial centers on the northern periphery of the massive Uinta Basin, a vast expanse of monochromatic Cretaceous-era rocks dotted with oil pumps, farms, ranches, Ute tribal lands, and wetland preserves that attract huge numbers of waterfowl.

BROWNS PARK

For a real backcountry adventure, consider a visit to **Browns Park**, an isolated valley on the Green River where a number of mountain man rendezvous took place in the early 1800s – it became a haven for outlaws such as Butch Cassidy in the 1860s. The best way to reach the site is the **Jones Hole Scenic Backway**, a 40-mile (65km) four-wheel drive trip that begins just north of Vernal (Browns Park Road). Allow lots of time for this drive: The road (impassable in winter) climbs 2,600ft (800 meters) to Diamond Mountain Plateau, then picks up **Browns Park Scenic Backway** down Crouse Canyon. A short side trip takes you to the **John Jarvie Historic Ranch** (summer Wed–Sat 10am–3pm) a ranch and store owned in the 1880s by a well-liked Scotsman who was later murdered in Browns Park. Contact the BLM in Vernal (170 S 500 East, tel:

Dinah the Pink Dinosaur welcomes you to Vernal City.

DINOSAUR, FLAMING GORGE AND THE HIGH UINTAS

435-781 4400; www.blm.gov) for more information. By far the most fun way to see Browns Park is on a river trip between Flaming Gorge and Dinosaur National Monument.

FLAMING GORGE–UINTAS SCENIC BYWAY

Running between Vernal and Manila on US 191 and UT 44 near the Utah–Wyoming border, the 82-mile (132km) **Flaming Gorge–Uintas Scenic Byway** ❹ (www.flaminggorgecountry.com) is a beautiful mountain drive. Fifteen interpretive wayside pullouts, and four nature trails highlight animals that live in eight different life zones over an elevation change of 7,000ft (2,100 meters). Two state parks on either side of the highway a few miles north of Vernal feature small reservoirs surrounded by a Jurassic landscape of bright, upended rocks. **Steinaker State Park** (tel: 435 789-4432; https://stateparks.utah.gov/parks/steinaker; daily summer 6am–10pm; winter 8am–10pm) has a nature trail that offers a good introduction to the geology and wildlife of the area. **Red Fleet State Park** (tel: 435-789 6614; https://stateparks.utah.gov/parks/red-fleet; daily summer 6am–10pm; winter 8am–5pm) named for its red sandstone formations, which do indeed look like ships on the water, has boating and camping.

A more rewarding detour is the 45-mile (72km) **Red Cloud/Dry Fork Scenic Backway Drive,** which runs north from Vernal on Dry Fork Canyon Road and eventually rejoins the Flaming Gorge Scenic Byway. The drive passes **McConkie Ranch**, a good place to view Fremont culture petroglyphs that are over 1,000 years old.

FLAMING GORGE NATIONAL RECREATION AREA

The scenic byway continues north into Flaming Gorge National Recreation Area (tel: 435-784 3445; www.fs.fed.us), named by explorer John Wesley Powell for its bright red canyons along the Green River. The river hasn't been free running since the dam at Red Canyon in Utah was completed in 1964. The resulting Flaming Gorge

Red Canyon, Flaming Gorge.

Reservoir forms the centerpiece of the recreation area, with the Red Canyon Visitor Center ❺ (Red Canyon Road, off UT 44; tel: 435-789 1181; Mon–Fri 10am–5pm, Sat and Sun 9am–6pm; with exceptions; free) boasting a dramatic overlook and attractive nearby campground.

Before you reach Red Canyon, US 191 branches off the scenic byway northeast at **Greendale Junction**. The meadows to the west are a great place to glimpse elk, moose, and deer in early morning and evening. US 191 continues toward Flaming Gorge Dam, passing the turning to **Swett Ranch Historical Homestead** (on FS 158; Memorial Day–Labor Day daily 9am–4pm), and several Forest Service campgrounds. Campers will find excellent facilities at Firefighters' Memorial Campground, which commemorates "smokejumpers" who gave their lives in this fire-altered landscape.

FLAMING GORGE DAM

US 191 take you to the southeast corner of the **Flaming Gorge Reservoir** and the 502ft (153-meter-) high **Flaming Gorge Dam** ❻, which backs up the Green River where the Uinta Mountains meet the Red Desert of Wyoming. The dam was dedicated in 1964 and is 1,285ft (393-meters) long and 131ft (40-meters) wide at the base. Tours are offered daily from the Flaming Gorge Visitor Center (tel: 435-885 3135; mid-Apr–mid-Oct daily 9am–5pm; free). Stop at one of the overlooks off US 191 on the east side of the dam for breathtaking sunset views. You'll find some of Utah's best fishing here. Trout, bass, catfish, and other stocked species grow to huge size in the reservoir.

River trips on the Green River begin beneath the dam (Dinosaur River Expeditions; https://dinosaurriverexpeditions.com). Rafts and kayaks meander gently through canyons and a series of broad openings, or "holes," so named by mountain men who trapped beaver and traded with Native Americans in Browns Park in the 1830s. River runners of all ages will enjoy floating the flat water and gentle rapids here. A pleasant trip of one to three days takes you through the authentic Wild West – 1,000-year-old Fremont culture sites, a national wildlife refuge, historic ranches, outlaw hideouts, and high desert scenery of quiet, mesmerizing beauty.

THE HIGH UINTAS

Back on the Flaming Gorge–Uintas Scenic Byway west of Red Canyon (US 44), continue on to the bridge at Sheep Creek Overlook where, during August and September, bright-red kokanee salmon return to Sheep Creek to spawn in huge numbers. Ten-mile (16km) **Sheep Creek Geologic Scenic Backway Loop** (forking off UT 44), a must-see for any visitor to Flaming Gorge, offers numerous delights: glimpses of kokanee salmon; the chance to see reintroduced bighorn sheep on the steep cliffs; and a close

Flaming Gorge Dam.

look at the Uinta Fault, which has tilted billion-year-old Precambrian rocks into vertical strata.

Spirit Lake Scenic Backway begins at the southern end of the Sheep Creek loop and is your best bet for reaching the **High Uintas Wilderness Area** ❼ from Flaming Gorge. The 17-mile (27km) dirt road passes Ute Fire Lookout Tower (tel: 435-781 5260; Memorial Day–Labor Day daily 10am–4pm), built by the Civilian Conservation Corps in the 1930s, and dead-ends at Spirit Lake, which features a rustic lodge and campground, a restaurant, horseback riding, and trails leading into the High Uintas Wilderness.

The northern end of the Sheep Creek loop is about 4.5 miles (7km) south of **Manila** ❽, where UT 44 joins WY 530/UT 43 on the north side of the Uintas. Manila is the headquarters of the Ashley National Forest Flaming Gorge Ranger District (25 UT 43; tel: 435-784 3445; www.fs.fed.us; Mon–Fri 8am–4.30pm, Memorial Day–Aug Sat 9am–3pm). It has a visitor center at the junction of UT 44 and UT 43, where you can pick up info on traveling into the recreation area, which sprawls northward into Wyoming.

From Manila you can continue north toward the Wyoming side of Flaming Gorge via WY 530 or head northwest on WY 414 to historic Fort Bridger on I-80. If you're interested in seeing the west side of the Uintas, drive west on I-80 and drop south on UT 150, also known as **Mirror Lake Scenic Byway**. This paved route is a complete contrast with the east side of the mountains, and attracts a largely urban crowd from Salt Lake City to its many trails, campgrounds, and mountain vistas.

UINTAH AND OURAY RESERVATION

The homeland of the Ute Tribe, the **Uintah and Ouray Indian Reservation** (www.utetribe.com) occupies large swathes of northeast Utah, with its headquarters at **Fort Duchesne** ❾, 25 miles southwest of Vernal. The Utes maintain a low profile in the area and are most visible at their annual **Northern Ute Indian Powwow** during the July 4th weekend and **Thanksgiving Powwow** in November, both held at Fort Duchesne. You may also encounter them taking part in the **Dinosaur Roundup Rodeo** (http://vernalrodeo.com) held in Vernal in July, which commemorates the region's Wild West heritage.

Within the reservation, a 12-mile (19km) stretch of the Green is protected as **Ouray National Wildlife Refuge** ❿ (19001 E Wildlife Refuge Road, Randlett; tel: 435 545-2522; www.fws.gov/refuge/ouray; 1 hour before sunrise to 1 hour after sunset) home to hundreds of resident and migratory bird species. A nine-mile (14km) self-guided auto tour route takes in a variety of habitats, providing superb wildlife viewing; primarily ducks, geese, cranes, herons, and a variety of shorebirds.

> **Fact**
> Travel in to the Uintas Mountains farther on foot or pack animal and you'll reach the High Uintas Wilderness surrounding Utah's highest mountain, 13,528ft (4,123-meter) Kings Peak. It's a challenging hike to the summit from the Henry's Fork trailhead in northern Utah: a 28-mile (45km) return route that takes 13 to 14 hours to complete.

The Uinta Mountains.

Goblin Valley State Park.

CENTRAL UTAH

Desert canyons, ghost towns, and villages with a Scandinavian flavor await travelers in the state's varied heartland.

Native American petroglyph of an owl.

Deseret, as Utah was once known to faithful Mormons, is a word from the Book of Mormon for the honey bee, symbolizing the industry the Saints brought to the task of building towns, growing food, creating successful businesses, and making the desert "bloom like a rose." The best place to understand this industriousness is central Utah, where farmers, ranchers, and miners have successfully harnessed the natural resources of the mountains and deserts since the mid-1800s.

Tintic Mining District, which grew up around Eureka in the Great Basin in 1869, was once one of the top three producers of precious metals in the state, with a total production of about 16,654,377 tons valued at $570 million during its century of operation. Equally wealthy was Carbon County, on the far side of the Wasatch Plateau in Castle Country. It has been called "Eastern Utah's Industrialized Island" by historian Philip Notarianni whose Italian forebears were among the thousands of immigrants who came to Utah to work in the coal mines in Helper and Price and stayed. Nowhere else in rural Utah is more cosmopolitan in character than Castle Country, nor as rich in natural and cultural history, from the thousands of dinosaur bones that have been unearthed at Cleveland–Lloyd Quarry to desert canyons throughout the scenic San Rafael Swell.

Immigrant "towns" contrasted dramatically with the larger Mormon culture, which, although drawn from around the world, emphasized assimilation rather than segregation. Yet few immigrants leave their culture behind, as is abundantly clear for visitors driving through the rural heartland of Sanpete Valley along Scenic Byway 89. In the 1850s and 1860s, Mormon converts from Norway, Sweden, and Denmark founded neatly laid-out small towns in this agricultural valley between the Wasatch Plateau and the San Pitch Mountains.

Mule deer, Nine Mile Canyon.

Isolated from the rest of Utah, Sanpete's hardy old-world pioneers cobbled together a way of life that has sustained them for nearly 150 years. Even today, pioneer activities, such as rug weaving, pottery, furniture making, and handmade musical instruments thrive in studios all along US 89 in towns such as Moroni, Ephraim, and Manti. Here you'll find some of the most unique historic districts in the statey.

Goblin Valley State Park.

CASTLE COUNTRY

Ancient rock art, old-time mining towns and the stark beauty of the San Rafael Swell attract visitors to a land where dinosaurs – and outlaws – once roamed.

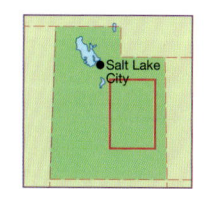

Main attractions
Cleveland-Lloyd Dinosaur Quarry
Goblin Valley State Park
Helper Museum
Horseshoe Canyon
Indian Canyon Scenic Byway
John Wesley Powell River History Museum
Little Wild Horse Canyon
Manti-La Sal National Forest
Nine Mile Canyon
Prehistoric Museum

Map on page 162

Nearly 100 million years before this landscape was pushed up by the same geologic episode that built the Rocky Mountains, the bone-dry San Rafael Swell was a sticky tropical swamp filled with supersized conifers, ferns and dinosaurs. Millions of years later, those same swamps would harbor so much coal and uranium that Castle Country would become Utah's most important center of coal mining and energy production. Today the chief attractions of this remote and rural section of Central Utah include huge caches of dinosaur bones at Cleveland-Lloyd Dinosaur Quarry and the Prehistoric Museum in Price; an extraordinary array of ancient Native American rock art in the San Rafael Swell and remote Nine Mile Canyon; the state parks and scenic drives in Manti-La Sal National Forest; and the sensational landscapes of Goblin Valley State Park and Little Wild Horse Canyon.

PRICE

The seat of Carbon County, the small city of **Price** ❶ was founded as a coal mining camp in the 1870s. Price is still a coal town but, after violent clashes between foreigners and Americans earlier in its history, it now proudly embraces its international roots. Mexican, Italian and Greek influences are particularly strong, reflected in Price's many inexpensive ethnic restaurants. The popular Greek Festival, held the second weekend in July, features Greek food, music, dancing and tours of the 1916 Hellenic Orthodox Church of the Assumption (61 S. 2nd St; tel: 435-637 0704; www.agoc.ut.goarch.org), Utah's oldest Greek Orthodox church.

Stop by the **Eastern Utah Tourism and History Association** (96 N. Carbon Ave; tel: 435-630 3699; www.eutha.org) to learn about local tours and area information before visiting the city's main attraction, the **Prehistoric**

Balanced rock at Nine Mile Canyon.

Castle Country

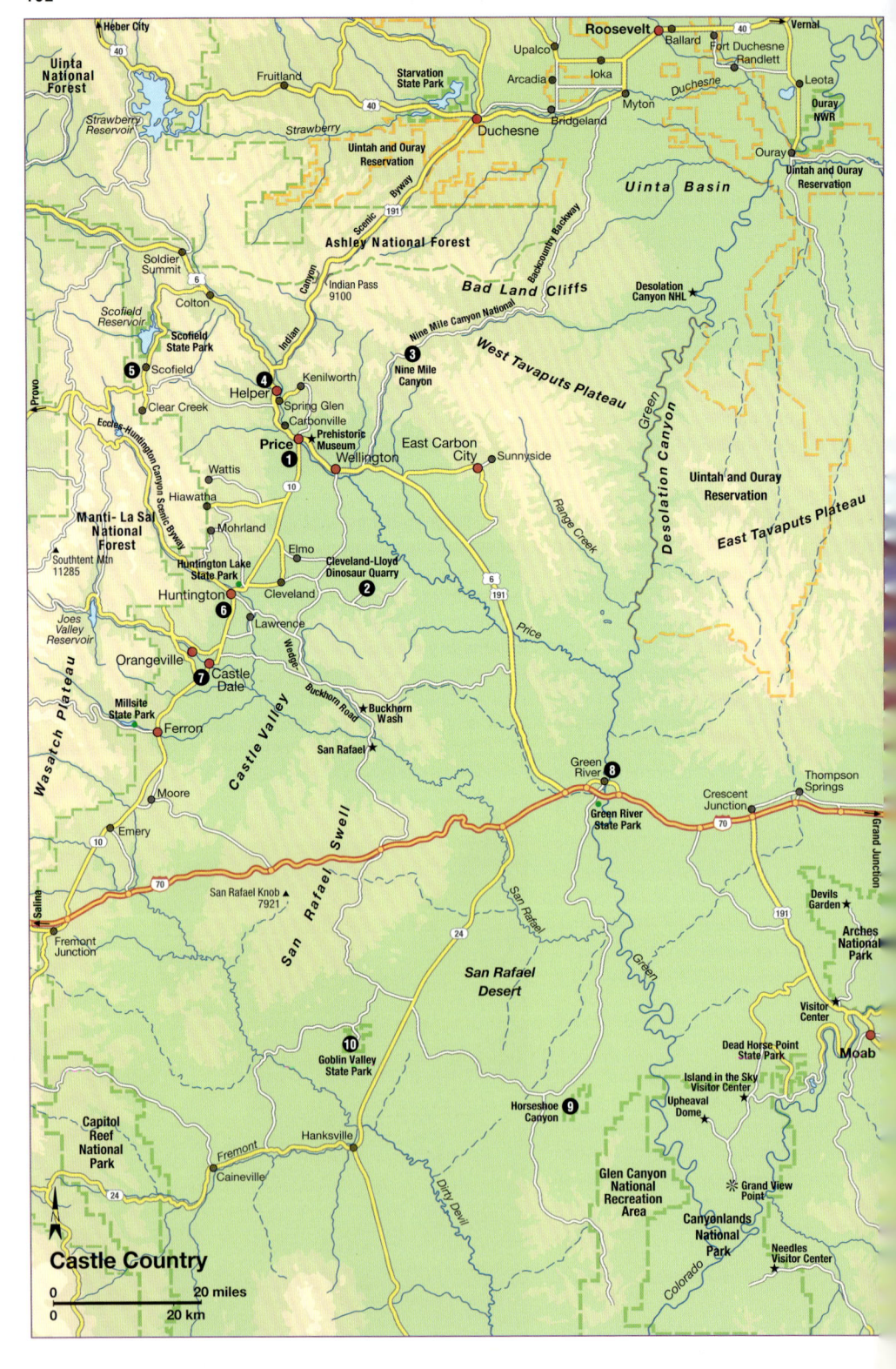

CASTLE COUNTRY | 163

Museum at USU Eastern (155 E. Main St, tel: 435-613 5060; https://eastern.usu.edu/museum; Sun–Wed 9am–5pm, Thu–Sat 9am–7pm; free). The museum's archaeology section has exhibits tracing the Native American presence in the area, including blow-up photographs of regional rock art and a full-size reproduction of the Barrier Canyon pictographs in the Horseshoe Canyon unit of Canyonlands National Park. Don't miss the "Pilling Figurines," 11 unbaked clay objects possibly used as fertility fetishes by the Fremont people, discovered in 1950 by Clarence Pilling on his ranch in Range Creek. The museum is also famous for its dinosaurs. The paleontology section is filled with enormous Allosaurus, Camptosaurus, Camarasaurus and Stegosaurus skeletons uncovered at **Cleveland-Lloyd Dinosaur Quarry** ❷ (see box page 163), a major dinosaur die-off site off UT 10, where more than 12,000 dinosaur bones have been uncovered. Unique to this museum are Early Cretaceous dinosaurs, found in the Cedar Mountain Formation, dating all the way back to about 120 to 110 million years ago.

Museum staff and volunteers have recovered more than 2,600 bones belonging to at least 10 new species of dinosaurs, ranging from 3 ft to 70 ft (1–21 meters) in length, including Utahraptor, Gastonia, Animantarx, Nedcolbertia and Eolambia. These highly specialized creatures occupied a unique ecological niche at the end of the dinosaur era. Much smaller than the better-known great lizards, Animantarx and Gastonia look almost like pony-size armadillos.

NINE MILE CANYON

Dubbed the "longest petroglyph art gallery" in the world, 46-mile (74 km) **Nine Mile Canyon** ❸ is littered with ancient Native American cave art, some 1,000 sites at last count. Created by the Fremont and Ute peoples, the art dates back almost 1,000 years. Nine Mile Canyon Road was paved in 2014, making access relatively easy – many sites are just off the road, like the Great Hunt Panel, with interpretive signs.

⏵ Eat

Price is a great place to eat if you love no-frills US diners with lots of character. For huge breakfast plates try Farlaino's Café (87 W. Main St; tel: 435-637 9217; Mon–Sat 7am–7pm). There's also Sherald's Frosty Freeze (434 E. Main St; tel: 435-637 1447; www.sheraldsfrostyfreeze.com; Mon–Sat 11am–8pm) for shakes and burgers.

Dinosaur tracks outside Moab.

⏵ THE DINOSAUR GRAVEYARD

A lumbering Camarasaurus wades into a pond to slake its thirst. As the dinosaur drinks, its stout, elephantine legs sink into the viscous clay. Struggling to escape, it only sinks deeper. The beast bellows an alarm, which lures three hungry allosaurs. The carnivores rush in to chomp the flanks of their prey, but before they can reach the helpless camarasaur, they too become mired in the swamp.

This scenario, or one much like it, played out some 147 million years ago at Cleveland-Lloyd Dinosaur Quarry (Apr–Oct Thu–Sun 10am–5pm), 30 miles (48 km) southeast of Price (with 13 miles/21 km of gravel road), the highlight of the western Dinosaur Diamond, a series of major dinosaur sites stretching from Moab, Utah, to Grand Junction, Colorado. More than 12,000 bones representing 70 individuals, including 44 allosaurs, the top predator of the Jurassic period, were uncovered at the quarry between 1939 and 1990. Stained jet black from manganese oxide in the groundwater, they constitute one of the most intriguing dinosaur die-off sites.

Visitors can see in-situ fossils and casts of other bones beneath two metal sheds over the quarry site. More bones, a mounted allosaur skeleton and an allosaur egg are displayed in a small visitor center. For the latest opening times, contact the BLM office in Price (tel: 435-636-3600) or visit www.blm.gov.

The road through the canyon begins in Wellington, just south of Price. Note that most of the land in the canyon is privately owned, and the only food and lodging is at historic **Nine Mile Canyon Ranch** (https://9mileranch.com), a western experience dubbed "bunk 'n' breakfast."

HELPER

Northwest of Price, sandwiched between railroad tracks and the highway, is historic **Helper** ❹. Like so many mining towns in the West, Helper is being revived by a community of artists. Every August, the historic district is shut down for the popular **Helper Arts Festival**, (www.helperartsfestival.com), which includes a plein air painting competition.

Helper's main visitor attraction is the **Helper Museum** (294 S. Main St; tel: 435-472 3009; Mon–Sat 11am–4pm; free), which occupies an old railroad hotel. Displays in the three-story building and adjoining outdoor park feature early 1900s dentist offices, a beauty salon and outlaw history. Model trains and old mining gear highlight Helper's rich mining and railroading past, which saw the development of ethnic enclaves, fights over miners' unions led by legendary activist Joe Hill, and three horrific mining disasters in 1900, 1924 and 1984.

US 191 continues north from Helper to **Duchesne** via 45-mile-long (72-km) **Indian Canyon Scenic Byway**, an enchanting route that offers a glimpse of the area's coal-mining past and amazing fall colors. US 191 passes the Castle Gate Power Plant and the old Castle Gate cemetery, where victims of the 1924 coal mine explosion are buried, then continues into **Ashley National Forest** via 9,100-ft (2,770-meter) Indian Pass.

MANTI-LA SAL NATIONAL FOREST

Some 16 miles (26 km) northwest of Helper, near the little town of **Colton** on US 6, is an entrance to **Manti-La Sal National Forest** (www.fs.usda.gov/mantilasal). Here UT 96 leads to **Scofield Reservoir**, the centerpiece of

San Rafael Swell.

Scofield State Park (tel: 435-448 9449; https://stateparks.utah.gov/parks/scofield; daily 6am–10pm) offering boating, swimming and fishing. Nearby is the historic mining town of **Scofield** ❺, where more than 100 miners were killed in an explosion in 1900. UT 96 joins UT 264 and then connects with UT 31, also known as **Eccles-Huntington Canyon Scenic Byway**. This is also the intersection for the north-south **Skyline Drive**, a scenic route across the 10,000-ft (3,000-meter) plateau with numerous forested campsites and hiking trails.

Heading south, UT 31 intersects with UT 10 at **Huntington** ❻, a mining town with a power plant producing electricity from coal mined on the plateau. **Huntington State Park** (tel: 435-687 2491; https://stateparks.utah.gov/parks/scofield; daily: summer 6am–10pm, winter 8am–5pm), encompassing a pristine reservoir next to the highway, is a good place for camping and birdwatching.

Some nine miles (15 km) south from Huntington, the **Museum of the San Rafael** (70 N 100 E St; tel: 435-381 3560; Mon–Fri 10am–4pm, Sat 10am–2pm;) livens the small town of **Castle Dale** ❼. It has its own glassed-in paleontology room, featuring mammoth and dinosaur skeletons, and an exhibit hall displaying local wildlife as well as arrowheads, spear points and the Sitterud Bundle, a collection of Native American artifacts dating from AD 1250–1450. The name of the museum refers to the San Rafael Swell, the high desert country that lies to the east of town. Further south, **Millsite State Park** (tel: 435-384 2552; https://stateparks.utah.gov/parks/millsite; daily: summer 6am–10pm, winter 8am–5pm) near Ferron also features a reservoir and campground popular with travelers on UT 10.

SAN RAFAEL SWELL

East of Castle Dale is the best-marked road into the desert-like **San Rafael Swell** (https://theswellutah.com) following the route of the Old Spanish Trail, used in the 1800s by Spanish traders and explorers John Gunnison and John C. Frémont. At Buckhorn

⊙ THE WILD BUNCH IN UTAH

It was early April, 1897. Outlaw Butch Cassidy had been hanging around the mining town of Castle Gate, near Price, Utah, for nearly a week. With his blond hair and clean-cut good looks, the affable young cowboy stood out from the town's residents, many of them non-English-speaking miners of European birth. Every day, Butch visited a saloon, chatted with the patrons, then rode his lively gray mare to meet the train. Rumor had it that Butch, a skilled horseman, and his companion, Elza Lay, were using the steep trails to train their mounts for an upcoming race. The story held water. Horses in Indian Canyon were an anomaly; it was so narrow the train could hardly make it through. Most of the population simply walked.

Townspeople had heard of Butch Cassidy and the Wild Bunch, of course. Word of their daring robberies in Wyoming and Colorado had spread throughout the West, but no one knew what the thieves looked like and they had never yet struck in Utah. Just in case, the Pleasant Valley Coal Company, owners of the Castle Gate Mine, had taken the precaution of varying the delivery schedule for payrolls. A holdup seemed highly unlikely under the circumstances.

Butch's cover held, and on April 21 his patience paid off. While meeting the train, he noticed that the bags being unloaded were heavier than usual and, pulling a six-gun, successfully held up the paymaster and his two assistants. Among the witnesses were several hundred men waiting for their paychecks, but no one made much of a move to stop the thieves, and with the town's telegraph wires cut by Butch, word of the robbery took a while to get out.

Butch and Elza dodged a posse from Castle Dale and Huntington. Along the way, the outlaws were helped by other gang members and ranchers who gave them fresh horses. South of Price, they rode through 70 miles (110 km) of the San Rafael Desert, until they reached Robber's Roost, in what is now the Maze district of Canyonlands National Park. Today, there are few signs of the Wild Bunch and other self-styled "businessmen" who dominated the rugged San Rafael Swell country in the late 1800s. Time and the vast wilderness of the Tavaputs Plateau have swallowed up these Wild West characters, making them seem larger than life.

PLACES

> **◎ Fact**
>
> A variety of river companies in Green River offer pricey but exhilarating multi-day trips on the river. Holiday River Expeditions (2075 E Main St; tel: 800-624 6323, www.bikeraft.com), for example, offers a 4-day whitewater rafting excursion through Lodore Canyon, and a 5–6 day raft and kayak trip through Desolation Canyon, beginning with a scenic flight over the Tavaputs Plateau.

Manti-La Sal National Forest.

Flat, turn south to view some of the area's best Archaic pictographs in **Buckhorn Wash**. The badly vandalized paintings, made about 6,000 years ago, were completely restored in 1995 and are an area highlight today.

Buckhorn Wash emerges at **San Rafael River Campground**, an unshaded but well-maintained BLM campground on the San Rafael River, the only one in this part of the Swell. Just to the east, the river cuts through **Little Grand Canyon**, a lightly visited but stunning gorge that well deserves its name. Continuing south the road brings you out to I-70, just west of **Black Dragon Wash**, one of several pictograph panels you can reach from the highway.

GREEN RIVER

The nearest visitor facilities on this scenic stretch of I-70 are at **Green River ❽**, which is set on the waterway of the same name and has become a haven for river runners, who descend on the town in droves year-round. Like other towns in these parts, Green River grew up around mining and the railroad and boomed briefly following World War II, when uranium was discovered. Today, it has reinvented itself as a tourist stop with plentiful gas stations, lodgings and eateries. If you're passing through Green River in the late summer and fall, be sure to stop and buy one of the delicious sweet melons grown in the area – the annual Green River Melon Days Festival takes place on the third weekend of September (https://www.melon-days.com).

The big attraction in Green River is the carefully thought-out **John Wesley Powell River History Museum** (1765 E. Main St; tel: 435-564 3427; http://johnwesleypowell.com; daily 9am–5pm). Named for the man who first explored the Green and Colorado Rivers, in 1869 and 1871, this airy museum is a homage to river aficionados and their watercraft, from historic figures like Powell to guides like Bert Loper. Inside the lobby doors, you'll find **Emery County Information Center**, where you can get maps and help with trip planning. South of the bridge is **Green River State Park** (tel: 435-564 3633; https://stateparks.utah.gov/parks/green-river; daily: summer 7am–10pm, winter 8am–5pm), which sits on the river and has a nine-hole golf course and numerous campsites amid the tamarisks.

HORSESHOE CANYON

Parts of the wild western section of **Canyonlands National Park** (see page 231; www.nps.gov/cany), may be reached overland from US 24, just west of Green River. Drive south through what's known as Sinbad Country, the extraordinary, uptilted landscape of the San Rafael Swell, until you reach Temple Junction, named for the highest point on the Reef, 6,773-ft (2,064-meter) Temple Mountain. East of the junction, a 30-mile (48-km) graded dirt road takes you to the **Horseshoe Canyon** ❾ section of Canyonlands National Park, where you can view the remarkable **Great Gallery Pictographs** via a strenuous hike (7 miles/11 km roundtrip; 6hr). From here a series of old ranch and mining tracks take you overland past **Hans Flat Ranger Station** (tel: 435-259 2652; Mon–Fri 8am–4.30pm) and into the Maze country that once sheltered the Wild Bunch. A four-wheel-drive is essential for deeper explorations of this rough country. Bring food, water, extra gas and spare tires. This is a very remote area.

West of Temple Junction is the paved road that leads directly into the heart of the San Rafael Swell, passing Archaic and Fremont rock art panels, old mines, wilderness study areas, wild horse herds and **Swasey's Cabin**, a backcountry ranch built by the highly "entrepreneurial" Joe Swasey in 1921 (the cabin can also be reached from I-70, exit 131).

GOBLIN VALLEY STATE PARK

If the wilder sections of the desert seems too intimidating (and never underestimate this country; its remoteness, heat and aridity can make it very dicey in summer), base yourself in delightful **Goblin Valley State Park** ❿ (tel: 435-275 4584; https://stateparks.utah.gov/parks/goblin-valley; daily 6am–10pm), which offers numerous comforts for the self-sufficient traveler in an awe-inspiring setting at the edge of the San Rafael Swell. The park is set about 20 miles (32 km) from UT 24 via paved roads and has everything even a neophyte backcountry explorer might desire: plenty of well-conceived, clean campsites with attractive metal gazebos, showers, toilets and everything else you could possibly need, plus easy to access trails and knock-your-socks-off scenery that has starred in numerous movies.

The "goblins" are actually eroded red Entrada sandstone, the same formation found in Cathedral Valley in nearby Capitol Reef National Park. The campground is sheltered right below them, in the far valley, and is much more intimate than you would expect. Friendly on-site rangers are passionate about this place and love to share information with visitors. Despite its remote setting, the park is quite popular with campers (the whole campground is occasionally reserved by movie crews); reserving a site ahead of time is advisable. Bring your mountain bike, hiking shoes and a camera, and plan on spending a couple of nights as there is plenty to explore.

If you've still some energy, tackle **Little Wild Horse Canyon** a short drive west via dirt road, a classic slot canyon which gets extremely narrow in places with beautifully sculpted walls. You can walk up the canyon and back, or make an eight-mile loop by crossing over and descending Bell Canyon. Castle Country doesn't get much better than this.

The Three Sisters Hoodoos, Goblin Valley State Park.

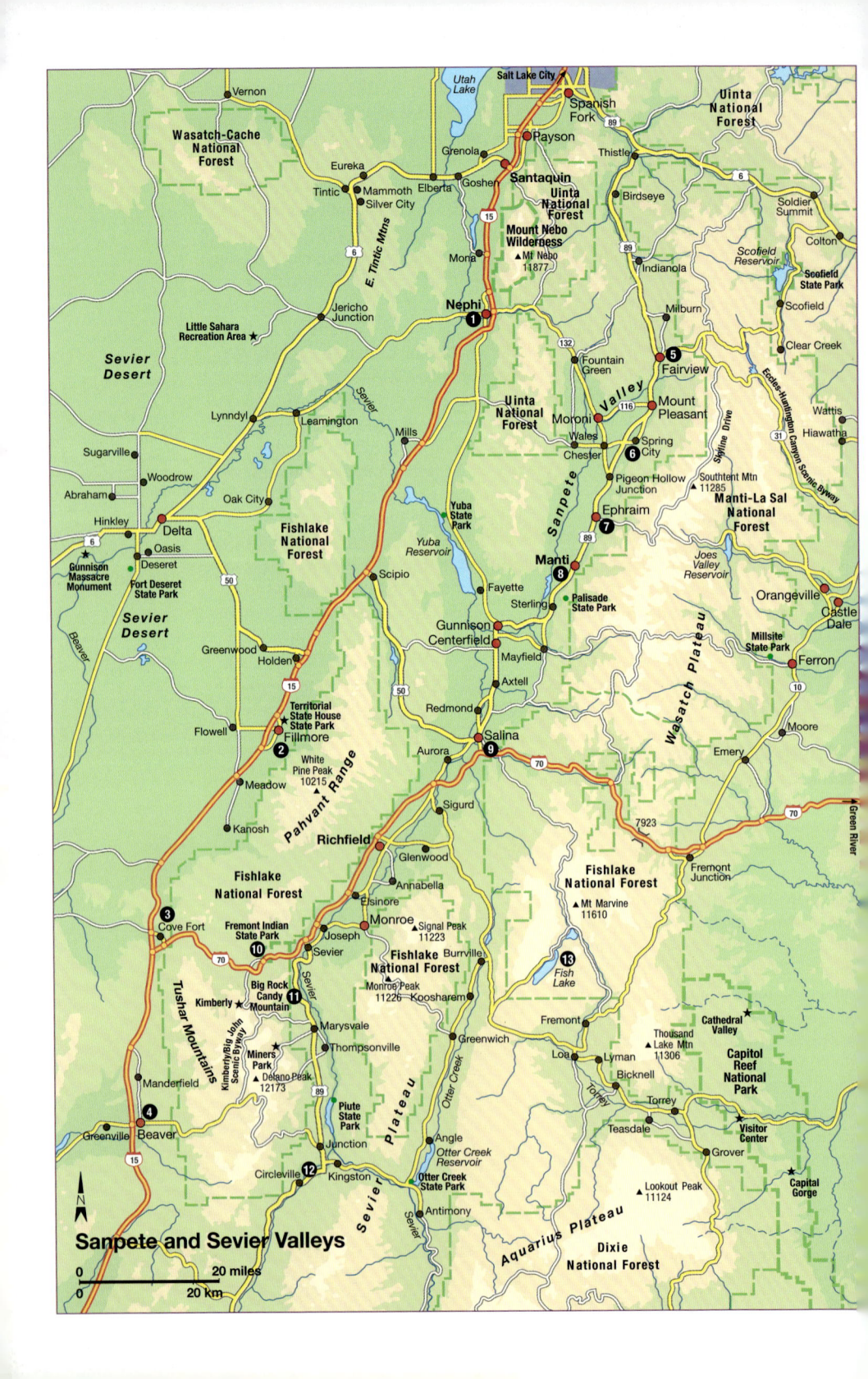

Sanpete and Sevier Valleys

SANPETE AND SEVIER VALLEYS

Scandinavian immigrants have left their stamp on this region of farms and ranches settled by Mormon pioneers in the mid-19th century.

Main attractions
Big Rock Candy Mountain
Butch Cassidy Childhood Home
Fairview Museum of History and Art
Fremont Indian State Park and Museum
Manti
Nebo Loop National Scenic Byway
Territorial Statehouse State Park Museu

Map on page 168

Most travelers heading south through Utah drive I-15, a fast, modern freeway running parallel to the yawning Great Basin and the high mountain ranges and plateaus that together make up what tourism officials call Panoramaland. But east of I-15, life settles into the slow lane. It's more rewarding to explore US 89, Utah's award-winning "Mormon pioneer cultural corridor," which passes through the isolated Sanpete Valley, then drops into the scenic valley of Sevier River, south of I-70, the gateway to southern Utah. On the way you'll pass through pretty Mormon towns and villages like Ephraim, home to Snow College and several art galleries, and Manti, where there is a stunning Mormon Temple and several pioneer museums. You can also enjoy the activities at Big Rock Candy Mountain, visit the Butch Cassidy Childhood Home, and explore the trails and scenic byways of tranquil Fishlake National Forest.

THE I-15 CORRIDOR

The sights along I-15 south of Utah Lake are few and far between. The Salt Lake City metropolitan area peters out at Spanish Fork, southeast of Utah Lake, giving way to long stretches of desert freeway punctuated by small towns in the shadow of mountain highlands. **Nephi** ❶ is home to July's **Ute Stampede**, one of Utah's most popular rodeos. In quiet, staid **Fillmore** ❷, you'll find the 1855 territorial state capitol, the oldest government building in Utah, protected now as **Territorial Statehouse State Park Museum** (50 W Capitol Ave; tel: 435-743 5316; https://stateparks.utah.gov/parks/territorial-statehouse; Mon–Sat 9am–5pm). At the junction of I-15 and I-70, blink and you'll miss **Cove Fort** ❸ (tel: 435-438 5547; www.placestovisit.lds.org; Mon–Sat 10am–6pm, Sun noon–5pm; free), an 1867

Sevier River.

> **Fact**
>
> Tickets for the Ute Stampede Rodeo in Nephi usually go on sale in April – you can buy them online (tel: 435-623 7102; https://utestampederodeo.com), and get a small early-bird discount. The rodeo runs for three days at the Juab County Fairgrounds (400 W Center St), with tickets for reserved seats running $14–16.

way station built by Mormon pioneers from volcanic rock and now operated by the LDS Church. Even farther south is **Beaver** ④, with over 200 historic buildings from its heyday as a gold and silver mining town adjacent to the Tushar Mountains, the third-highest range in Utah.

SANPETE COUNTY

Agricultural Sanpete County may well be Utah's most traditional Mormon stronghold. It attracted so many Scandinavian immigrant Mormon pioneers in the 1850s and 1860s that it was dubbed "Little Denmark." Today, the Scandinavian stamp is everywhere – in historic buildings now housing bed-and-breakfasts, mom-and-pop cafes, museums, art studios, and shops, as well as in the folklore, and deadpan, self-deprecating humor for which the region's Scandinavian communities are known.

Start your tour in **Payson**, at the northern end of **Mount Nebo National Scenic Byway**, which travels for 38 miles (61km) behind 11,877ft (3,620-meter) **Mount Nebo**, the highest peak in the Wasatch range. The winding road passes through oaks and aspens in **Uinta–Wasatch–Cache National Forest** for fabulous views of Mount Nebo Wilderness, Utah Valley, and the Wasatch Mountains. Most people drive the byway in late October, when fall colors really pop.

At UT 132, turn east into the Sanpete Valley, passing through **Fountain Green**, a camping site for Mormon pioneers in the 1850s. A few miles farther is **Moroni**, originally named Mego and Sanpitch, after local Ute leaders, and later renamed for the angel who led LDS Church founder Joseph Smith to the golden plates on which the Book of Mormon was recorded. From Moroni, take a detour north on UT 116 to pick up US 89 near **Fairview** ⑤, where a historic school now houses the homegrown **Fairview Museum of History and Art** (85 N 100 East; tel: 435-427 9216; https://fairviewmuseum.org; Tue–Thu noon–5pm, Fri–Sat 11am–5pm; free). Exhibits in the main building tell the sad but all-too-familiar

The scenic Nebo Loop.

19th-century tale of conflicts between Utes and whites in settling the valley, while highlighting the unique world view the newcomers brought with them. The modern building next door houses a Columbian mammoth skeleton and local art, while the original Fairview City Hall, built in 1900, should be part of the museum by the end of 2023.

SANPETE VALLEY

Although the towns in Sanpete Valley are just a few miles apart, each has developed separately, giving every community an individual look. A wealth of 19th-and early 20th-century buildings made from local limestone and often adorned with traditional Scandinavian carved wood and stained glass are slowly being restored. South of Fairview, the attractive Main Street of **Mount Pleasant**, which prospered with the arrival of the railroad, is still intact, with many buildings dating from 1880 to 1905.

At nearby **Spring City** ❻, the second oldest community in Sanpete County, the whole town is on the National Register of Historic Places and has become an artist haven. A little off the highway, it has several attractive bed-and-breakfasts and artist studios. The town hosts **Heritage Days** (www.friendsofhistoricspringcity.org) each spring, with tours of historic homes and studios, wagon rides, and a barbecue.

Another Biblical-sounding town – **Ephraim** ❼ – is home to **Snow College** (www.snow.edu), which was founded in the 1880s in a two-story stone building on Main Street that has also served as a mercantile and community center. The two-year college now has 4,000 students and is well regarded in the state. Ephraim was founded in 1854 and, at one time, 90 percent of the town's population hailed from Denmark. The meticulously restored former ZCMI store now houses the **Ephraim Co-Op Mercantile Association** (96 Main St; tel: 435-283 6654; www.ephraim-coop.org), showcasing the work of local artisans. If you're interested in Southwest contemporary art, check out **Granary Arts** (86 Main St; tel: 435-283 3456;

Manti Utah Temple.

www.granaryarts.org; Wed–Sat 11am–5pm; free), set in a classic limestone building. Other artists can be visited in working studios in town. The **Scandinavian Festival** (http://scandinavian-festival.org) is held in Ephraim every Memorial Day weekend.

Manti ❽, founded in 1849 at the invitation of Timpanogos Chief Walkara (aka Walker), is the oldest town in Sanpete County and the county seat. It is best known for its imposing **Mormon Temple** (200 E 510 North) built at a cost of $1 million between 1877 and 1888. The temple's mix of Victorian architectural styles echoes those found in other early Mormon towns in the Midwest, and it is certainly one of the most photogenic buildings in the area. Only "worthy" Mormons may enter the building. Non-Mormons can visit **Pioneer Park** (100 N 75 West; tel: https://pioneer-parkephraim.weebly.com; May–Sept Mon–Sat, call to confirm hours), anchored by the 1862 Historic Hansen House. Learn more about Manti at **John Patten DUP Museum** (300 N 100 West; tel: 435-851 0012), an 1854 pioneer rock house that serves as the town museum.

SEVIER VALLEY

The Scandinavian-influenced Sanpete Valley gives way to the Sevier River valley at **Salina** ❾, where US 89 meets I-70. If time permits, stop at **Miss Mary's Museum** (204 S 100 East; tel: 435-529 3968; late May–late Oct Tue–Fri 11am–3pm), which tells the story of Mary McCallum, a missionary and teacher who ministered to the needs of Japanese American internees at the remote Topaz Relocation Center during World War II.

One museum in the Sevier Valley that you should not miss is the **Fremont Indian State Park and Museum** ❿ (3820 Clear Creek Canyon Road; tel: 435-527 4631; https://stateparks.utah.gov/parks/fremont-indian; Mar–Nov daily 9am–5pm; Dec–Mar Mon–Sat 9am–5pm), 24 miles (39km) southwest of **Richfield** in the foothills of the Pahvant Mountains. During construction of the interstate highway

Butch Cassidy's childhood home.

⊘ CONFLICT IN THE SANPETE VALLEY

Native Americans had been living in Utah long before the arrival of the Mormons in the 1840s. Chief Walkara's welcome in the Sanpete Valley rapidly chilled when he clashed with antislavery Mormons over land disputes and the Ute practice of selling captured children from other Indigenous groups to Spanish traders. When the Walker War erupted in 1853 (after a relation of Walkara was killed in a trade dispute), settlers across the region took shelter in three forts built from logs and stone. Ute attacks occurred at Fillmore, Fountain Green, Santaquin, and Manti, and included the burning of Spring City. Fatal encounters with angry Native Americans didn't affect only Mormons. In 1853, Captain John Gunnison, an American surveying the newly acquired US territory, was killed by Native Americans nearby. The town of Gunnison is named for him. Though the skirmishes ended in 1854, tensions remained, flaring again in the Tintic War (1856) and notably during the Black Hawk War (1865–1872). This was named for the fierce young Ute leader who, together with other starving Native Americans, raided cattle herds and killed whites in an attempt to drive the Mormons from the Sanpete Valley. The long-running war was eventually settled by federal troops. Several Ute bands were then banished from their homeland to a reservation in the desolate Uintah Basin, a far cry from the lush valley in which they once roamed.

in 1985, archaeologists discovered a thousand-year-old Fremont village and hundreds of rock art panels on the walls of Clear Creek Canyon. Inside the visitor center are exhibits of reconstructed pit houses, pottery, and other artifacts. Three trails lead to pictograph panels. The park sponsors popular events, including a Mountain Man Rendezvous, atlatl (spear-thrower) competitions, and pottery workshops. US 89 continues south opposite the park and follows the Sevier River into dramatic red-rock country. Even amid southern Utah's canyon scenery, the historic cold-springs resort of **Big Rock Candy Mountain** ⓫ (4550 US-89, Sevier; tel: 435-326-2031; https://candymountainresort.com) stands out for its whimsical colors and huge profile, rising sharply above the river (the region was allegedly named after Harry McClintock's famous country song in 1928). Stop at the rustic resort for refreshments, float trips on the river and whitewater rafting, UTV rentals, canopy zipline course, and Adventure Park in the summer. West of **Marysvale**, the 6.5-mile-long (4km) Canyon of Gold scenic drive (aka Bullion Canyon Rd) takes you up Bullion Canyon to **Miners Park** (May–Oct daily; free) an open-air museum in the Tushar Mountains. Pick up a brochure at the start of this drive interpreting old mines and mill sites. Miners Park has mining exhibits and makes a good picnic spot.

Just outside **Circleville** ⓬ is the **Butch Cassidy Childhood Home** (24hr; free) the restored 1863 log cabin that served as the boyhood home of famed outlaw Robert Leroy Parker, alias Butch Cassidy, between 1880 and 1884. It was here the young Mormon planned his escape from a life of grinding poverty by changing his name to that of mentor Mike Cassidy, a ranch hand and sometime rustler who taught Butch the tricks of the trade.

FISHLAKE NATIONAL FOREST

Another scenic drive into mining country begins at Junction, a few miles north of Circleville. UT 62 runs east through dramatic Kingston Canyon, a rugged volcanic gorge, to the fishing and boating haven of **Otter Creek State Park** (tel: 435-642 3268; https://stateparks.utah.gov/parks/otter-creek; daily summer 7am–6pm; winter 9am–5pm). UT 62 connects with scenic UT 24, the main highway between pretty Sigurd and Loa, at the far end of the Torrey River valley. A left turn onto **Fishlake Scenic Byway** (UT 25) will take you into **Fishlake National Forest** (www.fs.usda.gov/fishlake) and to **Fish Lake** ⓭ (tel: 435-896 9233) itself, one of the state's premier hunting and fishing spots (with six developed campgrounds, and cabins). It has plentiful mackinaw and rainbow trout in summer and ice fishing in winter. Elk, deer, black bears, cougar, and moose can be found in the woods and peaks around here, as well as wild turkey and mountain goats.

> **Tip**
> An alternative route south begins at Fremont Indian State Park, where the 40-mile (64km) Kimberly/Big John Scenic Byway (Forest roads 113 and 123) winds into the Tushar Mountains to the old mining camp of Kimberly. The camp closed in 1907 and is now a ghost town (the byway ends at UT 153 about 16 miles/26km east of Beaver).

Fishlake National Forest.

📷 RODEOS

Bad-tempered bulls and bucking broncos ridden by lean, laconic, tobacco-spitting types clad in tight blue Wrangler jeans and plaid shirts. If this is your idea of the key ingredients of a rodeo, then you've got it absolutely right. This, happily, is one sporting spectacle that has changed very little over the years, and it remains a true cultural bastion in Utah.

BRONCS, BULLS AND BARRELS

The main rodeo events are the spectacular bull-riding and bronc-riding competitions. Each ride is scored according to how hard the animal bucks and how well the cowboy rides – while keeping one hand swinging free in the air at all times. A minimum eight seconds is the time required to earn a score. Calf-roping is another crowd favorite, for its combination of daring, skill and speed. A cowboy pursues the calf on horseback, hurls a lasso around its neck, dismounts at a full run then tackles the animal to the ground before trussing three of its legs together, thus rendering it immobile. Sounds like an afternoon's work, but in fact under 10 seconds is considered a good effort. Cowgirls often feature in the barrel-riding, which demands great riding skills as competitors turn tight figure-eights around barrels at a full gallop. Among other events are races for kids, the grand tradition of the rodeo being that everyone can be involved.

The traditional lassoing technique hasn't changed much at all over the years.

A cowboy roping cattle with a lasso.

A cowboy riding a bull at a rodeo in Bluff.

Ruby's Inn Rodeo Grounds.

Utah's top rodeos

Ever since 1934, the Ute Stampede Rodeo at the Juab County Fairgrounds in Nephi has been one of the state's premier events, held over three days in mid-July (tickets usually go on sale starting mid-April). The event is kicked off by a carnival and live concerts, followed by the opening rodeo events. Communal breakfasts, craft shows, parades, fun runs, a golf tournament, car show, and beauty contest take place in addition to the main rodeo competitions.

Ogden Pioneer Days Rodeo (also July) is another major event, featuring some of the best bareback bronc riding, barrel racing, tie-down roping, steer wrestling and bull riding anywhere.

The Utah Days of '47 Rodeo (https://utahdaysof47rodeo.com) takes place on Pioneer Day (July 24), at Utah State Fairpark in Salt Lake City. One of the oldest rodeos in Utah is the Golden Spike Rodeo (www.goldenspikerodeo.com), which takes place in August at Box Elder County Fairgrounds, in Tremonton. There's also the family-friendly Strawberry Days Rodeo (https://strawberrydaysrodeo.com), held in June in Pleasant Grove since 1921, under the shadow of Mount Timpanogos.

Utah State Fair Park.

...ull gets away during a rodeo event.

...ccessfully lassoing cattle during a rodeo event.

Bonneville Salt Flats.

THE GREAT BASIN

The harsh desert lands southwest of the Great Salt Lake yield ghost towns, shimmering salt flats, intriguing museums, and other unexpected sights.

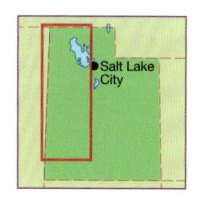

In the heat of the day, mirages shimmer on the salt flats like the ghosts of an ancient sea. Mountain ranges rise from the silvery illusions like the islands of Atlantis, their summits crowned with dark, distant forests that look less real than the mirages themselves. In a landscape lacking the bare essentials to sustain life, the air itself dances. The only part of the Great Basin of west-central Utah that travelers routinely see is the I-80 corridor, one of the longest, hottest and emptiest freeways in America. Most motorists are en route to California or West Wendover, the tiny "Sin City" on the Nevada state line just 90 minutes from Salt Lake City. But if time and temperament allow, there are several detours off the main drag that lead to intriguing museums, ghost towns, stark deserts, and island-like mountains in the vast Bonneville Salt Flats.

GREAT SALT LAKE – SOUTH SHORE

About 15 miles (24km) west of Salt Lake City is the exit for **Great Salt Lake State Park** ❶ (tel: 801-828 0787; https://stateparks.utah.gov/parks/great-salt-lake; park daily sunrise–sunset; visitor center Mon–Fri 11am–7pm, Sat–Sun 9am–8pm). The park consists of a 300-slip sailboat marina and miles of wide, grayish-white beaches along the lake's south shore. On summer weekends, city folks by the thousands pack the beach to bob like apples in the dense salt water and walk barefoot in the strange, squeaky sand, called oolite, which is made of the waste of billions of tiny brine shrimp coated in salt.

A hundred years ago, the lakeshore was the site of several elaborate beach resorts. One offered steamboat rides. Another had an elegant restaurant, a nightclub and a covered boardwalk. The most spectacular was Saltair, built in 1893 in a whimsical architectural style, with broad staircases, towers topped

Main attractions
Bonneville Salt Flats
Deseret Peak
Great Basin National Park
Great Salt Lake State Park
Little Sahara Recreation Area
Mammoth
Rio Tinto Kennecott Visitor Experience
Topaz Museum

Map on page 178

Deseret Peak.

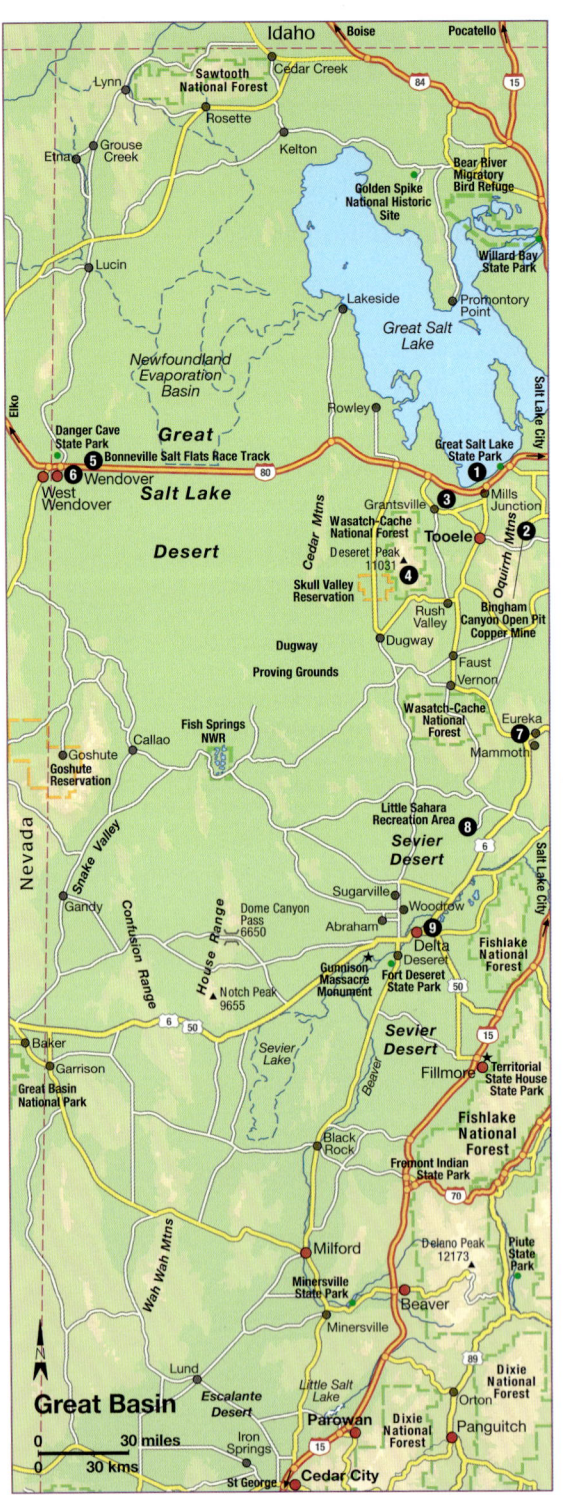

by bulbous Russian-style domes, and a ballroom under a five-story neo-Moorish atrium. Amusement park rides provided family entertainment, and dining options ranged from a fancy restaurant to picnic tables along the water. But with gradually declining water levels, the widening beach revealed a disadvantage of oolite sand: under the constant trampling of bathers' feet, it turned into foul-smelling mud. The resorts were gradually abandoned and, by the 1940s, demolished. Saltair, the last one left standing, was destroyed by fire in the 1960s. Today, a smaller reproduction of **Saltair Resort** (http://thesaltair.com) stands on the site, the resort's trademark copper-clad Russian domes glinting in the sun. Conceived as a bed-and-breakfast, the new incarnation of Saltair has turned out to be something of a white elephant, though it is occasionally used as a pop music concert venue.

Just 11 miles (18km) southwest from the park lies **Mills Junction**, site of the **Historic Benson Grist Mill** (325 UT 138; tel: 435-882 7678; http://bensonmill.org; May–Oct Thu–Sat 10am–6pm; free), built in 1854 by Brigham Young to grind grain for Tooele County farmers. Cabins, an old-fashioned blacksmith shop, and a museum can be found at the site.

Another easy side trip 30 miles (48km) south of the park leads to the **Bingham Canyon Open Pit Copper Mine** ❷, the largest excavated site on the planet. More than three-quarters of a mile deep (1.2km) and 2.5 miles wide (4km), the copper pit has produced in excess of 20 million tons of copper since it opened in 1903, along with a fortune in gold, silver, and molybdenum. In total, the pit has produced more tonnage of commercial metals than the California, Comstock Lode, and Klondike gold rushes combined. View the pit from the **Rio Tinto Kennecott Visitor Experience**, a visitor center perched on the rim (12732 Bacchus Highway, Herriman; tel: 801-252 3234; www.riotinto.com; Apr–Oct daily 9am–4pm). From here it's another 10 miles (16km) on UT 138 to **Grantsville** ❸, where you can visit the morbidly fascinating **Donner-Reed Museum** (90 N Cooley St; tel: 435-884 3411; www.donner-reed-museum.org; by appointment only). Most people familiar with Western history know the grizzly tale of the Donner party, the ill-fated pioneers who were trapped by snow in the Sierra Nevada of California, eventually resorting to cannibalism to survive (see page 39). The museum preserves the possessions that the party threw away on their hellish trek across Utah, which follows roughly the same route that I-80 takes today.

Six miles (10km) south of Grantsville, South Willow Canyon Road turns off from the Mormon Trail Road, providing access to an isolated section of Uinta–Wasatch–Cache National Forest around 11,031ft (3,362-meter) **Deseret Peak** ❹, the high point of the **Stansbury Mountains** and one of the tallest summits in the Great Basin. The peak is set within a designated wilderness area and can be climbed only on foot or horseback. The 3.5-mile (5.5km) trail from Loop Campground in South Willow Canyon gains 3,650ft (1,110 meters) in elevation as it ascends into cool aspen and fir forests and alpine meadows spangled with wildflowers. The summit offers what may well be the most spectacular view from any Utah mountaintop, a 360-degree panorama that takes in the Wasatch Front, the Great Salt Lake, the full expanse of the salt flat desert, and the vast wastelands of the military munitions testing ranges. It's possible to drive across the adjoining Onaqui Mountains via the **Fisher Pass** (aka Johnson Pass) on UT 199, further south at Rush Valley. The road was built in 1920 as part of the Lincoln Highway, America's first cross-country road.

GREAT SALT LAKE DESERT

To the west, I-80 runs straight as an arrow for some 75 miles (120km) across the **Great Salt Lake Desert**. The barren, sugar-white salt flats are a remnant of Lake Bonneville, an inland sea the size of Lake Michigan that partly evaporated 15,000 years ago. Dubbed the **Bonneville Salt Flats**, this is a fragile 30,000-acre (121 sq km) resource (12 miles/19km long and 5 miles/8km wide) administered by the Bureau of Land Management (www.blm.gov). The paved access road to the Salt Flats is reached by taking Exit 4 off I-80, dead-ending after about 3 miles/5km (it's open year-round and is free to visit). Travel on the actual salt flats from here is at your own risk and is only recommended when the surface is entirely dry. This is also the setting for the **Bonneville Salt Flats Race Track** ❺ (tel: 801-977 4300; www.bonnevilleracing.com), where automobiles have been setting land speed records since 1914. Pressed up against the Utah–Nevada state line is the little town of **Wendover** ❻, most of whose 1,600 residents work at adjacent Wendover Air Force Base or the nearby potash mines. The town's main street is lined with modest mom-and-pop motels, now prospering thanks to the cluster of casino resorts

> **Tip**
>
> Note that the Bingham Mine Overlook (free) on the southwest side of the Bingham Canyon Open Pit has been closed since 2021 due to landslides. The drive along Butterfield Canyon (July–Sept only) from Herriman, or up Middle Canyon Road from Tooele, 15 miles (24km) to 7,780ft (2,370-meter) Butterfield Pass, is still spectacular however (the whole route is paved).

Bingham Copper Mine.

Fact

The first unofficial land speed record at Bonneville, set by celebrity daredevil Teddy Tetzlaff in 1914, was 142.8mph (229.18km/h); in 1970, Gary Gabelich's rocket car *Blue Flame* reached 622.4mph (1,001.7km/h), which is still the record for Bonneville, though a speed of 763mph (1,227.9km/h) was set by Andy Green in 1997 at Black Rock Desert in Nevada.

"Wendover Will" welcomes you to Wendover.

that loom just inches from the state line in West Wendover, Nevada. For those interested in exploring the backcountry, the unpaved 54-mile (87km) **Silver Island Mountains Backcountry Byway** heads north along the edge of the Great Salt Lake Desert. The byway starts at I-80 Exit 4 and passes **Danger Cave State Park**, where archaeologists have discovered evidence of human habitation from 11,000 years ago, the oldest such site in Utah. The park is undeveloped; the cave entrance is blocked with an iron gate to prevent vandalism.

THE US 6 CORRIDOR

Another route across Utah's Great Basin is US 6, dubbed "the loneliest highway in America." Running roughly southwest from I-15 to the Nevada border, it's a passage into the stark beauty of the western desert.

Eureka ❼, 35 miles (56km) southwest of Spanish Fork, was the center of the silver-rich Tintic Mining District. Today, this village of weather-beaten shacks and boarded-up storefronts has a single tourist attraction: the **Tintic Mining Museum** (241 W Main St; tel: 435-433 6842; https://tintichistoricalsociety.org; Wed, Fri, and Sat noon–5pm; free), which occupies the historic railroad depot and the old city hall. Among the exhibits are the interior of a typical miner's home, a replica of the Eureka City Courthouse, and a scale model of a silver mine. About 3 miles (5km) south of Eureka is the ghost town of **Mammoth**. Though not completely abandoned (there are still about 60 residents), it's a mere shadow of the bustling mining camp that stood here in the 1890s.

Just off US 6, about 35 miles (56km) southwest of Eureka, is the **Little Sahara Recreation Area** ❽ (tel: 435-743 6811; www.blm.gov), the largest expanse of sand dunes in Utah, with "Sand Mountain" standing 700ft (215-meters) high. The dunes owe their existence to wind-borne sand scoured from the Sevier Desert to the southwest and deposited at the foot of the **Tintic Mountains**. The recreation area, a favorite of off-road vehicle enthusiasts, also has a 9,000-acre (3,600-hectare) nature preserve where only hikers are allowed. There are four campgrounds as well as picnic areas.

GREAT BASIN NATIONAL PARK

Situated in Nevada, just over the Utah border, Great Basin National Park (tel: 775-234 7331; www.nps.gov/grba) encompasses a fascinating array of ecosystems, ranging from low-lying, sun-blasted desert to the stony crags of 13,063ft (3,982-meter) Wheeler Peak. The park's best-known feature, Lehman Caves, is a limestone cave complex filled with stalactites, stalagmites, and other bizarre rock formations. Ranger-guided tours are available.

On the surface, the Wheeler Peak Scenic Drive winds up the mountain to an overlook with sweeping views of the surrounding landscape. From here, a demanding 5-mile (8km) trail leads intrepid visitors to the summit. One of the highlights of driving the mountain road is getting a close-up view of Great Basin bristlecone pines, some more than 4,000 years old. Slow growth rates and unremitting winds account for the trees' gnarled appearance.

Another highlight is Lexington Arch. Quite different from the sandstone arches of southern Utah, the existence of this 75ft (23-meter-) high limestone span baffles geologists. Some theorize that it is the remnant of a cavern eroded from entrances at both ends.

The park is about 100 miles (160km) west of Delta via US 6/50. It has a visitor center at Lehman Caves (daily 8am–5pm, with exceptions) and primitive campgrounds.

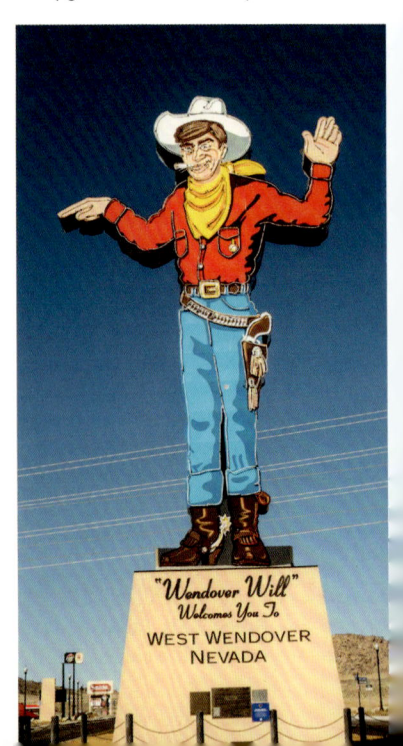

Farther along US 6, in the little town of **Delta**, is the **Great Basin Museum** (45 W Main St; tel: 435-864 5013; https://greatbasinmuseum.com; Mon–Sat 10am–5pm, with exceptions; free), with Native American and pioneer artifacts and a collection of historic photographs. Next door, the **Topaz Museum** (55 W Main St; tel: 435-864 2514; https://topazmuseum.org; Mon–Sat 10am–5pm; free) has an excellent exhibition on the Topaz Relocation Camp, where more than 8,000 Japanese Americans from California were confined during World War II. Topaz Camp was situated about 17 miles (27km) northwest of town – there's not much left, though the site is open to visit, with a small monument to those interred here (guided tours on request at the museum).

South of Delta, near the tiny town of **Deseret**, is the remains of **Fort Deseret**. The undeveloped site encompasses the ruins of an adobe fort built as a defense against the Paiute during the Black Hawk War of 1865–72. The fort was never attacked, though local settlers huddled within its walls for about a month. After the war, the structure was occupied by Native Americans, who used it for shelter and storage. The **Gunnison Massacre Monument**, about 6 miles (10km) farther south, memorializes the killing of a US government survey party by Utes during an earlier conflict, the Walker War of 1853. Historians still debate whether the local Mormons, who resented federal incursions into Utah, warned the surveyors of hostile Native Americans or simply sent them to their deaths. From Delta, US 6 (with US 50) runs about 100 miles (160km) across the barren expanse of the **Sevier Desert**, where the usually dry bed of Sevier Lake extends southward for nearly 40 miles (65km). Travelers with an adventurous spirit and a rugged vehicle can follow the unpaved 50-mile (80km) **Notch Peak Loop** into the **House Range**. The route crosses the mountains at 6,430ft (1,960-meter) **Dome Creek Pass** and then follows the western slope back to US 6. The highway passes through the picturesque **Confusion Mountains** before descending into the **Snake Valley** near the state line. **Great Basin National Park** is 18 miles (29km) across the border in Nevada.

Deseret Peak.

Rock formation in Glen Canyon.

SOUTHERN UTAH

Rock is the leitmotiv of this otherworldly landscape – layers and layers of it, rearranged by time and the elements.

A hoodoo in Canyonlands National Park.

In 1869, after a two-month journey down the Green River from Wyoming, an expedition led by explorer John Wesley Powell reached the confluence of the Green and Colorado Rivers, one of the most remote spots on the North American continent. Here, in the heart of what Powell called "the Great Unknown," both rivers lay deep within the earth, imprisoned by sheer cliffs of their own making, part of a mile-high, 130,000-square-mile (330,000-sq-km) elevated geophysical province known as the Colorado Plateau.

Today, travelers can drive across southern Utah in a matter of hours on paved roads, but there remains no fast route to appreciating the beauty and scope of Utah. Nature, rules here, in a continually metamorphosing landscape whose predominant feature is bare sedimentary rock rearranged by volcanism along deep faults and eroded by water, weather and time.

Within a 250-mile (400-km) radius lie 12 national parks, 14 national monuments, seven tribal parks, 17 wilderness areas, seven state parks and six national forests – such a wealth of extraordinary destinations, it has been dubbed the Grand Circle. Southern Utah is the meeting place of three deserts and a series of progressively higher plateaus on its west side known as the Grand Staircase. East of the Colorado River and above the San Juan River, southeastern Utah is even more remote. This is the heart of Canyon Country, preserved in Canyonlands and Arches National Parks, Glen Canyon National Recreation Area and Monument Valley, centerpiece of the Navajo Nation.

Kanab town.

Interstates 15 and 70 and scenic byways 89, 12, 24, 95 and 191 wrap around this broken country of arches and natural bridges; standing fins of rock; monoclines, anticlines, synclines and laccoliths; collapsed salt valleys; and cool forested volcanic peaks and drifting mesa tablelands. The population is sparse, the few towns of any consequence – St. George, Kanab, Escalante, Torrey, Hanksville, Green River, Moab, Monticello, Blanding and Mexican Hat – many miles apart and determinedly Mormon. It is country difficult to travel through and easy to get lost in, as human travelers, from prehistoric desert nomads to an increasing number of outdoor lovers, can attest. That, for most, is its greatest attraction.

Kolob Canyon.

ZION NATIONAL PARK AND THE ST. GEORGE AREA

Soaring cliffs, sandstone monoliths and narrow canyons are a few of the attractions that lure travelers to this spellbinding red-rock wilderness.

Main attractions

Brigham Young Winter Home
Checkerboard Mesa
Coral Pink Sand Dunes State Park
Kolob Canyons
Maynard Dixon Home and Studio
Pipe Spring National Monument
Riverside Walk (Zion Narrows)
Snow Canyon State Park
Zion Canyon Scenic Drive

Maps on pages 186, 192

Set in the rocky heart of southern Utah's convoluted canyon country, **Zion National Park** ① is nature at its most eloquent, a dramatic juxtaposition of towering sandstone monoliths, narrow slot canyons, fast-flowing water, dense greenery and myriad wildlife. From afar, the park's enormous buttes and domes rise like temples beckoning the faithful. Up close, its sheltering walls offer a protected sanctuary. For the Mormon settlers who came here in the mid-1800s, this seemed to be Zion, "the Heavenly City of God." A national park since 1919, Zion attracts millions of "worshippers" annually who marvel at the extraordinary geology and natural beauty found in these precipitous canyons. Beyond the park there's more natural beauty on display in a series of state parks and across the state line in the Arizona Strip, as well as some fascinating historical Mormon sights.

SOUTH ENTRANCE

The best way to Zion is from the west, via St George and **Hurricane**, along UT 9, following the course of the pretty Virgin River through spick-and-span villages into the park's **South Entrance**, which adjoins the gateway community of **Springdale**. In 2000, the community of Springdale and Zion National Park unveiled an integrated transportation and visitor services plan that has won awards as a model for how public-private partnerships can work elsewhere in the park system. The linchpin of this plan is a two-loop, free shuttle system, usually operating from March through November (plus weekends in February and March, and the last week in December). The **Springdale Line** (aka town shuttle) departs Majestic View Lodge and runs about 3 miles (5 km) to the pedestrian entrance at Zion Canyon Village mall (near the visitor center), stopping at nine locations in Springdale.

Zion National Park.

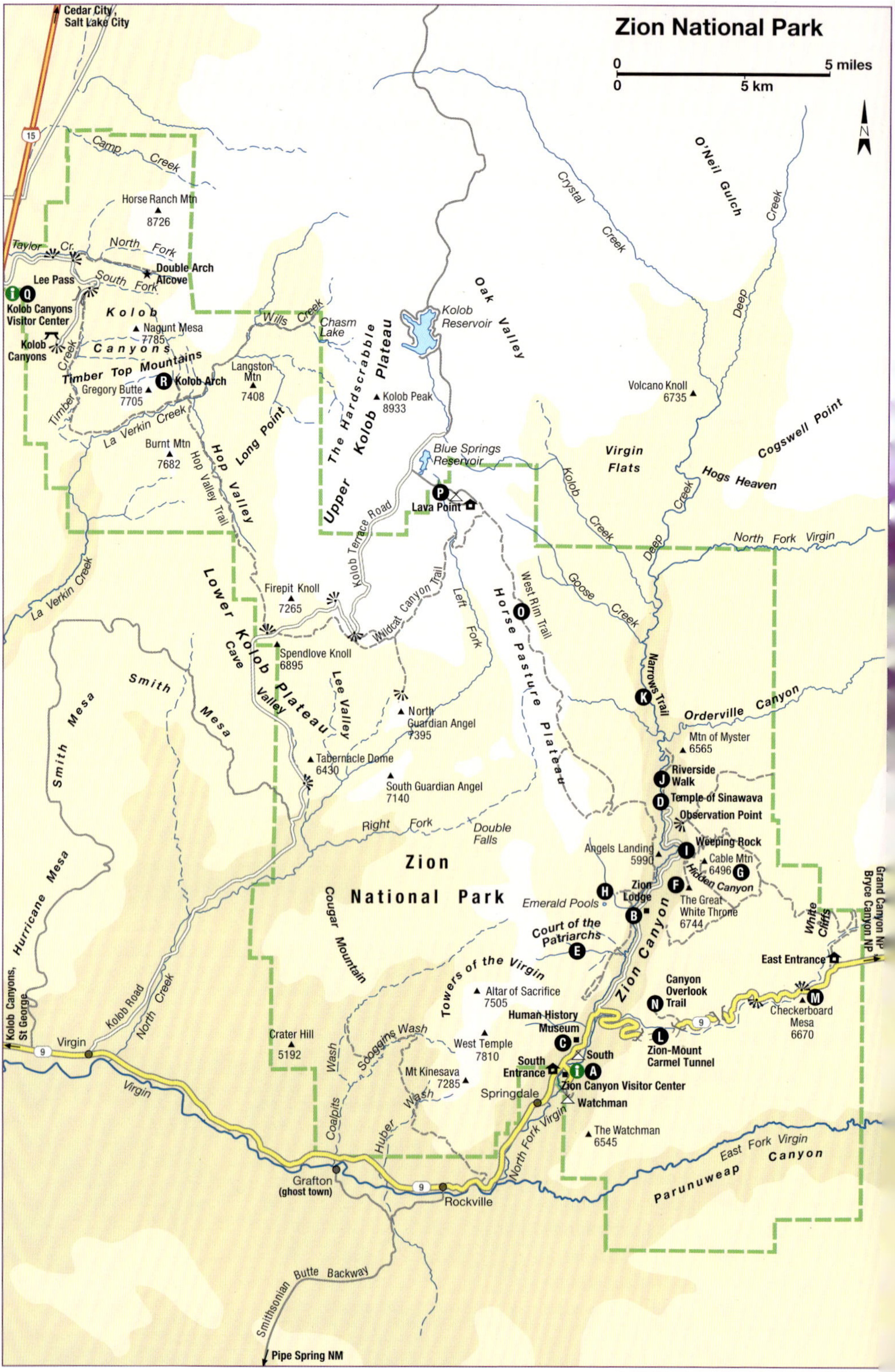
Zion National Park
0 5 miles
0 5 km
N
Cedar City, Salt Lake City
15
Camp Creek
Horse Ranch Mtn 8726
Taylor Cr.
North Fork
Double Arch Alcove
Lee Pass
South Fork
Kolob Canyons Visitor Center
Kolob Canyons
Kolob Canyons
Nagunt Mesa 7785
Wills Creek
Chasm Lake
Timber Top Mountains
Kolob Arch
Gregory Butte 7705
Timber Creek
Langston Mtn 7408
La Verkin Creek
Burnt Mtn 7682
Hop Valley
Hop Valley Trail
Long Point
The Hardscrabble
Upper Kolob Plateau
Kolob Peak 8933
Kolob Reservoir
Oak Valley
Crystal Creek
O'Neil Gulch
Creek
Deep
Volcano Knoll 6735
Cogswell Point
Virgin Flats
Hogs Heaven
Blue Springs Reservoir
Lava Point
Kolob Terrace Road
Kolob Creek
Deep Creek
North Fork Virgin
La Verkin Creek
Firepit Knoll 7265
Lower Kolob Plateau
Wildcat Canyon Trail
Left Fork
West Rim Trail
Horse Pasture Plateau
Goose Creek
Spendlove Knoll 6895
Smith Mesa
Smith Mesa
Smith Mesa
Cave Valley
Lee Valley
North Guardian Angel 7395
Narrows Trail
Orderville Canyon
Mtn of Myster 6565
Tabernacle Dome 6430
South Guardian Angel 7140
Riverside Walk
Temple of Sinawava
Observation Point
Right Fork
Double Falls
Angels Landing 5990
Weeping Rock
Cable Mtn 6496
Hidden Canyon
Zion National Park
Zion Lodge
The Great White Throne 6744
Emerald Pools
Hurricane Mesa
Cougar Mountain
Court of the Patriarchs
Zion Canyon
White Cliffs
Grand Canyon NP
Bryce Canyon NP
East Entrance
Towers of the Virgin
Altar of Sacrifice 7505
Canyon Overlook Trail
Checkerboard Mesa 6670
Kolob Canyons, St George
Kolob Road
North Creek
Human History Museum
9
Virgin
Crater Hill 5192
Scoggins Wash
West Temple 7810
Zion-Mount Carmel Tunnel
South
South Entrance
Zion Canyon Visitor Center
Watchman
Mt Kinesava 7285
Wash
Springdale
Virgin
Coalpits Wash
Huber
North Fork Virgin
The Watchman 6545
East Fork Virgin
Parunuweap Canyon
Grafton (ghost town)
Rockville
Smithsonian Butte Backway
Pipe Spring NM
A B C D E F G H I J K L M N O P Q R

The **Zion Canyon Line** (aka park shuttle) runs 7.7 miles (12.4 km) from Zion Canyon Visitor Center to the top of Zion Canyon at the Temple of Sinawava (45min), via several major trailheads and sights. The 60-seat buses run from around 6am to 9pm and arrive every few minutes during the peak summer season.

It's possible to park at the Zion Canyon Visitor Center, but the lot fills up early (often before 7am in summer). Otherwise, just park at one of several paid lots next to hotels and restaurants in Springdale, hop aboard the Springdale shuttle and go directly to the visitor center to pick up the Zion Canyon shuttle. The virtue of the shuttle system for busy sightseers is that you can effectively enjoy a pleasant, two-hour narrated bus tour of one of the most popular national parks (free with park entrance) and still easily get on and off at major attractions in the canyon to hike popular trails and visit historic Zion Lodge. Best of all, narrow Zion Canyon remains a quiet, idyllic Southwest river canyon, where the emphasis is on appreciating nature, scenery and walking.

ZION CANYON VISITOR CENTER

Zion Canyon Visitor Center Ⓐ (8am–5pm; to 6pm spring and fall, to 7pm in summer; tel: 435-772 3256), just inside the park boundary in the shadow of the **Watchman**, **West Temple** and **Towers of the Virgin** peaks, is sited on the south bank of the East Fork of the Virgin River. The handsome building has been constructed in a harmonious neo-rustic architectural style using native sandstone and heavy timbers, echoing the architecture of the 1930s, much of it carried out by the Civilian Conservation Corps, which built lodges and other infrastructure in Zion and Springdale. Modern touches include passive solar and twin state-of-the-art evaporative cooling towers that make the building a pleasant haven when summer temperatures soar into the triple digits.

From here, the role of water in shaping Zion is obvious. From the

Fact
Zion National Park (www.nps.gov/zion) is open 24 hours, throughout the year, though visitor centers and other facilities tend to open 8am–5pm daily. Admission is $35 per vehicle, valid for seven days (motorbikes $30; individuals hiking or cycling $20; aged 15 and under are free). If visiting more than one national park, buy the Interagency Annual Pass ($80).

ZION: A GEOLOGICAL HISTORY

Dramatically eroded sedimentary rocks are what give Zion its character and have led to its fame. Eight different rock strata may be found in the vicinity, all of which were deposited over a period of 260 million years, as geologic instability and changing climates and topography brought a succession of inland seas, lakes, rivers, streams, volcanic debris and even a dune-filled desert into the region. It is the latter that was responsible for the park's dominant rocks, the sheer, creamy-pink Navajo Sandstone cliffs, which reach a height of 2,200 ft (671 meters). But it's the corrosive power of flash-flooding rivers, ephemeral waterfalls and seeping water that is primarily responsible for the deep canyons found at Zion. Hard though it is to believe, the North Fork of the Virgin River (a modest-sized tributary of the Colorado River), which rises at 9,000 ft (2,750 meters) on the tableland of the Markagunt Plateau just north of Zion, carved Zion Canyon.

Beginning some 15 million years ago, the southern Colorado Plateau underwent a period of violent geologic activity that caused it to break and weather along faults into distinctive plateaus. The Hurricane Fault, a southern spur of the Wasatch Fault, rivals California's San Andreas Fault for activity. Zion is riddled with fractures in the soft rocks, which, combined with water erosion, account for the unusual U shape of its canyons and the great spalling arches (locally called "bridges") in its sheer walls. The Virgin River cut into its course as the land rose around it, scouring soft rock and bearing away sediments. The Colorado and its tributaries remove strata from this portion of the uplifted Colorado Plateau at differing rates, giving the canyon country a colorful, stepped look, referred to as the Grand Staircase.

The reds and pinks (and, occasionally, yellows and browns) found in the rocks at Zion generally result from iron within the rock, which has been washed through by percolating groundwater. Dark streaking, as on the Altar of Sacrifice, occurs when water falling over sheer precipices leaches minerals from vegetation or caprock. Weathering of organic material on rock faces also causes shiny "desert varnish," fixed by bacteria on the face of the rock, perhaps the most dramatic of all rock coatings in the Southwest.

> **Tip**
>
> Note that Zion Canyon Scenic Drive is closed to private vehicles (but not bicycles) when park shuttles are operating (UT 9, Kolob Terrace Road, and Kolob Canyons Scenic Drive remain open to cars year round).

riverside patio, you can listen to the river burbling over rocks and trickling through irrigation ditches while you plan your visit to the park using outdoor interpretive panels or listen to a ranger talk. Inside the building, short films give an overview of the park, and the large bookstore sells maps, books and other interpretive materials. Staffed kiosks offer registration for Zion Lodge and backcountry permits, required for overnight backpacking trips in the park and backcountry hikes in such places as the Subway and Mystery Canyon. Canyoneering, a sport that involves rappelling into narrow slot canyons, is wildly popular in Zion, and you may have difficulty getting a permit for the best-known hikes if you don't reserve ahead of time. Back-country hikers in Zion can now reserve and pay for permits and camp sites on the park website (www.nps.gov/zion) but permits must be picked up in person at Zion Canyon Visitor Center Wilderness Desk or the Kolob Canyons Visitor Center (see below).

Checkerboard Mesa.

PARK ACCOMMODATION

There are two developed campgrounds in Zion Canyon itself. The 176-site **Watchman Campground** (open year-round) and 117-site **South Campground** (open Mar–Oct) just beyond the visitor center. Sites at both can be reserved by calling tel: 877-444 6777 or visiting www.recreation.gov. Reservations are required since the campground is full nearly every night in the summer. The primitive 6-site **Lava Point Campground** next to the West Rim Trail on Kolob Terrace Road is open only May to September, has no water, and sites can also be reserved (two weeks in advance; same contacts). The log-framed **Zion Lodge** Ⓑ (tel: 435-772 7700 ; www.zionlodge.com) in Zion Canyon was built in the 1920s by the now-defunct Utah Parks Company to accommodate well-heeled park visitors and is now on the National Register of Historic Places. With its ice-cream fountain, pleasant gift shop, manicured lawns, shady trees and woodsy cabins, it's a good spot to take a breather or get something to eat or drink. Just don't expect to stay here without reservations; bookings must usually be secured a year in advance. Most people spend the night in one of the many inns, motels and bed-and-breakfasts in pretty little Springdale, which also has an excellent assortment of restaurants, from juice bars and espresso joints to steak houses and nouvelle cuisine.

ZION CANYON

The first shuttle stop after the visitor center is the **Zion Human History Museum** ⒞ (9am–5pm, to 7pm in summer), housed in the old park visitor center. The museum tells the human story of Zion from the Virgin Anasazi and Kaibab Paiutes who used the park seasonally to Mormon pioneers like the Behunin, Heaps and Rolfe families who first homesteaded the canyon, across from Zion Lodge, in 1862. The 6-mile (10-km) Scenic Drive up the canyon proper begins at the stone bridge where Pine Creek joins the North Fork of the Virgin River (aka Canyon Junction – shuttles only stop here on the way back), then heads north, paralleling the tree-lined banks of the Virgin River all the way to the amphitheater of the **Temple of Sinawava** ⒟ and the popular **Riverside Walk**. Within this short drive are the **Court of the Patriarchs** ⒠, the **Great White Throne** ⒡ and **Cable Mountain** ⒢, as well as shady hiking trails surrounded by dripping rocks and colorful hanging plants. From here, you can set out on longer hikes into the high country, or simply dream away the day deep in the canyon paddling in the river shallows.

Three short hiking trails – to **Emerald Pools** ⒣ (2 miles/3 km) and **Weeping Rock** ⒤ (1½ miles/2 km) – meander through side canyons populated by singleleaf ash, manzanita, cliff rose and Gambel oak. Here, contact between the porous Navajo Sandstone and impervious Kayenta river sandstones and shales below it has created seeping rocks, known as springlines, which are home to delightful "hanging gardens" of mosses, ferns, monkeyflowers and columbines, as well as the park's unique Zion snail. Another

Three sandstone peaks in the west of Zion Canyon known as the Three Patriarchs.

leitmotiv of the park is sacred datura or jimsonweed, known locally as Zion lily, a poisonous, white-trumpeted flower that opens at night along waysides. Other trails, most of them found close to Zion Lodge, lead to famous landmarks, such as the **Court of the Patriarchs** (300 ft/90 meters), **Angels Landing** (5 miles/8 km) and **Hidden Canyon** (2 miles/3 km, between Cable Mountain and the Great White Throne). Eight-mile (13-km) **Observation Point Trail** skirts the base of Cable Mountain before climbing through woodlands, offering stunning views of the Great White Throne, Cable Mountain, the West Rim, Angels Landing and Zion Canyon.

ZION NARROWS

At the end of Zion Canyon Scenic Drive, beyond the Temple of Sinawava, the walls of the canyon tighten to form the **Zion Narrows**, a stunning slot canyon through the sandstone carved by the North Fork of the Virgin River (2,000 ft/600 meters high and in places only 20 ft/6 meters wide). Hiking up the shallow stream at least part of **Riverside Walk** Ⓙ (2.2 miles/3.5 km return) is a highlight of the park. Serious hikers can extend the trek up to 9.4 miles/15.1 km (round-trip) up to Big Spring or Orderville Canyon on the **Narrows Trail** Ⓚ. In spring, when snowmelt is greatest, or during summer rainstorms, don't even think of wading up here – during heavy rainstorms, flash floods may funnel through the canyon at the speed of a runaway train, destroying everything in their path. Plan to make the trip in dry summer months, and even if you are just wading the southern section from the end of Riverside Walk, get a weather forecast before starting out. The Narrows Trail is in the riverbed, so be prepared to stay wet for hours in a chilly, sunless environment. Don't try to do the whole hike in one day – wading through water for eight hours is grueling. Reserve a campsite inside the canyon and enjoy the hike.

THE EAST RIM

It's a 10-mile (16km) scenic drive to the East Rim of Zion via the **Zion-Mount Carmel Highway** (UT 9), which follows Pine Creek, a tributary of the Virgin River. The road climbs in dramatic zigzag fashion through the canyon until it enters the 1-mile-long (1.6-km) **Zion-Mount Carmel Tunnel** Ⓛ, built in 1930 to shorten the route between Zion and Bryce Canyon and Grand Canyon National Parks. (Note: There are strictly enforced size restrictions on vehicles using the tunnel, and no bikes or pedestrians are allowed. Check with the park in advance.) Just before you reach the tunnel, the road passes beneath a huge blind alcove known as the Great Arch of Zion.

On the other side of the tunnel, you climb to an elevation of 7,000 ft (2,000 meters), where the highway passes through a landscape of marvelously eroded formations, which are exactly what they look like: "petrified" sand

Sonoran Desert Tortoise in Snow Canyon State Park.

dunes. The most distinctive is spectacular **Checkerboard Mesa** ⓜ, a huge, creamy giant with crosshatched surfaces caused by horizontal cross-bedding in the dunes and later deepening of vertical fractures by water erosion. If you have time (and can find a parking space), hike the **Canyon Overlook Trail** ⓝ (1 mile/1.6 km round-trip) next to the East Portal of the Zion-Mount Carmel Tunnel. It sits directly above the Great Arch of Zion and offers an unusual view of Zion Canyon and a superb introduction to some of Zion's key natural features.

KOLOB TERRACE

The central Kolob Terrace area of the park is accessible via the Kolob Terrace Road that heads north from the town of Virgin (15 miles/24 km west of Zion Canyon Visitor Center). The 22-mile (35-km) drive up to the Lava Point Campground offers mesmerizing views, especially of the canyon formed by the Left Fork of North Creek, aka "the Subway". A more strenuous way to get there is the one-way 13-mile (21-km) **West Rim Trail** ⓞ, which links Zion Canyon with **Lava Point** ⓟ through breathtaking mountainous country. Extend the trip by taking Wildcat Canyon Trail into the beautifully carved Finger Canyons of the Kolob Plateau.

KOLOB CANYONS

Kolob Canyons is the remote northwestern section of Zion National Park, accessed via Exit 40 off I-15. Check in at **Kolob Canyons Visitor Center** ⓠ (daily 8am–5pm; tel: 435-772 3256) before taking the 5-mile (8-km) scenic drive through the folded and eroded vermilion-colored cliffs. A lot of people miss visiting Kolob Canyons because of its distance from the main park, but there are some fascinating hikes in this section, including a strenuous, 14-mile (23-km) round-trip to 310-ft (94-meter) **Kolob Arch** ⓡ, the world's longest natural arch.

THE ARIZONA STRIP

Base yourself in Springdale for a few days and explore southwestern Utah's

Waterfall at Temple of Sinawava.

ⓞ ZION'S PARKITECTURE

Almost as memorable as Zion's naturally sculpted cliffs and canyons are the many examples of the rustic architecture preserved in the park. This building style dominated park architecture in the 1920s and 1930s and required buildings and other man-made structures to match their surroundings in scale, materials and color. The 1930 Pine Creek Bridge, for example, is an acknowledged work of art made entirely of Navajo Sandstone with a cemented rubblestone core and hand-hewn sandstone slabs reflecting all the colors of Zion – tan, brown, pink, red, purple, even green.

Much of this attractive "parkitecture" was built by young recruits in the Civilian Conservation Corps, organized during the Great Depression as a government-sponsored labor force. This was more than a make-work program designed to assist unemployed youth. The young men of "Roosevelt's Tree Army" embodied a resurgence of America's pioneer ethic and native optimism. In Zion, the Corps constructed trails, houses and park buildings and cut and shaped stone at a quarry a mile west of Springdale. They also built and maintained irrigation ditches, providing a visible link between the pioneers and the young men who sought to emulate them years later.

scenic byways and backways. The unpaved **Smithsonian Butte National Back Country Byway** (9.25 miles/ 15 km) links Rockville with UT 59 on in the **Arizona Strip**, passing **Grafton** on the south side of the river, a ghost town that was abandoned after the Great Flood of 1861–62. For years, Rockville residents, descendants of the original settlers, looked after the town and farmed adjoining fields. The whole town is now preserved as a historic site. Roadside interpretive signs can be found opposite the townsite, on UT 9, just before you get to Rockville.

The scenic backway offers an excellent shortcut to the Arizona Strip, which gets its name from the narrow swath of Arizona that borders Utah between the Grand Canyon and the Vermilion Cliffs. Drive east on UT 59 into Arizona, where the highway changes number to AZ 389. After 30 minutes, you'll reach **Pipe Spring National Monument** ❷ (406 Pipe Springs Rd, Fredonia, AZ; tel: 928-643 7105; www.nps.gov/pisp; visitor center daily 8am–5pm in summer, 8.30am–4.30pm in winter, tours every 30 minutes in summer), one of those small but fascinating units that abound in the park system but often get overlooked. Prehistoric Virgin Anasazi people, Kaibab Paiutes (whose reservation surrounds Pipe Spring), and early western settlers were all attracted to this spot because of the natural springs that come bubbling up the Sevier Fault in the Vermilion Cliffs. Pipe Spring is a fortified ranch built by the Mormons in 1870 to accommodate the Church's burgeoning cattle herds. During the 1880s, it served as a hideout for the wives of polygamous elders in nearby communities like Fredonia and Kanab, which were under surveillance by the federal government.

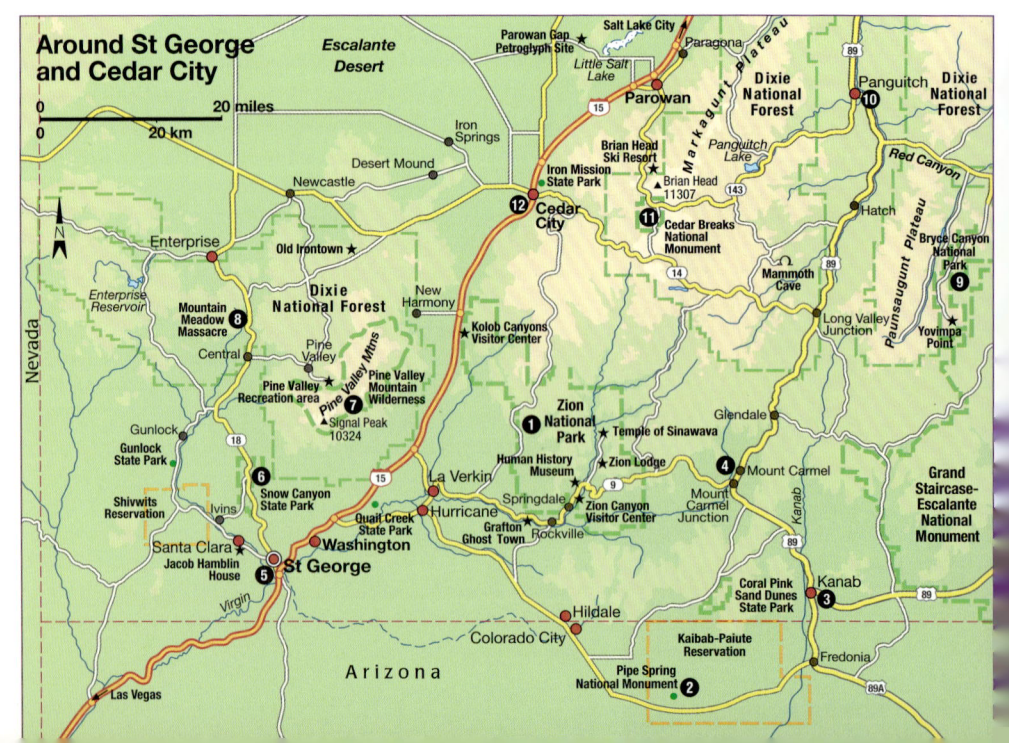

The fort and its outlying cabins, corrals, pens and ponds have been preserved very much as they were in their heyday, when Anson Winsor and his wife constructed the two modest stone houses that were dubbed Winsor Castle (a punning reference to Winsor's British roots). Pipe Spring served as a base for John Wesley Powell, the Colorado River explorer, during his survey of the region in 1871-72. Descendants of the original Kaibab Paiute and Anglo settlers still live in the area and maintain a strong attachment to Pipe Spring. The administrative offices of the Kaibab Band of Paiutes is across the road, and the Indigenous group operates a small campground next to the park, holds a powwow in October, and offers guided hiking tours of rock art sites. The group and the National Park Service are also involved in a joint partnership: a museum in the park visitor center containing 12 exhibits interpreting the Ancestral Pueblo, Kaibab Paiute and Mormon cultures.

Directly ahead is the AZ 389/US 89 junction in the tiny Mormon hamlet of **Fredonia**, which has a smattering of homestyle restaurants and motels. From here, you can either drive south to the Kaibab Plateau to visit the North Rim of the Grand Canyon or head north on US 89 to Kanab, just over the border back in Utah.

KANAB AND AROUND

Kanab ❸, at the crossroads of US 89 and 89A, is a fine place to spend the night, have a meal, and explore the surrounding canyons, which, for decades, have been used as backdrops in the movies. The Glen Canyon Conservancy, which supports public lands such as adjoining Grand Staircase-Escalante National Monument, operates the **Kanab Visitor Center** (745 East US 89; tel: 435-644-1300; www.canyon-conservancy.org; Tue–Sat 9am–4pm), where you can get information on the area. Return to Zion by heading north on US 89, turning left onto UT 9 at Mount Carmel and driving into the park through the East Entrance. Just south of Mount Carmel is a turnoff for **Coral Pink Sand Dunes State Park** (Sand Dunes Rd, off UT 43; tel: 435-648 2800; https://stateparks.utah.gov/parks/coral-pink; daily, sunrise–sunset), a 3,730-acre (1,510-hectare) expanse of rust-colored dunes deposited by winds funneled at great speed through a notch in the mountains. The park is a favorite with drivers of motorcycles and ATVs. A section is reserved for hikers, though in summer the dunes are sizzling hot.

Blink-and-you'll-miss-it **Mount Carmel** ❹ was a favorite of famed western artist Maynard Dixon, who, in the 1940s, spent his summers here, painting the Grand Staircase and other colorful formations that are now called Maynard Dixon Country. Between May and October each year, volunteers offer guided tours of the rustic **Maynard Dixon Home and Studio** (2200 State St; tel: 435-648 2653; www.thunderbird-foundation.com; mid-Apr to mid-Nov daily 10am–5pm; tours by appointment). The foundation also sponsors an annual three-day gala featuring 15 to 20 artists and an art sale at Dixon's former home.

AROUND ST. GEORGE

Kanab is an excellent base for day trips to sites on the east side of the Markagunt Plateau, such as Zion,

> **Tip**
>
> Docents at the main LDS sites in St George tend to be friendly, older Mormons, volunteering to fulfil their "second mission" – designed to bring converts into the Church. If you already have a religious affiliation, be sure to say so, to avoid any efforts at proselytizing.

Coral Pink Sand Dunes State Park.

Pipe Spring, Cedar Breaks, Bryce Canyon and Grand Staircase-Escalante National Monument. More convenient to the I-15 corridor, though, is **St. George** ❺, southwestern Utah's largest town and, at two hours from Las Vegas and four hours from Salt Lake City, the area's fastest growing community. Founded in 1861 by members of the Cotton Mission and known as Utah's Dixie because of its moderate winters, St. George was chosen by Brigham Young as the site of his **Winter Home** (67 W. 200 North; tel: 435-680 2283; Mon–Sat 9am–6pm, Sun noon–6pm; free). Here, Young oversaw construction of the dazzlingly white **St. George Temple** and the sandstone **St. George Tabernacle**, both completed in the 1870s by workers who, incidentally, were fed by meat and cheese from Pipe Spring's dairy herds. Only Mormons in good standing may enter the Temple, but the adjoining **Visitors' Center** is open to all and is a good place to find out more about the LDS faith (490 S. 300 East; daily 9am–9pm; tel: 435-673 5181; free). You can also take a guided tour of the Tabernacle (Mon–Sat 9am–6pm, Sun noon–6pm; tel: 435-680 2283).

Artifacts from the town's pioneer days are exhibited at the Daughters of Utah Pioneers' **McQuarrie Memorial Museum** (145 N. 100 East; tel: 435-628 7274; https://dupstgeorge.org; Mon, Tue, Thu–Sat 10am–5pm, 11am–3pm in Dec; free). The museum, Winter Home, Temple, Tabernacle and other historic buildings are within walking distance of **Ancestor Square** in the town center. Ancestor Square includes several historic buildings that have been converted to restaurants, stores and businesses. You may also enjoy strolling around the Dixie Technical College (https://dixietech.edu) campus, south of Main. Like Southern Utah University in Cedar City, it is a four-year college and hosts cultural events, including a popular arts festival. Located on the northern edge of the Mojave Desert (with its characteristic Joshua trees), St. George gets pretty hot in summer, but with 10 golf courses, a premium store outlet and other attractions, it's a good base for visitors.

If you have time, take the drive west of St. George to several important natural and cultural attractions. In the pastoral, fruit-growing town of **Santa Clara**, you can visit the **Jacob Hamblin Home** (3325 Hamblin Dr; tel: 435-673 2161; Mon–Sat 9am–6pm, Sun noon–6pm; free), built by the famous Mormon missionary and friend of John Wesley Powell, in 1862. A 24-mile (37-km) loop from St. George takes you to **Snow Canyon State Park** ❻ (1002 N. Snow Canyon Rd, Ivins; tel: 435-628 2255; https://stateparks.utah.gov/parks/snow-canyon; daily 6am–10pm), which combines red Navajo Sandstone and lava formations in a unique setting. The surreal landscape around Snow Canyon has been a favorite with filmmakers for years. John Wayne made

Brigham Young's winter home.

ZION NATIONAL PARK AND THE ST. GEORGE AREA | 195

several movies here. Camping, picnicking and horseback riding are available; several backcountry hikes offer an excellent opportunity to observe specially adapted desert plants and animals, such as desert tortoises, a rarely seen endangered species found in the hot, dry country around St. George.

The lava formations in Snow Canyon came from the volcano that built adjoining 10,324-ft (3,147-meter) **Pine Valley Mountain** ❼, the imposing peak that looms over St. George. **Pine Valley Recreation Area** in Dixie National Forest is a good place to escape the sizzling summer temperatures at lower elevations and has excellent cross-country skiing in winter. You can take longer hikes and backpack in the adjoining 50,000-acre (20,000-hectare) **Pine Valley Mountain Wilderness**.

MOUNTAIN MEADOWS MONUMENT

UT 18 continues all the way to **Gunlock Reservoir**, a popular fishing spot. Before you get there, the highway passes through a large, quiet grassy valley where the wind always seems to be moaning. This is **Mountain Meadows** ❽ (https://mmmf.org) where the worst (and least talked about) atrocity in Mormon history took place in 1857, at a time when tensions between Mormons and the federal government were causing widespread anxiety. Fear turned to tragedy when a party of emigrants bound for California passed through southern Utah and harassed Mormon farmers and Native Americans. In anger, a group of Paiutes and Mormons led by John D. Lee cornered the emigrants in Mountain Meadows, lured them out with a promise of safe passage, and then massacred 120 people, sparing only the youngest children. After evading capture for 20 years, Lee was forced by the LDS Church to surrender to authorities, and was tried, found guilty, and executed atop his own coffin at the site of the massacre. A somber granite monument records the names of the emigrants who perished.

St. George Utah Temple.

⊘ ZION FLORA AND FAUNA

Four different life zones are to be found in the 3,650–8,725-ft (1,100–2,650-meter) elevations at Zion, encompassing desert, riparian, woodland and coniferous forest. In the low, dry areas of the canyons, heavy-fruited prickly pear cactus is found alongside desert residents, such as whip-tailed and desert spiny lizards, slow-moving chuckwallas and, occasionally, western rattlesnakes.

The river is a perfect refuge when temperatures reach 100°F (38°C) or higher in summer. Throngs of Fremont cottonwoods, box elders, willows and velvet ash crowd its banks, sharing the location with bank beavers, gnatcatchers and insects, as well as footsore hikers. The high country supports ponderosa pine, Rocky Mountain juniper and sagebrush, as well as oak, Douglas fir, quaking aspen and numerous wildflowers.

At twilight, you may glimpse a coyote, mule deer or bighorn sheep. Animals like mountain lions and bobcats are rarely encountered. Your companions throughout much of the park will be squirrels, camprobbing ringtails and noisy ravens and pinyon jays, whose chatter usually drowns out the melodic descant sonata of canyon wrens and other songbirds. During the summer rainy season, the full impact of water on rock is evident. Torrents pour off vertical rock faces in magnificent waterfalls, and the swollen Virgin River speeds noisily over and around boulders.

Bryce Canyon National Park.

BRYCE CANYON AND THE CEDAR CITY AREA

Erosion has sculpted a landscape of knobs, "hoodoos," and desert scenery in a corner of Utah where visitors also find such unexpected attractions as a ski resort and Shakespearean festival.

A geologic fantasyland of multi-colored spires, natural bridges, gravity-defying arches, precariously balanced rocks and sky-filled windows carved deeply into the soft, pastel-hued cliffs of the Paunsaugunt Plateau, **Bryce Canyon National Park** ⑨ is part of southern Utah you'll long remember. To the Paiute people who have lived in the region for centuries, the remarkable formations of Bryce Canyon came into being in legendary times, when the animal people so displeased powerful Coyote that he turned them to stone. Ebenezer Bryce, a Scottish Mormon who homesteaded the Paria Valley below the cliffs in 1875–76, is said to have been more prosaic about the series of carved amphitheaters towering above him, complaining that it was "a hell of a place to lose a cow!" In fact, Bryce Canyon can be explained by the weathering action of water and repeated freezing and thawing on the east-facing edge of a lofty plateau. Beyond the park you'll find equally stunning landscapes in Red Canyon and Cedar Breaks on the wild and beautiful Markagunt Plateau, while Cedar City is enlivened by its student population, art museum, and surprisingly rich spread of sports and cultural festivals.

The Fairyland Loop in Bryce Canyon National Park.

BRYCE CANYON GEOLOGY

The Pink Cliffs of Bryce Canyon form the sixth and uppermost "step" of the Grand Staircase, which ascends in color-coded formations – oldest to youngest – from the Grand Canyon to the Paunsaugunt Plateau, more than 100 miles (160km) and an ascent of 5,000ft (1,500 meters). The rocks, which were pushed up, cracked and broken into plateaus by faults 15 million years ago, originated as sediments laid down over millions of years, when a succession of inland seas, lakes,

◎ Main attractions
Brian Head Ski Resort
Bryce Canyon National Park
Cedar Breaks National Monument
Cedar City
Parowan Gap Petroglyph Site
Red Canyon
Utah Shakespeare Festival

Maps on pages 192 and 198

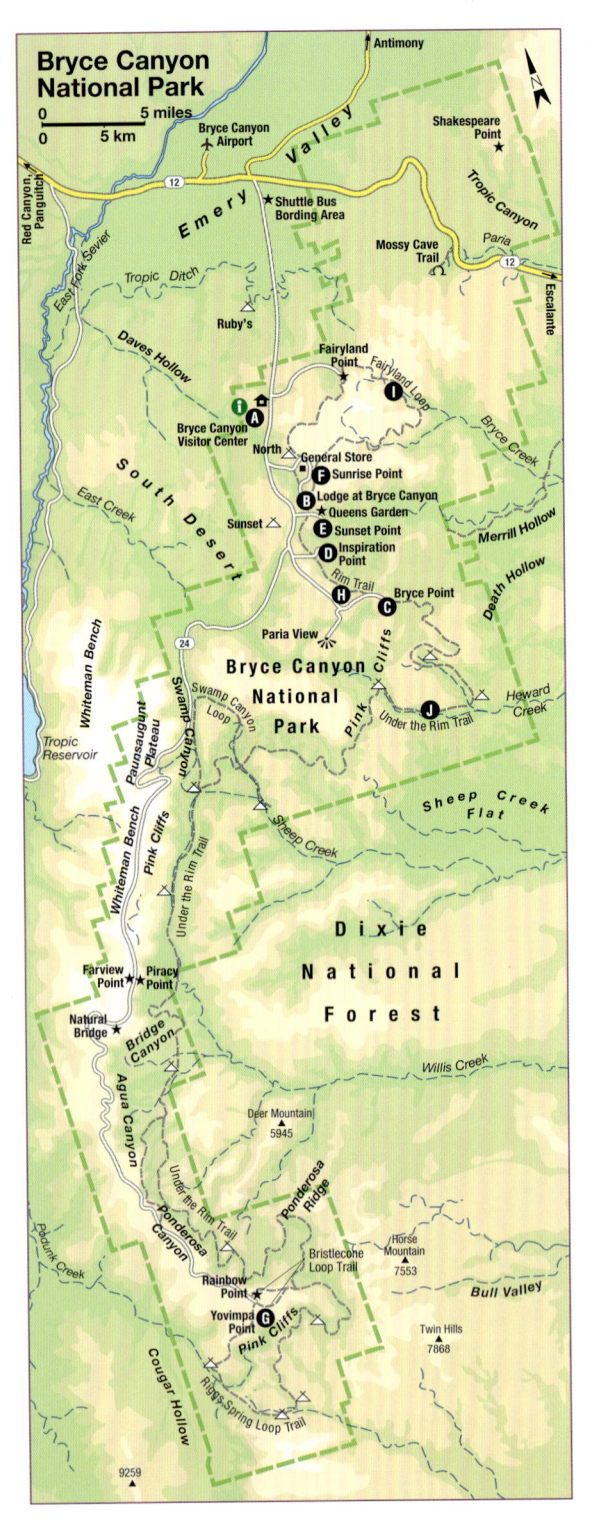

rivers, streams, and even a dune-filled desert covered the Southwest. Over time, the sediments hardened into rock, colored by manganese and iron. Today, weathering has oxidized these minerals into the blues, reds, purples, and yellows that bathe the rocks in a wash of pastel hues.

Bryce's Pink Cliffs are the youngest sedimentary rocks in the area, the result of silt, sand, and the limey skeletons of creatures that lived in the ephemeral freshwater lakes that formed here 55 million years ago, just before geologic activity began pushing up the Colorado Plateau. Forty million years later, when southern Utah began to split into its characteristic plateaus, these rocks, known as the Claron Formation, were exposed to the action of water speeding down the eastern edge of the Paunsaugunt Plateau. In what is today a semi-arid country, there is an irony in the role water has played in creating the eerie "hoodoos" and other "rock-candy" formations that crowd the park's amphitheaters.

EXPLORING THE PARK

Plan to spend at least a day here. Between April and October, large shuttle buses make it easy to get around what is usually a very crowded park, where spaces in small parking lots are often at a premium during peak hours. The **Bryce Canyon Shuttle** runs from Bryce Canyon City and stops at all the main viewpoints in the main canyon in around 50 minutes, beginning with the Visitor Center and including Inspiration Point, Sunset Point, and Bryce Lodge.

The shuttle is voluntary but offers numerous benefits. For example, driving into Bryce has become expensive ($35 per car). If you are alone, you can almost halve that cost and see the park more efficiently by taking the shuttle from the Park and Ride facility at Bryce Canyon City (Stop 1), or at several other stops in town (including Ruby's Inn) – you can also park at the Visitor Center

BRYCE CANYON AND THE CEDAR CITY AREA

(Stop 6) then take the bus, but you'll pay full price. The shuttles are free with your entrance fee or park pass.

The stone-and-timber **Bryce Canyon Visitor Center** Ⓐ (tel: 435-834 5322; daily mid-May–Sept 8am–8pm; Oct–early Nov and mid-Mar–early May 8am–6pm; mid-Nov–early Mar 8am–4.30pm) is an airy space that evokes the rustic park architecture of the 1920s. The park museum inside has exhibits on the natural and cultural history of Bryce, and there is a large bookstore. Rangers at the information desk will help you get the most out of your trip.

BRYCE CANYON ACCOMMODATION

Bryce has two campgrounds. The largest and busiest, **North Campground**, is entirely on a reservation system in summer (late May–Sept; first come, first served rest of year). Its 100 RV and tent sites can be reserved through www.recreation.gov up to six months ahead. If you're in a tent, the 100-site **Sunset Campground** (mid-Apr–Oct) east of the viewpoint of the same name, is much quieter because noisy RV generators are restricted (neither campground has hookups). Sunset is on a first-come, first-served basis, so try to arrive early to snag a site. If you plan on hiking, this campground offers easy access to the Sunset Viewpoint trailheads, across the road. The **Lodge at Bryce Canyon** Ⓑ (tel: 435-297 2757; www.brycecanyonforever.com; Apr–Nov), built in the 1920s by the Utah Parks Company, offers a step back into the past that may be worth the splurge. The dark, woodsy lodge with the wavy-shingled roof was designed by railroad architect Gilbert Stanley Underwood, who was responsible for rustic "Parkitecture" lodges in what were then the new parks of Zion, Cedar Breaks, and Bryce Canyon. Of these only 114-room Bryce Canyon Lodge survives. It is on the Register of Historic Places. Book at least six months ahead (preferably a year ahead); this lodge is very popular. Even if you're not staying here, take a look inside the lobby. You'll get a feel for what traveling used to be like in the golden age of tourism. The restaurant is a good stop for lunch if you're here for only a day.

BRYCE CANYON SCENIC DRIVE

The 18-mile (29km) scenic drive that runs north-south through the park follows the edge of the 8,000ft (2,438-meter) plateau through forests of ponderosa pine and summer wildflowers, such as Indian paintbrush, skyrocket gilia, and penstemon. The first 3 miles (4.8km) of the road take in the **Bryce Amphitheater**, and the four most popular overlooks in the park: **Bryce Point** Ⓒ, **Inspiration Point** Ⓓ, **Sunset Point** Ⓔ, and **Sunrise Point** Ⓕ. Longer visits take in the full length of the main road (aka Southern Scenic Drive) to Rainbow Point (at the end), Natural Bridge, and other viewpoints. The highest spot in the park is **Yovimpa Point** Ⓖ (9,115ft/2,778

> ### ⓘ Fact
> Bryce Canyon National Park (www.nps.gov/brca) is open 24 hours year-round. The visitor center and other facilities tend to open from 8am daily, with closing ranging between 4.30 and 8pm depending on the season. Admission is $35 per vehicle, valid for seven days (motorbikes $30; individuals hiking or cycling $20; aged 15 and under are free). If visiting more than one national park, buy the Interagency Annual Pass ($80).

Red Canyon, Dixie National Forest.

meters), just before Rainbow Point. Here, the ponderosa pine gives way to subalpine conifers such as white fir and blue spruce. Rare bristlecone pines – some more than 1,000 years old – grow in exposed areas. The pleasant 1-mile (1.6km) Bristlecone Loop trail meanders through the trees to the overlook at Rainbow Point.

In the evenings, you will encounter mule deer grazing by the roadside; during the day, rodents such as ground squirrels and prairie dogs are commonly sighted. Utah prairie dogs, an endangered species, are protected here but rarely seen. Out of sight but not out of mind are the shy mountain lions that prey on deer – their numbers diminished by destruction of habitat, but their presence still felt on the plateau. The skies are patrolled by red-tailed hawks and ravens, whose languid, circuitous flight is in sharp contrast to the quick, darting forays of cliff swallows. In the forests, jays jabber loquaciously from the pines, their iridescent blue feathers flashing among green needles.

The wildlife on the canyon bottom varies considerably from that on the moister, cooler rim. Pinyon and juniper trees grow alongside sagebrush, clinging tenaciously to pockets of soil in bare rock ledges. Runoff comes and goes swiftly here; there is little to hold it as it courses down steep precipices toward the Paria River, and thence to the Colorado River.

HIKING TRAILS

Even if you have only a short time, get out of your car and hike down into the amphitheaters along one of the superb intersecting trails, which start from the overlooks. The easy 11-mile (18km) **Rim Trail** links the scenic overlooks in the Bryce Canyon Amphitheater. The strenuous 8-mile (13km) **Fairyland Loop** has views into Fairyland and Campbell Canyons near the park entrance. From Sunrise Point, you can descend the cliffs 320ft (98 meters) on the easy 1.4-mile (2km) round-trip **Queen's Garden Trail** and, if you wish, join up with the moderately strenuous **Navajo Loop Trail** (1.3 miles/2km round-trip), which descends

Natural bridge rock formation in Bryce Canyon National Park.

steeply from Sunset Point 520ft (160 meters) and proceeds through the clustered formations of Silent City. Hiking through these strange carved rocks is one of life's great novelties. You won't soon forget the sight of an out-of-place Douglas fir yearning toward the sunlight from a narrow corridor on Navajo Loop Trail, nor should you miss taking a guided moonlit hike among these phantasmagoric rocks, if you visit at the right time of year. If you want a longer hike, the strenuous, 5.5-mile (9km) **Peekaboo Loop** starts at Bryce Point and meanders through the amphitheater's otherworldly formations. For overnight trips, the **Under-the-Rim Trail** ❾ runs 23 miles (37km) from Bryce Point to Yovimpa Point through some of the most remote and wildlife-rich country in the park. Be sure to consult the park rangers before attempting long backcountry hikes. Permits are required for overnight backpacking.

RED CANYON

Leaving Bryce, head west on UT 12 through **Red Canyon**, Bryce's pretty little sister. **Dixie National Forest** runs a **visitor center** (tel: 435-676 2676; www.fs.usda.gov/dixie; Fri–Mon 9am–6pm, Tue–Thu 10am–3pm) here and the Red Canyon Campground (first come, first served) makes a decent alternative for overnight campers if Bryce Canyon is full. There are many other hiking and camping options in the 2-million-acre (800,000-hectare) Dixie National Forest surrounding Bryce. **Panguitch** ❿, a few miles north of the US 89/UT 12 junction, meaning "big fish" in Paiute, has gas, food, lodging, and other visitor services in its pleasant downtown. Continue west on UT 143 to reach several campgrounds and lakeside resorts in the high country.

If you're headed for I-15, an even better idea is to drive south on UT 89, then west on UT 14, a beautiful drive at any time of year, across the 11,000ft (3,350-meter) -high Markagunt Plateau. The Markagunt Plateau is where southern Utahans come to escape the heat, and you'll find many attractions, including resorts, campgrounds, lodges, lakes, trails, and viewpoints.

> **Tip**
> Cedar Breaks National Monument is open year-round, but access varies by season – snow can block roads between December and May. Cross-country skiers and snowshoers can follow two marked trails through the park in winter and backcountry areas above the rim are open as well.

Cedar Breaks National Monument.

CEDAR BREAKS NATIONAL MONUMENT AND ENVIRONS

The undisputed highlight is **Cedar Breaks National Monument** ⓫ (4730 UT 148, Brian Head; tel: 435-586 9451; www.nps.gov/cebr; new visitor center expected to open in 2023). This tiny gem, just off UT 14 on UT 148, preserves another highly eroded amphitheater of Claron Formation rock, but because the amphitheater is deeper, the coloration somewhat different, and descent into it discouraged, it complements a trip to Bryce rather than takes the place of it.

Cedar Breaks is best known for its extravagant wildflower displays, including lupine sneezeweed, yarrow and sunflowers, which begin adorning the meadows in July, shortly after the park reopens. Summer brings a rush of wildlife, which ranges from scurrying pikas, chipmunks, squirrels, and marmots to stealthy mountain lions and coyotes. Mule deer browse on lush high-country meadows. Ravens and violet-green swallows swoop past colorful cliffs, and chattery Clark's nutcrackers and Steller's jays feast on the seasonal bounty of pine nuts.

The Historic LDS Rock Church in Cedar City.

A 5-mile (8km) scenic drive follows the rim of the amphitheater and has numerous overlooks. **Alpine Pond Trail** (1 mile/1.5km long) takes you through a cool, moist forest of spruce and fir. A completely different hike skirts the rim of the amphitheater past a large stand of thousand-year-old bristlecone pines clinging precariously to bare rock at **Spectra Point**, and out along the **Wasatch Ramparts**. The park's clean, quiet, 25-site Point Supreme Campground is a real find. Nicely screened sites in the conifers open onto high-country meadows heavily used by wildlife. A truly idyllic spot.

In summer, you can continue north on UT 148 to UT 143, which leads to **Brian Head**. At 11,307ft (3,446 meters), this is the highest point on the plateau. In winter, **Brian Head Ski Resort** (tel: 435-677 2035; www.brianhead.com) makes an excellent, little-known alternative to Sundance and other ski resorts in the Wasatch Mountains east of Salt Lake City. Brian Head is the highest ski resort in Utah and has 71 runs, eight chair lifts, and a snowboard park. It offers a wide array of condos, hotel rooms, and restaurants and is open year-round. UT 143 continues 14 miles (23km) to the sleepy Mormon community of **Parowan**, the oldest town in southern Utah. From here, take I-15 south 18 miles (29km) to Cedar City.

CEDAR CITY AND ENVIRONS

Three and a half hours south of Salt Lake City, **Cedar City** ⓬ is home to the award-winning **Utah Shakespeare Festival** (351 W Center St; tel: 800-752 9849; www.bard.org), held over a nine-week period each summer in a specially built Elizabethan theater on the campus of Southern Utah University. The Shakespearean Festival is only one of the many events that have transformed this clean-cut Mormon town into a popular tourist destination. The self-described Festival City USA is also host to the Utah Midsummer Renaissance Faire (www.umrf.net), Red Rock Film Festival, Simon Fest Theatre Co (https://simonfest.org), and Utah Summer Games (https://utahsummer-games.org).

Cedar City has come a long way from its pioneer roots. To find out more about the town's history, stop at **Frontier Homestead State Park Museum** (635 N Main St, tel: 435-586 9290; https://frontierhomestead.org; daily summer 9am–7pm; fall and spring until 6pm; winter until 5pm; charge), which commemorates the men of the Deseret Iron Company (many of them miners from Liverpool, England, who were "called" to help establish Cedar City in 1851. Low-tech but charming, the museum tells the story of the Iron Mission, which failed in 1860 and was supplanted by farming, ranching, and other typical Mormon pursuits. Among the exhibits are numerous old wagons and carriages from 1850 to 1920, as well as the William H. Palmer Collection of Southern Paiute basketry, clothing, tools, and other items collected by a prominent Cedar City Mormon in the 1940s.

Other samples of Palmer's Paiute basketry – nearly a lost art among surviving Paiutes – are on display in the Gerald R. Sherratt Library on the attractive campus of **Southern Utah University** (351 S Main St; tel: 435-586 7700; www.suu.edu/library), founded in 1897. A sizeable population of Southern Paiutes live locally on reservations in southern Utah and Nevada. The headquarters of the Paiute Indian Tribe of Southern Utah is in downtown Cedar City. The group holds an annual Paiute Restoration Gathering in June to celebrate its reinstatement as an "official" Native American Indigenous group.

Also on campus, the **Southern Utah Museum of Art** (13 S 300 West; tel: 435-586 5432; www.suu.edu/suma; Mon–Sat June–Sept 10am–8pm; Oct–May 11am–6pm; free), which features the artwork of regional artists as well as a 2,000-object permanent collection – including work by local artist Jimmie F. Jones and prints by Renoir, Dalí, Hokusai, Thomas Hart Benton, and others.

The famous Zipper Glyph, a calendar and map for solar alignments.

◷ PAROWAN GAP PETROGLYPHS

Evidence of prehistoric occupation is found throughout the Cedar City area. At least two of the area's pioneer settlements, Paragonah and Summit, were built on late Fremont sites dating to between AD 1000 and 1300, and there is evidence of human use dating back to the Late Archaic period, several thousand years ago.

Both Archaic and Fremont culture remains can be viewed at the 2-mile-long (3km) Parowan Gap Petroglyph Site, 15 miles (24km) northwest of Cedar City. Parowan Gap separates Cedar Valley to the west and Parowan Valley to the east and lies along a route used by Native Americans and wildlife crossing the Red Hills. The rock art at Parowan Gap is some of the best in Utah and is on the National Register of Historic Places. The images of mountain sheep, bear claws, snakes, lizards, and other animals indicate it may have been connected to hunting rituals.

To reach the site from Parowan, head west at 400 North under I-15 and continue for 10.6 miles (17km) to Parowan Gap. From Cedar City, go north on Main Street or take I-15 Exit 62, then follow signs for UT 130 north for 13.7 miles (22 km), and turn right 2.5 miles (4 km) on a gravel road near milepost 19. Parking is available at the western end of the Gap.

Slot canyon in Grand Staircase-Escalante National Park.

GRAND STAIRCASE-ESCALANTE NATIONAL MONUMENT

Follow a river corridor or rugged backcountry road through extraordinary red-rock canyons rich with desert life and adorned with ancient pictographs.

Main attractions
Anasazi State Park Museum
Cottonwood Canyons Scenic Backway
Escalante Canyons
The Grand Staircase
Grosvenor Arch
Hell's Backbone
Kodachrome Basin State Park
Phipps Arch

Map on page 206

"Yup! You Gotta Get Wet." The sign on the north bank of the Escalante River elicits big grins. On any desert pilgrimage to southern Utah's famed Escalante Canyons, a river baptism is the price of admission to heaven. There'll be additional toll-takers later on – bush-whacking through willow thickets, scrambling over boulders, squeezing through water-carved narrows, creeping over the slippery sandstone known as slickrock, and slogging through deep sand. The **Grand Staircase–Escalante National Monument** ❶ is remote and wild country. You'll barely have to leave one of the monument's paved highways or graded interior backroads to find yourself deep within the most rugged terrain imaginable. There's only one designated trail: a 6-mile (10km) round-trip hike to spectacular 126ft (38-meter) **Lower Calf Creek Falls** between Escalante and Boulder. Other "trails" are unmarked routes through often narrow desert canyons carved by rivers, streams, and washes.

HISTORY
The Ancestral Puebloan and Fremont cultures frequented this region for thousands of years, experts at farming the rugged land and building granaries to store their crops. It was one of the last regions in the continental United States to be mapped, when members of John Wesley Powell's second expedition to the West traveled overland from Kanab in 1871–72 to survey the area. They named the Escalante River after Father Silvestre Vélez de Escalante, a Spanish padre who traversed the area in 1776, though he never saw the river. Even today, with a sprinkling of small Mormon ranching and farming communities on the periphery, the area remains essentially pristine, adjoined by Capitol Reef National Park to the northeast, Glen Canyon to the

The lesser goldfinch.

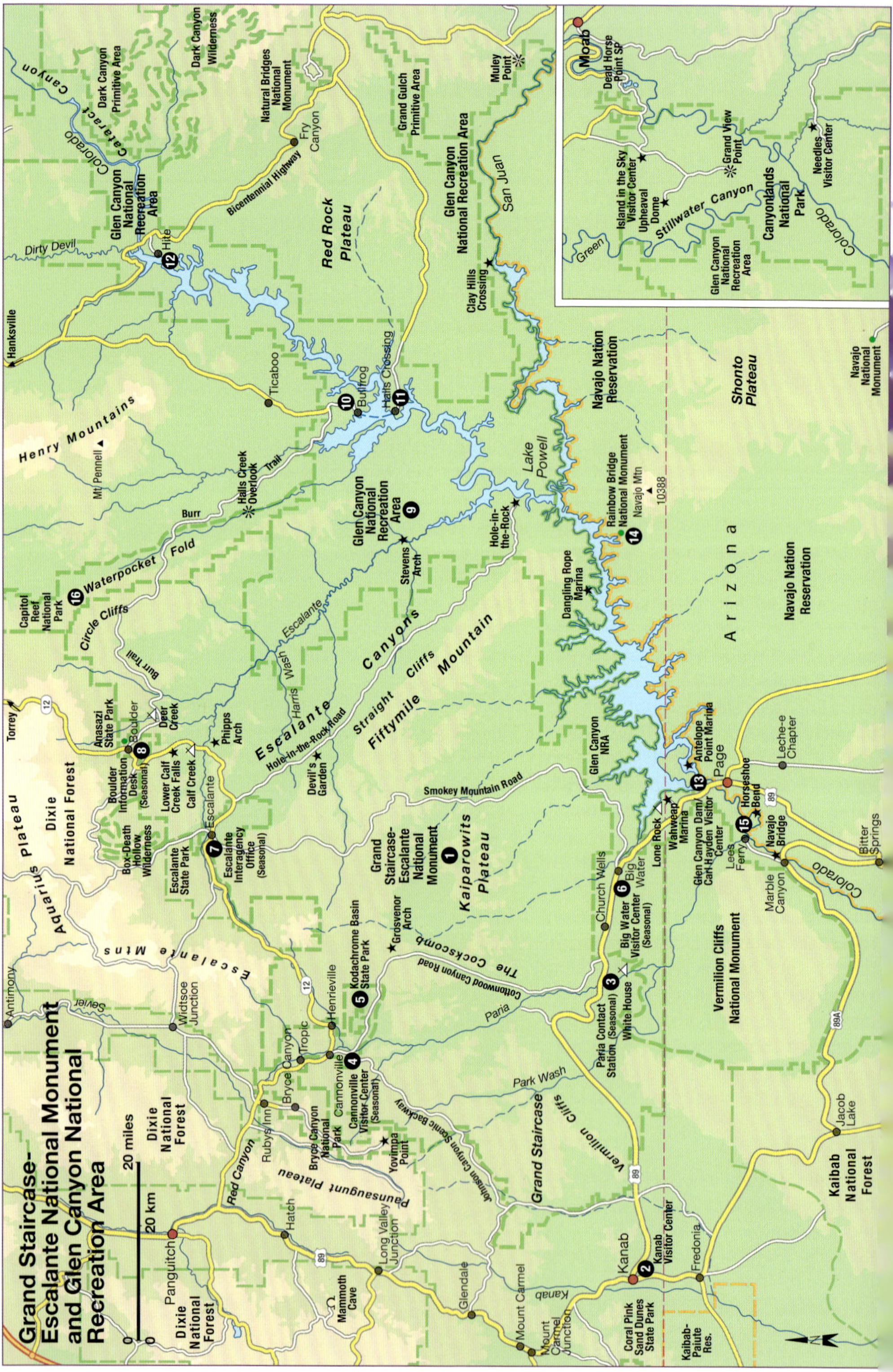

Grand Staircase-Escalante National Monument and Glen Canyon National Recreation Area
0 20 miles
0 20 km
Panguitch
Dixie National Forest
Mammoth Cave
Hatch
Long Valley Junction
Glendale
Mount Carmel
Mount Carmel Junction
Kanab
Coral Pink Sand Dunes State Park
Kaibab-Paiute Res.
Kanab Visitor Center
Fredonia
Red Canyon
Rubys Inn
Bryce Canyon
Bryce Canyon National Park
Paunsaugunt Plateau
Yovimpa Point
Johnson Canyon Scenic Backway
Cannonville Visitor Center (Seasonal)
Cannonville
Tropic
Henrieville
Kodachrome Basin State Park
Grosvenor Arch
Grand Staircase
Vermilion Cliffs
Park Wash
Paria
Paria Contact Station (Seasonal)
White House
Cottonwood Canyon Road
The Cockscomb
Big Water Visitor Center (Seasonal)
Church Wells
Big Water
Vermilion Cliffs National Monument
Jacob Lake
Kaibab National Forest
Marble Canyon
Lees Ferry
Navajo Bridge
Bitter Springs
Glen Canyon Dam/Carl Hayden Visitor Center
Horseshoe Bend
Page
Lone Rock
Wahweap Marina
Antelope Point Marina
Leche-e Chapter
Colorado
Antimony
Widtsoe Junction
Sevier
Escalante Mts
Aquarius Plateau
Dixie National Forest
Box-Death Hollow Wilderness
Escalante State Park
Escalante
Escalante Interagency Office (Seasonal)
Boulder Information Desk (Seasonal)
Lower Calf Creek Falls
Calf Creek
Boulder
Anasazi State Park
Torrey
Deer Creek
Burr Trail
Phipps Arch
Escalante
Hole-in-the-Rock Road
Devil's Garden
Smokey Mountain Road
Grand Staircase-Escalante National Monument
Kaiparowits Plateau
Straight Cliffs
Fiftymile Mountain
Canyons
Harris Wash
Escalante
Glen Canyon NRA
Circle Cliffs
Capitol Reef National Park
Waterpocket Fold
Burr
Trail
Halls Creek Overlook
Mt Pennell
Henry Mountains
Stevens Arch
Glen Canyon National Recreation Area
Hole-in-the-Rock
Dangling Rope Marina
Lake Powell
Rainbow Bridge National Monument
Navajo Mtn
10388
Arizona
Navajo Nation Reservation
Shonto Plateau
Navajo National Monument
Ticaboo
Bullfrog
Halls Crossing
Red Rock Plateau
Hanksville
Hite
Dirty Devil
Glen Canyon National Recreation Area
Bicentennial Highway
Fry Canyon
Natural Bridges National Monument
Grand Gulch Primitive Area
Clay Hills Crossing
San Juan
Muley Point
Dark Canyon Primitive Area
Dark Canyon Wilderness
Cataract Canyon
Moab
Dead Horse Point SP
Island in the Sky Visitor Center
Grand View Point
Upheaval Dome
Green
Stillwater Canyon
Canyonlands National Park
Needles Visitor Center
Glen Canyon National Recreation Area
12
89
89A

GRAND STAIRCASE-ESCALANTE NATIONAL MONUMENT

southeast and Bryce Canyon to the west.

The scientific implications of such a vast, intact ecosystem have become increasingly clear in recent decades. In September 1996, President Bill Clinton set aside Grand Staircase–Escalante as the country's first national monument overseen by the Bureau of Land Management. Encompassed within its 1.9 million acres (7,610 sq km) are an almost intact fossil record in exposed geological formations; flora and fauna adapted to five life zones and numerous microenvironments; and thousands of pristine archaeological sites spanning 10,000 years.

PLANNING A VISIT

Be sure to stop at one of the monument's visitor centers or ranger stations for information about backcountry road conditions, which change quickly after storms, and to pick up overnight backcountry permits, get help planning your trip, and attend lectures by experts on park topics in summer. The visitor centers and ranger stations are in or near the outlying towns: **Big Water**, **Cannonville**, **Escalante**, **Kanab**, and **Paria**.

All the nearby towns have a modest selection of gas, food, and lodging. An expanding number of approved outfitters offers low-impact backpacking, mountain biking, horse-back riding, llama trekking, fishing, hunting, four-wheel drive tours, and back-country survival courses. Bear in mind that distances between towns are great and even paved highways are lightly traveled. Make sure your car is in good working condition, keep your gas tank topped up, and bring spare tires. Carry a gallon of water per person per day (and drink it) and extra food. And don't forget a first-aid kit. Prepare to be self-sufficient; no services are available inside the monument.

If you're heading off-road, a compass, GPS unit, topographical map, and route-finding skills are essential. Be advised that cell phones do not work in many places in the monument. Spring and fall offer cooler hiking temperatures and are blessedly free of biting flies, mosquitoes, and tiny insects known as no-see-ums. Too much or too little water is the norm here, and what water one finds is notoriously unreliable or contaminated by chemicals. On the other hand, watch out for flash floods year-round, especially in summer when daily thunderstorms send surges through slot canyons with vertical walls hundreds of feet high. Last but most important: Be sure to let someone know where you're going, when you expect to return, and whom to call if you don't.

CAMPING

There are three small primitive campgrounds next to the main highways – **Calf Creek** (off UT 12, 15 miles/24km east of Escalante; tel: 435-826 5499; first come, first served), **Deer Creek** (Burr Trail Road, 7 miles/11km from Boulder; tel: 435-826 5499), and **White House** (2 miles/3km off US 89, on White House Road/BLM751; tel: 435-644

> **Fact**
>
> Grand Staircase–Escalante National Monument (tel: 435-644 1200, www.blm.gov) is open 24 hours year-round. The visitor centers and other facilities tend to open daily from 9am to 4pm (restricted hours in winter). Admission is free (it's not a National Park) but permits (also free) are required for all overnight stays (obtainable from visitor centers). Most campgrounds charge a small fee.

Canyon near Hell's Backbone Road.

1300) – as well as several developed campgrounds in adjoining state parks and national forests. Primitive camping is allowed throughout the monument (with an overnight permit) within 50ft (15 meters) of roads and at designated areas in the backcountry.

THE GRAND STAIRCASE

Grand Staircase–Escalante National Monument is divided into three large, contiguous geologic provinces. The easy-to-reach **Grand Staircase** section protects a 3,500ft (1,000-meter-) high geological "staircase" of rock strata, rising from the North Rim of the Grand Canyon to Cedar Breaks National Monument in southwestern Utah. In these massive color-coded cliffs and terraces, the Paria River and other Colorado River tributaries have carved a landscape of isolated mesas, valleys, buttes, and narrow canyons homesteaded by settlers in the 19th century. The **Kanab Visitor Center** ❷ (745 E UT 89, Kanab; tel: 435-644 1300; Tue–Sat 9am–4pm in summer; with exceptions) is located in Kanab in the Grand Staircase section, a good place to start your visit if you're coming from the west.

Forty-four miles (71km) east of Kanab, on US 89, is **Paria Contact Station** ❸ (intersection of UT 89 and White House Trailhead, between mile markers 20 and 21; tel: 435-689 0801; Mar–Oct daily 8am–4.30pm) adjoining the Paria Wilderness, a premier slot canyon that exits at the Colorado River in the northwest section of Glen Canyon National Recreation Area (pickup Paria Canyon Overnight permits at the Contact Station).

The Grand Staircase section of the monument has two lightly traveled day hikes that make a pleasant introduction to the area. To reach the trailheads, drive north 16 miles (28km) on the paved **Johnson Canyon Scenic Backway**, east of Kanab, and turn on the 34-mile (58km) dirt **Skutumpah Road Scenic Backway** heading east. You can also get there by driving north on US 89 from downtown Kanab to **Glendale**, an old coal-mining town, then heading west on **Glendale Bench Road**. Lick

Kodachrome Basin State Park.

GRAND STAIRCASE-ESCALANTE NATIONAL MONUMENT | 209

Wash and Willis Creek are halfway between Cannonville and Kanab. Both offer moderate hiking in deep, narrow canyons filled with stands of Douglas fir. Ask at the Kanab or Cannonville visitor centers for more information.

KAIPAROWITS PLATEAU

The middle section, the 800,000-acre (320,000-hectare) **Kaiparowits Plateau**, adjoins the Grand Staircase to the east and is the most remote and inaccessible area of the monument. The Kaiparowits' rugged isolation has preserved an extraordinary fossil and archaeological record in the younger rocks of the Cretaceous period. It is situated between the Straight Cliffs and a distinctive tilted formation known locally as the Cockscomb, which run 42 miles (68km) east to Glen Canyon National Recreation Area. **Cottonwood Canyons Scenic Backway**, the mainly dirt 46-mile (74km) route separating the Grand Staircase and Kaiparowits provinces, links US 89 with UT 12, the two paved highways encircling the monument.

At the north end of Cottonwood Road, you'll find the folksy **Cannonville Visitor Center** ❹ (10 Center St, Cannonville; tel: 435-826 5640; mid-Mar–mid-Nov Wed–Sun 9am–4pm), which interprets the rich human history of the monument, from the Fremont and Paiute to Mormon homesteaders.

Nine miles (15km) south of Cannonville, where the dirt Cottonwood Road rejoins pavement, is **Kodachrome Basin State Park** ❺ (tel: 435-679 8562; https://stateparks.utah.gov/parks/kodachrome-basin; daily 6am–10pm), named by writer Jack Breed in a 1949 *National Geographic* article extolling the beauties of the area. The park protects 67 unique stovepipe-shaped formations known as "sand pipes" and several natural arches; 8 miles (13km) south of the park is **Grosvenor Arch**, a rare double rock span. The nicely developed Basin Campground has showers and lots of tent and RV sites and makes a good base for touring the central section of the monument.

US 89 provides a scenic 77-mile (124km) link between **Kanab**, Utah, and **Page**, Arizona. A few miles before you get to Page, look for the turnoff for the **Big Water Visitor Center** ❻ (20 Revolution Way, Big Water; tel: 435-675 3200; mid-Mar–mid-Nov Thu–Mon 9am–4pm), which is located at the base of the rough and often impassable **Smoky Mountain Road** across the Kaiparowits Plateau. Built in the shape of a nautilus shell, this exquisite small facility has a native plant garden, sculptures, interpretive panels and dioramas interpreting the marine reptiles, dinosaurs, and early mammals of the late Cretaceous Period excavated from atop the Kaiparowits in the 1990s.

ESCALANTE CANYONS

The easternmost section of the monument is **Escalante Canyons**, which protects the maze of canyons cut by the Escalante River from the Aquarius Plateau to Lake Powell. The Escalante Canyons have long been the main attraction on the monument, offering riverside

The Devils Rock Garden.

hikes, slot canyons, bizarre rock formations, breath-taking vistas, and historic roads. If you've never been here before, you'll learn more about this vast maze of stone and stay safest if you hire a local outfitter to introduce you to the area and help pack your gear. You can go the traditional route with horses, but a more unusual option is to use llamas, which need far less water than horses and can carry up to 120lb (55kg) of gear. With their cushiony, two-toed feet, they have about as much impact on fragile desert soils as deer and are possessed of remarkably docile temperaments.

The busy **Escalante Interagency Visitor Center** ❼ (755 W Main St, Escalante; tel: 435-826 5499; Thu–Tue 9am–4pm; with exceptions) anchors the monument on the east side and offers in-depth information and trip planning for the Escalante Canyons and Glen Canyon National Recreation Area.

The Escalante Basin begins east of Escalante, between the 1,100ft (335-meter) Straight Cliffs of the Kaiparowits Plateau and the great drop-off of the Waterpocket Fold. On either side of UT 12, the torqued and twisted knobs of Navajo Sandstone roiling to the horizon are almost enough to bring on sea sickness. Near its confluence with Calf Creek, the Escalante River appears in a blaze of preternaturally green vegetation at the foot of ruddy sandstone. The water is only about 10ft (3 meters) wide and usually only knee-deep, but don't laugh – this qualifies as a river in Canyon Country. Its headwaters are on the 11,000ft (3,350-meter) Aquarius Plateau, from whence the Escalante drops toward its conjunction with Lake Powell. If the water gods had their way, this would be a straight shot, but Mother Earth has shrugged her shoulders at such plans and wrinkled the area in a series of uplifts, or monoclines, that have forced the river and its tributaries to cut deep, labyrinthine canyons.

Several side canyons lead to the river. On the north side, Deer Creek and The Gulch are popular access points. They join the **Burr Trail Scenic Backway**, the old rancher's road that starts in Boulder as a 31-mile (50km) paved road below the Circle Cliffs, then turns

Highway 12 scenic byway in Calf Creek Recreational Area.

⊘ EVERETT RUESS

Born in California in 1914, adventurer, artist, and writer Everett Ruess took to the road as a teenager along with thousands of other men seeking work during the Depression. Unlike them, though, Ruess came from a family of means: he simply traveled for the joy of it, sending home regular missives about his passion for the Arizona and Utah wilderness, the people he met and his faithful pack mule, Nemo.

On trips home, he befriended photographers Ansel Adams and Dorothea Lange and painter Maynard Dixon. Although the Bohemian life attracted him, his brooding temperament and love of wilderness drew him deeper into Utah's backcountry. In a final letter to his brother Waldo, he wrote: "I have not tired of the wilderness; rather I enjoy its beauty and the vagrant life I lead more keenly all the time. I prefer the saddle to the streetcar and star-sprinkled sky to a roof, the obscure and difficult trail leading into the unknown to any paved highway, and the deep peace of the wild to the discontent bred by cities." In November 1934, at the age of 20, he made his last journey (with two donkeys), vanishing into Davis Canyon in what is today Grand Staircase–Escalante National Monument. His fate remains unknown, but his love of Canyon Country continues to inspire modern-day adventurers.

to dirt as it crosses the Waterpocket Fold in Capitol Reef and continues into Glen Canyon National Recreation Area. On the south side, you can reach Harris Wash from the 57-mile (92km) **Hole-in-the-Rock Scenic Backway**, which was blasted by Mormon pioneers in the winter of 1879 on their epic mission to colonize southeastern Utah.

HIKING THE CANYONS

An easy, 15-mile (24km) overnight trip can be made along the Escalante River between Escalante and Calf Creek for great views of an arch, a natural bridge, and Native American granaries and rock art. Continue down the canyon for longer trips; five days is usually enough time to reach Glen Canyon National Recreation Area and explore side canyons. If you stick close to the Escalante River, you won't have to sprinkle bread crumbs to find your way back. Cattle have pounded out a trail along the riverbank that's easy to follow. You'll ford the silty river numerous times, so wear good river sandals or light boots and bring spare footwear and dry socks.

Water and other erosional forces have sculpted myriad cliffs, alcoves, arches, bridges, slots, and hoodoos. Cross-bedded Navajo Sandstone, the remnant of a 190-million-year-old desert, reaches precipitously to the rim and catches fire at sunrise and sunset. Beneath the rosy Navajo, the maroon Kayenta siltstone erodes into ledges, forcing the canyon to step back in terraces and benches. Even more dramatic than the Navajo (if that's possible) is the fiery orange Wingate Sandstone, which appears deeper in the canyon and reaches its most stunning expression in the fractured Circle Cliffs to the northeast. Lengthening shadows bring out the tapestry effect on sandstone. Pour-offs have washed out manganese and iron in the rock, creating "desert varnish" fixed to cliff faces by bacteria.

The eye is constantly drawn up to the cliffs, then back down to the feet, where your passage may send crickets jumping or a dozing lizard scurrying from the undergrowth.

About 2 miles (3km) down the canyon from the UT 12 bridge, a side

> **Tip**
>
> Watch out for "cryptobiotic crusts" in sandy areas of the canyons. These dark soils are made up of strands of cyanobacteria, lichen and algae that hold moisture and nitrogen and prevent erosion. This is where life begins in the desert, but it's easily destroyed by careless feet. To avoid "crypto," walk in washes or on slickrock.

Grosvenor Arch.

canyon to the south follows Phipps Wash. Head east in a box canyon to view 40ft (12-meter-) high **Phipps Arch**, a magnificent natural span. You'll need to scramble up several hundred feet of crumbly ledges and slickrock to reach the arch, but it's worth the effort. This is a great place for a picnic or for close encounters with turkey vultures and red-tailed hawks, which soar upon thermals through the canyon.

ESCALANTE CANYONS FLORA AND FAUNA

Over the burbling of the river, listen for the descending serenade of the canyon wren accompanied by the fluting notes of robins. Egrets and herons visit at times, along with dainty water ouzels that dip for insects in the shallows. Graceful white-throated swifts swoop down to the river from cliff nests in acrobatic dives. The cliffs are also home to more than 20 raptor species, which use tree snags and ledges as staging areas for skyline sorties. Perhaps you'll be lucky enough to see a golden eagle soaring into the morning sun and follow its shadow on a cliff as it spirals. Though formidable predators, these majestic birds are no match for peregrine falcons, which, along with condors released along the Vermilion Cliffs, are the great comeback story here. It's not unknown for lightning-fast peregrines to attack and kill eagles. More than three-quarters of the monument's plants and animals use riparian corridors like this one.

The bank of the Escalante River is a grabby tangle of tamarisk, willow, box elder, and thorny Russian olive. Scouring rushes and horsetails poke up from the shallows. Growing along the trail are woody sagebrush, rabbitbrush, greasewood, and four-wing saltbush interspersed with orange-red globemallow, vermilion Indian paintbrush, scarlet gilia, skyrocket, and purple-headed woolly vetch. On higher ledges, dwarf pinyon and juniper, Gambel oak, old man sage, and roundleaf buffaloberry find purchase in soil pockets.

In side canyons, giant Fremont cottonwoods wrap rubbery limbs around

Slot canyon known as Signing Canyon on the Burr Trail.

boulders and stretch toe roots into warm pools skittering with water striders and polliwogs. When you least expect it, you'll happen upon miniature hanging gardens of moss, ferns, and eye-dazzling columbines, monkey-flowers and shooting stars crowding around dripping springs in the canyon walls. The water percolates down through porous sandstone. The constant dripping undermines the overlying sandstone cliffs, which crack along joints, then peel away like an onion, leaving behind huge alcoves that will one day become arches. Various creatures find refuge here: elusive bighorn sheep, timid mountain lions scanning for deer, coyotes sniffing around for cottontails and jackrabbits, and rodents like the desert-adapted kangaroo rat, which recycles all its water from seeds.

BOULDER AND ENVIRONS

If you're arriving from the north, you'll find information in the little ranching community of Boulder at the start of the historic Burr Trail. The monument's **Boulder Contact Station** ❽ (tel: 435-335 7382; mid-Mar–mid-Nov daily 9am–5pm) is on the north end of town at **Anasazi State Park Museum** (460 N UT 12, tel: 435-355-7308; https://stateparks.utah.gov/parks/anasazi; daily 9am–5pm). This park preserves a huge pueblo known as the Coombs Site, one of the most important archaeological sites in the area – Ancestral Puebloans occupied the site between 1050 and 1175.

On the south side of town is the beginning of **Hell's Backbone**, the precipitous backroad that used to be the main link between Boulder and Escalante. Climbing a steep graveled road, this route (used by mule trains carrying mail until the 1940s) crosses **Box-Death Hollow Wilderness** and has spectacular views. Two gorgeous forest service campgrounds – **Posey Lake** (FR 154; tel: 877-444 6777; www.recreation.gov) and **Blue Spruce** (FR 145; first come, first served) – offer the best camping in the area. Don't attempt this road in bad weather. Ask about conditions before setting out.

Spires in the desert in Kodachrome Basin State Park.

⊘ ANCIENT TREASURES

Some of the most memorable sights in the canyons are the dwellings, granaries, stone-working sites, and rock art panels left behind by the Fremont and Kayenta Branch Puebloan cultures who lived here between AD 100 and 1300. The Fremont dug snug pit houses with warm southern exposures on deer and elk migration routes, gathered plants seasonally, raised corn, and appear to have subsisted on water from *tinajas*, or "potholes." The Kayenta Branch Puebloan culture were pueblo builders who erected the large Coombs Site now preserved in Anasazi State Park in nearby Boulder. The village here is thought to have flourished from 1160 to 1235, with a maximum population of around 250. It's estimated that more than 20,000 archaeological sites are situated within the Grand Staircase–Escalante National Monument, many protected by their remote locations.

Pecked and painted rock art panels display strong Fremont characteristics – wide-shouldered human-like figures with round shields, headdresses and ear bobs, accompanied by bighorn sheep, animal tracks, handprints, joined-hand figures, and concentric circles. It's hard not to admire the resourcefulness and artistry of these hardy people, though not everyone shares the sentiment, as is heartbreakingly apparent when you come upon sites desecrated by vandalism.

Glen Canyon Dam.

GLEN CANYON NATIONAL RECREATION AREA

Boaters ply a watery labyrinth in this sprawling park centered on a man-made lake in the heart of southern Utah's slickrock wilderness.

Managed by the National Park Service since 1972, **Glen Canyon National Recreation Area** ❾ preserves 1,960 square miles (5,076 sq km) in and around the Colorado River and its major tributaries – the San Juan, Paria, Dirty Devil and Escalante Rivers – which, since 1963, have been backed up behind Glen Canyon Dam at Page, Arizona. Although it sees most of the visitation, 252-square-mile (653-sq-km) Lake Powell represents only 13 percent of the park. Glen Canyon also includes many square miles of mesas, mountains and desert canyons cut by the rivers prior to inundation beneath the reservoir. Below Glen Canyon Dam, the Colorado River continues to flow for 15 miles (24 km) to Lee's Ferry in Arizona, offering white-water rafting in the lower reaches of the park.

LAKE POWELL

Since 2000, recreation in Glen Canyon National Recreation Area has been an unfolding work-in-progress. Lake levels have plummeted below capacity due to an extended drought; by 2022 it was around 180 ft (55 meters) below full pool – just 28 percent of its full capacity, putting in to question its ability to create hydropower in the future. But as the lake has dropped, hiking and primitive camping on new beaches and side canyons is once again becoming popular. Some of the best are in the spectacular Escalante Canyons in the northern reaches of the lake, where places like Cathedral in the Desert, named by geologist John Wesley Powell on his river expedition down the Colorado in 1869, are worthy destinations in themselves.

History and archaeology buffs will be thrilled to discover the cultural remains of Archaic and ancient Pueblo people, 19th-century pioneers and contemporary Native American Indigenous people reappearing from the

Horseshoe Bend near the Colorado River.

Main attractions
Glen Canyon Dam
Horseshoe Bend
John Wesley Powell Memorial Museum
Lake Powell

Map on page 206

Fact

Glen Canyon National Recreation Area (tel: 928-608 6200, www.nps.gov/glca) is open 24 hours, throughout the year, though the visitor center and other facilities tend to open from 9am to 5pm daily, with seasonal variations. Admission is $30 per vehicle, valid for seven days (motorbikes $25; individuals hiking or cycling $15; aged 15 and under are free). The Interagency Annual Pass ($80) is valid here.

Lake Powell.

receding waters like the mythical lost city of Atlantis. Glen Canyon, once mourned as "The Place No One Knew" by activists opposed to the construction of Glen Canyon Dam, is beginning to reemerge of its own volition even as the dam faces an uncertain future.

Despite its depleted state, Lake Powell – the second-largest man-made lake in the Western Hemisphere – remains the big attraction at Glen Canyon for the more than two million visitors who come here annually. The dam that created this vast reservoir was authorized by the Colorado River Storage Project Act in 1956, a water-sharing arrangement between the western states of California, Nevada, Wyoming, Utah, Colorado, Arizona and New Mexico. Although it is overextended, the dam project has provided water storage, flood control, irrigation, river regulation and hydroelectric power, which, in the years since, have paid for the cost of construction.

Lake Powell extends 186 miles (299 km) upstream from the dam and has 1,960 miles (3,154 km) of shoreline – longer even than the West Coast of the United States. Water activities, such as boating, water skiing, wind surfing, swimming and fishing, predominate and are served by five marinas: **Bullfrog**, **Wahweap**, **Dangling Rope** (which was closed through 2022 due to low water levels), **Hall's Crossing** and **Antelope Point Marina** in Arizona (537 Marina Parkway, Navajo Route 22B; tel: 928-645 5900; https://antelopepointlakepowell.com), a joint project with the Navajo Nation, whose vast reservation adjoins Lake Powell to the south.

BULLFROG

If you're arriving at Lake Powell from Utah in summer, **Bullfrog Resort and Marina** ⑩ (UT 276, Bullfrog; tel: 435-684 3000) is your best bet. Less than five hours from Salt Lake City, it offers both full services and the perfect introduction to the quiet beauty of Glen Canyon in the northern sector of the park. You'll find almost everything you will need at Bullfrog and nearby Ticaboo – accommodations, a campground, a large marina, a swimming beach, restaurants, gift shops, boat tours, a gas station, a fuel dock, convenience stores and a medical clinic. Bullfrog is one of three marinas renting houseboats (with Wahweap and Antelope Point), a popular option with vacationers. You can also rent kayaks and other small watercraft as well as fishing gear. Largemouth and striped bass, black crappie, catfish, bluegill and walleye predominate in Lake Powell; trophy-sized rainbow trout thrive in the cold waters below the dam.

Your first stop at Bullfrog should be **Bullfrog Visitor Center** (UT 276-North Bullfrog; tel: 435-684 7423; usually open May–Sept, check park website for latest hours), a pleasant haven adjoining the medical clinic. The visitor center interprets the natural and cultural history of the region with state-of-the-art displays, video programs and a helpful staff who can give

GLEN CANYON NATIONAL RECREATION AREA | 217

you tips on exploring the surrounding area. It has exhibits on desert animals and the alcove villages left behind by ancient Pueblo people.

Among the most interesting exhibits is a full-sized diorama of a slot canyon, a common geological feature in Canyon Country, where floodwater cuts straight down through sandstone, leaving behind narrow, winding subterranean passageways with cool, sandy bottoms. The best-known slot canyon in the area is photogenic Antelope Canyon, on the south side of the lake near Page. There are several good slot canyon hikes near Bullfrog, too. You'll find them off the Burr Trail; inquire at the visitor center for directions.

HALL'S CROSSING AND HITE

On the eastern side of the lake, **Hall's Crossing** ⓫ has a marina (tel: 435-684 7000), boat launch, ferry landing, campground and store. **Hall's Crossing Boater Contact Station** (open 8am–6pm intermittently in summer) has exhibits on boater information and safety, geology and the history of the village. This remote spot was named for one of the Hole-in-the-Rock pioneers, Charles Hall, who operated a ferry across the Colorado River in the late 19th century. Business was slow, and Hall stopped running the ferry after three years, just before a gold rush in Glen Canyon would have kept him busy.

Beginning in 1945, another historic ferry was operated by Arthur Chaffin at **Hite** ⓬, the northernmost community in Glen Canyon. Situated at the junction of the Dirty Devil and Colorado Rivers, Hite was named for 19th-century prospector Cass Hite, who first came here in 1883 with Navajo headman Hoskaninni, after asking the Monument Valley leader to show him where the Navajo found silver for their jewelry. Two earlier prospectors with a similar interest had been killed in Monument Valley three years earlier, but fortunately

Hite, Hoskaninni was willing to show him the place on the south side of the Colorado River where he had found gold dust in the riverbank.

Dandy Crossing, as Hite called the spot, was quickly mobbed by prospectors but, sadly, there was never

> **Tip**
>
> Normally, the **Charles Hall Ferry** runs between Bullfrog and Halls Crossing (tel: 435-684 7000; www.udot.utah.gov), connecting the two halves of UT 276 across Lake Powell in around 25 minutes. However, since 2021 water levels have been too low to the run the ferry. Check the UDOT website for the latest. Otherwise, it's a 2-hour 30-minute drive (125 miles/201 km) to the other side of the lake.

Rock formations in Lake Powell.

> **Tip**
>
> Note that tours of the 710-ft-high (216-meter) Glen Canyon Dam and power plant have not been offered since the beginning of the COVID epidemic in 2020 (check the park website to see if they have resumed). Walk across the bridge for the best views of the dam and the canyon.

sufficient gold to make up for the difficulty of extracting it in such remote country. Two corporations – one run by mining engineer Robert Stanton at Bullfrog Creek and one by Charles Spencer at Lee's Ferry – made a major attempt. All eventually gave up, leaving their equipment to rust along the river and eventually be drowned by Lake Powell.

Modern travelers now cross the river via a suspension bridge along US 95. Lake levels have been so low that Hite – once a waterfront village – has turned into a ghost town. The boat launch is closed, but anyone with even a passing interest in desert rivers will want to drive this way to see how quickly the river is reclaiming the mudflats from the lake. **Hite Ranger Station** (tel: 435-684 2457) is open intermittently but has outdoor interpretive displays about the historic village.

GLEN CANYON DAM

The southern section of the lake and recreation area lies across the border in Arizona, where the **Glen Canyon Dam** on US 89 holds back the Colorado River and makes the whole thing possible. **Carl Hayden Visitor Center** [13] (tel: 928-608 6200; daily 8am–6pm in summer; 8am–5pm spring and fall; 8am–4pm winter), next to the dam, has exhibits, interpretive presentations, a bookstore and information on hiking side canyons and arranging river trips.

When it was begun in 1956, Glen Canyon Dam had the blessing of almost everyone concerned. By the time it was finished in 1963, conservationists such as Sierra Club's David Brower and writer Wallace Stegner had belatedly recognized that Glen Canyon was comparable in grandeur to anything – including the nearby Grand Canyon – on the Colorado Plateau. Today, many people believe that the drowning of Glen Canyon and its rich natural and cultural history was an unspeakable ecological tragedy and are advocating dismantling the dam. But while both biologists and politicians investigate ways to mitigate the effects of the dam on the downstream environment, nature has intervened, rapidly drying up the lake during a period of drought that, as of this writing, shows no signs of abating.

That said, Glen Canyon Dam is an extraordinary structure. It was built over seven years at a cost of $187 million and is the second-largest dam in the United States (after Hoover Dam, downstream at Lake Mead, Nevada). The canyon it occupies was shaped to fit the dam, not the other way around, and hundreds of rock bolts were installed by high scalers to reinforce the canyon walls and prevent rock slabs from falling. The dam designers thought of almost every eventuality. Groundwater, seeping through fractures in the sandstone, enters tunnels in the dam at 2,600 gallons (9,800 liters) a minute and is diverted through weirs and troughs and discharged to the river below. Massive diversion tunnels on either side of the dam regulate water releases during times of seasonal flood.

Glen Canyon National Recreation Area.

GLEN CANYON NATIONAL RECREATION AREA

The dam can generate 1.3 million kilowatts of electricity through hydroelectric power, most of which is used to power the megalopolis of Phoenix and other Southwest cities. Hydrologists estimate that if the drought continues, hydropower at Glen Canyon Dam could be eliminated within the next few years, affecting millions of households. Daily, icy waters from deep below Lake Powell are released from behind the dam to coincide with peak usage times in western cities. This type of operation, known as "peaking," means that the river level below the dam rises and falls by as much as 14 ft (4 meters) a day, depending on the season. This has heavily impacted the downstream environment of the Colorado River, whose ecology was adapted to the free-flowing river. No longer can spring floods scour the riverbank and rebuild beaches. The warm, silty-red waters (for which the Colorado was named) are a thing of the past. Warm-water native fish species, such as the razorback sucker and humpback chub, are now federally listed endangered species, along with the southwest willow flycatcher, a small, drab, gray bird that nests in native willows that have been largely replaced by exotic tamarisk, or salt cedar, along the riverbank.

PAGE, AZ

Civil War veteran and geologist John Wesley Powell, for whom Lake Powell was named, was the first to travel down the free-flowing Colorado River in 1869. Using the Mormon community of Kanab, Utah, as a base, he returned for a second, shorter trip in 1872, photographing many features in the canyons as well as Navajos, Paiutes and other native people whom he used as guides. In his subsequent report, Powell was the first to write about the need for a realistic federal water policy for the West.

Powell's legacy is celebrated at the charming **John Wesley Powell Memorial Museum** in **Page**, across the river (6 N. Lake Powell Blvd; tel: 928 640 3900; www.canyonconservancy.org; Mon–Sat 8am–6pm). A Grandma's-attic type of place, the museum displays old drawings and photos from Powell's life and

The Rainbow Bridge National Monument.

⊘ RAINBOW BRIDGE

Rainbow Bridge National Monument (tel: 928-608 6200; www.nps.gov/rabr; open year-round, sunrise to sunset; free) set deep in the heart of Glen Canyon, is a 100-mile (160-km) round-trip by boat from Wahweap Marina near Page. Although it is possible to hike overland from Navajo Mountain, using a Navajo guide, the 14-mile (23-km) trail is unmarked, rugged and shadeless and not recommended for those who aren't in good shape or accustomed to hot desert hiking. You must obtain a permit from Navajo Parks and Recreation in Window Rock (tel: 520-871 6647; https://navajonationparks.org) before starting out.

Traditionally, most people visit Rainbow Bridge by boat – the problem is that the lake is now so low, there is no dock access to the shoreline near the bridge. Independent boats and small vessels beach at their own risk – contact B&T Marine in Page for boat rentals (https://www.bandtmarine.com). Concessionaires normally run popular, all-day boat trips from Wahweap for about $125–130 per person, but tours are suspended until water levels improve – visit www.lakepowell.com for the latest. If the tours are running, visitors must hike 4 miles (6.4 km) round-trip to view Rainbow Bridge, so wear sturdy shoes, a hat and sunscreen, and bring plenty of water. Rainbow Bridge is sacred to local Indigenous people. The National Park Service urges visitors to approach the bridge with respect and refrain from walking beneath it.

HIDDEN LIFE

> The biological soil crust known as cryptobiotic soil (Greek for "hidden life") is one of the quiet miracles of the Glen Canyon National Recreation Area.

"Crypto," as it's known, is a living community of mutually beneficial organisms, working together to reduce erosion, retain water, and encourage soil fertility. An astonishing 75 percent of the Colorado Plateau is covered in this ancient building block of life. Cryptobiotic communities are dominated by cyanobacteria (blue-green algae), one of the oldest life-forms on earth, as well as lichens, mosses, microfungi, bacteria and green algae. Cyanobacteria and microfungi protect themselves from sharp sand grains by secreting a sticky mucilage around their cells that helps glue soil particles in place. Mosses and lichens put down small roots that anchor the soil and keep it from blowing away.

When it rains, these organisms absorb up to 10 times their volume in water and then release it slowly into the soil. Frost-heaving roughens the surface of cryptobiotic soil, further slowing rainwater runoff. Mature cryptobiotic crusts are easy to recognize: the soil is dark, mounded, crumbly and filled with plants. Less easy to see are young soils, which look like a sandy crust.

Cryptobiosis also allows living things to shut down metabolic activity and lie dormant until conditions are favorable — a survival tactic widespread among microscopic life-forms found in potholes, the depressions atop sandstone cliffs. Potholes are carved by desert downpours that collect in depressions and dissolve the cementing minerals between grains of sand, allowing them to be removed by wind and rain.

Thousands of tiny plants and animals live in these temporary aquatic habitats. Only single-celled organisms survive in small, shallow pools. Slightly larger potholes may contain water bears, rotifers, nematodes and water mites. The largest pools contain the most diversity: fairy shrimp, water fleas and other small crustaceans; snails; mosquito larvae; diving beetles; and water boatmen.

FIGHTING TO SURVIVE

Because rainfall is sporadic on the Colorado Plateau, many pothole dwellers have evolved survival tactics that allow them to lie dormant indefinitely, then quickly revive and reproduce before rainwater evaporates.

Some fairy shrimp complete their entire life cycle in as little as four days. Once laid, fairy shrimp eggs withstand dehydration. Rotifers, tardigrades and nematodes can dry up and survive at any time in their life cycle.

Hiking, camping, bicycling, and off-road driving are destroying cryptobiotic crusts and pothole life in Canyon Country. Crushed cryptobiotic crusts contribute less nitrogen and organic matter to the ecosystem, dry out, and blow away, forming sand dunes that bury other healthy soils. Recovery can take up to 250 years. Bicycle and tire tracks are particularly damaging because they form a continuous strip and channelize water flow that quickly washes away soil. Pothole life is also fragile and easily disturbed. Never wade in a pothole, use it for washing or drinking, or even walk, ride, or drive through a dry pothole, if you can avoid it.

Lake Powell.

voyages, geological displays and Native American artifacts. Among the many items of interest is Powell's old bedstead, a wooden dory rowboat used by Mexican Hat river runner Norm Nevills, the largest collection of phosphorescent rocks in the world and the complete skeleton of a giant predatory marine reptile called a plesiosaur, which lived about 90 million years ago, when this region was inundated by a huge interior seaway.

Page has grown from a makeshift shantytown for dam workers into far northern Arizona's largest community, with a variety of lodgings and restaurants. From here, you can arrange trips on Lake Powell, boat tours to **Rainbow Bridge** ⑭, tours of Antelope Canyon and Monument Valley, and the nearby Grand Canyon. **Wahweap Marina** (100 Lake Shore Dr; tel: 928-645 2433; www.lakepowell.com), just west of the dam on the other side of the river, is the main access for the lake and has full facilities. Primitive camping is available at nearby **Lone Rock Beach**, back over in Utah.

MARBLE CANYON AND LEE'S FERRY, AZ

Busy Wahweap is a popular venue for partying boaters and vacationers. For a more back-to-nature experience, head south on US 89, then north on US 89A to **Marble Canyon**. When it opened in 1929, the narrow, 467-ft-high (142-meter) Navajo Bridge over the Colorado was the highest steel structure in the world. A wider bridge was opened in 1997 for automobiles, and you can walk across the old structure. The small **Navajo Bridge Visitor Center** (daily 9am–5pm; tel: 928-608 6200) is an impressive piece of desert architecture, with pueblo-style sandstone walls and a fine little bookstore.

Behind the dramatic Vermilion Cliffs is **Lee's Ferry** ⑮, once a ferry crossing operated by John D. Lee, a prominent Mormon elder. Lee was sent here personally by LDS Church President Brigham Young after being implicated in the 1857 Mountain Meadows Massacre of an emigrant wagon train bound for California. At the mouth of the Paria River is Lee's old homestead, **Lonely Dell Ranch**, a pretty spot with a log cabin, a blacksmith shop, ranch house and shady orchards. There is a campground at Lees Ferry, several quaint lodgings and restaurants. The historic **Spencer Trail**, which was built as a shortcut over the Vermilion Cliffs in 1910 by a miner and trader named Charles Spencer, makes an interesting day hike while you're in the area. You can reach the rim of these steep cliffs in one to two hours, depending on your physical condition. By now, you'll probably be champing at the bit to get on the river itself. Wilderness River Adventures (tel: 800-528 6154; www.riveradventures.com) offers single-day and multiday river trips from below Glen Canyon Dam to Lee's Ferry and beyond. From the dam, you'll pass through **Horseshoe Bend**, an entrenched meander, or gooseneck, cut by the river into the sedimentary rocks. From Lee's Ferry, you can continue through Grand Canyon National Park, whose boundary adjoins Glen Canyon to the west.

Balanced rock near Lee's Ferry in Glen Canyon National Recreation Area.

Fruita barn at Capitol Reef National Park.

CAPITOL REEF NATIONAL PARK

A wrinkle in the earth's crust runs through this intensely colorful park where "sleeping rainbows", "golden thrones" and other formations appear to be illuminated from within.

Main attractions
Bicknell Theater
Boulder Mountain
Capitol Reef Scenic Drive
Capitol Gorge
Cathedral Valley Driving Loop Tour
Fruita Historic District
Loop-The-Fold Driving Tour
Muley Twist Canyon

Maps on pages 206 and 224

For many people, the desert Southwest seems like a vast dry ocean that stretches endlessly in every direction, its rocky floor occasionally interrupted by broad troughs, tablelands, snowcapped mountains and maze-like canyons. But in Utah, the paradox of ocean imagery amid intensely arid land goes one step farther, for here, rolling in long, colorful, petrified breakers across a desert basin, is one of the most dramatic geologic features on the American continent: the Waterpocket Fold, a 100-mile-long (160-km) warp on the earth's surface that neatly bisects southeastern Utah, from volcanic Thousand Lake Mountain in the north to man-made Lake Powell in the south. In between, 378-square-mile (979-sq-km) **Capitol Reef National Park ⓰** preserves 75 miles (120 km) of the Waterpocket Fold, its native plants and animals, and the artifacts of the Fremont people and Mormon pioneers who made the area their home.

CAPITOL REEF GEOLOGY

Most visitors are intrigued by the Waterpocket Fold. How did it come to be here? Geologists believe that it was created about 65 million years ago, when a period of geologic activity deep below the earth's surface began wrenching the low-lying landscape of western America into its present contorted form. It is generally thought that massive movements along the junction of the Pacific and North American Plates around that time forced up the Sierra Nevada in California and continued to reverberate eastward, squeezing the miles of sedimentary rocks that had accumulated across the Southwest.

The monolithic Colorado Plateau rose slowly under this pressure, and a series of steep, north-south monoclines, or folds, began to form across

A storm brewing at Capitol Reef National Park.

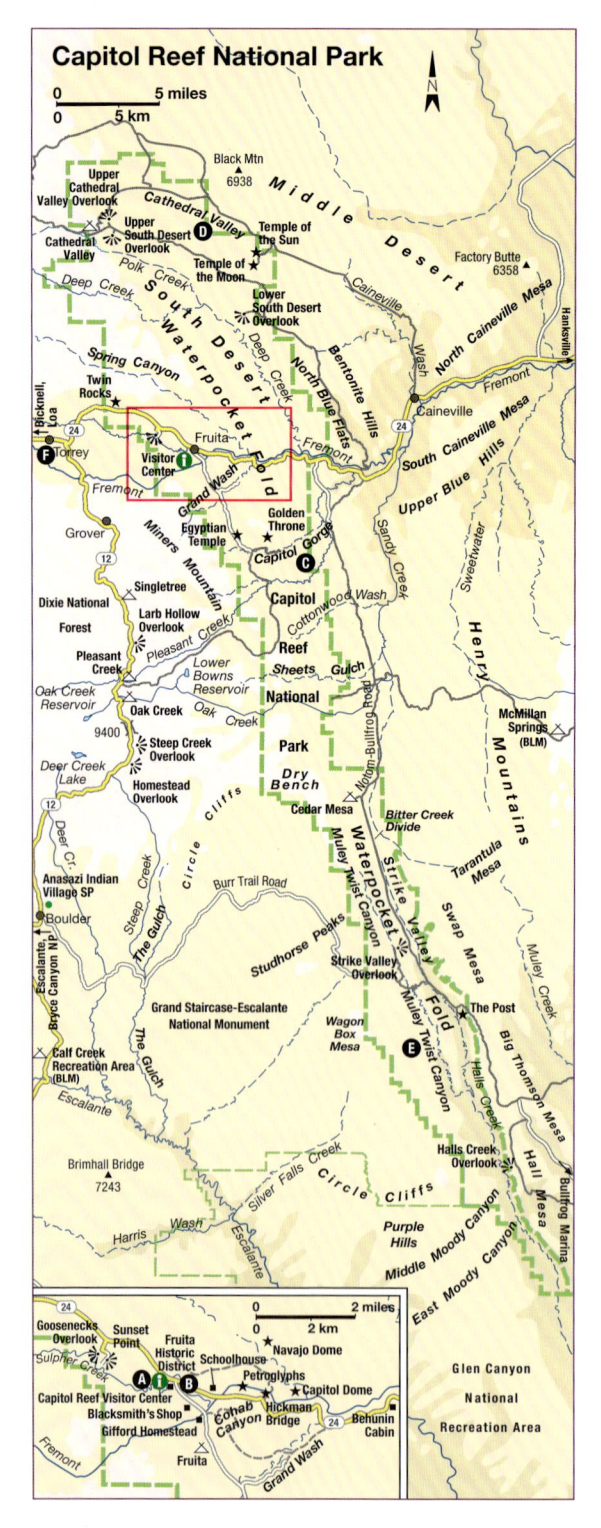

its surface, of which the Waterpocket Fold is one of the most spectacular examples. The exposed rock surfaces soon became vulnerable to weathering. Wind and water carved the rainbow-colored cliffs, spires, natural bridges, arches and hogbacks that characterize Capitol Reef today.

PARK HISTORY – FRUITA

Though the Utes had been coming here for hundreds of years, geologist and Civil War veteran Major John Wesley Powell was the first American to systematically explore the area, in 1872. He noted the way depressions in the "slickrock" filled with life-giving rainwater and dubbed the formation the Waterpocket Fold. The first permanent homesteader was Niels Johnson in 1880, with the establishment of the Fruita Town & Land Company four years later by William E. Pabor considered the official foundation of the town of **Fruita** – today it's technically a ghost town, but what remains serves as the national park's headquarters.

Fruita eventually comprised 10 families, some of whom were polygamists wishing to live quiet, self-supporting lives away from the glare of government disapproval. Names like Cohab Canyon linger, commemorating these early settlers. The Mormons' preoccupation with land and government is also reflected in the name they gave the area of the Waterpocket Fold in which they had settled – Capitol Reef. In their eyes, the central section of the Fold welled up like an ocean reef, while one of its larger domes was a dead ringer for the US Capitol. Other unusually eroded rocks sparked equally descriptive names – Chimney Rock, Golden Throne, Egyptian Temple and the Castle.

With a reliable water source at hand, the residents were able to harvest plentiful supplies of apricots, peaches, cherries and apples, which they used for their own consumption or sold to neighboring towns, transient miners, cowboys and even outlaws. Butch Cassidy and the Wild Bunch, who hid out in nearby Loa and east of the park in a remote area known as Robber's Roost, were customers. Cassidy carved his signature on the wall of a side canyon, along with many other early miners, surveyors, explorers and homesteaders. A number of inscriptions are preserved at **Pioneer Register**, visible on the popular hike through Capitol Gorge. The earliest historic signatures are those of two prospectors who passed through in 1871.

Fruita residents prospered even as downriver communities like **Caineville**, snugged into the low-lying badlands, struggled with flooding. In 1884, they built a notorious wagon road known as the "Blue Dugway" through Capitol Gorge, crossing the nearly impassable ridges and smooth domes of the Waterpocket Fold to link Torrey on the west with settlements on the east. Every year, enterprising farmers hauled their produce to markets in Price and Ritchfield. It was an extraordinary undertaking, considering that in 1910 the 10-mile (16-km) wagon trip to Torrey, the closest settlement, took no less than 90 minutes – in good weather.

Growing all their own food, residents weathered the Great Depression far more successfully than the rest of the United States. Still, the community remained isolated and, in the 1930s, boosters proposed that part of the present national park be set aside as Wayne Wonderland State Park in an effort to bring visitors to the area. Instead, the area was designated a national monument in 1937 and later incorporated into the larger Capitol Reef National Park in 1971. Fruita's last few residents departed in the 1960s.

EXPLORING THE PARK

Capitol Reef is one of the lesser-known parks in the Southwest – a plus for outdoor enthusiasts who are put off by the crowds at Grand Canyon and Zion. It adjoins Grand Staircase–Escalante National Monument and Glen Canyon National Recreation Area to the south and is halfway between Bryce Canyon and Canyonlands National Parks. It is easily reached from UT Scenic Byway 12 to the south or from I-70 to the north. UT 24 cuts across the middle of the park, following the winding Fremont River beneath sheer sandstone cliffs. On the east, these cliffs open into a series of humpbacks, known to the Paiutes as "the sleeping rainbow." Roads on either side of the Waterpocket Fold swing south from UT 24, providing numerous possibilities for exploring the park by car, bicycle or on foot.

Because it follows the Fold, the park is much longer than it is wide and can be divided roughly into three sections: the rugged, remote northern section of Cathedral Valley paralleling the northeastern exposure of the Fold; the accessible Escarpment section, encompassing park headquarters at Fruita, the Fremont River and a particularly scenic portion of the Fold; and

> **Tip**
> Capitol Reef National Park (www.nps.gov/care) is open 24 hours, throughout the year, though the visitor center and other facilities tend to open from 8am–4.30pm daily. Admission is $20 per vehicle, valid for seven days (motorbikes $15; individuals hiking or cycling $10; aged 15 and under are free). The Interagency Annual Pass ($80) is valid here.

Chimney Rock, Capitol Reef National Park.

the southernmost section of the park, the Waterpocket District above Bullfrog Basin in Glen Canyon, where the great rock waves of the Fold reach 1,500 ft (460 meters) in height and are cut by a labyrinth of deep canyons.

This is a park that inspires strong emotions. It is remote and desperately hot and dry in summer (unless you find yourself caught in a summer downpour, when most of the park's scant 7 inches/18 cm of precipitation falls). To keep cool, either view the park from your car or stick to one of the day hikes off the Scenic Drive south of Fruita and UT 24, such as those at **Grand Wash**, **Capitol Gorge**, the **Goosenecks Overlook**, **Sunset Point** and **Hickman Bridge**. If you do hope to explore the park on foot, bring adequate weather protection, water, food and backpacking equipment; supplies are not available in the park. There are numerous places where you can hike and camp off-trail. Plan your trip carefully before venturing out by obtaining a free backcountry map from rangers at the visitor center.

A young mule deer, Capitol Reef National Park.

THE ESCARPMENT

If you haven't been to Capitol Reef before, start your visit in the **Escarpment** section of the park on UT 24. Park headquarters is in the pretty little former Mormon community of Fruita, which sits next to an emerald belt of cottonwoods, tamarisks and willows along the Fremont River. Views here are incredible, especially after a summer rainstorm. You'll be surrounded on all sides by cliffs of Navajo Sandstone atop the sheer Wingate Sandstone, which have been moulded by erosion into domes, buttes, pillows and knobs that contrast with a startling blue sky.

Stop first at the **Capitol Reef Visitor Center** Ⓐ (tel: 435-425 3791; daily: Apr–Nov 8am–4.30pm, Dec–Mar 9am–4pm;) to pick up self-guided tour leaflets and hiking information, view exhibits, and buy books and maps. If you plan to do any backcountry driving on the Bullfrog-Notom Road to Lake Powell, the Burr Trail in the southern part of the park, or in Cathedral Valley, be sure to ask about road conditions before setting out. These high-clearance roads wash out after bad weather and are not recommended at such times.

The 200-acre (80-hectare) **Fruita Historic District** Ⓑ includes the 1896 one-room **Schoolhouse**, the 1908 **Gifford Homestead**, the **Blacksmith's Shop**, barns and the historic **Fruit Orchards**, containing roughly 3,000 trees, the most extensive in the National Park System. If you spend the night in the park's grassy campground (highly recommended; 71-site **Fruita Campground** is the only developed campground in the park), you can stroll the trails linking these historic structures and pick fruit in the orchards as it comes into season. The peaches are especially tasty.

The tree-lined banks of the Fremont River also provide shade on days when temperatures approach 100°F (37°C). The river and the shallow pools at the base of seeping sandstone walls are

CAPITOL REEF NATIONAL PARK | 227

an oasis where trees and water-loving plants, such as columbines, monkeyflowers and ferns grow. They are also popular haunts for mule deer, warblers, ringtail cats, frogs and other desert denizens who come to drink and splash during cool desert evenings and mornings. In winter, you can sometimes surprise a mountain lion or bobcat emboldened by the lack of visitors.

It is a mistake to imagine that the desert is devoid of life. In reality, the many creatures, large and small, that live here have adapted to a life beneath rocks, in underground burrows, or hidden in narrow canyons, where sunlight and human visitors rarely interrupt their privacy. On the slippery cliffs towering above the river, pinyon and juniper trees struggle with the elements, sending roots into pockets of soil. These dune-deposited rocks were laid down in a vast desert roughly 190 million years ago and, over time, compressed into mineralized rocks several miles thick.

The 8-mile (13-km) **Scenic Drive** south of Fruita takes you through the dramatic western exposure of the Waterpocket Fold into Grand Wash and Capitol Gorge, two water-carved, sheer-walled canyons. Along the drive, older rocks of the Shinarump Conglomerate, Chinle and Moenkopi formations reveal their ancient origins in sluggish streams and rivers during the time of the dinosaurs. In **Capitol Gorge** G (and along a roadside trail off UT 24) is 1,000-year-old rock art left behind by prehistoric Fremont people between AD 700 and 1250. These first residents of Capitol Reef cultivated fields of hardy corn along the fertile floodplain and stored crops in granaries in side canyons. They hunted bighorn sheep and deer and made unique moccasins from the hide, using a deer's dewclaw for traction on the heel. Their early pottery was unpainted gray or black, with raised or tooled surfaces. Later, they began to decorate this grayware with black paint – similar to Mesa Verde ceramics – possibly as a result of contact with Ancestral Pueblo neighbors to the south.

CATHEDRAL VALLEY

Abundant evidence of geologic activity is on view in the northern section of the

The highway from Torrey, Utah to Capitol Reef National Park.

⊙ THE MAN BEHIND THE PARK

Ephraim Portman Pectol was the owner of a store in Torrey and served as a Mormon bishop there from 1911 to 1928. He enjoyed exploring Capitol Reef and collecting Fremont artifacts, which he displayed in a small private museum inside his store.

In 1921, Pectol organized a boosters club in Torrey, with the sole aim of promoting the scenic attractions of Wayne County. The club mounted a major media campaign, using articles and photographs of the area to drum up nationwide interest for a park. Wayne Wonderland Club paid Salt Lake City photographer J. E. Broaddus to take a series of promotional photographs and travel around lecturing on Wayne Wonderland.

Pectol's long campaign to establish Wayne Wonderland National Monument succeeded soon after he was elected to the legislature in 1933. Four years later, Capitol Reef National Monument was set aside by President Franklin D. Roosevelt. It was expanded and upgraded to a national park in 1971. Sleeping Rainbow Ranch, a former dude ranch and motel along Pleasant Creek belonging to Lurt Knee and his wife Alice, was passed to the park in 1978. In 2008 it was refurbished as the Capitol Reef Field Station, a scientific research center collecting data on the large number of endemic plant species found in the area.

> **Tip**
>
> In the remote northern section of the park, you can stay at the primitive six-site Cathedral Valley Campground (free) close to Upper Cathedral Valley Overlook, and another campground at summer-only **Elkhorn** (first-come first-served) in Fishlake National Forest, outside the park limits.

park. East of the Waterpocket Fold, the enormous drainage area of **Cathedral Valley** D fans southeast from the base of Thousand Lake Mountain in the South Desert, where more recent volcanism and glaciation have built and sculpted the high country beyond Capitol Reef. In this extremely arid section of the park, accessible only on foot or by four-wheel-drive, thick layers of red Entrada sandstone have been whittled by erosion into 500-ft (150-meter) spires that seem to guard the rugged landscape. The exposed location is home to only the hardiest desert plants. Burrowing creatures such as kangaroo rats, jackrabbits and cottontails have found a way to survive here – even though these same animals form the diet of gray foxes, coyotes, mountain lions, golden eagles, ravens and other peripatetic desert dwellers.

Most visitors drive the 57.6-mile (92.7 km) **Cathedral Valley Driving Loop Tour** (allow 6–8 hours), beginning on Hartnet Road east of the visitor center, though the route requires fording the Fremont River; do not attempt to cross during periods of high water.

Golden Throne, Capitol Reef National Park.

WATERPOCKET DISTRICT

For "desert rats" used to the rigors of hiking over naked slickrock, the **Waterpocket District** at the southernmost tip of the Fold is the most alluring. It can be reached via the dirt **Notom-Bullfrog Road**, which runs down the east side of the Fold all the way to Bullfrog Marina at Lake Powell, or by turning off at Boulder along UT 12 and crossing the famous **Burr Trail Road**, the 34-mile (58-km) paved route across the Waterpocket Fold built by rancher John Atlantic Burr in the late 1800s. The full 124-mile (199 km) **Loop-The-Fold Driving Tour** from the visitor center in Fruita usually takes 4–6 hours.

On this southern exposure of the Waterpocket Fold, Capitol Reef adjoins the wilderness that surrounds the Escalante River and its canyons in Grand Staircase–Escalante National Monument, and here the true meaning of canyon country becomes apparent. The best way to explore the region is to hike south from the intersection of Burr Trail and Notom-Bullfrog Road through 16-mile (26-km) **Muley Twist Canyon** E. This route takes you through steep canyon narrows to an exceptionally wild area of the park around Lower Halls Creek where, for a few years in the early 1880s, Hole-in-the-Rock pioneer Charles Hall ferried passengers across the Colorado River.

The Burr Trail Road south from the Notom-Bullfrog junction remains unpaved for another 3.3 miles (5.3 km) to the park boundary, then continues (paved) for 32.5 miles (52.3 km) to Bullfrog Marina in Glen Canyon National Recreation Area (see page 216).

TORREY AND ENVIRONS

If, like many visitors, you're traveling east on UT 24 through Capitol Reef to Moab – all in one long day – it's easy to miss much of what makes the park and surrounding area so special. That takes a bit more time. Instead, plan to spend the night in the park's campground or in nearby Torrey and explore Wayne County – an area that is 97 percent public land.

Tiny **Torrey** F, a mile west of the UT 12/24 junction, is a quintessential Mormon ranching and farming community, complete with irrigation ditch and a historic LDS church. But that doesn't mean culture has passed it by. It has a modest but worthwhile art gallery, an enterprising visitors bureau (https://capitolreef.org), an organization that offers seasonal public lectures on topics of local interest, the area's only four-star bed-and-breakfast, an annual Cowboy Music and Poetry Festival, and several high-end restaurants whose chefs serve farm-raised trout from nearby Loa and organic produce from Mesa Farm (https://mesafarm-market.com) in Caineville.

The technicolor country surrounding Capitol Reef has long attracted writers and artists. Zane Grey and Wallace Stegner found inspiration in the redrocks, as did artists Maynard Dixon and comic-book illustrator Dick Sprang, who drew his most famous character, Batman, while living here.

In the 1970s, Salt Lake City travel writer Ward Roylance fell in love with the Capitol Reef area and moved here with his wife. Until his death in 1993, Roylance fought tirelessly to preserve the area. His book, *Enchanted Wilderness,* is a little-known classic and led to the founding of the nonprofit **Entrada Institute** (70 S. 200 West St; http://www.entradainstitute.org), dedicated to preserving the red-rock country and its heritage through arts and education. The Institute is a Torrey fixture, offering public workshops, readings, demonstrations and lectures every weekend in July and August on topics such as rock art, astronomy, the environment and historical characters. Entrada occupies part of Roylance's hand-built, pyramid-shaped home. The nearby **Torrey Gallery** (160 W. Main St; tel: 435-425 3909; www.torreygallery.com) displays Navajo rugs and works by Bonnie Posselli, Doug Snow and other Utah artists.

Continue west on UT 24 through **Bicknell**, where you can view the 1890s **Nielsen Grist Mill** from a roadside interpretive pullout. Bicknell has a few places to stay and eat, but the town has seen better days. In does boast one of the smallest cinemas in the region, the restored 1947 **Bicknell Theater** (11 E. Main St; tel: 435-425 3493; www.thebicknelltheater.com), still showing new releases, and the Reel Bites Café serving hot sandwiches, fruit smoothies and ice cream.

There are numerous hiking and camping opportunities in Dixie National Forest on **Boulder Mountain** (off UT 12 between Boulder and Torrey) and Fishlake National Forest on **Thousand Lake Mountain**, north of Bicknell. For more information, contact the Fishlake National Forest headquarters (115 E. 900 North St, Richfield; tel: 435-896 9233). The cool, forested mountains, reaching 12,000 ft (3,660 meters) in elevation, are reason enough to stick around Torrey when the temperatures at lower elevations soar.

Egyptian Temple, Capitol Reef National Park.

Canyonlands National Park.

CANYONLANDS NATIONAL PARK

The Green and Colorado rivers converge in the heart of Canyon Country, where ancient pueblo ruins combine with enthralling landscapes and lots of recreational opportunities.

Canyonlands sprawls at the physical and emotional center of the geologic province known as the Colorado Plateau. Here, across a tilted, tiered, and carved rock stage, one of nature's longest-running dramas plays every day – an epic in which rock, river, weather, and finely adapted living things all have equal roles.

Stewart Udall, who as US Secretary of the Interior was midwife to the congressional bill that created **Canyonlands National Park** ① in 1964, described the region as "a vast area of scenic wonders and recreational opportunities unduplicated elsewhere on the American continent or in the world." You will certainly need to plan your trip to this 527 sq mile (1,365 sq km) park carefully, as it is divided into four distinct units – Island in the Sky, the Needles, the Maze, and the converging Green and Colorado rivers – all of which deserve equal consideration. For Horseshoe Canyon, see page 167.

EXPLORING THE PARK

If you have only a day, the 6,000ft (1,830-meter) plateau of **Island in the Sky**, situated in the northern part of Canyonlands atop the Y created by the conjoining rivers, offers sweeping views of the park, a visitor center, interpretive talks, the primitive Sky Campground (Willow Flat), and short, rugged hikes to salt domes, arches, and other geologic features. No water is available; be sure to bring plenty with you. The road to this unit begins 7 miles (10km) north of Moab, then southwest from UT 313 for another 25 miles (40km). Float trips above the confluence of the Green and Colorado rivers – one of the most pleasurable ways to experience the park – are popular, as are mountain biking and four-wheel driving.

You can arrange trips into Canyonlands with park concessionaires,

Main attractions
Dead Horse Point State Park
Grand View Point Overlook
Green and Colorado River trips
The Maze
The Needles District
Upheaval Dome
White Rim Road

Maps on pages 232 and 250

Dead Horse State Park.

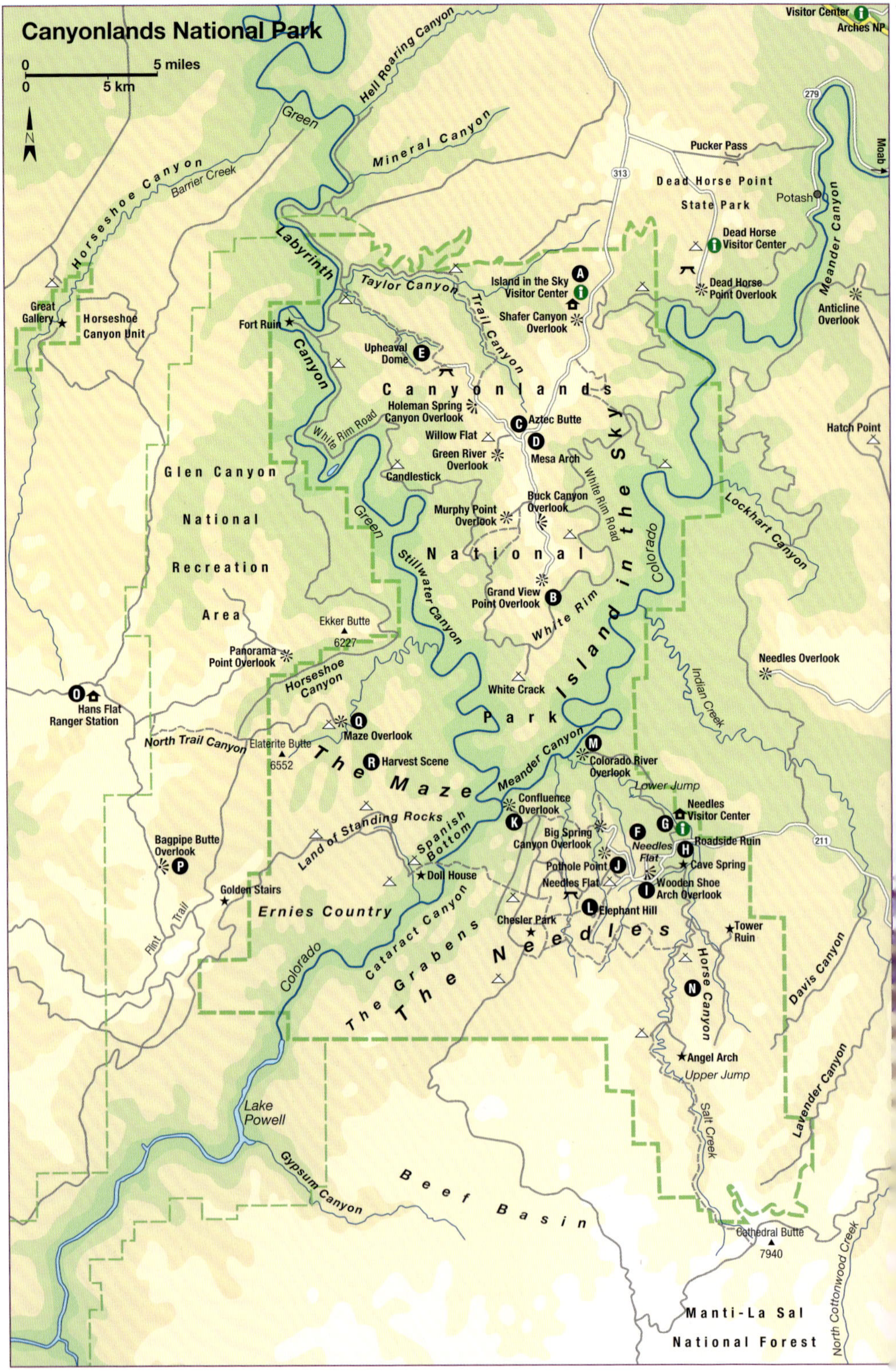
Canyonlands National Park
0 5 miles
0 5 km
N
Visitor Center
Arches NP
Hell Roaring Canyon
Green
Mineral Canyon
Horseshoe Canyon
Barrier Creek
279
Moab
Pucker Pass
313
Dead Horse Point
State Park
Potash
Dead Horse Point
Visitor Center
Dead Horse Point Overlook
Meander Canyon
Anticline Overlook
Labyrinth
Taylor Canyon
Island in the Sky Visitor Center
Great Gallery
Horseshoe Canyon Unit
Fort Ruin
Shafer Canyon Overlook
Trail Canyon
Canyon
Upheaval Dome
Canyonlands
Holeman Spring Canyon Overlook
Aztec Butte
White Rim Road
Willow Flat
Mesa Arch
Green River Overlook
Hatch Point
Candlestick
Glen Canyon
National
Recreation
Area
Buck Canyon Overlook
White Rim Road
Murphy Point Overlook
Green
Lockhart Canyon
Stillwater Canyon
National
Island in the Sky
Colorado
Grand View Point Overlook
White Rim
Ekker Butte
6227
Panorama Point Overlook
Horseshoe Canyon
White Crack
Needles Overlook
Indian Creek
Hans Flat Ranger Station
Park
Maze Overlook
North Trail Canyon
Elaterite Butte
6552
The Maze
Harvest Scene
Meander Canyon
Colorado River Overlook
Lower Jump
Confluence Overlook
Needles Visitor Center
Land of Standing Rocks
Spanish Bottom
Big Spring Canyon Overlook
Roadside Ruin
211
Bagpipe Butte Overlook
Needles Flat
Pothole Point
Cave Spring
Doll House
Needles Flat
Wooden Shoe Arch Overlook
Golden Stairs
Elephant Hill
Ernies Country
Cataract Canyon
Chesler Park
Tower Ruin
Flint Trail
The Needles
The Grabens
Horse Canyon
Davis Canyon
Colorado
Angel Arch
Upper Jump
Lavender Canyon
Lake Powell
Salt Creek
Gypsum Canyon
Beef Basin
Cathedral Butte
7940
North Cottonwood Creek
Manti-La Sal
National Forest

located primarily in Moab or Green River; for a list, visit the park website or the multi-agency **Moab Information Center** (25 E Center St, Moab; tel: 435-259 8825; www.discovermoab.com; daily 8am–5pm).

The best way to see canyon country up close is to drive south 40 miles (64km) on US 191, then another 36 miles (56km) on UT 211 into the **Needles District**, where a dizzying array of sandstone arches, fins, buttes, spires, and canyons rival Ancestral Pueblo ruins and rock art for beauty and abundance. The Needles has an attractive, air-conditioned visitor center with exhibits and a bookstore; the 26-site Needles Campground; primitive backcountry campsites; and several unpaved roads and undeveloped hiking trails.

The remote **Maze District**, once described as "a 30 sq mile puzzle in sandstone," can only be reached by foot or four-wheel drive vehicle from west of the park (or from the river). If you're equipped with water, food, backpacking supplies, spare tires, and winches and are willing to spend extra time in the park's remote reaches, the Maze contains a rich variety of desert landscapes and rock art.

GREEN AND COLORADO RIVER TRIPS

For "river rats," there's no better way to go into the heart of this convoluted canyon country than to follow in the wake of explorer Major John Wesley Powell, who made daring runs down the Green and Colorado Rivers in 1869 and 1871–72. Both rivers are calm upstream of the river confluence, perfect for canoes and kayaks. Below the river confluence, the swollen Colorado erupts into roaring white water for the 14 miles (23km) that link sheer-walled Cataract Canyon with Lake Powell. River running here is challenging and carefully monitored by the National Park Service; only experienced river runners should attempt the trip independently. River Permits are required for flatwater or Cataract Canyon day-use or overnight trips through www.recreation.gov or in person from the Backcountry Permit Office in Moab (Mon–Fri 8am–4pm) or from any Canyonlands visitor center (minimum two days before launch). Overnight permits are valid for 14 days and include reserved campsites in the backcountry. Since Canyonlands is cold in winter and exceedingly hot and dry in summer, spring and fall are the most popular times. Local outfitters offer a variety of guided river trips (by jet boat, whitewater raft, kayak, or more sedate river boats); try Adrift Adventures of Canyonlands (www.adrift.net); Canyonlands by Night and Day (https://canyonlandsbynight.com); Mild to Wild Rafting (https://mild2wildrafting.com); or Wilderness River Adventures (www.riveradventures.com).

ISLAND IN THE SKY

Rock is the leitmotiv of Canyonlands. In order to understand its scope, drive

> **Fact**
> Canyonlands National Park (www.nps.gov/cany) is open 24 hours year-round. Each district has its own visitor center with operating hours that vary seasonally, but usually open daily 8am–5pm in the summer. Admission is $30 per vehicle, valid for seven days (motorbikes $25; individuals hiking or cycling $15; aged 15 and under are free). The Interagency Annual Pass ($80) is valid.

Island in the Sky, Canyonlands.

south from **Island in the Sky Visitor Center** Ⓐ (tel: 435-259 4712; late Mar–Oct daily 8am–5pm; mid-Feb–late Mar and Nov–Dec daily 8am–4pm; Jan–mid-Feb Thu–Mon 9am–4pm) to **Grand View Point Overlook** Ⓑ, which is the best place to survey the 360-degree panorama that unfolds before you. Hidden in the northeast are the soaring red-rock landmarks of Arches National Park. To the east rise the tall, volcanic crags of the La Sal Mountains, imposing yet inviting. Closer to the park, beneath Dead Horse Point State Park, loop the famous "goosenecks" of the **Colorado River**, marking the park's eastern border.

To the west, the equally contorted **Green River** winds through **Labyrinth Canyon**, its narrow meanders forming the boundary with Glen Canyon National Recreation Area. To the southwest, the Henry Mountains obstruct the view of Capitol Reef National Park, their great bulk looming beyond the Maze. The view south encompasses more than 100 miles (160km) of drifting tablelands and swirling canyons, including the junction of the Colorado and Green Rivers, bound on either side by the eroded sandstone of The Needles and the tortuous passages of The Maze. The scenic drive to Grand View Point offers several places for stopping and hiking. Short trails to **Aztec Butte** Ⓒ (2 miles/3 km) and **Mesa Arch** Ⓓ (800 meters) are clearly marked by piles of rock, or cairns, on the slickrock.

Just below this sky island is the **White Rim Road**, a circuitous, 100-mile (160km) dirt trail that was used by prospectors mining uranium in the colorful Chinle Formation in the 1950s. This popular mountain bike and four-wheel drive route follows a bench of White Rim Sandstone through prime bighorn sheep territory. Note that you must get a day-use permit to traverse White Rim Road; 50 permits are allowed each day for vehicles, and 50 for mountain bikes (25 via www.recreation.gov and 25 in person from visitor centers the day before your trip).

Plants struggle to survive in this arid environment – in cracks in the rock and in fragile, "brown sugar" patches of cryptobiotic soil. Although it doesn't look like much, cryptobiotic soil is a primary building block of all living things in canyon country. It is actually a community of mutually beneficial living organisms – lichens, mosses, microfungi, and blue-green algae – that work together to reduce erosion, increase water retention, and encourage soil fertility. These hummocks protect young pinyons, junipers, blackbrush, grasses, and wildflowers and allow them to root, stabilize the desert soil, and prosper. As they say in these parts: "Don't Bust the Crust." Keep to the trail or bypass these sensitive soils by walking in sandy washes and on the rocks. Adaptable reptiles, such as whip-tailed lizards, and ground squirrels, canyon mice and other gnawing creatures are found on the plateau. They make fine fare for peripatetic coyotes and gray foxes and alert sky patrollers, such as eagles, ravens, and red-tailed hawks.

Washer woman arch in Utah's Canyonlands National Park.

CANYONLANDS NATIONAL PARK

The rocks in this park contain a color-coded record of sediment deposited over the past 300 million years, in a succession of seas, beaches, deserts, rivers, and streams. But the accounting is not complete; more than a vertical mile of recent strata has already been borne away by the youthful enthusiasm of the Colorado and Green Rivers, which began scouring the land as the massive Colorado Plateau was forced up. The topography is forever changing. As the sediment-laden rivers cut their paths, and ground water, ice, snow, and wind break down the rocks, the eroded beauty of Canyonlands will one day be merely a memory.

One of the best ways to confront the geologic processes that brought Canyonlands into being is to hike the trail to **Upheaval Dome** E, a short way from the main road in Island in the Sky. Just below you is a 1,500ft (460-meter) crater filled with a jumble of rocks. Some geologists believe this is a collapsed salt dome; others, the site of a meteor impact; still others a combination of the two.

The 11 layers of sedimentary rocks on display in Canyonlands sit uneasily on a layer of salt thousands of feet thick – the remnant of evaporated seas that lay trapped here 300 million years ago. As overlying sediments pressed down on this salt – the Paradox Formation – it became soft and mobile and began to move away from the weight. Highlands blocked it on the east, so it flowed west until it encountered ancient fault blocks that forced the salt to bulge upward, forming the cracked salt domes you see throughout the large Paradox Basin. Groundwater began to seep into the fractures, dissolving the salt and deepening the joints through many layers of sedimentary rocks. This weathering of sandstone has created memorable features throughout the park – some of the most spectacular are found in the carved, banded spires of Cedar Mesa Sandstone in The Needles.

THE NEEDLES

The turnoff for The Needles district lies 14 miles (23km) north of **Monticello**,

Dead Horse Point, Canyonlands National Park.

⊘ DEAD HORSE POINT STATE PARK

Situated next to the Island in the Sky district of Canyonlands, 5,250-acre (21 sq km) Dead Horse Point State Park (tel: 435-259 2614; https://stateparks.utah.gov/parks/dead-horse; daily 6am–10pm; visitor center daily 9am–5pm) has breathtaking views of the La Sal Mountains, eroded cliffs, mesas, buttes, and river canyons. At the base of the mesa is an enormous horseshoe bend, or entrenched meander, carved by the Colorado River.

Before the turn of the century, mustang herds ran wild on the mesas near Dead Horse Point. The promontory provided a natural corral used by cowboys for rounding up horses. The only escape was through a narrow, 30-meter "neck" of land controlled by fencing. Mustangs were then roped and broken, with the better ones being kept for personal use or sold to eastern markets.

According to one legend, a band of broomtails was left corralled on the Point. The gate was supposedly left open so the horses could return to the open range. For some unknown reason, the mustangs remained on the Point and died of thirst.

Dead Horse Point is a popular movie location; in 1991 it served as the backdrop for the final scenes of *Thelma and Louise*. The park has 10 miles (16km) of rim trails and a 21-site campground with developed facilities and makes a useful base for exploring the surrounding lands.

on US 191, where paved UT 211 follows Indian Creek to **Needles Flat** F. This is one of those rare places in Canyonlands blessed with deeper soils that allow Indian ricegrass, galleta, and other useful grasses to establish themselves. Until 1975, local cowboys ran their cattle here in winter, leaving behind line camps in shady overhangs such as Cave Creek.

After the **Needles Visitor Center** G (tel: 435-259 4711; mid-Feb–Nov daily 8am–5pm; Dec–mid-Feb Fri–Sat 9am–4pm), the scenic drive passes **Roadside Ruin** H, a small Ancestral Pueblo dwelling, and **Wooden Shoe Arch Overlook** I, which has views of a clog-shaped rock formation to the east. **Pothole Point** J is named for the depressions in the rock that trap rainwater for thousands of microorganisms, such as miraculous tadpole shrimp, which can survive even when water isn't present. The road ends at **Big Spring Canyon Overlook**, where a strenuous trail to **Confluence Overlook** K (10 miles/16.5km) begins.

From **Needles Campground**, a 3-mile (5km) unpaved spur leads to **Elephant Hill** L, and thence a dirt road takes you to the collapsing fins of the **Grabens** near the river – you need a permit to go to Elephant Hill and note that this is a very technical four-wheel drive road. The 5-mile (8km), round-trip **Chesler Park Trail**, which eventually passes through a meadow surrounded by eroded rocks, makes a good hike from Elephant Hill. The canyons and meadows of The Needles support many wood rats, chipmunks, squirrels, kangaroo rats, and other rodents, as well as horned larks and black-throated sparrows.

There are several places along the scenic drive to turn off and explore. One four-wheel drive road, beginning at the visitor center, takes you north to the **Colorado River Overlook** M. The sandy road is decent until the last 1.5 miles (2.4 km), when stair-step rocks and tight turns make for some nerve-wracking moments – park your four-wheel drive and walk down. Another short, unpaved spur south of the scenic drive leads to **Cave Spring Trail** (0.6 miles/1 km), which preserves a historic cowboy camp beside a spring. The camp is a reminder that much of Canyonlands was grazed by cattle and sheep from the late 1800s until well into the 20th century.

From Cave Spring, you will need a four-wheel drive vehicle or sturdy legs to explore sandy-bottomed **Salt Creek**, the only year-round riparian area in Canyonlands beside the Colorado and Green rivers. Salt Creek Road is closed beyond Peekaboo Spring (the site of a rock art panel) in order to protect park resources, and is often impassable due to deep sand, deep water, and quicksand – the **Salt Creek Canyon Trail** (22.5 miles/34km) continues south to Cathedral Butte. Salt Creek has more cultural remains of Ancestral Pueblo people, who lived here between about AD 1 and 1300, than anywhere else in the park. Salt Creek's main tributary, **Horse Canyon** N (which can be explored on

Upheaval Dome, Canyonlands National.

rough four-wheel drive road), also has hidden ancient Native American dwellings, the masonry structure of **Tower Ruin**, as well as the **Thirteen Faces**, red-and-white pictographs painted on the sandstone walls. Pueblo families farmed along ephemeral washes, now overgrown with willow, tamarisk, and cottonwood, but they continued to hunt small game and supplement meals with seeds, nuts, and edible plants. Surplus grain was stored in granaries built into hard-to-reach ledges. About 100 families lived in this area, probably using these cliff-side homes seasonally and farming atop the mesas in summer. Rock paintings found in these canyons portray large, mysterious, anthropomorphs, both shield-shaped and triangular, bejeweled and brightly painted in red, white, and sometimes blue. Images were also pecked into the walls. Here as elsewhere, you may look but not touch rock art. Disturbing artifacts is strictly prohibited. Archaeologists speculate that when life here became too tough sometime in the 1200s, the Ancestral Puebloans moved to farmlands along the Rio Grande and the Little Colorado, where their descendants still live.

THE MAZE

An even earlier culture has also been identified in Canyonlands: The Archaic people who hunted and gathered here between 10,000 and 2,000 years ago. You can go as far as **Hans Flat Ranger Station** O (tel: 435-719 2218; daily 8am–4.30pm), reached along a 46-mile (74km) unpaved road from UT 24 north of Hanksville. After that, you'll need a four-wheel drive to get around this incredibly tangled landscape, much of which can only be hiked.

Several long unpaved roads traverse wild country dotted with strangely named landmarks, which, in true Western style, arose from differing perspectives of Indigenous peoples, early adventurers, and poetic travelers. A road leads north to Horseshoe Canyon (see page 167), south to **Bagpipe Butte Overlook** P, then east along the Flint Trail to Ernies Country and the Land of Standing Rocks. From here you can hike through the **Doll House** above the river confluence and down into Spanish Bottom on the Colorado River. For a look into The Maze, backtrack to the Golden Stairs, then drive northeast to the **Maze Overlook** Q or hike the 14-mile (23km) **North Trail Canyon** to the overlook. A 3-mile (5km) trail leads into The Maze itself, where Archaic pictographs known as the **Harvest Scene** R reward your efforts. The Maze is the park's most pristine experience – a place where quiet desert residents, such as kit foxes, coyotes, and mountain lions, are bolder, and unexpected seeps deep in the canyons nourish throngs of maidenhair ferns, mosses, monkeyflowers, and columbines. It is rugged, beautiful country, but it can be treacherous. You need to be an experienced and well-prepared hiker or four-wheel driver (towing fees in Canyonlands start at $1,500). Err on the side of caution and talk to park rangers before attempting a trip.

> **Tip**
> Note that you must have a day-use permit for all trips on Elephant Hill Road and Salt Creek (Peekaboo)/Horse Canyon roads in the Needles district. Get one online (www.recreation.gov; $6) or at any visitor center (free) the day before your trip. Only 24 vehicles and 12 mountain bikes are permitted per day on Elephant Hill Road.

The Elephant Hill Trail in the Needles District of the Canyonlands National Park.

Arches National Park.

ARCHES NATIONAL PARK AND THE MOAB AREA

Mountain bikers, river runners, rock climbers and other adventurers come to play at a hip desert town surrounded by a beguiling sandstone wilderness.

◎ **Main attractions**
Delicate Arch
Devils Garden
Fiery Furnace
Landscape Arch
La Sal Mountain Loop
Panorama Point
Slickrock Trail
Utah Scenic Byway 128
Utah Scenic Byway 279
The Windows Section

Maps on pages 240 and 250

One of the pleasures of a trip across the Colorado Plateau is the way its ever-changing topography pushes us to understand our surroundings according to different rules, to change our sense of what is normal. **Arches National Park** ❷, with its world-renowned population of carved, salmon-colored arches, fins, spires, pinnacles and balanced rocks, is a case in point. Here, the very landmarks for which this park is famous are windows through which we experience the natural world in a new way. This 120-sq-mile (310-sq-km) desert park, 5 miles (8 km) north of Moab, is home to more than 2,000 natural arches and many other strangely eroded red-rock giants. Moab itself has become the outdoorsy capital of eastern Utah and a mountain biking and off-roading hub, with an excellent array of restaurants and motels. From here you can also explore some tantalizing scenic byways, taking in wetlands, trails, arches, and the remains of ancient Native American civilizations.

ARCHES GEOLOGY

Arches has the largest number of natural sandstone arches in the world, with many more being formed all the time – the fortuitous result of location, geology and water erosion. You might think that the explanation for the large number of shape-shifting rocks in this place is complicated, but you would be wrong. The key to this odd convention of geologic landmarks is salt – a common enough commodity, which here has given rise (quite literally) to this high-relief landscape.

The salt that lies below Arches was deposited 300 million years ago, when a succession of large, shallow seas lay landlocked by the Uncompahgre Uplift, the highlands to the east where the La Sal Mountains are today. As the climate gradually dried, the

Natural rock arches in Arches National Park.

> **Fact**
>
> Arches National Park (www.nps.gov/arch) is open 24 hours, throughout the year, though the visitor center and other facilities open depending on the season. It's a busy park – enter before 8am or after 3pm to avoid the heaviest traffic. Admission is $30 per vehicle, valid for seven days (motorbikes $25; individuals hiking or cycling $15; aged 15 and under are free).

seawater evaporated, leaving behind salt deposits thousands of feet thick in an enormous depression known as the Paradox Basin. Eventually, the highlands began shedding debris into the basin, which compacted there, cemented by calcium carbonate and other minerals. Its tremendous weight bore down on the underlying Paradox deposits, causing the salt, which is somewhat "plastic," to flow west, away from the burden. The movement stalled when the salt ran up against ancient fault blocks.

One of the most obvious of these faults can be seen in rocks opposite the visitor center, where a 2,500-ft (760-meter) displacement along the Moab Fault has exposed the fossiliferous strata of the ancient Honaker Trail Formation – a rare glimpse of the rocks that make up the park's basement. Unable to move farther, the salt layer domed up through the 12 layers of rocks lying on top of it, cracking the rocks and weakening the strata. Joints appeared along these fault lines, giving groundwater a chance to enter and dissolve the salt. Undermined by this erosion, the salt domes began to collapse. The low-lying Salt and Cache Valleys and the parallel lines of formations sweeping across them (most evident from overlooks in the nearby La Sal Mountains) are testimony to this ongoing weakening of loosely cemented sedimentary rocks.

It's not difficult to understand what happened next. The evidence can be found everywhere in Arches. Once water, ice and snow went to work on the rock, deepening and widening joints, all manner of oddly carved stones gradually emerged, of which the delicate spans of reddish-brown sandstone, known as natural arches, are some of the most interesting.

EXPLORING ARCHES

Unlike neighboring Canyonlands, which requires many visits to appreciate, Arches is small enough to experience in a day by way of its paved scenic drive, pullouts and many short trails, yet large enough to warrant longer explorations into the backcountry,

Balanced rock on La Sal Mountains.

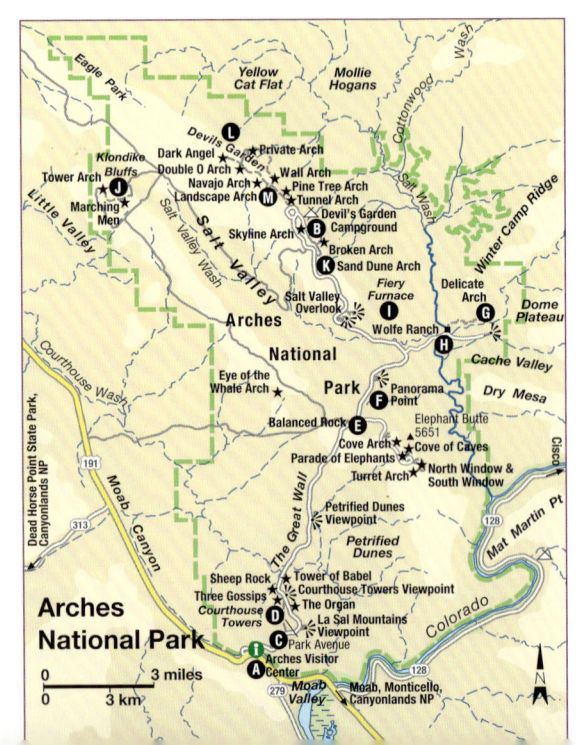

where its wild nature becomes apparent.

The entrance to Arches adjoins US 191, beyond the bridge over the Colorado River from Moab, which forms the southeastern boundary of the park. **Arches Visitor Center** Ⓐ (tel: 435-719 2299; Mar–Oct daily 8am–6pm, Nov–Feb daily 9am–4pm) is the place to pick up information, purchase books and maps, and watch a film on the park (every half hour). You can also sign up for ranger-led walks for the Fiery Furnace, a maze of convoluted rock fins just beyond Salt Valley, offered daily between April and October (Self-Guided Fiery Furnace Exploration Permits must be obtained at www.recreation.gov at least two days before your trip). Top off your water bottles here; water is only available at the visitor center and Devil's Garden Campground, 18 miles (29 km) north of the park entrance, at the end of the scenic drive.

Temperatures at this elevation reach 110°F (43°C) in summer, and thunderstorms and torrential rain are apt to swoop in suddenly. In winter, it is surprisingly frigid, with sub-freezing nighttime temperatures. The dry-rock landscape is occasionally transformed under a glittering white blanket of snow, making colors seem deeper and more intense – a great time to experience Arches with almost no other visitors. The area is subject to dramatic changes in temperature, which can fluctuate by 50°F (28°C) in a 24-hour period. Check the weather forecast before heading out, and take cover in your car if a thunderstorm blows in. Most of Arches is very exposed. On all hikes, bring plenty of water, wear sunscreen, a hat and sturdy hiking boots, and cover exposed skin in summer. The best time of day to hike is before 9am or in the evening. Night hikes are particularly beautiful. Naturally dark, unpolluted skies make star gazing a popular activity at Arches. The contrast of rock and sky makes this park an ideal location for viewing celestial events such as comets and eclipses.

PARK ACCOMMODATION

Many travelers have their hearts set on staying in **Devil's Garden Campground** Ⓑ (tel: 435-719 2299), an attractive 51-site area set amid the most popular arches in the park. Reservations (www.recreation.gov or tel: 1-877-444 6777) are essential March to October, when the campground tends to be full nightly. Reservations must be made at least four days ahead of your arrival (and up to six months in advance). Between November and February, all sites are first come, first served. Overnight stays in the backcountry require a permit, issued in person up to seven days in advance at the **Backcountry Permit Office** (2282 SW Resource Blvd, off US 191) two miles (3.2 km) south of Moab (not at Arches Visitor Center).

ARCHES SCENIC DRIVE

For a look at the many different types of arches and geologic phenomena in

Fiery Furnace, Arches National Park.

Tip

Timed reservations were required to visit Arches National Park Apr–Sept in 2022 (daily 6am–5pm) in a pilot scheme that is likely to be annual. Reserve at www.recreation.gov or by phone at tel: 877-444 6777. Once inside the park you can stay as long as you like (and even exit and re-enter the park on the same day).

Devils Garden Arch.

the park, take the scenic drive from the visitor center to **Devils Garden**, stopping to enjoy the viewpoints and short trails along the way. The first weathered rocks you encounter are the skyscraper-like monoliths in **Park Avenue** Ⓒ, so named because of the way their sheer walls jostle the skyline. Nearby, in the **Courthouse Towers** Ⓓ, are Sheep Rock, the Organ, the Tower of Babel and the Three Gossips, soaring giants composed of iron-rich Entrada sandstone, the principal rock layer in the park. Different rates of erosion in the three "members" of Entrada sandstone are responsible for the majority of features, with the lower Dewey Bridge Member crumbling easily beneath the harder Slick Rock Member. The uppermost layer, the white Moab Member, can be seen capping some of the higher landmarks. Underlying the Entrada are the swirling beds of cream-colored Navajo sandstone, whose ancient Sahara-like origins can easily be seen just beyond Courthouse Towers in the humped shapes of "petrified" sand dunes. In this open landscape, you get a great view of the 12,000-ft (3,600-meter) snowcapped La Sal Mountains, great laccoliths with hearts of lava, exposed by erosion in forested crags and peaks that dominate the eastern sky. Even if you don't have much time, park rangers recommend that you drive at least as far as the **Windows Section** (on a 2-mile/3.5-km paved spur road), for it is here that you can see the largest concentration of single and double arches, buttes, and windows, beginning with the gravity-defying **Balanced Rock** Ⓔ, just before the turning. Highlights include the North Window, Turret Arch, and Double Arch. Between May and August, Indian paintbrush, larkspur, sand verbena and other wildflowers blooming in front of the rocks are at their most photogenic. In the 1950s, irascible environmental activist Ed Abbey lived in a trailer next to Balanced Rock.

Back on the Scenic Drive just beyond the Windows Section turning, you can stop and take in much of the park at **Panorama Point** Ⓕ. The canyon of the Colorado River is visible on the park's southeast border. The green belt of willows, tamarisks and cottonwoods that grows long the waterway seems like a mirage at the edge of this sparsely vegetated salt valley, where only salt-tolerant plants like pickleweed and seepweed grow.

After Panorama Point, another spur road turns northeast for 3 miles (5 km), crossing an area of collapsed rocks of the more recent Dakota, Morrison and Mancos Formations. The road ends at a wheelchair-accessible trail that leads to a viewpoint of **Delicate Arch** Ⓖ, the world-famous symbol of Utah's red-rock country. Delicate Arch is actually not very tall – only 45 ft (14 meters) – but its location on the lip of a slickrock bowl gives it a dramatic bearing. For a close-up look, climb the steep trail to the arch – one of the most rewarding hikes in the park. The trail begins at a rudimentary cabin, the 1906 **Wolfe Ranch** ⓗ, which was home to Civil War veteran John Wesley Wolfe and his son. Wolfe came here for his health in 1888, but it's hard to understand why he settled in such a remote outpost so far from society. Maybe that was exactly the point. Canyon country seems to attract loners who value silence and the harmony of the desert. Near the cabin is an important rock art panel, containing pictographs depicting horses drawn by the Ute, the only place in the park with clear signs of their presence.

FIERY FURNACE AND DEVIL'S GARDEN

A few miles farther along the main Scenic Drive, you reach the flaming rock fins known as **Fiery Furnace** ⓘ, which explode with vibrant color at sunset. If time permits, sign up at the visitor center for this three-hour guided hike; it's one of the most spectacular backcountry hikes in the park but not a good idea to do alone. There is no marked trail through the radiating rocks, so it is quite easy to lose your way. The Fiery Furnace is popular with seasoned rock climbers who may enter (with permit) in a private group or with local outfitters.

Beyond Fiery Furnace, a left turn onto a gravel road leads 9 miles (14 km) across Salt Valley to **Klondike Bluffs** ⓙ, whose Marching Men and Tower Arch formations so impressed prospector Alexander Ringhoffer that he persuaded the railroad to conduct tours to the spot in 1923. Arches was named a national monument just six years later, though it did not become a national park until 1971. Klondike is now one of the least visited places in the park. A moderate 3.5-mile (5.5-km) trail leads to Tower Arch from a parking lot. Look for fresh deer tracks and occasional mountain lion tracks. Whistle loudly if you see the latter, to avoid any unexpected encounters.

Head back to the Scenic Drive to visit **Sand Dune Arch** ⓚ, which shelters a large sand dune at its base – a fun place for the family to romp. Nearby **Skyline Arch** demonstrates how

Lizard climbing the rocks in Arches National Park.

ⓞ ARCHES FLORA AND FAUNA

While out hiking in Arches National Park, stay on the trails. The desert floor is dotted with dark patches of cryptobiotic soil, composed of mosses, lichen, fungi and algae that retain moisture, protect against erosion, and provide nitrogen and other nutrients in which plants can grow. Once stepped on, this fragile, new soil, on which so much new life depends, is destroyed for centuries. Plants and animals must be very choosy about where they live in this difficult environment, jealously guarding their special places in an ongoing bid for survival. Desert creatures are generally nocturnal, venturing out only when the desert cools down. You are likely to hear the yip of coyotes at night, as they and gray foxes trot great distances in search of jackrabbits, cottontails, ground squirrels and the smaller rodents you may hear investigating your campsite at night. Rattlesnakes, collared lizards and other reptiles, which are unable to control body temperatures, doze beneath rocks and bushes at midday (so watch where you put your hands). The sheerest cliffs make good perches for lazy-winged golden eagles and red-tailed hawks, while the joyous song of the tiny canyon wren bounces off seeping sandstone walls decorated with colorful water-loving plants.

| Eat

Moab is a great place to eat. Moab Diner (189 S. Main St; tel: 435 259 4006; www.moabdiner.com; Mon–Sat 6am–10pm) knocks out great breakfasts, while Red Rock Bakery (74 S. Main St; tel: 435-259 5941; daily 6.30am–1pm) is the spot for homemade bread, bagel sandwiches, pastries.

quickly the rocks here can change. A major rockfall in November 1940 doubled its size overnight. The Scenic Drive ends at **Devils Garden** Ⓛ, where the park's densest array of arches and fins makes a fitting climax to any visit. Several easy trails meander among its soaring spans. A 1-mile (1.6-km) trail from the road leads to **Landscape Arch** Ⓜ, a 306-ft (93-meter) span of "desert varnished" beige rock, one of the longest natural arches in the world (the longest is in Zion National Park). You may continue from Landscape Arch to two other formations – **Double O Arch** and **Dark Angel**. A short side trail leads to massive **Navajo Arch** and the twin openings of **Partition Arch**.

MOAB AND ENVIRONS

Travelers on the Spanish Trail in the 1830s and 1840s forded the Colorado River just north of modern-day **Moab** ❸. Few towns in the Southwest have as beautiful and dramatic a setting as this bustling small town. Sheer sandstone cliffs form fortress-like walls on all sides, enclosing the town in a private world of red rock, verdant riverbanks and tidy houses fronted by ditches irrigating cottage gardens of hollyhocks and other colorful flowers. Moab has a typically Mormon, grid-like layout in its quaint historic downtown but has burst its confines to the south, spilling into Spanish Valley near the southern turnoff for the La Sal Mountain Loop.

The town's history is unusual. Members of the Elk Mountain Mission – one of many colonizing efforts in southern Utah in the 1850s and 1860s by the LDS Church – built a settlement here in 1855 near the Colorado River but were driven out by hostile Utes. By the time another group of Mormons succeeded in founding the town in 1878, a motley crew of homesteaders, rustlers, drifters and grifters had settled in, hoping to find their fortune at the end of the Civil War. Until well into the 20th century, Moab was a sleepy hamlet, miles from nowhere. And it might have stayed that way if it hadn't been for the atomic bomb. At the onset of the Cold War, the former U.S. Atomic Energy Commission (AEC), as part of a nationwide search for uranium, established a generous fixed price for uranium as an incentive to miners. Charlie Steen was the first to make a big strike. In an area south of Moab that the AEC had deemed "barren of possibilities," Steen discovered his Mi Vida mine, from which he shipped $100 million of uranium-235. Overnight Moab became the "Uranium Capital of the World," but by the 1980s the boom was over.

Mining today takes a very different form: that of mining for tourist dollars. Following the huge recreational boom of the postwar years, surplus army rafts were converted to river-running boats, four-wheel-drive Jeeps were used as recreational vehicles, and then, in the 1980s, the mounting popularity of mountain biking on slickrock trails put Moab on the outdoor recreation map. This boom appears to be here to stay. Since the 1990s the resident population

La Sal Mountain Loop.

of Moab has doubled – to more than 5,000 – with thousands more owning second homes in the area.

Moabites, a frisky, independent bunch who are always free with their opinions, grouse that with real estate prices and property taxes what they now are, they can barely afford to live here anymore. And the growing number of motels, fast-food outlets, over-priced eateries, brew pubs, espresso joints and T-shirt boutiques that have sprung up along Main Street certainly signals major changes. But one can't argue with success. Pretty little Moab is perfectly located for trips to Canyonlands and Arches National Parks, the Manti-La Sal Forest and other public lands nearby. It has become a bona-fide destination, complete with all the attendant headaches when a small rural town is "discovered" by outsiders.

Your first stop in town should be the multi-agency **Moab Information Center** (25 E. Center St; tel: 435-259 6111; www.discovermoab.com; daily 8am–5pm), where you can discuss your trip with rangers and choose books and maps from a large selection in the attractive bookstore. Afterward, consider strolling a half-block east to the enjoyable little **Moab Museum** (118 E. Center St; tel: 435-259 7985; https://moabmuseum.org; Tue–Sat 10am–6pm), a good place to learn more about the history of the area. You can continue your walk farther by following the Downtown Moab Historic Walking Tour brochure, available at the MIC.

SLICKROCK TRAIL

There is so much for outdoor lovers to do in Moab that they could easily spend weeks here and never tire of the possibilities. Immediately adjoining the town is the infamous **Slickrock Trail**, a 10.5-mile (15-km) mountain bike loop that begins about 2 miles (3 km) from the junction of Sand Flats Road and Mill Creek Drive in Moab and continues over surrounding sandstone mesas. This is Moab's most difficult mountain biking route, a Class IV. If you're new to the area, you should ride the 2-mile (3-km) practice loop first to test your skills (note: even this route isn't for novices). The Slickrock Trail is in the **Sand Flats Recreation Area** ❹ (Sand Flats Rd; tel: 435-259 2444) adjoining the La Sal Mountains, and has 110 primitive campsites. Bring water; none is available here.

Exposed sandstone in summer gets as hot as an oven. Heat exhaustion and stroke are common problems for hikers and mountain bikers, and there are deaths every year from people who misjudge their heat tolerance. Stay safe. Don't head out in the middle of the day. Stay in a group, wear a helmet, make sure your brakes are in good working order, and carry a first-aid kit. Anyone exercising in the desert in summer should drink at least a gallon (4 liters) of water a day, eat high-energy snacks, and keep skin covered and cool.

UTAH SCENIC BYWAY 128

Drivers and mountain bikers share the road on several scenic byways

Courthouse Towers in Arches National Park.

around Moab. **Utah Scenic Byway 128**, which begins 2 miles (3 km) north of Moab at the bridge over the Colorado River, winds for 45 miles (72 km) below 1,000-ft-high (300-km) red rocks carved by the river and includes a hiking trail, an old ranch used in the movies, and the historic Dewey Bridge at the confluence with the Dolores River. The BLM manages small campgrounds between the road and the riverbank. These sites in the thick tamarisk, or salt cedar, get hot and buggy in summer, a bit smelly, and suffer from road noise, but are a reasonable alternative to crowded national park campgrounds, at least for one night.

Three miles (5 km) from the bridge is **Grandstaff Trail**, which may be one of Moab's most pleasant day hikes. The moderately difficult 3.5-mile (5.5-km) trail, named for a 19th-century African-American named William Grandstaff who ran a ranch here, parallels a pretty creek beneath high cliffs and ends up at Morning Glory Arch, in the northern end of the Sand Flats Recreation Area.

Castle Rock and Priest and Nuns at La Sal Mountain Loop.

At Mile Marker 14 is the **Moab Museum of Film and Western Heritage** (tel: 866-812 2002; www.redcliffslodge.com; daily 7am–10pm; free), which is packed with movie memorabilia. The museum is located at Red Cliffs Lodge which, beginning in the John Ford era of the 1940s, has been a popular film location. *Wagon Master*, *Rio Grande*, *Comancheros*, *City Slickers*, *Thelma and Louise*, and more recently *Transformers: Age of Extinction*, *The Lone Ranger*, *John Carter* and the *Westworld* TV Series have all used the magnificent scenery surrounding the ranch as a backdrop. There are numerous other movie locations in the Moab area, including many in Arches and Canyonlands National Parks. Ask at the MIC for the Movie Tour brochure.

Two famous geological landmarks that have appeared in movies – **Castle Rock** and 1,500-ft-high (450-meter) **Fisher Towers** – can be seen at the start of the **La Sal Mountain Loop**, a 60-mile (97 km) paved scenic drive that begins on UT 128 (just after Red Cliffs Lodge), some 11 miles (18 km)

◎ THE SCRIBE OF THE DESERT

In 1956–57, iconoclastic writer Edward Abbey (1927–1989) worked as a seasonal ranger in Arches National Monument. A native of the Appalachian community of Home, Pennsylvania, Abbey had fallen in love with the Southwest while riding the rails and, after a stint in the army in Europe, moved west to attend the University of New Mexico.

While working at Arches, the erudite but curmudgeonly Abbey explored the backcountry and kept a journal. Ten years later, he transformed this material into a popular memoir, *Desert Solitaire: A Season in the Wilderness* (1968). Although he wrote 20 other books, including *The Monkey Wrench Gang*, a humorous eco-thriller, *Desert Solitaire* remains Abbey's masterpiece; a love letter to the desert and a rallying cry to stop the growth of "industrial tourism" in America's national parks before it is too late. "I see myself as an entertainer," he once said. "I'm trying to write good books... make people laugh, make them cry. Provoke them, make them angry. Make them think, if possible."

Friends and admirers delighted in Ed's humor, word play, penchant for philosophical debate, camaraderie and spirit of adventure, and felt a huge loss when he died in 1989. At his request, he was buried under a pile of rocks in the Sonoran Desert at an undisclosed location. His fondest wish was that he would be reborn as a buzzard and haunt the skies above the desert.

ARCHES NATIONAL PARK AND THE MOAB AREA

from the Moab bridge, and continues high into the La Sal Mountains. The scenic drive makes for a truly spectacular four-hour tour around Moab and is highly recommended. From high in the La Sals, there are several viewpoints with breathtaking vistas of the unique geology of southeastern Utah. You can see all the way to the **Canyon Rims Recreation Area**, adjoining the Needles District of Canyonlands, historically used by ranchers and increasingly popular with the thousands of four-wheel-drive, backpacking, rock climbing and camping enthusiasts that flood into southeast Utah each year. When Moab hits the 100°F (39°C) mark, there may be no more pleasant place than the La Sal Mountains, where you'll find picnic sites, lakes and several idyllic campgrounds set among the cool aspens and conifers. The loop exits onto US 191, eight miles (13 km) south of Moab.

UTAH SCENIC BYWAY 279

The BLM also manages many lesser-known natural and cultural sites. Closest to Moab is **Utah Scenic Byway 279**, also known as Potash Road, which begins 3 miles (5 km) north of Moab, off US 191, and parallels the Colorado River south for 17 miles (27 km). All along Potash Road are Native American rock art panels and several three-toed dinosaur tracks. Petroglyphs scratched into the dark mineralized "desert varnish" date to Archaic times, more than 3,000 years ago. There are also rare etchings by the Fremont people, whose homeland adjoined that of the Ancestral Pueblo people along the Colorado River about a thousand years ago.

Just past the petroglyphs and dinosaur tracks are several natural arches carved out of the sandstone. A 1.5-mile (2.5-km) hiking trail leads to the **Corona** and **Bow Tie** arches. Farther on is the aptly named **Jug Handle Arch**. The paved road ends at the Moab Potash Plant, which produces fertilizer from salt deposits below the earth's surface, and continues on a very rough road through to Canyonlands National Park (high clearance 4WD only). Near the plant is also the main put-in for river trips below the Island in the Sky district of Canyonlands. Outfitters offer day trips on the river, and if you have time, this is one of the most enjoyable ways to visit the sprawling, wild park. In just a day, you can float past the 2,000-ft-high (600-meter) cliffs below the "goosenecks" of the Colorado River. Outfitters usually offer lunch on the riverbank, then a bumpy Jeep ride back up to the mesa top, stopping at sites along the famous Shafer Trail before returning to Moab.

On the other side of the Colorado River, Kane Creek Blvd runs from Moab to the **Matheson Wetlands Preserve** (tel: 435-259 4629; daily sunrise–sunset), managed by The Nature Conservancy. This little-known gem is Utah's only Colorado River wetland and harbors some 200 species of birds, amphibians and aquatic mammals such as the beaver and river otter.

Double arch windows, Arches National Park.

Valley of the Gods.

SAN JUAN COUNTY

Mormon, Navajo and ancient Pueblo cultures intersect in Utah's southeast corner, a rough-hewn land of red-rock monuments, salmon-colored dunes and a gentle desert river.

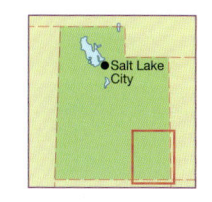

San Juan County occupies Utah's wild and witheringly beautiful southeast corner, a triangle bounded by the Colorado River to the west, Arizona and the Navajo Nation to the south, and Colorado to the east. It takes its name from the San Juan River, a tributary of the Colorado that runs east-west across the county, while most of its residents still make a living from ranching and farming in traditional Mormon communities founded by their forefathers. For visitors it's the county's stunning landscapes that provides the main draw, best experienced in a series of state parks and on scenic byways that cut though the wilderness – there's also ancient pueblo ruins, hoodoo rocks, Navajo trading posts and rafting and kayaking along the San Juan River. The real showstopper is Monument Valley, a mind-bending landscape of towering buttes and peaks that should be on everyone's bucket list.

EARLY HISTORY

Southeast Utah's tangled topography delayed European settlement of the region compared with other areas of the United States, but it has had a much longer human occupation than you might imagine. As early as 6,000 years ago, nomadic Desert Archaic hunter-gatherers wandered these canyons, living off the seasonal bounty of the desert and leaving behind their haunting paintings deep within the pale-walled canyons of Cedar Mesa Sandstone that is a hallmark of southeastern Utah. About 2,000 years ago, they were replaced by the region's first farmers. These early agriculturists built cool pithouses near washes and raised corn, squash and beans. They gathered their harvest in baskets, which has led archaeologists to dub them the Basketmakers. With the help of technologies from Mexico, such as agriculture, building with stone, making pottery, and ceremonies to

◉ Main attractions
Bluff
Edge of the Cedars State Park
Goosenecks State Park
Harts Draw Scenic Backway
Hoveenweep National Monument
Monument Valley
Natural Bridges National Monument
San Juan River trips
UT 95 (Bicentennial Scenic Byway)

Map on page 250

Mule Canyon Ruins.

Around Moab and San Juan County
0 20 miles
0 20 km
Grand Junction
Green River
Crescent Junction
Thompson Springs
Green River State Park
70
Salina
San Rafael
Green
191
Devils Garden
Arches National Park
2
Dewey Bridge
Colorado
128
Fisher Towers
Colorado River way RA Rec. Sites
Castle Rock
Red Cliffs Ranch Film Museum
Gateway
Dolores
San Rafael Desert
Visitor Center
Potash Road
279
3
Moab
4
Sand Flats Rec. Area
Dead Horse Point State Park
Matheson Wetland Preserve
Spanish Valley
La Sal Mtns Loop Road
La Sal Mtns
Mount Peale 12721
Island in the Sky Visitor Center
Upheaval Dome
Canyonlands National Park (Horseshoe Canyon Unit)
Manti-La Sal National Forest
Paradox
Grand View Point
Canyon Rims Recreation Area
La Sal Junction
Wilson Arch
Dirty Devil
1
Canyonlands National Park
Needles Visitor Center
Colorado
Canyon
Hanksville
Colorado
Summit Point
Cataract
Dark Canyon Primitive Area
Glen Canyon National Recreation Area
Hite
Monticello
5
Egnar
Ucolo
491
Abajo Mtns
Abajo Peak 11360
Eastland
Dove Creek
95
Lake Powell
Dark Canyon Wilderness
Manti-La Sal National Forest
Bicentennial Highway
191
Natural Bridges National Monument
8
Fry Canyon
7
Edge of the Cedars State Park
Blanding
6
Red Rock Plateau
Mule Canyon Ruins
95
Butler Wash Ruins
9
Bicentennial Highway
Kane Gulch Range Station
Moki Dugway Road
White Mesa
Canyons of the Ancients National Monument
Grand Gulch Primitive Area
10
Hovenweep National Monument
16
Hatch Trading Post
261
Cedar Mesa
Glen Canyon National Recreation Area
Clay Hills Crossing
San Juan
11
Valley of the Gods
Comb Ridge
Bluff
13
163
Montezuma Creek
Sand Island Rec. Area
163
Comb
San Juan
Aneth
12
Goosenecks State Park
Mexican Hat
Navajo Reservation
191
Navajo Reservation
163
Chinle Creek
Monument Valley
N
Oljeto
Goulding
Four Corners Monument Navajo Tribal Park
14
160
Visitor Center
15
Monument Valley Navajo Tribal Park
Arizona
160
Red Mesa
New Mexico
Kayenta
Mexican Water
Teec Nos Pos

ensure a good harvest, the ancestors of the modern Hopi and other Pueblo people became successful farmers. By the eighth century, people throughout the Four Corners were living in extended clans in small stone villages, or pueblos, built around a plaza. Even though they now lived above ground, they retained their strong spiritual connection to the earth by using underground rooms called kivas to plan ceremonies. They, too, left rock art on sandstone walls, depicting what was most important in their daily lives: game animals, water, corn, deities, fertility and the patterns of their travels across the land.

In the 1200s, Pueblo people from near Mesa Verde in southwestern Colorado began moving west into Utah, perhaps displaced by crowding and friction among neighbors, scarce natural resources due to a long drought, and a desire to seek safety amid the canyons of the Colorado River and its tributaries.

At Hovenweep and Canyons of the Ancients National Monuments on the Utah–Colorado border, they built unusual defensive villages of D-and C-shaped buildings with tower kivas, where unobstructed views could keep the people safe. Other clans pushed farther into Canyon Country and constructed single family units and granaries under overhangs that blended into the rocks. By 1300, for reasons known only to themselves, the people had left these homes, sealed their granaries, and moved south to Hopi, Zuni, Acoma and the Rio Grande pueblos, where their descendants remain today. Southeastern Utah is now home to the Navajo and Ute who have lived in the area for centuries, possibly arriving before the departure of the Pueblos, according to new evidence.

EUROPEANS ARRIVE

In 1776, two Franciscan priests from Santa Fe named Atanasio Domínguez and Silvestre Vélez de Escalante, were the first Spaniards to travel through the Colorado River country, searching unsuccessfully for a route to California. Spaniards named the Abajo ("low") and La Sal ("the salt") Mountains in southeastern Utah, as well as the Colorado River, during a visit to the Grand Canyon. In 1869 and 1871, geologist John Wesley Powell (1834–1902) became the first to run the length of the Colorado River in wooden dories, thrilling Americans back east with his account of a landscape he called "The Great Unknown."

Several years later, soldiers who had first visited the area as part of Kit Carson's roundup of Navajos during the 1864–68 Long Walk period returned, hoping to find rumored Navajo gold and silver deposits. They were killed by a party of local Native Americans. Soon afterward, prospector Cass Hite (1845–1914) arrived in Monument Valley, determined to learn the secrets of the Navajo. Fortunately for him, Chief Hoskannini (1828–1912) took a liking to him and showed him where gold could be found on the Colorado River. By the 1880s, Hite's was among a number of

Moki Dugway, scenic backway.

gold-mining operations on the Colorado, San Juan and other rivers that boomed briefly, then were abandoned due to the difficult terrain.

Other settlers, such as John Wetherill (1866– 1944) and his wife Louisa and Harry and "Mike" Goulding, were attracted by the Navajo themselves. They, and other adventurous entrepreneurs, built trading posts in remote areas on the new Navajo reservation and began trading flour, sugar, cloth, hardware and other necessities for Navajo crafts like silver jewelry and wool rugs. Acting as a bridge between Native Americans and the world beyond the reservation, they introduced visitors to Native American culture, even offering food and lodging in the early days, when roads through this area did not exist. Although Native Americans no longer need to shop at trading posts, most maintain close bonds with traders, whose support continues to open new and lucrative markets for Native American arts and crafts.

After World War II, mining again became big news in the region, after huge deposits of uranium were found in the Four Corners region. Recreation, too, began to take off. Enterprising locals like Mexican Hat resident Norm Nevills (1908–1949) and other river runners used wooden rowboat dories and government-surplus rubber rafts to transport paying visitors through previously inaccessible canyons. In Monticello, a young rancher's son named Kent Frost (1917–2013) and his wife Fern bought army Jeeps and almost single-handedly invented the craze for four-wheel-driving in Canyonlands National Park, a park they were instrumental in helping create in 1964.

Monticello

About an hour south of Moab, at the junction of US 191 and 491, the small town of **Monticello** ❺ is the county seat and a good place to begin your trip. It has good motels, a mix of down-home restaurants and cafés, and tourist facilities. Your first stop in Monticello should be the **Monticello Welcome Center** (216 S. Main St; tel: 435-587 2271; www.utahscanyoncountry.com; Wed–Mon 9am–6pm, with exceptions)

Valley of the Gods, near Bears Ears National Monument.

in the heart of downtown. It has good information on planning a trip to the area and a small **Frontier Museum** (free) in the barn next door with exhibits on the history of San Juan County.

HARTS DRAW SCENIC BACKWAY

The **Harts Draw Scenic Backway** through the Abajos (locally called the Blues) offers a little-known but spectacular shortcut into the Needles District of Canyonlands National Park. Look for West 200 St (County Rd 101), in downtown Monticello. This paved road quickly turns to dirt and winds up to Abajo Peak, passing through part of the 1.4-million-acre (570,000-hectare) **Manti-La Sal National Forest**, which contrasts dramatically with the desert vistas below. Spanish explorers were fooled into thinking the Abajos are low. In fact, they are quite high – more than 9,000 ft (2,700 meters) – and snow-covered in winter. They offer wonderful hiking and camping at two primitive campgrounds (Buckboard and Dalton Springs) between May and October. If you're visiting the area at that time of year, you may come upon cattle being rounded up in these parts. Cattle ranchers trail their cows and calves into the cool mountains to fatten up all summer in high-country pastures, then bring them down to corrals at lower elevations in September to ready them for market. The Harts Draw route also allows you to take a scenic backway to **Blanding** ❻, 30 miles (48 km) to the south – a good alternative to US 191.

BLANDING

Like Monticello, Blanding has decent lodgings, restaurants and other visitor facilities – stop by the **Blanding Visitors Center** (12 N. Grayson Pkwy; tel: 435-678 3662; www.visitblanding.com; Mon–Sat 8am–6pm, 10am–4pm in winter) for an overview. The whole town is built atop six large pueblos that were occupied between AD 825 and 1225. An excavated pueblo and rare great kiva can be viewed at the excellent **Edge of the Cedars State Park Museum** ❼ (660 W. 400 North St; tel: 435-678 2238; https://stateparks.utah.gov/parks/edge-of-the-cedars; Mar–Nov daily 9am–5pm), named for a clearing in the junipers, or "cedars," on the west side of town used as a cowboy camp. The modern museum has thoughtful exhibits that explore the links among the area's Ancestral Puebloan, Ute, Navajo and modern white residents. Also noteworthy are a large Ancestral Pueblo pottery collection donated by an early Blanding pioneer; a garden containing such native plants as beeweed and yucca used by early Native Americans; and whimsical iron sculptures by Bluff artist Joe Pachak evoking early Pueblo rock art.

Blanding was the scene of the West's last gun battle, in 1923, when a couple of Ute rustlers broke out of jail with the help of a Paiute named Old Posey. A posse chased them for two days before Posey was fatally wounded. A band of Utes, whose homeland originally was in southwestern Colorado, inhabits the

> **Tip**
>
> If you're planning on hiking on the 2.1 million acres (850,000 hectares) of land managed by the Bureau of Land Management (41 percent of the land base), be sure to stop at the **BLM Field Office** in Monticello (365 N. Main St; tel: 435-587 1500; Mon–Fri 7.45am–noon and 1–4.30pm) for information and the latest conditions.

Moonscape Overlook.

| Eat

Old school hamburger joint Patio Diner (95 N Grayson Pkwy; tel: 435-678 2177; https://patiodiner.com; Mon–Sat 11am–9pm) is a great place to eat in Blanding, open since 1959 – be sure to try Utah's famous "fry sauce" here (a combo of mayo, ketchup, and mustard).

Heron petroglyph, Cedar Mesa.

White Mesa Community south of Blanding (part of the larger Ute Mountain Ute Indigenous group).

UT 95 (BICENTENNIAL SCENIC BYWAY)

The highlight of this area is UT 95, which begins just south of Blanding and links that community with the tiny Mormon settlement of **Hanksville**, a gateway to Capitol Reef National Park and Grand Staircase-Escalante National Monument, the Maze district of Canyonlands, and the San Rafael Swell. Dubbed the Bicentennial Scenic Byway because it was completed in 1976, this 140-mile-long (225-km), paved route figured prominently in Edward Abbey's eco-terrorism novel *The Monkey Wrench Gang* and traverses rough topography above the San Juan River. It has plenty of attractions, from scenery and unusual geological formations to one of the Southwest's largest concentrations of Native American ruins, and several early pioneer communities. This route is part of the larger **Trail of the Ancients** scenic loop (www.trailoftheancients.com), highlighting natural and cultural sites throughout the region. Ask for a brochure at the Monticello or Blanding visitor centers.

Just west of Blanding, the highway cuts through one of the major topographical features of this region, **Comb Ridge**. This geological monocline was pushed up 1,000 ft (300 meters) in elevation by volcanic forces deep below the thick sedimentary rocks of Canyon Country. It runs 80 miles (130 km) north to south, from the Abajo Mountains to Kayenta, Arizona, and can be seen from miles away, domed up above the San Juan River. Its high ramparts provided plenty of headaches for the Hole in the Rock pioneers who tried to cross it in 1880. Stop at a viewpoint and take a closer look, instead of quickly driving on. You'll gain new respect for the wagon pioneers of the 19th century whose faith spurred them through some of the toughest country imaginable.

There are numerous places to get out and explore the area around Comb

○ HOLE-IN-THE-ROCK EXPEDITION

In 1879, a party of Mormons answered a call from their Church to establish a mission in Utah's unpopulated southeastern corner. Setting out from Escalante, 250 men, women and children, 80 wagons and a thousand head of cattle traveled overland across the rugged Escalante Canyons, searching for a route across the Colorado River, as winter approached.

Spirits remained high until the settlers reached the 1,200-ft-deep (365-meter) Colorado River gorge, where, for six weeks, men were forced to construct a wagon road down the vertical cliffs. Inch by inch, the wagons were lowered down the "road" using ropes, then taken across the 300-ft-wide (90-meter) river at a ford used in 1776 by the Dominguez-Escalante expedition.

On April 6, 1880, after enduring frigid winter conditions, the settlers reached the San Juan River, where they established Bluff City. The journey took six months, two babies were born, and no one died. In 1887, some Bluff pioneers moved north and founded Monticello. When Blanding was founded in 1910, Bluff was abandoned. Today, you can drive part of the Hole-in-the-Rock road in Grand Staircase-Escalante National Monument, passing landmarks like Dance Hall Rock, a natural amphitheater used for dancing by the pioneers. A four-wheel-drive vehicle is required for the final couple of miles to the Hole in the Rock itself.

Ridge. Two of the most interesting are roadside archaeological sites managed by the BLM preserving Pueblo cliff dwellings from the 13th century. Just before Comb Ridge, you'll pass **Butler Wash Ruins**, which are notable for their circular and rectangular kivas, showing influences from both the Mesa Verde area to the east and the Kayenta area to the south. You can see another set of ruins from the same era a few miles farther on at **Mule Canyon Ruins**. This small archaeological site has a partially reconstructed kiva and a residence unit. They can be viewed from a wheelchair-accessible trail. There are picnic tables at this site. Both are open year-round.

A few miles on is the turnoff for **Natural Bridges National Monument** ❽ (tel: 435-692 1234; www.nps.gov/nabr; 24hr daily), which preserves three natural bridges carved by a tributary of the Colorado River through White Canyon. Each of the three bridges in the monument – Sipapu, Kachina and Owachomo – can be seen along the 9-mile-long (15-km) **Bridge View Scenic Drive**, which starts at the small, solar-powered visitor center (daily 9am–5pm summer, Thu–Mon 9am–4pm winter) and loops around White Canyon. You can hike to the base of all three bridges from trailheads or all the way along the bottom of the canyon to visit each one. Watch for mountain lions in the thick brush; they and other animals are frequent visitors to this park. Natural Bridges has one of the nicest little campgrounds in the area. In summer, rangers offer interesting campfire talks on subjects ranging from herpetology to archeoastronomy.

If you continue driving northwest on UT 95, you'll pass over the Colorado River in Glen Canyon National Recreation Area and eventually reach Hanksville, where you'll find gas, food and lodging. The nearby Henry Mountains have plenty of primitive camping and hiking far from other people; there is also a buffalo herd here. For more information, stop at the BLM Henry Mountains Field Station (380 S. 100 West St, Hanksville; tel: 435-542 3461; Mon–Fri 8am–4.30pm).

CEDAR MESA (BEARS EARS NATIONAL MONUMENT)

To the south of Natural Bridges, in an area known as **Cedar Mesa**, the Trail of the Ancients Scenic Byway continues south from UT 95 along UT 261. Much of this wilderness area forms the **Bears Ears National Monument** (www.blm.gov/visit/bears-ears-national-monument), created in 2016 and co-managed by the Forest Service and BLM. You can learn more at the **Kane Gulch Range Station** ❾ (tel: 435-587 1510; Mar to mid-June and Sept–Oct daily 8am–noon), four miles (6.5 km) south of the UT 95/261 junction, which has interpretative displays and a bookstore. You can also get walk-in permits here; these are required to visit the canyons of Cedar Mesa and Butler Wash, or to camp overnight (you can also obtain these from www.recreation.

Anasazi cliff dwelling ruins at Butler Wash.

PLACES

> **Tip**
>
> A permit is required year-round to float any section of the San Juan River between Montezuma Creek and Clay Hills in southeast Utah. Permits are only issued through a pre-season lottery (for mid-Apr to mid-July) and advance reservations (Jan to mid-Apr, and mid-July to Dec). The San Juan River permit lottery and reservations are now available at www.recreation.gov. Check with the Monticello River Office (Mon–Fri 8am–noon; tel: 435-587-1544).

An example of river erosion, Goosenecks State Park.

gov by searching for "Cedar Mesa Permits", or in fee tubes located at prominent trailheads). You'll need a permit to hike into the **Grand Gulch Primitive Area** ❿, a world-class archaeological site to the west of Kane Gulch Range Station and UT 261 (limited to 20 people per day Mar–June and Sept–Oct). Hundreds of Basketmaker and Ancestral Pueblo dwellings and rock art sites, dating back 700 to 2,000 years, can be found beneath overhangs throughout this 52-mile (84-km) canyon, making it very special indeed. Some people hike the entire canyon one way and arrange a pickup on the San Juan River; most, however, explore for several days, staying in designated campsites near some of the best Pueblo ruins, then hike back out.

Further south along UT 261, don't miss the white-knuckle ride down the **Moki Dugway**, a mining road that switchbacks 1,100 ft (335 meters) down Cedar Mesa. At the bottom is the **Valley of the Gods** ⓫, a miniature and lesser-known version of Monument Valley, complete with a rough 17-mile (27-km) drive past hoodoo rocks weathered out of sandstone. A number of formations here have spiritual meaning for the Navajo. Hogan-shaped Lime Ridge, just to the north, for example, is said to have served as a prison for disobedient children placed there by the Sun Bearer. When they did not repent after four days, the Sun Bearer turned the hogan to solid rock. One can still hear crying near the rock, or so the locals say.

Before reaching **Mexican Hat**, take a detour to tiny **Goosenecks State Park** ⓬ (tel: 435-678 2238; https://stateparks.utah.gov/parks/goosenecks; daily 24hr) for an eye-popping view of the entrenched meanders, or Goosenecks, of the San Juan River in the dark gray Halgaito Shale below. There are no facilities or water here, but you can make camp on the headland. If you look carefully, you'll see river runners winding through the Goosenecks on their rafts.

SAN JUAN RIVER

San Juan River access is either at **Sand Island Recreation Area**, 3 miles (5 km) east of Bluff, or at Mexican Hat, 26 miles (42 km) downriver, just before the Goosenecks. You can raft 84 miles (135 km) to **Clay Hills Crossing**, camping on beaches below **Johns Canyon**, **Grand Gulch** and **Slickhorn Gulch**, before the river flows into Lake Powell. The stretch between Sand Island and Mexican Hat is popular for its Pueblo ruins, rock art and leisurely river running. The best time to go is during spring runoff in May; by late summer, the river is usually too low for rafting. A restrictive lottery system is in place for private trips on the San Juan River – it's easier to arrange a trip of one to six days with an approved commercial outfitter such as Wild Expeditions (tel: 435-672 2365; www.riversandruins.com).

Pretty little **Bluff** ⓭ (https://bluffutah.org), to the east via US 191 (or an 11-mile/18-km hike on the **Bluff River Trail**), has been reborn as an

SAN JUAN COUNTY | 257

artist haven. The remains of old **Bluff Fort** (www.hirf.org/fort.html; Mon–Sat 9am–6pm, Sun 11am–6pm; free), built by Hole in the Rock pioneers to defend themselves against Native American incursions, has been developed into a tourist attraction with reconstructed cabins representative of those built before 1895; in addition to the Visitor's Center (a replica of the co-op trading post), there's a traditional Navajo home, or hogan, actual wagons from the Hole in the Rock journey, the rebuilt log meetinghouse, the ruins of the Kumen Jones home, and the original Bluff Relief Society building. You can learn more about the archeology and cultural landscapes of the region at the **Bears Ears Education Center** (567 W. Main St; tel: 435-672 2402; https://bearsearsmonument.org; Thu–Mon 8am–4pm, closed July).

NAVAJO NATION

Bluff and Mexican Hat are on the edge of the 29,000-sq-mile (75,000-sq-km) **Navajo Nation** (www.navajo-nsn.gov) or Diné Bikéyah, that covers parts of Utah, Arizona and New Mexico. **Montezuma Creek**, on the San Juan River just east of Bluff via UT 162, is a primarily Navajo settlement. Head south across the river from here on Red Mesa Road (UT 35) to join US 160 in Arizona, the main east-west route across the northern reservation. Some 15 miles (24 km) east of the junction is the Navajo community of **Teec Nos Pos**, which has a nice little trading post (daily 8am–6pm) selling Navajo arts and crafts. Turn north here on US 160 to visit **Four Corners Monument Navajo Tribal Park** ⑭ (tel: 928-206 2540; https://navajonationparks.org; daily: May–Sept 8am–6.45pm, Oct–Mar 8am–4.45pm, Apr 8am–5.45pm), the only place in the United States where four states – Utah, Colorado, Arizona and New Mexico – join. There is a modest visitor center but no water. Vendors from local Navajo and Ute families sell fry bread and arts and crafts.

MONUMENT VALLEY

Many travelers head south on US 163, going through homely Mexican Hat and crossing the San Juan River into the Big Rez just north of Monument Valley, which sits astride the Utah–Arizona line. **Monument Valley Navajo Tribal Park** ⑮ (tel: 435-727 5870; https://navajonationparks.org; daily: Mar–Aug 6.30am–7.30pm, limited hours rest of year; visitor center daily 8am–5pm) is one of those places everyone should see at least once, especially at sunrise or sunset, when the wind-carved red De Chelly Sandstone monoliths, scattered Ancestral Pueblo ruins, and traditional Navajo who live among them are at their most photogenic.

Begin at the visitor center, which has exhibits about the Navajo as well as water and restrooms. The View Restaurant has good food and great views of the park through enormous picture windows. Monument Valley Trading Post sells Navajo arts and crafts, books and other gifts. The 17-mile-long (27-km), unpaved scenic drive into the valley takes about two hours. The dusty, rutted road

> ◎ **Tip**
>
> If you plan to hike or camp on the south side of the San Juan River, on Navajo Nation land, you will need a permit from Navajo Parks and Recreation – purchased at the time of arrival (at Monument Valley, Four Corners, or Window Rock, AZ) or online at https://navajonationparks.org.

Valley of the Gods.

may be driven by passenger cars but becomes impassable after rain. Inquire before setting out. Be sure to bring plenty of water and food with you. These are not available along the tour route.

A tour booklet for the scenic drive is available in the store. It has information on 11 overlooks, including **John Ford Point**, made famous by the director of Western films such as *Stagecoach*, *Cheyenne Autumn* and *She Wore a Yellow Ribbon*. **Sand Springs**, Monument Valley's only water source, offers glimpses of a hogan, corrals, sheep and goats, and local residents dressed in traditional velveteen blouses, broomstick skirts and silver-and-turquoise jewelry. Off-road hiking, biking, camping, horseback riding and driving are allowed only with a registered Navajo guide. Several companies offer reasonably priced two-hour, five-hour and overnight Jeep and van tours. Sign-up at the visitor center and nearby **Gouldings Lodge** (https://gouldings.com). If you want to meet Monument Valley residents, this is your best bet. You'll also see some of the 100 small ruins built by ancient Pueblo people, known to the Navajo as the Anasazi, or "Enemy Ancestors".

You'll find an ATM, supermarket, gas station, convenience store, campground, restaurant and gift shop at Gouldings Lodge, west of UT 163, at the foot of Oljato Mesa. In 1923, Colorado-raised Harry Goulding and his wife "Mike" bought a patch of former Paiute land, pitched a tent, and began trading with the Navajo out of the back of a horse-drawn wagon. In the 1930s, they built a stone trading post and began publicizing the area to famous Hollywood directors like John Ford. Goulding's original trading post, adjoining the modern Goulding's Lodge, is now **Goulding's Trading Post Museum** (open on request). The first floor is much as Mike Goulding left it when she died in the 1990s. The second floor displays movie stills and memorabilia from films shot in Monument Valley. A cabin used by John Wayne in *She Tied a Yellow Ribbon* in 1949, aka "Captain Nathan Brittles Cabin," can be seen behind the post (it was once Mike Goulding's potato cellar).

HOVENWEEP NATIONAL MONUMENT

Hidden in the no-man's-land that straddles the Utah–Colorado border, the remote Ancestral Puebloan ruins at **Hovenweep National Monument** ⓰ (tel: 970-562 4282, www.nps.gov/hove; daily sunrise–sunset), offer a haunting sense of timeless isolation. While it preserves six distinct conglomerations of ruins, all sprouting from the rims of shallow desert canyons, easy access is restricted to Little Ruin Canyon, behind the visitor center (June–Oct daily 9am–5pm; May daily 9am–4pm; Nov–Apr Thu–Mon 9am–4pm). A mile-long loop trail offers good views of the largest ruins, including the grandly named Hovenweep Castle, constructed around 1200 AD. No accommodation, petrol or food is available.

Hovenweep National Monument.

NAVAJO ART

Hubbell Trading Post is the epicenter of Navajo art and is still one of the best places to experience this tradition today.

Historic trading posts abound on and around the Navajo Nation, many built soon after the Navajo reservation was established in 1868. The reservation's most famous trading post is Hubbell Trading Post (www.nps.gov/hutr) in Ganado, Arizona. Now a national historic site, it was established in 1878 by Lorenzo Hubbell. With partner C. N. Cotton, Hubbell reinvigorated arts and crafts among the Navajos. He hired Mexican silversmiths to teach Navajo men how to work silver and encouraged women to switch from weaving blankets to more saleable rugs.

By the early 1900s, catalogs selling various grades of weavings marketed Hubbell's Ganado rugs as far as New York City. His biggest buyer was hotelier Fred Harvey who furnished his hotels along the railroad line with Native American art and popularized Native American tourism in the Southwest.

Hubbell Trading Post has changed little over the years. Visitors enter a low, cool, brick building into the "bullpen," where Bluebird flour, coffee, tobacco, canned fruit, calico and other goods are still prized items among the Navajo. Women continue to bring in rugs they have woven to trade for necessities. Surrounded by textiles in the famed rug room, the traders work closely with families, urging women to continue weaving and developing new talent.

Hubbell wasn't the only trader to develop a unique style of weaving associated with his trading post. Other traders also got in on the act, and today you'll find a range of regional styles, including Ganado, Teec Nos Pos, Wide Ruins, Two Grey Hills and Burntwater styles. In Monument Valley, you'll find pictorial rugs featuring Yei or Yeibichei dancers and scenes from daily Navajo life. The biggest prize of all are rare historic rugs, such as Navajo Slave rugs, Eye Dazzlers and other patterns dating back to the 18th and 19th centuries.

Turquoise, sacred to the Navajo, ranges in color from robin's-egg blue to blue-green and can be found throughout the reservation. The stones are shaped by jewelers into disks, nuggets, pendants and other forms and set into silver to make necklaces, bracelets, earrings, watch bands and belt buckles.

Round woven baskets made from sumac are used in Navajo ceremonies and are prized by every family. Baskets are traditionally woven by Navajos and Southern Paiutes on the Shonto Plateau area, just south of Lake Powell. A tightly woven basket starts at about $150. The best baskets on the reservation can be found at Blue Mountain Trading Post in Blanding (www.bluemountainrvpark.com) and Twin Rocks Trading Post (https://twinrocks.com) in Bluff, both run by the Simpson family. The Simpsons champion the work of Mexican Hat basketmaker Mary Black, whose award-winning basketry is now nationally known. These two trading posts also specialize in contemporary pictorial and mosaic rugs developed with Navajo artists.

A Navajo woman weaving at the Hubbell Trading Post.

The road leading to Monument Valley.

UTAH
TRAVEL TIPS

TRANSPORT

Getting There 262
    By Air 262
    By Road 262
    By Rail 262
Getting Around 263
    By Rail 263
    By Road 263

A – Z

Accessible travel 265
Accommodations 265
Admission charges 267
Age restrictions 267
Budgeting for your trip 267
Children 267
Climate 267
Crime and safety 268
Customs regulations 269
Eating out 269
Electricity 270
Embassies and consulates 270
Emergencies 270
Etiquette 270
Festivals 270

Health and medical care 271
Internet 272
LGBTQ+ travelers 272
Maps 272
Media 272
Money 272
Opening hours 273
Postal services 273
Public holidays 273
Religious services 273
Shopping 273
Smoking 273
Tax 273
Telephones 274
Time zones 274
Tourist information 274
Tour operators and
    travel agents 275
Visas and passports 275
Websites and apps 275
Weights and measures 275

FURTHER READING

History and society 276
Fiction and Poetry 277

TRANSPORTATION

GETTING THERE

By Air

Many people choose to fly into Salt Lake City International Airport, 4 miles (6km) west of downtown, then continue their trip by rented car. Several international airlines connect Salt Lake with parts of North America, Mexico/Central America, Europe, and Asia. Delta flies nonstop from Calgary, Toronto and Vancouver in Canada, and from London and Paris in Europe. From other parts of the world, you'll have to change planes in Chicago, Dallas/Fort Worth, on the West Coast (typically LA) or East Coast (usually New York or Atlanta).

Salt Lake City Airport is connected to the city center by trams on the TRAX Green Line (tel: 801-743 3882; www.rideuta.com). Alternatively, taxis and shuttles also run into town via Xpress Shuttles (tel: 801-596 1600; https://expressshuttleutah.com/), while Canyon Transportation (tel: 801-255 1841; https://canyontransport.com) serves the ski areas.

By Road

From Canada or Mexico, passing through customs and immigration at the US border can be a lengthy process, with line ups of an hour or two not uncommon on weekends, though the crossings between Montana and the Canadian provinces of Alberta and Saskatchewan tend to be lowkey. If possible, avoid the border, traveling in either direction, on Friday or Sunday late afternoons and evenings.

The major bus company with routes into the US is Greyhound Lines. Some routes end or begin at a Canadian or Mexican city just over the border, where you can subsequently transfer to a local carrier, but there are also special direct services to cities like Salt Lake. For further details, contact Greyhound at tel: 1-214-849 8100, or www.greyhound.com.

Delta Airlines at the Salt Lake City International Airport (SLC).

By Rail

Amtrak offers one direct passenger train route into Utah: the California Zephyr which runs once daily

⊙ Airlines

Air Canada
Tel: 1-888-247 2262
www.aircanada.com
Air France
Tel: 1-800-237 2747
www.airfrance.com
Alaska Airlines
Tel: 1-800-252 7522
www.alaskaair.com
Allegiant Air
Tel: 702-505 8888
www.allegiantair.com
American Airlines
Tel: 1-800-433 7300
www.aa.com
British Airways
Tel: 1-800-247 9297
www.britishairways.com
Delta Air Lines
Tel: 1-800-221 1212
www.delta.com
Frontier Airlines
Tel: 1-801-401 9000
www.flyfrontier.com
Icelandair
Tel: 1-800-223 5500
www.icelandair.com
JetBlue
Tel: 1-800-538 2583
www.jetblue.com
Lufthansa
Tel: 1-800-645 3880
www.lufthansa.com
Southwest Airlines
Tel: 1-800-435 9792
www.southwest.com
United Airlines
Tel: 1-800-864 8331
www.united.com
WestJet
Tel: 1-888-937 8538
www.westjet.com

TRANSPORTATION | 263

Railroad crossing in Utah.

between Chicago and Emeryville (San Francisco), via Denver, to Provo, Green River, Helper, and Salt Lake City. Salt Lake station is downtown at 320 S Rio Grande Ave.

Amtrak's USA Rail Pass allows you to hop-on/hop-off between 10 segments over 30 days

Both first-class and coach accommodations are available, each with dining cars. For further information, telephone the nearest train station or contact Amtrak at 1-800-USA-RAIL or www.amtrak.com.

GETTING AROUND

Though it is possible to travel around the Utah by bus, renting a car is far more convenient, and will allow exploration of national parks and isolated towns and destinations not covered by public transportation.

By Rail

In Utah, the FrontRunner (www.rideuta.com) commuter rail system runs from Ogden to Provo along an 82-mile (132km) corridor serving Salt Lake City, Orem, Farmington, and the Utah Valley.

By Road

Buses

Greyhound provides limited services in Utah (mostly in cooperation with Salt Lake Express; https://saltlakeexpress.com), with buses from Salt Lake City (300 S 600 West St) to Boise via Ogden (1 daily), to Las Vegas via Provo, Fillmore, Beaver, Cedar City, and St George (2 daily); and to Blanding via Green River, Moab, Monticello, Price, and Provo (2 daily). Logan and Vernal are also served once daily.

Budget carrier Flixbus (www.flixbus.com) now operates services between Salt Lake City, Provo, and Ogden.

Park City

A free comprehensive bus system operates daily in Park City between 6am and 2.30am (www.parkcity.org). The six routes are color-coded (download the Park City mobile bus app for convenience).

Salt Lake City and Utah Valley

Local buses and TRAX trams (trolleys) are operated by the Utah Transit Authority (tel: 801-743 3882, www.rideuta.com); journeys within the downtown area are free (tell the driver you intend to stay in the free zone when you board).

Regular UTA buses run every day between 6.30am and 7.30pm from Salt Lake City to the Cottonwood canyons resorts during winter (services are less frequent in summer); from downtown, take the Blue TRAX line to Midvale Fort Union Station, then transfer to the Ski Bus for Brighton and Solitude, or the one for Alta and Snowbird. The trip takes around one hour.

Driving

To really appreciate Utah, you'll need a car. Renting is usually straightforward: foreign drivers' licenses are valid in the USA. Driving is on the

Greyhound bus.

Heritage railroads

While the US West is served by few regular passenger trains, the region does boast several "heritage railroads," restored railways that offer rides on old trains (sometimes steam) on often very scenic stretches of track – most only operate in the summer months. In Utah, **Heber Valley Railroad** (www.hebervalleyrr.org) runs steam trains, and the **Golden Spike National Historical Park** (www.nps.gov/gosp) operates replicas of the original steam trains that met at Promontory Summit on May 10th, 1869.

right and seat belts are mandatory, as are child seats.

Salt Lake City sits at the heart of Utah's interstate network, with I-80 running west to Nevada and east into Wyoming, and I-15 running north into Idaho and south to Las Vegas in Nevada. I-70 cuts across Colorado from Denver into central Utah. Other than those relatively swift connectors, driving long-distance can be very slow, though the roads are rarely busy beyond the congested Utah Valley. If you plan on driving into remote areas or in heavy snow, mud, or severe weather, it's best to use a four-wheel drive vehicle with high clearance.

Highway speed limits and other laws differ slightly from state to state in the USA; in Utah top limits range between zippy 75 and 80mph (121–129km/h). The American Automobile Association (AAA) is a

Rules of the Road

Besides remembering to drive on the right, there are few other safety considerations to keep in mind. While the USA has an extensive and modern system of highways, most of which are well numbered and clearly marked, at times it is very helpful to know your north from south and your east from west.

Speed limits are posted in miles per hour (mph) and they vary from 20 to 35 mph (32–56km/h) in built-up areas to between 75 and 80mph (121–129km/h) on highways.

Headlight rules also differ between states. In Utah, headlights must be turned on when you cannot see at least 1,000ft (305 meters) in front of you.

In all US states you may turn right at a red traffic light (except where prohibited by a sign), after coming to a full stop and making sure that the way is clear before you do so.

School buses display flashing lights before stopping and after leaving a stop; by law you must stop (from either direction), until everyone is clear of the road and the bus is moving.

good source for information and driving regulations (www.aaa.com).

If you are traveling from Canada check with your insurer before you depart to make sure it covers you during your stay in the US. Finally, a word of caution: If your car breaks down on a back road, do not attempt to strike out on foot, even with water. A car is easier to spot than a person and provides shelter from the elements. If you don't have a cell phone or your phone doesn't work, sit tight and wait to be found.

Car rentals

All the major international car rental companies have offices throughout Utah and rentals can be easily arranged before arriving in the US. Call the following firms, toll-free, for information:

Alamo
Tel: 1-888-233 8745
www.alamo.com
Avis
Tel: 1-800-352 7900
www.avis.com
Budget
Tel: 1-800-214 6094
www.budget.com
Enterprise
Tel: 1-855-266 9565
www.enterprise.com
Hertz
Tel: 1-800-654 4173
www.hertz.com
National
Tel: 1-844-393 9989
www.nationalcar.com
Sixt
Tel: 1-888-749 8227
www.sixt.com
Thrifty
Tel: 1-800-334 1705
www.thrifty.com

Motor homes (RV)

No special license is necessary to operate a motor home (or recreational vehicle – RV for short), but they aren't cheap. When you add up the cost of rental fees, insurance, gas, and campsites, renting a car and staying in motels or camping may be less expensive. Keep in mind, too, that RVs are large and slow and may be difficult to handle on narrow mountain roads. If you plan to rent a camper/recreational vehicle in July and August you should book 3–4 months in advance.

Both companies listed below offer pick-up and drop-off in Salt Lake City.

El Monte RV
Tel: 1-888-337 2214
www.elmonterv.com
Cruise America
Tel: 1-800-671 8042
www.cruiseamerica.com

Cycling

Though the altitude (and the ups and downs) can make cycling in Utah a challenge, plenty of visitors do travel the region by bike. Popular routes include Salt Lake City through Colorado to Denver or Pueblo, but it's crucial to avoid major highways. For information about dedicated bike trails see "The Outdoors Experience," (see page 101).

Salt Lake City's and Ogden's bike share program is GREENbike (www.greenbikeutah.org), with stations all over both downtowns; 24-hour passes are $7 (unlimited 30min trips; $5 for each 30min thereafter). Summit Bike Share (www.summitbikeshare.com) offers a similar service in the Park City region.

National car rental booth at SLC airport.

A

Accessible travel

By international standards, the USA is exceptionally accommodating for travelers with mobility concerns or other physical disabilities. By law, all public buildings, including hotels and restaurants, must be wheelchair accessible and provide suitable toilet facilities. Most street corners have dropped curbs (less so in rural areas), and most public transport systems include subway stations with elevators and buses that "kneel" to let passengers in wheelchairs board.

The Americans with Disabilities Act (1990) obliges all air carriers to make the majority of their services accessible, and airlines will usually let attendants of travelers with disabilities accompany them at no extra charge.

Almost every Amtrak train includes one or more coaches with accessible accommodation. Guide dogs travel free. Be sure to give 24 hours' notice. Hard of hearing passengers can get information on tel: 800-523 6590 (TTY/TDD).

Greyhound, however, has its challenges. Buses are not equipped with lifts for wheelchairs, though staff will assist with boarding (intercity carriers are required by law to do so), and the "Helping Hand" policy offers two-for-the-price-of-one tickets to passengers unable to travel alone (carry a doctor's certificate). The American Public Transportation Association, in Washington, DC (www.apta.com), provides information about the accessibility of public transport in cities.

The American Automobile Association (http://aaa.com) produces a mobility guide, while the larger car-rental companies provide cars with hand controls at no extra charge, though only on their full-sized (most expensive) models; reserve well in advance.

Resources

Visit the state tourism website for information (www.visitutah.com/plan-your-trip/accessible-utah), or visit the useful independent site https://barrierfreeutah.com. Wheelchair Getaways (www.accessiblevans.com) in Salt Lake City will meet you at the airport with a fully-accessible, ramp-equipped rental van. Common Ground Outdoor Adventures (http://cgadventures.org) provides outdoor recreational opportunities, while the Courage Reins Therapeutic Riding Center (https://couragereins.org) in Highland offers therapeutic horseback riding and other equine-based activities. Wasatch Adaptive Sports (https://wasatchadaptivesports.org) provides winter and summer recreational pursuits. For Salt Lake County Parks & Recreation's Adaptive Program visit https://slco.org/adaptive.

In addition, see the Society for Accessible Travel and Hospitality (SATH; https://sath.org), a nonprofit travel-industry group, for information on accessible travel and tourism. Mobility International USA (www.miusa.org), offers travel tips and operates exchange programs; it also serves as a national information center on disability.

The "America the Beautiful Access Pass" (www.nps.gov/planyourvisit/passes.htm), issued without charge to US citizens and permanent residents with a permanent disability, gives free lifetime admission to all US national parks. It can only be obtained in person at a federal area where an entrance fee is charged; you'll have to show proof of permanent disability, or that you are eligible for receiving benefits under federal law.

Accommodations

Accommodations in Utah are much the same as in the rest of the US, albeit with a bigger choice of cabins and campgrounds in the national parks. If you're visiting anywhere with large numbers of tourists, such as Salt Lake City and the surrounding canyon ski resorts or the better-known national parks in southern Utah, such as Zion, Arches and Bryce, you'll generally find plenty of expensive boutique hotels, cozy inns, chain motels, family-run bed-and-breakfasts, all-inclusive resorts and spas, and self-catering condominiums and house rentals. In between, it can often feel like a wasteland, if you're just passing through, with lodgings tending toward bare-bones family-owned motels, out-of-the-way bed-and-breakfast operations in historic homes, and dude and working ranches where you'll often sit down with a Mormon family at breakfast.

Reservations are essential in the busy summer months. Almost all hotels, motels, and resorts accept major credit cards, but it's a good idea to check in advance, especially if you travel in remote areas. Most hotels are now completely smoke-free, so if you require a smoking room, make sure to ask.

Hotels and motels

Motels, or "motor hotels", tend to be found beside the main roads away from city centers, and are thus much more accessible to drivers. Budget hotels or motels can be pretty basic, but in general standards of comfort are uniform – each room comes with a double bed (often two), a TV, phone, and usually a portable coffeemaker, plus an attached bathroom. For places with higher rates, the room and its fittings simply get bigger and include more amenities, and there may be a swimming pool, and extras such as irons and ironing boards, or premium cable TV (HBO, Showtime, etc). Almost all hotels and motels now offer free Wi-Fi, albeit sometimes in the lobby only.

The least expensive properties tend to be family-run, independent "mom-and-pop" motels, but these are rarer nowadays. When you're driving along the main interstates there's a lot to be said for paying a few dollars more to stay in motels belonging to the national chains. These range from the ever-reliable and cheap Super 8 and Motel 6 through to the mid-range Days Inn and La Quinta, up to the more commodious Holiday Inn Express and Hampton Inn.

Few budget hotels or motels bother to compete with the ubiquitous diners by offering full breakfasts, although most will provide free self-service coffee, pastries, and if you are lucky, fruit, or cereal, collectively referred to as "continental breakfast."

Bed-and-breakfast

Staying in a bed-and-breakfast is a popular, often luxurious, alternative to conventional hotels in Utah. Some establishments consist of no more than a couple of furnished rooms in someone's home, and even the larger ones tend to have fewer than 10 rooms, sometimes without a TV or phone, but often laden with potpourri, chintzy cushions, and an assertively precious Victorian atmosphere. If this cozy, twee setting appeals to you, there's a range of choices throughout the state, but keep a few things in mind. For one, you may not be an anonymous guest, as you would in a chain hotel, but may be expected to chat with the host and other guests, especially during breakfast. Also, some enforce curfews, and take a dim view of guests stumbling in after midnight after an evening's partying. The only way to know the policy for certain is to check each bed-and-breakfast's policy online – there's often a lengthy list of do's and don'ts.

.The price you pay for a bed-and-breakfast always includes breakfast (sometimes a buffet on a sideboard, but more often a full-blown cooked meal). The crucial determining factor is whether each room has an en suite bathroom; most provide private bath facilities, although that can damage the authenticity of a fine old house. At the top end of the spectrum, the distinction between a "boutique hotel" and a "bed-and-breakfast inn" may amount to no more than that the latter is owned by a private individual rather than a chain.

Historic hotels and lodges

Throughout Utah, many towns still contain historic hotels. So long as you accept that not all will have up-to-date facilities to match their period charm, these can make wonderfully atmospheric places to spend a night or two. In addition, several national parks feature long-established and architecturally distinguished hotels, traditionally known as lodges, that can be real bargains thanks to their federally controlled rates. The only drawback is that all rooms tend to be reserved far in advance. Among the best are Zion Lodge in Zion National Park, The Lodge at Bryce Canyon, and Goulding's Lodge in Monument Valley.

Guest ranches

Guest, or dude, ranches range from working cattle operations with basic lodging to full-fledged "resorts with horses" that have swimming pools, hot tubs, tennis courts, massage treatments, all-terrain vehicles, and other amenities. Most ranches offer horseback riding lessons, guided pack trips, hearty Western cowboy and chuckwagon cookouts with spontaneous cowboy poetry and storytelling around a campfire, and entertainment like rodeos and square dancing. If traveling with a family, be sure to ask about a children's program. As you'd expect, family-oriented Utah is very kid-friendly, and many resorts have children's playgrounds, basketball hoops and other sports facilities. Recommended options include Sorrel River Ranch Hotel & Spa Resort, Zion Ponderosa Ranch Resort, and Zion Mountain Ranch.

Hostels

Hostel-type accommodation is not as plentiful in the US as it is in Europe, but provision for backpackers and low-budget travelers does exist in Utah. Unless you're traveling alone, most hostels cost about the same as motels; stay in them only if you prefer their youthful ambience, energy and sociability. These days, many hostels are independent, with no affiliation to the HI-AYH (Hosteling-International-American Youth Hostels; http://hiusa.org) network (like the Lazy Lizard Hostel in Moab). The few hostels that do belong to HI-AYH tend to impose curfews, limit daytime access hours, and segregate dormitories by sex. A dorm bed in a hostel usually costs $20–45 per night. In Utah, camping makes a cheap – and exhilarating – alternative. Alternative methods of finding a cheap room online are through www.airbnb.com and the free hosting site www.couchsurfing.org.

National parks and camping

The ideal way to see Utah – especially if you're on a low budget – is to camp in state and federal campgrounds. While hotel-style lodges are found only in major parks, every park or monument tends to have at least one well-organized campground. Often, a cluster of motels can also be found not far outside the park boundaries. National parks and monuments are often surrounded by tracts of national forest – also federally administered but much less protected. These too usually hold appealing rural campgrounds. Public campgrounds range in price from free (usually when there's no water available, which may be seasonal) to around $35 per night. If you're camping in high season, either reserve in advance or avoid the most popular areas.

With appropriate permits – subject to restrictions in popular parks – backpackers can also usually camp in the backcountry (a general term for areas inaccessible by road). Backcountry camping in the national parks is usually free. Before you set off on anything more than a half-day hike, and whenever you're headed for anywhere at all isolated, be sure to inform a ranger of your plans, and ask about weather conditions and specific local tips. Carry sufficient food and drink to cover emergencies, as well as all the necessary equipment and maps. Check whether fires are permitted; even if they are, try to use a camp stove in preference to local materials. In wilderness areas, try to camp on previously used sites. Where there are no toilets, bury human waste at least 6in in the ground and 100ft (30 meters) from the nearest water supply and campground. The goal of low-impact/no-impact backpacking is to leave the area in the same condition as you found it, if not better. Don't break branches, level the ground, or alter the landscape in any way. Take away all trash, including toilet paper.

Admission charges

Most museums and art galleries in Utah charge admission, but discounts are generally available for children, students, and senior citizens – most adult charges range $10–25, museums in the bigger cities such as Salt Lake tend to charge the higher rates. The main exception is for sites operated by the LDS (Mormon) Church, which are usually free.

National Parks and most state parks also charge admission (usually per vehicle), and these can add up fast: Zion National Park and Bryce Canyon for example, both cost $35 each, while Arches and Canyonlands are $30, though this covers seven days of entry in each park. It you intend to visit more than two national parks, consider buying an Annual Pass for $80, from any federal site or via the USGS store (https://store.usgs.gov/pass/index.html). US citizens or permanent residents ages 62 or over can purchase a $80 Lifetime Senior Pass or a $20 Annual Senior Pass.

Age restrictions

You must be at least 21 years of age or older to purchase alcohol or tobacco products in the USA. It's generally much easier to buy alcohol in Utah than it used to be, from grocery stores, convenience stores, and on draft at bars and restaurants. In Utah you can drive a car from the age of 16, but most rental companies will not rent cars to anyone under 21 (and sometimes under 25).

B

Budgeting for your trip

The daily costs for an average traveler in the Utah vary considerably across the state. For stays in Salt Lake City, or at one of the bigger lodges in the national parks, the comfortable daily cost per person (assuming two people sharing a room) should be about $250 ($150 for hotel, $20 for breakfast, $25 for lunch, $50 for dinner, and $10 for transport/gas). Staying in smaller towns and parks, especially if camping, will cut costs dramatically; to around $30 (camping) or $90 (motel), $10 on transport, and $40 (or much less self-catering) for food for the day. In most places a beer will cost $6–8, and a glass of wine a bit more.

C

Children

Two words of advice about traveling with children in Utah: first, be prepared and, second, don't expect to cover too much ground. Overall, Utah – like the rest of the US – is very child and family-friendly, with reduced admission fees at most attractions and kid-friendly activities, menus and more, but be sure to take everything you need. Backcountry towns may be quite small and remote; supplies may be limited. If you need baby formula, special foods, diapers, or medication, carry them with you. It's also a good idea to bring a general first-aid kit for minor scrapes and bruises. Games, books, and crayons help kids pass the time in the car. Carrying snacks and drinks in a day pack will come in handy when kids (or adults) get hungry and there are no restaurants nearby.

Give yourself plenty of time. Remember, kids don't travel at the same pace as adults. They're a lot less interested in traveling from point A to point B than in exploring their immediate surroundings. What you find fascinating (an art museum), they may find boring. And what they think is "really cool" (the game room at the hotel), you may find totally uninteresting.

Inquire about special children's programs at parks, museums, and other attractions. Be sure that wilderness areas, ghost towns, and other backcountry places are suitable for children. Are there abandoned mine shafts, steep stairways, cliffs, or other hazards? Are there special precautions in regard to wildlife? Is a lot of walking necessary? If so, will it be too strenuous for a child? Are strollers permitted? Are food, water, shelter, bathrooms, and other essentials available at the site?

Avoid dehydration by having children drink plenty of water before and during outdoor activities, even if they don't seem particularly thirsty. Put a wide brimmed hat and high-SPF (at least 30 SPF) on children to protect them from the sun. Don't push children beyond their limits. Rest often, provide plenty of snacks, and allow for extra napping.

Climate

Utah spans a wide range of climate and life zones but is mostly a desert state with sunny skies, low humidity, and limited precipitation. Climate varies widely with elevation. Climbing 1,000ft (300 meters) is equivalent to traveling 300 miles (500km) northwards. Conditions atop the highest peaks are akin to those in the Arctic.

Between the mountain ranges, Utah's climate is semiarid. Yearly precipitation ranges from 5–10in (13–26cm) in the Great Basin and along the Colorado River, and an average 8–14in (20–37cm) at elevations of 5,000–7,000ft (1,500–2,100 meters). In the Wasatch and other mountain ranges rainfall totals climb to more than 50in (130cm). These big variations allow for a wide choice of recreational activities in Utah, from pleasant desert hiking and river running during the winter months in the south to snowboarding and skiing in the north.

Spring (March to May)
The spring thaw usually begins in March in the mountains, though

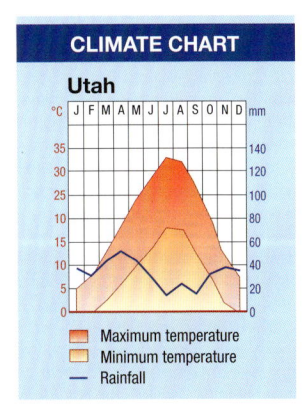

CLIMATE CHART
Utah
°C | J F M A M J J A S O N D | mm
- Maximum temperature
- Minimum temperature
- Rainfall

snow lingers well into July on the highest peaks and mountain passes.

Summer (June to August)

Summer weather begins in late June or early July. Most rain falls in brief, intense thunderstorms during the summer season, when small streams, dry washes, and narrow canyons are prone to flash floods. Violent electrical storms are common on desert peaks during summer afternoons.

Low elevations throughout this desert state sizzle under extremely hot temperatures in summer, hitting the 90s and 100s (32°–38°C) regularly and barely dropping to the 60s and 70s (15–21°C) at night. Many residents escape the heat by spending time at second homes in the mountains, where summer daytime temperatures are usually pleasant, dropping by roughly 5°F (3°C) for every 1,000ft (330 meters) climbed, and hovering in the 40s and 50s (4°–10°C) at night. Nights in the mountains can be chilly even in July and August, and winds are often brisk, so bring a sweater or jacket. Snow, hale, and sleet are possible at the highest elevations at any time of year.

Fall (September to October)

Autumn begins in September, a lovely period of sunny days, chilly nights, and spectacular colors on the forested slopes of the Wasatch Front, High Uintas, and Colorado Plateau.

Winter (November to February)

Winter sets in by late November, though ski areas in northern Utah sometimes open as early as late October (with the aid of snow-making machines) and close in June. With no moderating influences, desert winters are also very cold and often sunny, although the Salt Lake Valley often suffers from a winter inversion layer that brings smog to the Wasatch Front. Only the extreme southern part of the state, around St George, has daytime temperatures averaging above freezing in winter; the Colorado Plateau and mountains frequently post sub-zero temperatures during the winter months and plummet even farther at night. Snowfall at lower elevations is sporadic and often dusts red rocks briefly before melting during warm spells between storms. Annual snowfall in excess of 500in (1,270cm) is common in the ski areas of the Wasatch Mountains, creating what Utah used to call "the greatest snow on earth." Winter storms roll into Utah from the Pacific, lose moisture over Great Salt Lake, and then dump piles of the light, dry powder for which the Wasatch Mountains are famous.

What to wear

With few exceptions, Western dress is informal. A pair of jeans or slacks, a polo, or button-down shirt, and boots or shoes are appropriate at all but the fanciest places and events. Shorts and light shirts are suitable for most situations in the warmer months, though it's always a good idea to have a sweater or jacket for evenings, high elevations, or overly air-conditioned shops, and restaurants.

Many destinations in Utah require some walking, often on rough ground, so be sure to bring good walking shoes or sandals as well as a sturdy pair of hiking shoes or boots for rugged trails. A thin, inner polypropylene sock and a thick, outer wool sock will help keep your feet dry and comfortable. If blisters or sore spots develop, quickly cover them with moleskin or surgical tape, available at most pharmacies or camping supply stores. Good river sandals are important for river trips. A high-factor sunblock, wide-brimmed hat, and polarized sunglasses are advisable too, even if the day starts out cloudy. The sun is merciless in desert areas and at high elevations.

Crime and safety

Many areas of Utah are best enjoyed on foot and it is generally very safe to walk the streets or hike in the national parks. Crime rates across the region have been falling for many years and are generally very low. However, you should be careful when sightseeing, shopping, and moving about, especially after dark. Whenever possible travel or hike with another person. Avoid deserted areas. Never leave your luggage unattended at the airport, at your hotel, or anywhere else. If you are not driving, always lock your car and don't leave luggage, cameras, and other valuables in view. Lock them in the trunk. At night, try to park in lighted areas.

Never leave money, jewelry, or other valuables in your hotel room, even if only for a short time. Don't carry around extra cash. Use credit cards whenever possible. When making purchases avoid making a display of large amounts of cash.

If involved in a traffic accident, remain at the scene. It is illegal to leave the scene of an accident. Use your mobile phone or ask a passing motorist to call the police, then wait for emergency vehicles to arrive. Driving under the influence of alcohol carries stiff penalties, including fines and jail in Utah. Wearing seat belts is required. Children under four must be in a child's safety seat.

Wildlife safety

Realistically, your biggest irritations while hiking are likely to be mosquitoes and flies, and traveling in Utah is far safer than wandering around most cities. Mosquitoes, huge deer flies, and clouds of cedar gnats (midges), or "no-see-ums", begin hatching in May and June on the Colorado Plateau and in river canyons, making life miserable for hikers, campers, and river runners. If you can plan a trip in March or April, before these insects emerge, or fall, when they are gone for the year, you'll be much more comfortable. Insect repellents seem to have little effect, nor do most folk remedies. Your best bet is to carry and wear specially designed mesh headgear fine enough to keep out no-see-ums and be sure to keep tents tightly zippered.

Cougars (mountain lions) can pose a threat (between 2020 to 2021 there were 118 "incidents" with cougars and seven were euthanized in Utah, but proper attacks are very rare) – unlike bears, the best strategy with cougars is to try and fight them off (they usually avoid groups altogether).

Sidewinder, Great Basin, and other Western rattlesnakes are the only Western snake species in Utah and are usually seen in Upper Sonoran Desert regions of the state, if at all. Fatalities from snakebites are very rare – wear proper boots and if you do disturb a snake back away so that it has room to move freely. Even the most venomous bites can be treated successfully if you receive immediate medical attention (call 911 or notify park staff). Only about 3 percent of people bitten in the modern era by a rattlesnake die, and these are mainly small children.

Ironically, more tourists get hurt by otherwise fairly harmless animals, almost always because they get too close when taking a photo. Never ever approach wildlife; stay at least 25 yards (23 meters) away from animals such as bison and elk.

Wilderness safety

Every year people underestimate remote desert backcountry areas in southern Utah, such as Grand Staircase-Escalante National Monument, where adventurous hikers regularly get lost in enchanting but mazelike slot canyons and jeopardize not only their own lives but those of search-and-rescue teams looking for them. Never enter wild areas without adequate planning and letting someone know your plans (if it's a last-minute trip, at least leave a note of your expected itinerary and travel time in your car). Know how to use a topographical map and compass, and don't rely on GPS satellite devices or cell phones; they rarely work in remote canyon country or the mountains. Protect yourself from the elements, depending on the season, and carry a backpack containing any necessary medicines and the so-called Ten Essentials: a gallon of water per person per day, adequate high-energy foods, matches or other fire starter, flashlight, mirror, topo map, compass, whistle, warm clothing, and first-aid kit. Realistically assess your physical and emotional resilience before setting out, avoid traveling alone, and, it's worth reiterating: always let someone know where you are planning to go and when you plan to return. It may save your life.

Ghost towns and old mines

Travelers in Utah should exercise caution around old buildings and abandoned mines. Structures may be unstable and the ground may be littered with broken glass, nails, and other debris. Mine shafts are particularly dangerous. Never attempt to enter a mine shaft or cave unless accompanied by a park ranger or other professional.

Flash floods

Sudden downpours - even those falling miles away from your location - can fill canyons and dry riverbeds with a roaring torrent of water and mud that will sweep away everything in its path. Travelers should be especially careful during the summer "monsoon" season.

Avoid hiking or driving in arroyos or narrow canyons, and never try to wade or drive across a flooded stream. If rain begins to fall or you see rain clouds in the distance, move to higher ground. It's impossible to outrun or even outdrive a flash flood. Act before the water level begins to rise.

Lightning

In Utah, lightning is the number one life-threatening weather hazard. Stay alert for fast-changing weather conditions. It doesn't have to be raining where you are for lightning to be a threat. Avoid being the tallest object in the area and stay away from other tall objects such as a small group of trees. If hiking in the mountains, go early in the day, before thunderstorms develop. Above tree line, there are few places to take cover. If you are in the mountains when a storm is moving in, descend from high points. If you can't get away from an exposed area, make yourself as small as possible, crouching down or perching on a small rock with insulation such as a poncho or foam pad under you, your feet touching rock and your hands clasped around your knees. Never seek shelter under a lone tree, in a shallow cave, or under a rock overhang. Your car is the safest place to be if you are away from a building.

Customs regulations

Everyone entering the United States must go through Customs. Be prepared to have your luggage inspected and keep the following guidelines in mind:
1. There is no limit to the amount of money you can bring into the US. If the amount exceeds $10,000 (in cash and other monetary instruments), however, you must file a special report.
2. Any objects brought for personal use may enter duty-free.
3. Adults may enter with a maximum of 200 cigarettes, or 50 cigars, or 2 kilograms of tobacco, and/or 1 liter of alcohol duty-free.
4. Gifts valued at less than $400 can enter duty-free.
5. Agricultural products, meat, and animals are subject to complex restrictions; to avoid delays, leave these items at home unless absolutely necessary.
6. Illicit drugs and drug paraphernalia are strictly prohibited. If you must bring narcotic or habit-forming medicines for health reasons, be sure that all products are properly identified, carry only the quantity you will need while traveling, and have either a prescription or a letter from your doctor.

E

Eating out

In Salt Lake City, you can pretty much eat whatever you want, whenever you want, thanks to the ubiquity of restaurants, diners, bars, and street carts selling food well into the night. Also, along all the major highways and on virtually every town's main street, restaurants, fast-food joints, and cafés try to outdo one another with bargains and special offers. Whatever you eat and wherever you eat it, service is usually prompt, friendly, and attentive - thanks in large part to the institution of tipping. Waiters depend on tips for the bulk of their earnings; 15 to 20 percent is the standard rate, with anything less sure to be seen as an insult.

Broadly, steaks and other cuts of beef are prominent in Utah, over items such as fresh seafood, though local trout and kokanee salmon are ubiquitous throughout the state. Wild game, including bison and elk, is also popular (often served as burgers or in chili). Mexican food (or at least the Tex-Mex version) is also incredibly popular, with even small towns serving up nachos, tacos,

Betty's Cafe, Vernal.

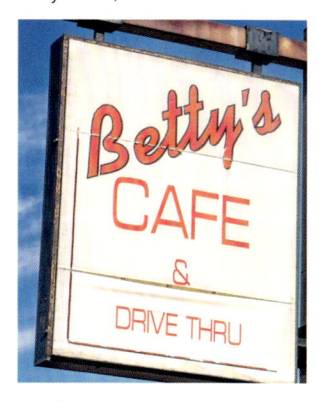

cheese enchiladas, and burritos from one or two holes-in-the-wall. Native American hybrids such as Navajo tacos are also common (the tacos are made of fry bread rather than tortillas), while Utah also claims to have invented "fry sauce" – a blend of ketchup and mayonnaise that tastes similar to Thousand Island Dressing. Bear Lake is the capital of raspberries – raspberry shakes are a beloved local tradition. Salt Lake City is proud of its home-grown Crown Burgers chain, but regardless of where you go, you'll find a good range of authentic diners where the breakfast plates are huge and the burgers handcrafted and tasty. Visitors to Utah's internationally famous national parks represent a huge in-season market for would-be restaurateurs, and world-class cuisine can now be found in even the remotest desert towns in canyon country, such as Boulder, Torrey, and Moab. At its best, this is food with heart, inspired by world cuisine, the Native American and Mormon cultures that have called Utah home, and the chefs' love of the desert.

Electricity

Most wall outlets have 110-volt, 60-cycle, alternating current. A transformer is necessary if you are using European or 220-volt equipment (most smartphones and computers accept both currents these days, and hairdryers tend to be the biggest problem for travelers).

Embassies and consulates

In the USA:
Australia: 1145 17th St NW, Washington, DC, 20036, tel: 202-797 3000, https://usa.embassy.gov.au.
Canada: 501 Pennsylvania Ave NW, Washington, DC 20001, tel: 202-682 1740, https://www.international.gc.ca.
Ireland: 2234 Massachusetts Ave NW, Washington DC 20008, tel: 202-462 3939, https://www.dfa.ie/irish-embassy/usa.
New Zealand: 37 Observatory Circle NW, Washington, DC 20008, tel: 202-328 4800, https://www.mfat.govt.nz.
South Africa: 3051 Massachusetts Ave NW, Washington, DC 20008, tel: 202-232 4400, https://www.saembassy.org.
UK: 3100 Massachusetts Ave NW, Washington, DC 20008, tel: 202-462 1340, https://www.gov.uk.

US embassies overseas:
Australia: Moonah Place, Yarralumla, Canberra, ACT 2600, tel: 02-6214 5600
Canada: 490 Sussex Drive, Ottawa, Ontario K1N 1G8, tel: 613-688 5335
Ireland: 42 Elgin Road, Ballsbridge, Dublin 4 tel: 01-668 8777
New Zealand: 29 Fitzherbert Terrace, Thorndon, Wellington 6011, tel: 04-462 6000
South Africa: 877 Pretorius St, Arcadia, Pretoria, tel: 012-43 4000
UK: 33 Nine Elms Lane, London, SW11 7US, tel: 020-7499 9000

Emergencies

In case of an emergency dial 911 for police, fire, ambulance or any other emergency. If you dial the operator "0" and state the nature of the emergency you can receive some assistance.

Etiquette

Good manners are valued in Utah: hold doors open for people following you; don't jump the line; let people get off public transportation before you get on; offer your seat to older passengers or pregnant women. Show respect when visiting churches – keep your voice down and ask before taking photos.

F

Festivals

On July 4, America's Independence Day, the entire state takes time out to picnic, drink, salute the flag, and watch or participate in fireworks displays, marches, beauty pageants, eating contests, and more, all to commemorate the signing of the Declaration of Independence in 1776.

January (Park City)
Sundance Film Festival (https://festival.sundance.org)
Established in 1978, America's premier event for indie movie makers features dramatic and documentary features and short films, as well as showcasing multimedia installations and performances. The festival began as the Utah/US Film Festival but was renamed in 1991 after Robert Redford's character the Sundance Kid from the film Butch Cassidy and the Sundance Kid (Redford was one of the early sponsors of the festival).

Late January (Ogden)
Hof German Fest (www.hofgermanfest.com)
This annual German-themed festival is held in honor of Ogden's twin city of Hof, Germany. It usually encompasses two to three days of authentic German food (wiener schnitzel, bratwurst, and knockwurst), German-style dances, polka bands, and craft booths.

Late May (Ephraim)
Scandinavian Festival (http://scandinavianfestival.org)
The West's biggest celebration of Scandinavian culture and heritage (expect to see lots of Viking helmets), with parades, food markets, quilt show, car show, and the hilarious "Viking on a Bike Parade."

Early June (Salt Lake City)
Utah Pride Parade & Festival (https://utahpridecenter.org)
The first Sunday of June each year sees an exuberant parade of floats, singers, and dancers celebrate the city's LGBTQ+ community. The festival continues with art, food and drinks, and performance art.

Early June (Salt Lake City)
Utah Blues Festival (www.utahbluesfest.org)
The region's premier blues festival offers two days of live music from some of the best artists in the country, at the Gallivan Center in downtown Salt Lake City.

Late June (Salt Lake City)
Utah Arts Festival (https://uaf.org)
Held over four days at Library Square over six stages, with over 170 artists and more than 200 performances – everything from film showings to live rock, classical music, and bluegrass/folk.

Late June to early Oct (Cedar City)
Utah Shakespeare Festival (www.bard.org)
Founded in 1961, this summer long festival of the Bard sees the campus of Southern Utah University put on a seven- or eight-show repertory of plays every year; half by Shakespeare or his contemporaries, the rest from more modern sources.

Early July (Price)
Greek Festival (https://agoc.ut.goarch.org/greek-festival)
Boisterous celebration of Greek heritage and culture organized by the Assumption Greek Orthodox Church – Greek food always plays a big part in the festivities, as well as live music and dancing.

Late July to late August (Park City)
Beethoven Festival Park City (www.beetfestut.org)
Utah's oldest classical music festival was founded in 1984 by violist Leslie Harlow and has since presented over 850 chamber music concerts, in several venues all over Park City, including free performances in the city park and Park City Community Church.

July 24 (Salt Lake City)
Days of '47' Parade (www.daysof47.com)
Utah's Pioneer Day is celebrated in Salt Lake City with this colorful parade, featuring huge floats that commemorate the history of the state – there's also a huge fair, food, music, and games.

Early August (Garden City)
Bear Lake Raspberry Days Festival (https://gardencityut.us/raspberrydays)
This celebration of the raspberry harvest (which usually begins in July) runs over three days next to Bear Lake, with a parade, live concerts, pie eating contest, rodeo, bingo, pancake breakfasts, fireworks, and lots of arts and crafts.

Late August (Helper)
Helper Arts Festival (www.helperartsfestival.com)
Tiny Helper has put on this annual showcase of art, music, and film since 1994 – all the performances are free. There's also a children's art yard, and an arts and crafts market.

Mid-September (Salt Lake City)
Utah State Fair (www.utahstatefair.com)
Utah's annual state fair at the dedicated Utah State Fairpark also includes an entertaining rodeo, a huge food fair, live concerts, and a huge skatepark.

Late September (Green River)
Melon Days (www.melon-days.com)
Green River has been celebrating its annual melon crop since 1906, with live concerts, craft and snack stalls, special activities for kids, and tons of delicious, fresh watermelon to sample.

H

Health and medical care

Being ill in America is a very expensive affair. Make sure you are covered by medical insurance while traveling in Utah. The US has an excellent, but private healthcare system. An ambulance can cost $1,000, emergency room treatment can rise from $300 to $15,000 incredibly fast (fees for drugs, appliances, supplies, and the attendant physician are all charged separately), and just seeing a local doctor or dentist will be at least $100. In most cases you'll have to pay up front and claim insurance later. For minor ailments it's not worth the expense of seeing a doctor, but you need insurance anyway, mainly to cover you in case of an accident or serious illness (especially if skiing or mountain biking) – operations and emergency treatment can cost tens of thousands of dollars. Should you find yourself requiring a doctor or dentist, ask if your hotel has links to a local practice, or search online. In general, inoculations aren't required for entry to the USA, though check the latest regulations at https://travel.state.gov.

Altitude sickness
Remember that the air is thinner at higher elevations. Unless properly acclimated, you may feel uncharacteristically winded. If you experience nausea, headache, vomiting, extreme fatigue, light-headedness, or shortness of breath, you may be suffering from altitude sickness. Although the symptoms may be mild at first, they can develop into a serious illness. Return to a lower elevation and try to acclimate gradually.

Water
It's always a good idea to carry a little more water than you think you'll need when hiking. The rule of thumb is a gallon a day (4.5 liters) per person, more in extreme conditions. Drink at least a quart at the start of a hike (around a liter) and prevent dehydration by drinking at regular intervals while you're on the trail even if you don't feel particularly thirsty. Don't wait until you've become dehydrated before you start drinking. All water taken from natural sources must be purified before drinking. Giardia is found in water (even crystal-clear water) throughout Utah and can cause severe cramps and diarrhea. The most popular methods of purifying water are using a water purification tablet, a water-purification filter (both available from camping supply stores), or by boiling water for at least 15 minutes.

Sunburn
The sun can be fierce, even on a cool day. Protect yourself by using a high-SPF sunscreen and wearing a wide-brimmed hat and sunglasses, even if the day starts out cloudy. Sunshine reflected off snow can cause serious burns even on the coldest days. Wear sunglasses or ski goggles at all times.

Overheating
Heat exhaustion and heat stroke are very real possibilities when hiking in southern Utah's desert country in summer. Every year, several mountain bikers and hikers traveling on slickrock around Moab die of heat stroke within a few miles of town.

Overheating often comes on insidiously. The body normally deals with excess heat by sending more blood closer to the skin's surface, causing reddening and sweating to bring body temperature down. That mechanism frequently gets overwhelmed when temperatures are high and conditions arid, so that sweat evaporates rapidly without your even realizing you're getting overheated. Eventually, the body loses its ability to control temperature. Initially, skin may become pale and clammy, then, as full-blown heat stroke begins, it gets red and dry and sweating stops. In summer, keep skin cool and moist by keeping exposed skin covered in damp breathable cotton clothing. Wear a wet bandanna around the neck, mist your face and other exposed areas with a portable spray bottle, and, if you feel dizzy, unwell, or shaky, immediately pour copious amounts of water over your head, or find a cool (but not cold) water source for full immersion, to prevent full-blown heat stroke. Be very conservative about outdoor recreation in hot summer conditions. Better to be safe than sorry.

Pharmacies

Pharmacies are widely available throughout Utah – almost every town has one, though only big cities such as Salt Lake City tend to have 24-hour branches.

I

Internet

Almost all hotels and many coffee-shops and restaurants in towns offer free Wi-Fi for guests, though some upmarket hotels charge for access. The main exception is in national and state parks, and wilderness areas throughout Utah – though things are gradually improving, Wi-Fi and often cell phone coverage can be spotty or non-existent. If you are going to require Wi-Fi access, always ask in advance of your stay – don't assume it's available.

L

LGBTQ+ travelers

The LGBTQ+ scene in America is huge, albeit heavily concentrated in the major cities – though Salt Lake City boasts an active community, in rural areas things are a lot more conservative. Though active discrimination is unusual, LGBTQ+ travelers should exercise due diligence to avoid hassles and possible aggression. Utah Pride Center (https://utahpridecenter.org) is a good resource.

M

Maps

Accurate maps are indispensable in Utah, especially when one is leaving paved roads. Road maps can be found at bookstores, convenience stores and gas stations. Free maps may be available by mail from state or regional tourism bureaus.

Maps of national parks, forests and other public lands are usually offered by the managing governmental agency. Good topographical maps of national parks and forests are available from Trails Illustrated (www.natgeomaps.com/trail-maps/trails-illustrated-maps); these maps are often in bookstores, or available online. Extremely detailed topographical maps of the state are available from the U.S. Geological Survey (https://www.usgs.gov/products/maps). Topo maps are usually available in higher-end bookstores and shops that sell outdoor gear, such as REI in Salt Lake City and outfitters in southern Utah.

Media

The two major newspapers in Salt Lake City are now both weeklies, albeit with daily online editions: the *Salt Lake Tribune* (www.sltrib.com) and the *Deseret News* (http://deseretnews.com). Most of the smaller towns in Utah have local newspapers. The *Standard Examiner* (https://www.standard.net) printed in Ogden has a wide circulation. Also available are *The New York Times, Los Angeles Times, Washington Post, USA Today*, and *Wall Street Journal*.

Local publications

Canyon Country Zephyr (www.canyoncountryzephyr.com)
The future of this long-time bimonthly looked uncertain in 2022.
City Weekly (www.cityweekly.net)
Salt Lake City's free alternative weekly covers the city's arts and entertainment.
The Times-Independent (Moab) www.moabtimes.com. Weekly hometown newspaper.
Salt Lake City Magazine
www.saltlakemagazine.com.
Published monthly.
Southern Utah News (Kanab)
www.sunews.net.
The Spectrum (St George)
www.thespectrum.com.
Utah Business
www.utahbusiness.com.
Focuses on what's happening in the Salt Lake City business community.
Utah Life Magazine
www.utahlifemag.com.
Bimonthly travel and entertainment information.

Television

Cities and many large towns have their own local TV stations in addition to the usual national networks and cable stations. Complete listings appear in daily newspapers or online.

Money

The US dollar comes in $1, $2, $5, $10, $20, $50, and $100 denominations. One dollar comprises one hundred cents, made up of combinations of one-cent pennies, five-cent nickels, ten-cent dimes, and 25-cent quarters.

The big bank names are Capital One, Chase, Bank of America, Citibank, Wells Fargo, and US Bank. With an ATM card, you'll be able to withdraw cash just about anywhere, though you'll be charged $2–5 per transaction for using a different bank's network. Foreign cash-dispensing cards linked to international networks, such as Plus or Cirrus, are also widely accepted – ask your home bank or credit card company which branches you can use.

Credit and debit cards are the most widely accepted form of payment at major hotels, restaurants, and retailers, even though a few smaller merchants still do not accept them. You'll be asked to show some plastic when renting a car, bike, or other such item, or to start a "tab" at hotels for incidental charges; in any case, you can always pay the bill in cash when you return the item or check out of your room. It's advisable to arrive with at least $100 in cash (in small bills) to pay for ground transportation and other incidentals.

Tipping

As in most parts of the United States, service personnel rely on tips for a large part of their income. Your gratitude in the form of a tip is not only appreciated, it's also expected, especially in restaurants, where 15 to 20 percent is standard. When sitting at a bar, you should leave at least a dollar per round for the barkeeper; more if the round is more than two drinks. Hotel porters and bellhops should receive at least $2 per piece of luggage, more if it has been lugged up several flights of stairs. About 15 percent should be added to taxi fares, rounded up to the nearest 50 cent or dollar. It is not necessary to tip chamber maids unless you have an extended stay in a small hotel or resort. Tipping is not always necessary in cafeterias and other self-service or fast-food

A – Z | 273

restaurants, but do tip if you feel the service you have received is worth it.

O

Opening hours

Standard business hours are 9am to 5pm Monday through Friday. Many banks open a little earlier, usually 8.30am, and nearly all close by 3pm. A few have Saturday morning hours. Post offices tend to be open from 8am to 5pm Monday through Friday and between 8am and noon on Saturdays. Big city post offices may have extended hours. Most stores keep weekend hours and may stay open late one or more nights a week. As a general rule, most museums are open Tuesday to Sunday, 10am to 5 or 6pm, though most have one night per week where they stay open at least a few hours longer. On national public holidays banks and offices are likely to be closed all day, and some shops will be closed or have reduced hours.

P

Postal services

Even the most remote towns are served by the US Postal Service (www.usps.com). Smaller post offices tend to be limited to business hours (Mon–Fri 9am–5pm), although central, big-city branches may have extended weekday and weekend hours.

Stamps are sold at all post offices and at some convenience stores, filling stations, hotels, and transportation terminals, usually in vending machines.

In the US, the last line of the address includes the city or town and an abbreviation denoting the state ("UT" for Utah, for example). The last line also includes a five-digit number – the zip code – denoting the local post office. It is very important to include this, though the additional four digits that you will sometimes see appended are not essential. You can check zip codes on the US Postal Service website.

Public holidays

Government offices, banks and post offices are closed on public holidays. Public transportation usually runs less frequently on these days.

January 1: New Year's Day
January 15: Martin Luther King, Jr.'s Birthday
Third Monday in February: Presidents Day
March/April: Easter Sunday
Last Monday in May: Memorial Day
July 4: Independence Day
First Monday in September: Labor Day
Second Monday in October: Columbus Day
November 11: Veterans Day
Fourth Thursday in November: Thanksgiving Day
December 25: Christmas Day

Utah celebrates Pioneer Day on July 24 to commemorate the arrival of Brigham Young and the first Mormon pioneers in the Salt Lake Valley. Many shops will be closed. Parades and other festivities are held in Salt Lake City and in towns and cities throughout the state.

R

Religious services

Freedom of religion in the US is guaranteed in the First Amendment to the United States Constitution; while there is no official religion, Christianity, specifically Protestantism, dominates. In Utah, Mormons account for over 55 percent of residents. There are also smaller Roman Catholic congregations and tiny communities of Jews, Muslims, Hindus, and other religious faiths.

S

Shopping

Utah offers plenty of shopping opportunities – from the malls and boutiques of Salt Lake City and Park City, to the arts and crafts stands of small towns across the desert plains and mountains. Shopping opportunities in Salt Lake City include indoor malls downtown like City Creek Center (https://shopcitycreekcenter.com) and the Gateway (https://atthegateway), and the big box stores along Main Street like H&M and Macy's. The Central City neighborhood is known for its art galleries and Trolley Square (www.trolleysquare.com), an indoor mall featuring both high street brands and designer boutiques. There's also Millcreek, 8 miles (13km) south of downtown, especially good for outdoor and hiking gear.

Outside Salt Lake City, travelers will find a surprising variety of art galleries, Native American jewelry stores, clothing shops, and craft stands at ski resorts and small towns throughout the state. For almost all purchases, state taxes will be applied.

Smoking

Smoking in public is generally frowned upon in the US, though the slightly less invasive practice of vaping (e-cigarettes) has taken off in recent years. In Utah, smoking is banned in workplaces, schools, childcare facilities, restaurants, bars, retail stores, and recreational/cultural facilities – you must be 21 or older to buy tobacco products.

Marijuana and other drugs

Over recent years, the legalization of marijuana (cannabis) for recreational purposes has been introduced in several US states. Though its neighbor Colorado was one of the first to legalize, it is still very much **illegal in Utah**, where even being under the influence of marijuana is a misdemeanor that can land you in jail. Also note that all other recreational drugs remain illegal at both state and federal level, and even possession of a tiny amount can get you into serious trouble.

T

Tax

Most items you buy will be subject to state – not federal – sales tax, which has a 4.85 percent base rate in Utah. In addition, counties and cities add to that rate – currently in Utah this tends to be 1.25 percent for a minimum sales tax of 6.10 percent in most places. Still more local taxes can be added on top of that (for mass transit, highways, etc), so that the Salt Lake City combined total rate is 7.75 percent and Park City's is 9.05 percent, the highest in Utah. Hotel taxes are usually slightly different and vary from county to county, beginning with a 0.32 percent statewide "transient room tax" and ranging up to 6 percent or more.

Telephones

Public telephones are becoming rare thanks to the explosion of cell phone use, but you should still find them at highway rest areas, service stations, motels, and restaurants. The quickest way to get assistance is to dial 0 for the operator; local calls usually cost 25 cents and can be dialed directly. Rates vary for long-distance calls, but they can also be dialed directly with the proper area code and country code.

If you are planning to take your mobile phone (more often called a cell phone in America) from outside the USA, you'll need to check with your service provider whether it will work in the country: you will need a tri-band or quad-band phone that is enabled for international calls (all iPhones and most smartphones should be okay). Non-North American residents that use their home cell phone will probably incur hefty roaming charges for making calls and will be charged extra for incoming calls. Many travelers turn off voicemail and data roaming before they travel. If you have a compatible (and unlocked) GSM phone and intend to use it a lot, it can be much cheaper to buy a US SIM card ($10 or less) to use during your stay. AT&T (www.att.com) is your best bet. Some networks also sell basic US flip phones (with minutes) for as little as $25 (no paperwork or ID required).

Calling home from the USA

For country codes not listed below, dial 0 for the operator, consult any phone directory or log onto www.countrycallingcodes.com.
Australia 011 plus 61 plus area code minus its initial zero.
New Zealand 011 plus 64 plus area code minus its initial zero.
Republic of Ireland 011 plus 353 plus area code minus its initial zero.
South Africa 011 plus 27 plus area code.
UK 011 plus 44 plus area code minus its initial zero.

Time zones

The continental US is divided into four time zones. From east to west, later to earlier, they are eastern, central, mountain, and Pacific, each separated by one hour. Utah is on mountain standard time, seven hours behind Greenwich mean time. On the first Sunday in April, Utahns set the clock ahead one hour in observation of daylight savings time. On the last Sunday in October, the clock is moved back one hour to return to standard time. Neighboring states are also in the mountain time zone except Nevada, which, like California, is in the Pacific time zone. Note: Arizona does not observe daylight savings time and, during the summer, is in the same time zone as California. Glen Canyon National Recreation Area, which spans the Utah–Arizona line but is headquartered in Page, Arizona, is one hour behind Utah in summer.

Tourist information

Each region has its own tourist office. These offer prospective visitors a colossal range of free maps, leaflets, and brochures on attractions from overlooked wonders to the usual tourist traps. You can either contact the offices before you set off, or, as you travel around the country, look for the state-run "welcome centers," usually along main highways close to the state borders. In addition, visitor centers in most towns and cities – often known as the "Convention and Visitors Bureau," or CVB – provide details on the area, as do local chambers of commerce in almost any town of any size.

Statewide
Utah Office of Tourism
https://www.visitutah.com
Utah Travel Council
https://www.utah.com

Northern Utah
Bear Lake Convention and Visitors Bureau
69 N Paradise Parkway Bldg A, Garden City; tel: 800-448 2327
https://bearlake.org
Box Elder County Tourism and Community Development
1 S Main St, Brigham City; tel: 877-390 2326
www.visitboxeldercounty.com/tourism
Cache Valley Visitors Bureau
199 N Main St, Logan; tel: 435-755 1890
www.explorelogan.com
Davis County Tourism
61 S Main St, Farmington; tel: 801-451 3237
https://discoverdavis.com
Duchesne County Chamber of Commerce
50 E 200 South St, Roosevelt; tel: 435-722 4598
www.uintabasin.org
Heber Valley Chamber of Commerce
475 N Main St, Heber City; tel: 435-654 3666
www.gohebervalley.com
Park City Chamber of Commerce
1850 Sidewinder Drive No. 320, Park City; tel: 800-453 1360
www.visitparkcity.com
Tooele County Chamber of Commerce
154 S Main St, Tooele; tel: 435-882 0690
https://tooelechamber.com
Uintah County Travel and Tourism
152 E 100 North St, Vernal; tel: 800-477 5558
www.dinoland.com
Explore Utah Valley
220 W Center St, Suite 100, Provo; tel: 800-222 8824
www.utahvalley.com
Visit Ogden
2411 Kiesel Ave No. 401, Ogden; tel: 801-255 8824
www.visitogden.com
Visit Salt Lake
90 S West Temple, Salt Lake City; tel: 801-534 4900
www.visitsaltlake.com

Central Utah
Carbon County Tourism
751 E 100 North, Suite 2600, Price; tel: 435-636 3701
www.castlecountry.com
Millard County Tourism
460 N Main St, Fillmore; tel: 435-743 7803
https://millardcounty.com
San Pete County Tourism
191 N Main St, Manti; tel: 435-835 4321
www.sanpete.com
Sevier County Tourism
250 N Main St, Richfield; tel: 435-893 0400
www.sevierutah.net

Southern Utah
Beaver County Travel Council
105 E Center St, Beaver; tel: 435-438 6482

A – Z | 275

https://ramblersutah.com

Capitol Reef Country/Wayne County Tourism
Junction Highway 12 and 24, Torrey; tel: 800-858 7951
https://capitolreef.org

Garfield County Travel Council
55 S Main St, Panguitch; tel: 800-444 6689
www.brycecanyoncountry.com

Grand County Economic Development Office
125 E Center St, Moab; tel: 435-259 8825
www.discovermoab.com

Greater Zion Convention & Tourism Office
20 N Main St, Suite 105, St George; tel: 435-634 5747
https://greaterzion.com

Kane County, Utah Office of Tourism
78 S 100 East St, Kanab; tel: 435-644 5033,
https://visitsouthernutah.com

San Juan County Economic Development and Visitor Services
117 S Main St, Monticello; tel: 800-574 4386
www.utahscanyoncountry.com

Visit Cedar City
581 N Main St, Cedar City; tel: 435-586 5124
https://visitcedarcity.com

Parks and wilderness areas

Bureau of Land Management
491 N John Glenn Road, Salt Lake City; tel: 801-320 8300
www.blm.gov/office/salt-lake-field-office

National Park Service Southwest Region
1100 Old Santa Fe Trail, Santa Fe; tel: 505-988 6016
www.nps.gov

Utah State Park and Recreation Division
1594 W North Temple St, Suite 116, Salt Lake City; tel: 801-538 7220
https://stateparks.utah.gov

U.S. Forest Service (Salt Lake Ranger District)
6944 S 3000 East St, Salt Lake City; tel: 801-733 2660
www.fs.usda.gov

Tour operators and travel agents

The United States Tour Operators Association has a comprehensive listing of US tour operators; visit their website at https://ustoa.com. For hiking, biking, skiing, and kayaking in Utah:

G Adventures
Tel: 212-228 6655/1-888-800 4100; www.gadventures.com

Rocky Mountain Tours (ski trips)
Tel: 800-525 7547; www.rockymountain-tours.com

Western Spirit Cycling Adventures
Tel: 435-259 8732; https://westernspirit.com

Wildland Trekking
Tel: 928-223 4453/1-800-715 4453; https://wildlandtrekking.com

UK

Contiki Holidays
Tel: +41 22-929 9216 from Europe; www.contiki.com

Travelpack
Tel: 020-8585 4080; www.travelpack.com

V

Visas and passports

Under the Visa Waiver Program, citizens of Australia, Ireland, New Zealand, and the UK do not require visas for visits to the US of 90 days or less. You will, however, need to obtain Electronic System for Travel Authorization (ESTA) online before you fly, which involves completing a basic immigration form in advance. Do this only on the official US Customs and Border Protection website: at the time of writing the website was https://esta.cbp.dhs.gov/esta, but note that similar sites that might seem official will charge you more and are a scam. There is an official processing fee of $4, and a further $17 authorization fee once the ESTA has been approved (for a total $21, all paid via credit card online). Once given, authorizations are valid for multiple entries into the US for two years (or until your passport expires, whichever comes first) – it's recommended that you submit an ESTA application as soon as you begin making travel plans (in most cases the ESTA will be granted immediately, but it can sometimes take up to 72 hours to get a response). You'll need to present a machine-readable passport to Immigration upon arrival. Note that ESTA currently only applies to visitors arriving by air or cruise ship: Crossing the land border from Canada, those qualifying for the Visa Waiver Program do not need to apply for ESTA – instead you must fill in an I-94W form, though this may change in future. Canadians now require a passport to cross the border (no need to apply for ESTA), but can travel in the US for up to a year without a visa or visa waiver.

W

Websites and apps

Airbnb: airbnb.com
America's premier site for apartment, individual rooms, or mansion rentals.

GasBuddy: www.gasbuddy.com
Useful for long-distance drives in the region: operates apps and websites that list real-time fuel prices at thousands of gas stations across the United States.

Incident Information System: https://inciweb.nwcg.gov
This site provides instant updates on extreme weather that affects the whole US.

National Park Service: https://www.nps.gov/index.htm
The Park Service website details the main attractions of the national parks, plus opening hours, the best times to visit, admission fees, hiking trails, and visitor facilities.

Visit The USA: www.visittheusa.com
The US's official tourist website has useful tips and travel information on the Rockies region.

Weights and measures

Despite efforts to convert to metric, the US still uses the Imperial System of weights and measures – in areas near the Canadian border you will occasionally see miles converted to kilometers.

1 inch = 2.54 centimeters
1 foot = 30.48 centimeters
1 yard = 0.9144 meter
1 mile = 1.609 kilometers
1 pint = 0.473 liter
1 quart = 0.946 liter
1 ounce = 28.4 grams
1 pound = 0.453 kilogram
1 acre = 0.405 hectare
1 square mile = 259 hectares
1 centimeter = 0.394 inch
1 meter = 39.37 inches
1 kilometer = 0.621 mile
1 liter = 1.057 quarts
1 gram = 0.035 ounce
1 kilogram = 2.205 pounds
1 hectare = 2.471 acres
1 square kilometer = 0.386 square mile

FURTHER READING

It would be hard to argue for Utah as a literary hotbed, though to be sure the rugged lands and postcard images have fired the imagination of many, from the first Native Americans to Wallace Stegner and on. The books below include those most evocative of the Utah backdrop, as well as ones that should prove most entertaining and useful during your trip. The majority should be easy to find on the internet or can be ordered by your favorite bookstore.

HISTORY AND SOCIETY

Butch Cassidy: The True Story of an American Outlaw by Charles Leerhsen. The most recent biography of Cassidy, born Robert LeRoy Parker into a Mormon family in Beaver, Utah, in 1866, is one of the best, shedding light on what motivated the rustler and bank robber.

A History of Utah's American Indians by Forrest S. Cuch, ed. This comprehensive history of Utah's complex and diverse Native American peoples remains the classic study, covering the state's official six recognized Indigenous groups and many others with essays by several experts.

Ancient North America by Brian M. Fagan. Archaeological history of America's Indigenous peoples, from the first hunters to cross the Bering Strait up to first contact with Europeans.

The Book of the Navajo by Raymond Locke. An excellent introduction to the history, mythology traditions, and contemporary culture of the Navajo. Locke died in 2002, but his book is still one of the best.

Brigham Young: Pioneer Prophet by John G. Turner. Essential reading for anyone interested in the origins of the "Mormon State" in Utah. Turner provides a fascinating portrait of the Mormon's greatest leader.

Bury My Heart at Wounded Knee by Dee Brown. Still the best narrative on the impact of white settlers pushing westward on Native Americans.

Cinema Southwest: An illustrated Guide to the Movies and their Locations by John Murray. Film buffs will enjoy this guide to all the classic films shot in Utah and its neighboring states, from Westerns to *Avatar*.

Exploration of the Colorado River and Its Canyons by John Wesley Powell. Thrilling account of Powell's momentous journey down the Green and Colorado rivers in 1874, taking in much of modern-day Utah.

Send us your thoughts

We do our best to ensure the information in our books is as accurate and up-to-date as possible. The books are updated on a regular basis using destination experts, who painstakingly add, amend and correct as required. However, some details (such as opening times or travel pass costs) are particularly liable to change, and we are ultimately reliant on our readers to put us in the picture.

We welcome your feed back, especially your experience of using the book "on the road", and if you came across a great new attraction we missed.

We will acknowledge all contributions and offer an Insight Guide to the best messages received.

Please write to us at:
**Insight Guides
PO Box 7910
London SE1 1WE**

Or email us at:
hello@insightguides.com

It Happened in Utah by Tom Wharton. The Utah edition of the "It Happened In" series is crammed with historical anecdotes from early pioneers to the 2002 Salt Lake Olympics.

It's Your Misfortune and None of My Own by Richard White. Dense, authoritative and all-embracing history of the American West, which debunks the notion of the rugged pioneer by stressing the role of the federal government.

Life Is Just What You Make It by Donny Osmond. Fans of the Osmonds, Utah's first family of light entertainment, will enjoy this autobiography, which recounts Donny's upbringing in Ogden and his family's rise to super stardom in the 1970s. See also **Might As Well Laugh About It Now** by equally beloved sister, Marie Osmond.

Mormon America: The Power and the Promise by Richard Ostling and Joan K. Ostling. Fascinating look at what lies behind Mormon beliefs, rituals and the modern-day church in Utah, with special attention given to LDS wealth and business interests.

Mormon Country by Wallace Stegner. A collection of 28 essays focusing on Mormon life and the wide range of non-believers who lived in Mormon country in the late 19th and early 20th centuries. There are some great tales here, and Stegner tells them superbly.

The Mormon Experience: A History of the Latter-day Saints by Leonard Arrington and Davis Bitton. Still one of the best overall histories of the Mormons in North America and especially their community in Utah.

The Mountain Meadows Massacre by Juanita Brooks. Detailed and enlightening account of the Mormon massacre of 120 California-bound emigrants in 1857, offering insights into the background of the conflict, and the attempt to cover it up. Brooks also wrote the entertaining **Quicksand and Cactus: A Memoir of the Southern Mormon Frontier**.

Outlaw Tales of Utah: True Stories of Utah's Most Famous Robbers, Rustlers, and Bandits by Michael Rutter. Entertaining account of the state's roster of 19th century cattle rustlers, train robbers, and other assorted outlaws, from Butch Cassidy and the Wild Bunch to Kid Curry.

Red: Passion and Patience in the Desert by Terry Tempest Williams. This collection of essays and stories by the respected Utah author

makes the case for the preservation of Utah's wild and as yet mostly unspoiled Canyon Country. See also Williams' memoir, *Refuge: An Unnatural History of Family and Place*.
Tales of Canyonlands Cowboys by Richard Negri. Product of a series of illuminating interviews with seven men and three women – cattle hands and ranchers – about life in southeastern Utah in the early 20th century.
Under the Banner of Heaven: A Story of Violent Faith by Jon Krakauer. The respected investigative journalist takes on fundamentalist Mormonism and polygamy in this tragic account of the 1984 murder of Brenda Lafferty.

FICTION AND POETRY

The 19th Wife by David Ebershoff. Historical drama set in the 1870s, inspired by the real life of Ann Eliza Young, one of Brigham Young's 54 wives, juxtaposed against a modern-day murder involving a polygamist family in Utah.
The Big Rock Candy Mountain by Wallace Stegner. This harrowing historical saga of the fictional Mason family in some ways mirrors Stegner's own life, especially the sections set in Salt Lake City. Stegner is probably the most famous author associated with Utah; see also the sequel *Recapitulation* and his autobiography *Wolf Willow*.

Cage of Stars by Jacquelyn Mitchard. Emotional revenge drama set in Cedar City, as Veronica "Ronnie" Swan must confront her Mormon parents for forgiving the man who murdered her two beloved sisters.
Children of God: An American Epic by Vardis Fisher. Fisher wrote popular novels set in the old Wild West from the 1930s through to the 1960s, and though his work can be hard to find today, it's extremely evocative of the period. This novel features the early history of the Mormons in Utah (Fisher was raised Mormon in Idaho). See also *Mountain Man* and *The Mothers: An American Saga of Courage*, the latter tells the story of the doomed Donner Party.
The Chinchilla Farm by Judith Freeman. Freeman's debut novel tells the story of Verna Flake, who flees her Mormon life in Utah for California and eventually Mexico. See also Freeman's excellent **Red Water**, a fictionalized account of the life of Mountain Meadows Massacre perpetrator John D. Lee through the eyes of some of his 19 wives.
Desert Quartet: An Erotic Landscape by Terry Tempest Williams. A journey of self-discovery in the canyons of southern Utah. A thought-provoking blend of drawings and stream-of consciousness poetry.
Don't You Marry the Mormon Boys by Janet Kay Jensen. This classic love story between a conventional Mormon and a fundamental

polygamist is beautifully handled by the Utah-based author.
The Giant Joshua by Maurine Whipple. This seminal work of Mormon fiction was published in 1941, a realistic tale of the harsh life experienced by especially female Mormon pioneers living in 19th-century southwestern Utah.
The Lonely Polygamist by Brady Udall. Tragicomic but enthralling tale of the trials of Golden Richards, a modern-day polygamist with four wives and 28 kids.
Riders of the Purple Sage by Zane Grey. This seminal Western novel, published in 1912, is set amongst the Mormon communities of Southern Utah in the 1870s, and follows the struggles of rich Mormon ranch owner Jane Withersteen and gunslinging Lassiter.
When the Emperor Was Divine by Julie Otsuka. Poignant tale based on the very real internment of Japanese Americans at Topaz in Utah during World War II – invaluable for anyone who visits the Topaz Museum in Delta.
Windows on the Sea and Other Stories by Linda Sillitoe. A collection of short stories centered around Mormon women. Sillitoe is another Utah author whose books are harder to find today (she was most popular in the 1990s), but her work is worth seeking out; see also *Sideways to the Sun* and her coverage of the "Mormon forgery murders."

CREDITS

PHOTO CREDITS

Adobe Stock 140, 141, 143, 144, 145, 146, 147, 148, 150, 151, 153, 154, 155, 156, 157, 158, 159T, 159B, 160, 161, 163, 164, 166, 167, 169, 170, 171, 172, 173, 174/175T, 176, 177, 179, 180, 181, 214, 215, 216, 217, 218, 219, 220, 221, 222, 223, 225, 226, 227, 228, 229, 230, 231, 233, 234, 235, 236, 237, 238, 239, 240, 241, 242, 243, 244, 245, 246, 247, 248, 249, 251, 252, 253, 254, 255, 256, 257, 258, 260, 262B, 262T, 263TL, 263TL, 264, 264/265, 269
iStockphoto 276
Public domain 20/21

Shutterstock 1, 4, 6ML, 6MR, 6BL, 6MR, 7TR, 7ML, 7MR, 7ML, 7BR, 7TL, 8BR, 8M, 8BL, 9TR, 9TL, 9BR, 10B, 10TR, 10TL, 11B, 11TL, 11TR, 12/13, 14/15, 16/17, 18, 19T, 19B, 22B, 22T, 23B, 23T, 24, 25, 26, 27L, 27R, 28, 29, 30, 31, 32, 33, 34R, 34L, 35, 36, 37, 38, 39, 40/41T, 40BL, 40BR, 41BR, 41TR, 41BL, 41ML, 42, 43, 44R, 44L, 45, 46, 47, 48, 49, 50, 51, 52/53T, 52BL, 52BR, 53ML, 53BR, 53BL, 53TR, 54, 55, 56, 57, 58, 59, 60, 61, 62, 63, 64, 65, 66, 67, 68, 69, 70/71T, 70BR, 70BL, 71ML, 71BR, 71BL, 71TR, 72, 73, 74, 75, 76, 77, 78, 79, 80, 81, 82, 83, 84, 85, 86, 87, 88, 89, 90, 91, 92, 93, 94/95T, 94BR, 94BL, 95ML, 95BR, 95BL, 95TR, 96, 97, 98, 99, 100, 101, 102, 103, 104, 105, 106, 107, 108/109, 110/111, 112/113, 114, 115T, 115B, 118, 119T, 119B, 120, 121, 123, 124, 125, 126, 127, 128, 129, 130, 131, 133, 134, 135, 136, 137, 138, 139, 149, 174BR, 174BL, 175ML, 175BR, 175BL, 175TR, 182, 183T, 183B, 184, 185, 188, 189, 190, 191, 193, 194, 195, 196, 197, 199, 200, 201, 202, 203, 204, 205, 207, 208, 209, 210, 211, 212, 213, 259, 263BR

COVER CREDITS

Front cover: The North Window at Arches National Park *Anthony Heflin/Shutterstock*
Back cover: Downtown Provo *Adobe Stock*
Front flap: (from top) Mount Timpanogos *Adobe Stock*; Rafting *Shutterstock*; Skiing at Deer Valley *Shutterstock*; petroglyphs at Mcconckie Ranch *Shutterstock*
Back flap: Northern Ute Veterans Memorial in Ballard *Shutterstock*

INSIGHT GUIDE CREDITS

Distribution
UK, Ireland and Europe
Apa Publications (UK) Ltd;
sales@insightguides.com
United States and Canada
Ingram Publisher Services;
ips@ingramcontent.com
Australia and New Zealand
Booktopia;
retailer@booktopia.com.au
Worldwide
Apa Publications (UK) Ltd;
sales@insightguides.com
Special Sales, Content Licensing and CoPublishing
Insight Guides can be purchased in bulk quantities at discounted prices. We can create special editions, personalised jackets and corporate imprints tailored to your needs.
sales@insightguides.com
www.insightguides.biz

Printed in China

All Rights Reserved
© 2023 Apa Digital AG
License edition © Apa Publications Ltd UK

First Edition 2022
Second Edition 2023

This book was produced using **Typefi** automated publishing software.

No part of this book may be reproduced, stored in a retrieval system or transmitted in any form or means electronic, mechanical, photocopying, recording or otherwise, without prior written permission from Apa Publications.

Every effort has been made to provide accurate information in this publication, but changes are inevitable. The publisher cannot be responsible for any resulting loss, inconvenience or injury. We would appreciate it if readers would call our attention to any errors or outdated information. We also welcome your suggestions; please contact us at: hello@insightguides.com

www.insightguides.com

Editor: Beth Williams
Copyeditor: Philippa MacKenzie
Author: Stephen Keeling
Picture Editor: Piotr Kala
Picture Manager: Tom Smyth
Cartography: Carte
Layout: Grzegorz Madejak
Indexer: Penny Phenix
Head of DTP and Pre-Press: Katie Bennett
Head of Publishing: Kate Drynan

CONTRIBUTORS

This new edition was commissioned by Beth Williams and edited by Philippa MacKenzie. It was thoroughly updated by Stephen Keeling.

This version builds on earlier work by Nicky Leach, Richard Harris and Edward A. Jardim. The book was indexed by Penny Phenix.

ABOUT INSIGHT GUIDES

Insight Guides have more than 45 years' experience of publishing high-quality, visual travel guides. We produce 400 full-colour titles, in both print and digital form, covering more than 200 destinations across the globe, in a variety of formats to meet your different needs.
Insight Guides are written by local authors, whose expertise is evident in the extensive historical and cultural background features. Each destination is carefully researched by regional experts to ensure our guides provide the very latest information. All the reviews in **Insight Guides** are independent; we strive to maintain an impartial view. Our reviews are carefully selected to guide you to the best places to eat, go out and shop, so you can be confident that when we say a place is special, we really mean it.

Legend

City maps
- Freeway/Highway/Motorway
- Divided Highway
- Main Roads
- Minor Roads
- Pedestrian Roads
- Steps
- Footpath
- Railway
- Funicular Railway
- Cable Car
- Tunnel
- City Wall
- Important Building
- Built Up Area
- Other Land
- Transport Hub
- Park
- Pedestrian Area
- Bus Station
- Tourist Information
- Main Post Office
- Cathedral/Church
- Mosque
- Synagogue
- Statue/Monument
- Beach
- Airport

Regional maps
- Freeway/Highway/Motorway (with junction)
- Freeway/Highway/Motorway (under construction)
- Divided Highway
- Main Road
- Secondary Road
- Minor Road
- Track
- Footpath
- International Boundary
- State/Province Boundary
- National Park/Reserve
- Marine Park
- Ferry Route
- Marshland/Swamp
- Glacier
- Salt Lake
- Airport/Airfield
- Ancient Site
- Border Control
- Cable Car
- Castle/Castle Ruins
- Cave
- Chateau/Stately Home
- Church/Church Ruins
- Crater
- Lighthouse
- Mountain Peak
- Place of Interest
- Viewpoint

INDEX

A

accessible travel 265
accommodations 265
activities 97. *See also* activities by name
admission charges 267
age restrictions 267
agriculture 26, 58
Alpine Loop Scenic Drive 143, 144
Alta 106
altitude sickness 271
American West Heritage Center 128
Anasazi State Park 213
Ancestral Puebloans 27
Anderson, May 67
Antelope Island 119
Antelope Island State Park 102, 121
  birdlife 121
  bison 122
  Frary Peak 121
  Garr Ranch 122
Apache 29
apps 275
Arches National Park 91
Arrington, Leonard 77
art galleries. *See* museums and galleries
Ashley, William H. 36
Astor, John Jacob 36
Athabascans 29

B

backpacking 266
ballooning 103
basketball 61, 134
Bear Lake 126
Bear River Migratory Bird Refuge 93, 127, 128
Beaver 170
Beaver Mountain 105
Beaver Mountain Ski Area 126
bed-and-breakfasts 266
Beus Canyon Trail 125
Bidwell, John 38
Big Cottonwood Canyon 139
Big Rock Candy Mountain 82, 173
bike routes 102
Bingham Canyon Open Pit Copper Mine 178, 179
birdlife and birdwatching 87, 90, 91
  Bear River Migratory Bird Refuge 127
  Bryce Canyon 200, 202
  California condor 89
  Great Salt Lake 121
  Ouray National Wildlife Refuge 157
bison 102
Blacksmith Fork Canyon 128
Blanding Dinosaur Museum 84
boating 98
Bonneville Salt Flats 179
Bonneville Salt Flats Race Track 179, 180
books 276
Box-Death Hollow Wilderness 213
Brian Head 106, 202
Bridal Veil Falls 144
Bridger, Jim 37, 48
Brigham City 128
brine shrimp 92
British immigrants 66
Browns Park 154
Browns Park Scenic Backway 154
Bryce Canyon National Park 101
  accommodation 199
  Bryce Amphitheater 199
  camping 199
  geology 197
  hiking trails 200
  hours and admission 199
  scenic drive 199
  shuttle bus 198
  viewpoints 199
  Visitor Center 199
  wildlife 200
Bryce, Ebenezer 67, 197
Buchanan, President James 50
budgeting for your trip 267
burros 153
Burton, Richard Francis 49
buses 263, 265
buses to Utah 262
business hours 273
Butch Cassidy Childhood Home 173
Butterfield Canyon 179
Butterfield Pass 179

C

cacti 91
camping 266
canoeing 233
canyoneering 102
Canyonlands National Park 26, 81, 91, 97, 101
  admission and passes 233
  Aztec Butte 234
  Bagpipe Butte Overlook 237
  Big Spring Canyon Overlook 236
  birdlife 234
  Cave Spring Trail 236
  Chesler Park Trail 236
  Colorado River Overlook 236
  Confluence Overlook 236
  Doll House 237
  Elephant Hill 236
  float trips 231
  geology 235
  Grabens 236
  Grand View Point Overlook 234
  guided river trips 233
  Hans Flat Ranger Station 237
  Harvest Scene pictographs 237
  Horse Canyon 236
  Island in the Sky 231
  Labyrinth Canyon 234
  Maze District 233, 237
  Maze Overlook 237
  Mesa Arch 234
  Moab Information Center 233
  Needles Campground 236
  Needles District 233, 235
  permits 233, 234, 237
  plantlife 234, 237
  Pothole Point 236
  Roadside Ruin 236
  Salt Creek 236
  Salt Creek Canyon Trail 236
  Thirteen Faces 237
  Tower Ruin 237
  Upheaval Dome 235
  visitor centers 233, 234, 236
  White Rim Road 234
  wildlife 234, 236, 237
  Wooden Shoe Arch Overlook 236
Canyons of the Ancients National Monument 28
Capitol Reef National Park 82, 101
Carbon County 159
car rental 263, 264
Carson, Kit 38
Cascade Springs Loop 145
Cassidy, Butch 40, 173
Castle Country 159
Castle Valley Ridge Trail 102
Cataract Canyon 97
Cedar Breaks National Monument 201, 202
  Alpine Pond Trail 202
  Spectra Point 202
  Wasatch Ramparts 202
  wildflowers 202
  wildlife and birdlife 202
Cedar City 202
  Frontier Homestead State Park Museum 203
  Paiute Restoration Gathering 203
  Red Rock Film Festival 203
  Simon Fest Theatre Co 203
  Southern Utah Museum of Art 203
  Southern Utah University 203
  Utah Midsummer Renaissance Faire 203
  Utah Shakespeare Festival 70, 202
  Utah Summer Games 203
cell phone coverage 272
Central Utah 159
Chaco civilization 27
children, traveling with 267
Church of Jesus Christ of Latter-day Saints 52, 61, 131. *See also* Mormons
Circleville 173
climate 88, 267
climbing 102
Clinton, President Bill 207

INDEX | 281

clothing 268
Colorado Plateau 19, 79, 89
Colorado River 85, 87, 88, 89, 98, 231, 233, 234, 235
Confusion Mountains 181
Connor, Colonel Patrick E. 56
consulates 270
copper mining 85
Coronado, Francisco Vázquez 33
cougars 268. *See* pumas
Cove Fort 169
Covid-19 61
crime 268
currency 272
customs regulations 269
cycling 264
Czerkas, Sylvia and Stephen 84

D

Danger Cave State Park 179
Dead Horse Point State Park 235
Deer Creek Reservoir 146
Deer Creek State Park 146
Deer Valley 106
Delta 180
Deseret 180
Deseret Peak 178
deserts 91
Devil's Slide 125
dialects 68
Dineh 29
Dinosaur Diamond 81
Dinosaur National Monument 79, 81, 151
  Canyon Visitor Center (Dinosaur, CO) 153
  Dinosaur Quarry Visitor Center 152
  Josie Bassett Morris Homestead 153
  Quarry Exhibit Hall 152
  Tour of the Tilted Rocks 153
dinosaurs 83, 84
Dinosaur town (CO) 153
disabilities, travelers with 265
Dome Creek Pass 181
Domínguez, Francisco Atanasio 35
Donner, George 39
Donner Party tragedy 39
driving 263
  accidents 268
  car rental 264
  from Canada 264
  rules of the road 264
  to Utah 262
drugs 273
dude ranches 266
Dugout Ranch 89

E

eating out 269
Eccles, David 67
Echo Park (CO) 153
Eckhart, Aaron 76
economy 61
electricity 270
embassies 270
emergencies 270

Emigration Canyon 138
Ephraim 70, 171
  Ephraim Co-Op Mercantile Association 171
  Granary Arts 171
  Snow College 171
Escalante Forest State Park 81
Escalante River 91, 205, 210
Escalante, Silvestre Vélez de 34
etiquette 270
Eureka 180

F

Fairview 170
festivals and events 70
  Beethoven Festival (Park City) 70
  bird-watching festival (Bear River Migratory Bird Refuge) 127
  calendar of events 270
  Dinosaur Roundup Rodeo (Vernal) 157
  Greek Festival (Price) 70
  Heritage Days (Spring City) 171
  Hof German Fest (Ogden) 71
  Living Traditions Festival (Salt Lake City) 66
  Melon Days (Green River) 71
  Northern Ute Indian Powwow (Uintah and Ouray Reservation) 157
  Paiute Restoration Gathering (Cedar City) 203
  Pioneer Day 70, 75
  Pioneer Day pageants 66
  powwows 31
  Raspberry Days Festival (Garden City) 70
  Red Rock Film Festival (Cedar City) 203
  Restoration Gathering (Cedar City) 31
  Salt Lake City Jazz Festival (Salt Lake City) 70
  Scandinavian Festival (Ephraim) 70, 172
  Sundance Film Festival (Park City) 71, 145
  Swiss Days (Santa Clara) 75
  Thanksgiving Powwow (Uintah and Ouray Reservation) 157
  Utah Arts Festival (Salt Lake City) 70
  Utah Blues Festival (Salt Lake City) 70
  Utah Midsummer Renaissance Faire (Cedar City) 203
  Utah Pride Parade & Festival (Salt Lake City) 70
  Utah Shakespeare Festival (Cedar City) 70, 202
  Utah State Fair (Salt Lake City) 71
  Utah Summer Games (Cedar City) 203
  Ute Bear Dance 65
  Ute Stampede (Nephi) 169, 170
  Wild Horse Festival 153
Fillmore 169

Fisher Pass 179
fishing 88, 156, 173
Fish Lake 173
Fishlake National Forest 173
Fishlake Scenic Byway 173
Fitzpatrick, Tom 37
Flaming Gorge Dam 60, 156
Flaming Gorge National Recreation Area 155
Flaming Gorge Reservoir 156
Flaming Gorge–Uintas Scenic Byway 155
flash floods 269
flights 262
flights, scenic 103
float trips 231
football 137
Fort Duchesne 157
fossils 80, 84
Fountain Green 170
Fremont culture 28, 203, 213
Frémont, John Charles 38, 45
further reading 276
fur trade 36
fur trappers 37

G

Gabelich, Gary 180
Garden City 70
geology 19
ghost towns 269
Gila monsters 93
Glen Canyon Dam 60
Glen Canyon National Recreation Area 84
Glendale 208
gliding 103
Godbe, George S. 67
Godbeite Movement 67
Golden Spike National Historic Site 129
gold rush 39
golf 146
Goodyear, Miles 39, 122
Gooseberry Mesa 102
Goshutes 29
Grand Staircase 85
Grand Staircase–Escalante National Monument 84
  activities 207
  Anasazi State Park Museum 213
  Boulder Contact Station 213
  Burr Trail Scenic Backway 210
  camping 207
  Cottonwood Canyons Scenic Backway 209
  cryptobiotic sensitive areas 211
  Escalante Canyons 209
  Escalante River 210
  flora and fauna 212
  geology 211
  Grand Staircase 208
  hiking 208, 211
  history 205
  Hole-in-the-Rock Scenic Backway 211
  hours, fees and permits 207
  Johnson Canyon Scenic Backway 208
  Kaiparowits Plateau 209

INDEX

Paria Contact Station 208
Phipps Arch 212
Skutumpah Road Scenic Backway 208
Smoky Mountain Road 209
visitor centers and ranger stations 207, 208, 209, 210
Grantsville 178
gratuities 272
Grayeyes, Willie 25
Great Basin 87, 177
Great Basin National Park (NV) 180
Great Salt Lake 38, 85, 93, 98, 119
Antelope Island State Park 121
Great Salt Lake State Park 177
Promontory Point 129
South Shore 177
Spiral Jetty 129
Great Salt Lake Desert 38, 119, 179
Green, Andy 180
Greendale Junction 156
Green River 85, 98, 156, 231, 233, 234
Melon Days 71
Green Valley Loop 102
guest ranches 266
Gunnison, Captain John 172
Gunnison Massacre Monument 181

H

Hafen, Lyman 77
Hamblin, Jacob 74
hang gliding 103
Hardware Wildlife Management Area 128
Hastings, Lansford W. 39
health 271
heat exhaustion 271
Heber City 146
Heber Valley 146
Heber Valley Historic Railroad 146
helicopter and airplane tours 103
Hell's Backbone 213
Henry Mountains 234
High Plateaus 79, 85
High Uintas Wilderness Area 156, 157
hiking 99
Beus Canyon Trail 125
footwear and equipment 100
Indian Trail 125
Logan Canyon 126
safety 99
Salt Lake City and environs 139
Hill, Joe 58
Hispanic immigrants 69
Historic Benson Grist Mill 178
Historic Union Pacific Rail Trail 102, 148
history
Black Hawk War 172
Escalante–Domínguez expedition 34
explorers 33
Fremont culture 203
modern age 55
Posey War 60

post World War II era 59
timeline 22
Tintic War 172
Utah War, 1857–58 50
Walker War 172
World War II 59
holidays, public 273
Homestead Crater 146
horseback riding 100
Horse Canyon 28
horses 28
wild 153
hostels 266
hot-air ballooning 103
hotels 265, 266
hot springs 146
houseboating 98
House Range 181
Hovenweep National Monument 28
hunting 173
Huntsville 125
Hyrum 128

I

I-15 corridor 169
ice climbing 144
Indian Trail 125
Industrial Workers of the World (IWW) 58
industry 60
insects 268
internet 272

J

Jackson, David 37
John Jarvie Historic Ranch 154
Jones Hole Scenic Backway 154
Jordanelle Reservoir 146
Jordanelle State Park 146
Josepa 64

K

Kaiparowits Plateau 209
Kanab 209
kayaking 98, 156, 233
Kayenta Branch Puebloan culture 213
Kayenta Formation 81
Kimberly-Big John Scenic Byway 173
Kodachrome Basin State Park 209
Kokopelli Trail 101

L

Lake Powell 98
La Sal Mountains 89
Latter-day Saints. *See* Mormons
leaf-peeping 139
Lee, John D. 51
Lehman Caves 180
Lexington Arch 180
LGBTQ+ community 63
LGBTQ+ travelers 272
lightening 269
Little Cottonwood Canyon 139
Little Sahara Recreation Area 180

Logan 127
Cache Daughters of Utah Pioneers Museum 127
Caine Lyric Theater 127
Ellen Eccles Theater 127
Logan Tabernacle 127
Logan Utah Temple 127
Nora Eccles Harrison Museum of Art 128
Utah State University 128
Utah Theater 128
Zootah at Willow Park 128
Logan Canyon 126
Logan Canyon Scenic Byway 126
Lone Peak wilderness area 145
Longabaugh, Harry. *See* Sundance Kid
López de Cárdenas, Captain García 33
Lower Calf Creek Falls 205

M

mail 273
Mammoth 180
Manila 157
Manti 172
John Patten DUP Museum 172
Mormon Temple 172
Pioneer Park 172
maps 272
marijuana 273
Markagunt Plateau 79, 201
Marriott, J. W. 76
Maryboy, Kenneth 25
Maryboy, Mark 25
Marysvale 173
McConkie Ranch 155
media 272
medical care 271
Merriam, C. Hart 89
Mesa Verde 27
Midway 146
Mills Junction 178
mines 269
mining 56, 60, 159
Mirror Lake Scenic Byway 157
Mojave Desert 87
money 272
Monte Cristo Range 125
Monticello 235
Monument Valley Navajo Tribal Park 81
Mormons 19, 30, 43, 57, 97, 131, 159, 170
Book of Mormon 53
British Mormon Mission 66
Hawaiian converts 64
origins of Mormonism 52
Mormon Tabernacle Choir 133
Moroni 170
Morris, Joseph 67
motels 265
motor homes 264
motor racing 179
mountain biking 101, 145
Mountain Green 125
mountain lions 268. *See* pumas
Mount Nebo 170
Mount Nebo National Scenic Byway 170

INDEX | 283

Mount Ogden 125
Mount Olympus 119
Mount Pleasant 171
Mount Timpanogos 145
movie and TV locations 149
museums and galleries
  Alf Engen Ski Museum (Park City) 148
  American West Heritage Center (Wellsville) 128
  Anasazi State Park Museum (Boulder) 213
  Beehive House (Salt Lake City) 133
  Cache Daughters of Utah Pioneers Museum (Logan) 127
  Church History Museum (Salt Lake City) 133
  Dinosaur Museum (Blanding) 84
  Discovery Gateway Children's Museum (Salt Lake City) 135
  Donner-Reed Museum (Grantsville) 178
  Fairview Museum of History and Art (Fairview) 170
  Fort Douglas Military Museum (Salt Lake City) 138
  Fremont Indian State Park and Museum (Sevier Valley) 172
  Frontier Homestead State Park Museum (Cedar City) 203
  Garr Ranch (Antelope Island State Park) 122
  George Eccles 2002 Winter Olympic Games Museum (Park City) 148
  Granary Arts (Ephraim) 171
  Great Basin Museum (Delta) 180
  Hill Aerospace Museum (Ogden) 124
  John Patten DUP Museum (Manti) 172
  Leonardo, The (Salt Lake City) 135
  Miners Park (Bullion Canyon) 173
  Miss Mary's Museum (Salina) 172
  Monte L. Bean Life Science Museum (Provo) 143
  Museum of Art (Provo) 142
  Museum of Paleontology (Provo) 143
  Museum of Peoples and Cultures (Provo) 142
  Museums at Union Station (Ogden) 123
  Natural History Museum of Utah (Salt Lake City) 137
  Nora Eccles Harrison Museum of Art (Logan) 128
  Ogden's George S. Eccles Dinosaur Park and Museum (Ogden) 124
  Park City Museum 147
  Pioneer Memorial Museum (Salt Lake City) 136
  Provo Daughters of Utah Pioneer Museum (Provo) 141
  Southern Utah Museum of Art (Cedar City) 203
  Springville Museum of Art (Springville) 143
  Territorial Statehouse State Park Museum (Fillmore) 169
  This Is the Place Heritage Park (Salt Lake City) 138
  Tintic Mining Museum (Eureka) 180
  Topaz Museum (Delta) 180
  Treehouse Museum (Ogden) 123
  Utah Field House of Natural History State Park Museum (Vernal) 154
  Utah Historical Society Museum (Salt Lake City) 135
  Utah Museum of Contemporary Art (Salt Lake City) 134
  Utah Museum of Fine Arts (Salt Lake City) 137

N

national parks and monuments 79
  admission charges 267
  Arches National Park 91
  Bears Ears National Monument 60
  Bryce Canyon National Park 90, 101
  camping 266
  Canyonlands National Park 81, 89, 91, 97, 101
  Canyons of the Ancients National Monument 28
  Capitol Reef National Park 82, 101
  Cedar Breaks National Monument 85, 201, 202
  Dinosaur National Monument 79, 81, 151
  Grand Staircase-Escalante National Monument 84
  Great Basin National Park (NV) 180, 181
  Hovenweep National Monument 28
  Timpanogos Cave National Monument 145
  Zion National Monument 60
  Zion National Park 88, 101
Native Americans 25, 33, 49, 63, 64, 172
nature preserves
  Fish Springs National Wildlife Refuge 90
  Lytle Ranch 88
  Red Cliffs Reserve 88
Navajo 29
Needles Flat 236
Nephi 169
newspapers 272
Nibley, Charles 67
Notarianni, Philip 159
Notch Peak Loop 181

O

Ogden 121
  25th Street Historic District 123
  bike share program 264
  Fort Buenaventura Park 122
  Hill Aerospace Museum 124
  history 55
  Hof German Fest 71
  Indigenous Voices Pow Wow 71
  Kayak Park 124
  Lagoon 124
  Museums at Union Station 123
  Ogden Nature Center 123
  Ogden River Parkway 124
  Ogden River Scenic Byway 124
  Ogden's George S. Eccles Dinosaur Park and Museum 124
  Peery's Egyptian Theater 123
  Treehouse Museum 123
Ogden Canyon 124
Ogden, Peter Skene 37
Olympic Winter Games 2002 61
opening hours 273
Otter Creek State Park 173
Ouray National Wildlife Refuge 157
overheating 271

P

Page (AZ) 209
Paiute people 29, 31, 197, 203
paleontologists, amateur 84
Panguitch 201
paragliding 103
Park City 141, 146
  Alf Engen Ski Museum 148
  Alpine Slide 148
  Beethoven Festival 70
  bike trails and rentals 102, 148, 264
  buses 263
  Canyons, The 148
  Deer Valley Resort 148
  Egyptian Theatre 147
  George Eccles 2002 Winter Olympic Games Museum 148
  hiking 148
  Historic Union Pacific Rail Trail 148
  horseback riding 148
  Main Street Historic District 147
  mountain biking 148
  Park City Mountain Resort 107, 147
  Park City Museum 147
  ski resorts 147
  Sundance Film Festival 71, 149
  Swaner Preserve & EcoCenter 148
  Sweeney Switchbacks 148
  Utah Olympic Park 107, 148
  winter sports 106
Park City Mountain Resort 106
Parker, Robert LeRoy.
  See Cassidy, Butch
Parowan 202
Parowan Gap Petroglyph Site 203
passports 275
Payson 170
petroglyphs 155, 203
pharmacies 272
phones 274
Pineview Reservoir 125

INDEX

pioneers 38
plantlife 87
Point of the Mountain Flight Park 103
politics 61
Pony Express National Historic Trail 90, 102
population 63
postal services 273
Powder Mountain 106
Powell, John Wesley 97, 205
powwows 31
Price Greek Festival 70
Provo 141
  Brigham Young University 142
  Covey Center for the Arts 142
  Monte L. Bean Life Science Museum 143
  Museum of Art 142
  Museum of Paleontology 143
  Museum of Peoples and Cultures 142
  Provo City Center Temple 142
  Provo City Library 142
  Provo Daughters of Utah Pioneer Museum 141
  Provo Farmers Market 142
  Sons of Utah Pioneer Village 141
Provo Canyon 144
Provo Peak 141
Provost, Étienne 37
public holidays 273
Pueblo people 27
pumas 94

R

rafting 97, 156, 173
railroad, transcontinental 55
rail travel 262, 263
Red Canyon 201
Red Cloud-Dry Fork Scenic Backway Drive 155
Red Fleet State Park 155
Redford, Robert 144, 149
religious services 273
Rendezvous Beach 126
restaurants 269
Richfield 172
Rio Tinto Kennecott Visitor Experience 178
Rivera, Juan Antonio María de 34
river running 233
rock art 213
rock climbing 102
Romney, Mitt 61, 76
Round Valley Trail 102
Ruess, Everett 210

S

safety 268
Salina 172
Saltair Resort 177
Salt Lake City 19, 30, 48
  Abravanel Hall 134
  airport 262
  Assembly Hall 133
  Avenues Historic District 136
  Beehive House 133
  bike share program 134, 264
  Bonneville Shoreline Trail 139
  Brigham Young Monument 133
  buses 263
  Capitol Hill 136
  Capitol Theater 134
  Cathedral of the Madeleine 136
  Central City 135
  Church History Museum 133
  City and County Building 135
  City Creek Canyon Trail 139
  City Creek Center 134
  Clark Planetarium 135
  Conference Center 133
  Discovery Gateway Children's Museum 135
  Downtown 134
  Emigration Canyon 137, 138
  Family History Library 133
  festivals and events 70
  Fort Douglas Military Museum 138
  Gallivan Center 134
  Gateway 135
  hiking 139
  history 56
  Hoberman Arch 138
  Hogle Zoo 138
  Hotel Utah 133
  Isaac Chase Home and Mill 136
  Joseph Smith Memorial Building 133
  Keith Brown Mansion 136
  LDS Temple 131
  Leonardo, The 135
  Liberty Park 136
  Lion House 133
  Living Traditions Festival 66
  Marmalade Historic District 136
  McCune Mansion 136
  Natural History Museum of Utah 137
  Olympic Cauldron Park 137
  Olympic Plaza 135
  Pioneer Day 70
  Pioneer Memorial Museum 136
  Pioneer Park 135
  Red Butte Garden 138
  Rice-Eccles Stadium 137
  Rio Grande Depot 135
  Salt Lake 2002 Visitor Center 138
  Salt Lake City Public Library 135
  Salt Palace Convention Center 134
  Seagull Monument 133
  Tabernacle 133
  Temple Square 131
  This Is the Place Heritage Park 138
  Thomas Kearns Mansion 136
  Tracy Aviary & Botanical Garden 136
  Trolley Square 135
  Union Pacific Depot 135
  University-Foothill District 137
  University of Utah 137
  Utah Historical Society Museum 135
  Utah Museum of Contemporary Art 134
  Utah Museum of Fine Arts 137
  Utah State Capitol 136
  Utah State Fair 71
  Vivint Arena 134
  Washington Park 135
  Wheeler Historic Farm 138
Salt Lake City International Airport 262
sand dunes 180
San Juan River 83
Sanpete County 170
Sanpete Valley 159, 171, 172
San Rafael Swell 87
Scandinavian immigrants 67
scorpions 93
scuba diving 146
sea monkeys 92
seasons 267
Sevier Desert 181
Sevier Valley 172
Sheep Creek Geologic Scenic Backway Loop 156
Shooting Star Saloon (Huntsville) 125
shopping 273
Shoshones 29
Silver Island Mountains Backcountry Byway 179
Silver Reef ghost town 85
skiing. See winter sports
skiing, cross-country 107
ski resorts 105
skydiving 103
Skyline Drive 87
Slickrock Trail 101
Smith, Davina 25
Smith, Hyrum 73
Smith, Jedediah 37
Smith, Joseph 43, 73
Smithson, Robert 129
smoking 273
Smoot, Reed 57
snakes 93, 268
Snake Valley 181
Snowbasin 106, 125
Snowbird 106
snowboarding 107. See winter sports
Snow Canyon State Park 102
snowfall 105
snow sports 105
soccer 137
spiders 93
Spirit Lake Scenic Backway 157
sport
  Olympic Winter Games 2002 63
Spring City 171
Springville 143
Stage Coach Inn State Park 90
Stansbury Mountains 179
state parks 60
  admission charges 267
  Anasazi 213
  Antelope Island 102, 121
  Danger Cave 179
  Dead Horse Point 235
  Deer Creek 146
  Escalante Forest 81
  Great Salt Lake 177
  Jordanelle 146
  Kodachrome Basin 209
  Otter Creek 173
  Red Fleet 155

Snow Canyon 102
Stage Coach Inn 90
Steinaker 155
Utah Lake 143
Wasatch Mountain 107, 146
Willard Bay 129
Steinaker State Park 155
Sublette, Milton and William 37
sunburn 271
Sundance 105
Sundance Film Festival (Park City) 145, 149
Sundance Film Institute 145
Sundance Kid 40
Sundance resort 144
Swett Ranch Historical Homestead 156
Syracuse 121

T

tax 273
telephones 274
television 272
Tempest Williams, Terry
An Unnatural History of Family and Place 93
Tetzlaff, Teddy 180
time zones 274
Timpanogos Cave National Monument 145
Tintic Mining District 159
Tintic Mountains 180
tipping 272
toads 93
Tony Grove Lake 127
tourism 60
tourist information 274
tour operators 275
trains 265
transport 262
Trappers Loop Road 125
travel agents 275

U

Udall, Stewart 231
Uintah and Ouray Reservation 31, 157
Uinta Mountains 79, 88, 157
Uinta–Wasatch–Cache National Forest 125, 139, 145, 170
University of Utah 137
uranium 59, 81
US 6 corridor 179
Utah Jazz basketball team 61, 134
Utah Lake 143
Utah Lake State Park 143
Ute people 29, 33, 141

V

vaping 273
Vélez de Escalante, Silvestre 205
Vernal 154
Virgin River 91
visas 275

W

Walker, Joseph 37
Wasatch Canyons 139
Wasatch Front 88, 119, 121
Wasatch Mountains 19, 79, 85, 102
Wasatch Mountain State Park 107, 146
Wasatch Plateau 87
water, drinking 271
weather 88, 267
Webb, Ann Eliza 51
Weber Canyon 125
websites 275
weights and measures 275
Wellsville 128
Wellsville Mountains 127
Wendover 179
what to wear 268
Wheeler Peak Scenic Drive 180
White Rim Trail 101
whitewater rafting 173.
  See rafting
Wi-Fi 272
Wild Bunch 40
wilderness safety 269
wildflowers 90
wildlife 91
  bison 122
  elk, winter feeding 128
  horses and burros 153
  Ouray National Wildlife Refuge 157
  pumas 94
  safety issues 268
  Wildlife Education Center 128
Willard Bay State Park 129
Williams, Terry Tempest 77
Winter Olympic Games 2002 106
winter sports , 10, 63
  Beaver Mountain Ski Area 126
  Brian Head Ski Resort 202
  cross-country skiing 107
  Park City 146, 147
  Salt Lake City environs 139
  Snowbasin resort 125
  Soldier Hollow 146
Wobblies 58
Woodruff 126
Woodruff, Wilford 51

Y

Yampa River 85
Young, Brigham 19, 45, 51, 73, 87, 131

Z

Zion National Park 88, 101

NOTES

NOTES

Utah's National Parks and Monuments
N
0 30 miles
0 30 km
Abbreviation Legend
NCA National Conservation Area
NHP National Historical Park
NHS National Historic Site
NM National Monument
NP National Park
NRA National Recreation Area
NWR National Wildlife Refuge
RA Recreation Area
SHP State Historic Park
SM State Monument
SP State Park
Idaho
Wyoming
Colorado
Nevada
Preston
Bear Lake
Bear Lake State Park-Rendezvous Beach
Bear
Sawtooth National Forest
Logan
Tremonton
Golden Spike National Historic Site
Wellsville
Hyrum State Park
Bear River Migratory Bird Refuge
Brigham City
Willard Bay State Park
Wasatch-Cache National Forest
Evanston
Lyman
Flaming Gorge Reservoir
Flaming Gorge National Recreation Area
Ogden
Great Salt Lake
Lost Creek State Park
Newfoundland Evaporation Basin
Morgan
Antelope Island State Park
Bountiful
Coalville
East Canyon State Park
Wasatch-Cache National Forest
Great
Jordan River State Park
Danger Cave State Park
Wendover
Great Salt Lake State Park
Salt Lake City
Rockport State Park
High Uintas Wilderness
Kings Peak 13528
Uinta Mountains
Browns Park National Wildlife Refuge
Salt Lake
Wasatch-Cache National Forest
Taylorsville
Park City
Ashley National Forest
Red Fleet State Park
Cedar Mtns
Steinaker State Park
Dinosaur National Monument
Deseret Peak 11031
Tooele
Riverton
Wasatch Mtn State Park
Heber City
Uintah and Ouray Reservation
Dinosaur Quarry Visitor Center
Vernal
Desert
Veterans Memorial State Park
Deer Creek State Park
Skull Valley Reservation
Roosevelt
Provo
Uinta National Forest
Ouray NWR
Utah Lake
Starvation State Park
Springville
Duchesne
Strawberry Reservoir
Uinta Basin
Uintah and Ouray Reservation
Wasatch-Cache National Forest
White
Fish Springs NWR
Uinta National Forest
Ashley National Forest
Green
Mount Nebo Wilderness
Nine Mile Canyon
Goshute Reservation
Scofield State Park
Nephi
Helper
West Tavaputs